Robert P. Goldman

Epic and Argument in Sanskrit Literary History

Essays in Honor of Robert P. Goldman

Edited by
SHELDON POLLOCK

MANOHAR
2026

First published 2010
Reprinted 2026

ISBN 978-81-7304-865-4

Published by
Ajay Kumar Jain *for*
Manohar Publishers & Distributors
4753/23 Ansari Road, Daryaganj
New Delhi 110 002

Printed at
Replika Press Pvt. Ltd.

Contents

Acknowledgements

I am very grateful to all the collaborators not only for their wonderful contributions in honor of a wonderful colleague, but for their patience in the face of the various delays accompanying the publication of this book.

Arthur Dudney, my research assistant at Columbia, did an extraordinary job helping with the editing and the production of the volume. I am also grateful to Ramesh Jain of Manohar Publishers and Distributors for his support and to my dear friend Shahid Amin of the University of Delhi for his good counsel.

New York
July 2009

SHELDON POLLOCK

Vidyāsāgaraḥ Suvarṇapuruṣaḥ: A Brief Survey of Robert P. Goldman's Scholarship

Robert P. Goldman's scholarly career spans four decades. As a teacher, research scholar, and administrator, he is well-known throughout the Indological world for his profound scholarship and learned personality. His primer of Sanskrit grammar [*Devavāṇīpraveśikā: An Introduction to the Sanskrit Language* (1980, 1987, 1999, 2002, 2004)], co-written with Dr. Sally Goldman, remains the standard text in many English-speaking classrooms where elementary Sanskrit is taught. Dedicated to the study of the Indian epics for much of his career, Professor Goldman is widely acknowledged as the foremost scholar of the Vālmīki *Rāmāyaṇa*. His service to the University of California at Berkeley has been instrumental in that program's continued success and, recently, he has lent a guiding administrative hand to numerous American students studying abroad through the programs of the University of California. Among his many awards and honors, some notable ones include: the Award for Distinguished Teaching at the University of California, Berkeley, in 1974 (one of the youngest awardees of this prestigious honor); Guggenheim Fellow (1978); recipient of the National Endowment of the Humanities grants (four times); visiting professor in Indian Philosophy and Religion at Wolfson College, Oxford University (1984-85); Honorary Fellow at Calcutta Sanskrit College (1992); and a longstanding member and trustee of the American Institute of Indian Studies. Two acknowledgements of his cumulative record stand out with special distinction: his fellowship with the prestigious American Academy of Arts and Sciences and his honorary appellation Vidyāsāgara ("Ocean of Learning"), a status accorded to him by the Mandākinī Saṃskṛta Vidvat Pariṣad, an Indian organization dedicated to traditional Sanskrit learning. Both of these honors testify to Professor Goldman's impact on the intellectual life of America and India. Both titles reflect his elegant fluency in communicating to English and Sanskrit audiences alike.

Professor Goldman is best known for his important work on the Sanskrit epics, the *Mahābhārata* and the *Rāmāyaṇa*. His scholarship from the past thirty years on these massive texts consistently demonstrates a thoughtful integration of literary, linguistic, philosophical, psychological, social, and political approaches. As chief editor and primary translator, he has spearheaded for several decades the *Rāmāyaṇa* Translation Project, a translation of the critical edition of the Vālmīki *Rāmāyaṇa* and its important Sanskrit commentaries. This project, bringing together distinguished Sanskrit scholars from three continents, has produced six of the seven projected volumes. The labor that has gone into this project is evident on every page of the work—from the illuminating prefaces and thoughtful translations to the exhaustive notes—and will reach completion with the translation (with Dr. Sally Goldman) of the Uttarakāṇḍa, the final book of the epic. Each volume reflects painstaking research involving scores of Sanskrit manuscripts and secondary works in Indian and European languages. The notes to the text represent the fruits of assimilating a diverse set of perspectives gained from decades of textual study, communication with academics and traditionally-trained Sanskrit scholars, and deep familiarity and engagement with the diverse artistic and religious communities of South and Southeast Asia. Perhaps the most elegant translation of what is arguably the most important document in the history of Asia and certainly one of the most important documents of world civilization, the *Rāmāyaṇa* Translation Project itself constitutes a grand achievement and about its utility and value—and indeed projected immortality—very little needs to be said to any scholar currently thinking and writing about the cultural life of pre-modern and early modern India.

Nearly a decade before the appearance of the first volume of the *Rāmāyaṇa*, Professor Robert Goldman published an influential monograph on the Bhārgavas of the *Mahābhārata*. During an illustrious career, he has edited nearly a dozen volumes (including all of the *Rāmāyaṇa* volumes), written over twenty long articles on Vālmīki's epic, another ten or so on the *Mahābhārata*, several on aspects of Vedic and Purāṇic literature, a learned foreword to his colleague P.S. Jaini's work on Jain soteriology, and at least two very important articles on translation and hermeneutics with respect to Sanskrit materials. Some of his most important essays have applied a critical lens to Indian cultural materials from the point of view of modern psychology. In most of these essays, Professor Goldman demonstrates his skill in teasing out the deep socio-psychic implications of texts like the Sanskrit epics by directly addressing the evidence the poems (and the readings of their audiences) themselves offer in light of living cultures that embody the legacy of these texts. Thus, the psychoanalytic exploration of the epics' human relationships ["Fathers, Sons, and Gurus: Oedipal Conflict in the Sanskrit Epics" (1978) and "Matricide, Renunciation, and Compensation in the Legends of Two Warrior Heroes of the Sanskrit Epics" (1982)]; the wide-ranging meditations on the reality/fantasy divide in the Indian literary and philosophical imagination ["Karma, Guilt, and Buried Memories: Public Fantasy and Private Reality in Traditional India" (1985), "The Serpent and the Rope on Stage: Popular, Literary, and Philosophical Representation of Reality in Traditional India" (1986), and "A City of the Heart: Mathurā and the Indian Imagination" (1986)]; the insightful analyses of the epic protagonists in their multifaceted representations as narrative portraits and psychologically complex beings [see especially "*Rāmaḥ Sahalakṣmaṇaḥ*: Psychological and Literary Aspects of the Composite Hero of Vālmīki's *Rāmāyaṇa*" (1980), "Vālmīki's Hanumān: Characterization and Occluded Divinity in the *Rāmāyaṇa*" (1994, co-written with Sally Goldman), and "Gods in Hiding: The *Mahābhārata*'s *Virāṭa Parvan* and the Divinity of the Indian Epic Hero" (1995)]; and the socio-sexual information and its broader implications reflected in the epic literature ["Transsexualism, Gender, and Anxiety in Traditional India" (1993), "Rāvaṇa's Kitchen: A Testimony of Desire and the Other" (2000) and "Resisting Rāma: Dhārmic Debates on Gender and Hierarchy and the Work of the Vālmīki *Rāmāyaṇa*" (2003)].

In each of these sets of articles, as in virtually every other critical study of his, there is a shared purpose (if not thematic concern) with the traditional commentators of the Sanskrit epics (from Nīlakaṇṭha to Govindarāja): to be fully cognizant of the intricate details of the surface text and yet to be fully open to the suggestive possibilities of underlying deep structures emerging repeatedly and hauntingly in episode after episode of these endlessly fascinating texts. So while several of the articles cited above offer his own interpretive insights, it is fitting that several other of his articles pointedly focus on the historical interpretations (and interpreters) with whom he shares an intellectual camaraderie. Thus, the theoretical piece on the Sanskrit commentarial tradition ["Translating Texts Translating Texts: Issues in the Translation of Popular Literary Texts with Multiple Commentaries" (1992)] happily supplements the detailed descriptions of the ardent precision of the "traditional" Indian hermeneutic mind in essays about the work of *Rāmāyaṇa* commentators ["*Sundare Kiṃ Na Sundaram*? The Genetic and Receptive Histories of the *Sundarakāṇḍa*" (1998-99), "Historicizing the *Rāmakathā*: Vālmīki's *Rāmāyaṇa* and its Medieval Commentators" (2005),"How Fast Do Monkeys Fly? How Long Do Demons Sleep?" (2006), and "To Wake a Sleeping Giant: Vālmīki's Account of the Life and Death of Kumbhakarṇa" (in Press)]. One needs only to scan the lengthy and detailed notes in the volumes on the *Sundarakāṇḍa* and *Yuddhakāṇḍa* translations to encounter the labors put forth to assess, embellish, and critique the contributions of the Vaiṣṇava commentators of the *Rāmāyaṇa*.

Finally, it is important and auspicious to note that Professor Goldman's intellectual legacy will ultimately and intimately be tied to the first and last of the great Indian poems, whose scope and reach continues to grow and change in India and elsewhere. His awareness of the poem's historical and contemporary significance is signaled in a number of essays from the past fifteen years ["The Vālmīki *Rāmāyaṇa* as a Source of Indian Cultural Integration" (1993), "Yāvat Sthāsyanti Girayaḥ: The *Ādikāvya* and the Legacy of Ṛṣi Vālmīki" (1998-99), "The Ghost from the Anthill: Vālmīki and the Destiny of the Rāmakathā in South and Southeast Asia" (2000), "Of Time and the Epic: The *Rāmāyaṇa*'s Trajectory from *ādikāvya* to National Epic" (2001), and "The *Rāmāyaṇa* and the Problem of an 'Asian' Cultural Area" (2003), "The Spirit of the Age: Social Vision and Historical Perspective in the *Mahābhārata* and the *Vālmīkirāmāyaṇa*" (2006), and "Expert Nation: An Epic of Antiquity in the World of Modernity" (in Press)].

What comes out in Professor Goldman's writing—and certainly in his lectures—is his unique ability to collapse the psychic distance between a world-perspective which, at first encounter, might seem totally unfamiliar but upon reflection reminds every reader of a shared humanity. It can be said of him what he once wrote about the mathematician and Indologist D.D. Kosambi ["D.D. Kosambi and a Marxist Critique of Sanskrit Literature" (1974)]: "For where he criticizes and even condemns, it is as one who knows well and views with sympathy and even fascination the object of his critique ... [He] laid a sort of groundwork which might, perhaps, encourage further, deeper study towards future radical analyses of much that is to be cherished in Indian culture." It is surely the case that, in the coming years, Professor Robert P. Goldman of the University of California at Berkeley will himself be the author and encourager of many more of these deeper studies toward radical analyses of much that is to be cherished in Indian culture.

University of Pennsylvania DEVEN M. PATEL

Selected Books and Articles

"D.D. Kosambi and a Marxist Critique of Sanskrit Literature," in *Marxist Influences and South Asian Literature.* Michigan: Michigan State University, 1974.

Gods, Priests, and Warriors: The Bhārgavas of the Mahābhārata. New York: Columbia University Press, 1977.

"Fathers, Sons, and Gurus: Oedipal Conflict in the Sanskrit Epics." *Journal of Indian Philosophy,* vol. 6, 1978, pp. 325-92.

Devavāṇīpraveśikā: An Introduction to the Sanskrit Language (with Sally Sutherland Goldman). Berkeley: Center for the South and Southeast Asia Studies, University of California, Berkeley, 1980.

"*Rāmaḥ Sahalakṣmaṇaḥ*: Psychological and Literary Aspects of the Composite Hero of Vālmīki's *Rāmāyaṇa.*" *Journal of Indian Philosophy*, vol. 8, 1980, pp. 11-51.

"Matricide, Renunciation, and Compensation in the Legends of Two Warrior Heroes of the Sanskrit Epics," in *Proceedings of the Stockholm Conference Seminar in Indological Studies. Indologica Taurinensia*, vol. 10, 1982, pp. 117-31.

"Karma, Guilt, and Buried Memories: Public Fantasy and Private Reality in Traditional India." *Journal of the American Oriental Society*, vol. 105, no. 3, 1985, pp. 413-25.

The Rāmāyaṇa of Vālmīki*: An Epic of Ancient India, Vol. I: Bālakāṇḍa.* Princeton: Princeton University Press, 1985. (Translator and editor, annotation with Sally J. Sutherland.)

"The Serpent and the Rope on Stage: Popular, Literary, and Philosophical Representation of Reality in Traditional India." *Journal of Indian Philosophy*, vol. 14, 1986, pp. 349-69.

"A City of the Heart: Mathurā and the Indian Imagination." *Journal of the American Oriental Society*, vol. 106, no. 3, 1986, pp. 471-83.

Foreword to P.S. Jaini's *Gender and Salvation: Jaina Debates on the Spiritual Liberation of Women.* Berkeley: University of California Press, 1990, pp. vii-xxiv.

"Translating Texts Translating Texts: Issues in the Translation of Popular Literary Texts with Multiple Commentaries." *Literary Studies East and West: Cross-cultural Perspectives: Selected Conference Papers.* East-West Center: University of Hawaii at Manoa, 1992, pp. 93-106.

"The Vālmīki *Rāmāyaṇa* as a Source of Indian Cultural Integration." In *Rāmāyaṇa and Rāmāyaṇa Studies.* Delhi: Sage Publications, 1993.

"Transsexualism, Gender and Anxiety in Traditional India." *Journal of the American Oriental Society*, vol. 113, no. 3, 1993, pp. 374-401.

"Vālmīki's Hanumān: Characterization and Occluded Divinity in the *Rāmāyaṇa.*" (With Sally Sutherland Goldman) *Journal of Vaiṣṇava Studies*, vol. 2, no. 4, 1994, pp. 31-54.

"Gods in Hiding: The *Mahābhārata's Virāṭa Parvan* and the Divinity of the Indian Epic Hero." In *Modern Evaluation of the Mahābhārata (Professor R.K. Sharma Felicitation Volume).* S.P. Narang, ed. New Delhi: Nag Publishers, 1995, pp. 73-100.

The Rāmāyaṇa of Vālmīki*: An Epic of Ancient India, Vol. V: Sundarakāṇḍa.* Princeton: Princeton University Press, 1996. (Translated, annotated, and edited with Sally J. Sutherland Goldman.)

"*Yāvat Sthāsyanti Girayaḥ*': The *Adikāvya* and the Legacy of Ṛṣi Vālmīki", *Journal of the Oriental Institute* (Baroda), vol. XLVIII, nos. 1-4, September 1998 & June 1999, pp. 1-20.

"*Sundare Kiṃ Na Sundaram?* The Genetic and Receptive Histories of the *Sundarakāṇḍa* of the Vālmīki *Rāmāyaṇa.*" *Journal of the Oriental Institute* (Baroda), vol. XLVIII, nos. 1-4, September 1998 & June 1999, pp. 83-106.

"Rāvaṇa's Kitchen: A Testimony of Desire and the Other." In *Questioning Rāmāyaṇas.* Paula Richman, ed. Delhi: Oxford University Press and Berkeley: University of California Press, 2000, pp. 105-16; 374-76.

"The Ghost from the Anthill: Vālmīki and the Destiny of the *Rāmakathā* in South and Southeast Asia." In *A Varied Optic: Contemporary Studies in the Rāmāyaṇa*, M. Bose, ed. Vancouver: Institute of Asian Research, University of British Columbia, 2000, pp. 11-30.

"Of Time and the Epic: The *Rāmāyaṇa*'s Trajectory from *Ādikāvya* to National Epic." In *Les Sources et le Temps.* F. Grimal, ed. Pondichery: Publications du Departement d'Indologie, 91 Institut Français de Pondichery, Ecole Française d'Extrême-Orient, 2001, pp. 211-27.

"The *Rāmāyaṇa* and the Problem of an "Asian" Cultural Area: Vālmīki's Values in India and Beyond." *Purāṇa*, vol. XLV, no. 1, January 2003, pp. 7-34.

"Resisting Rāma: Dharmic Debates on Gender and Hierarchy and the Work of the Vālmīki *Rāmāyaṇa.*" In *Rāmāyaṇa Revisited.* M. Bose, ed. New York: Oxford University Press, 2003, pp. 19-46.

"Historicizing the *Rāmakathā:* Vālmīki's *Rāmāyaṇa* and its Medieval Commentators," IIC Quarterly, IIC: Delhi, 2005.

"How Fast Do Monkeys Fly How Long Do Demons Sleep?" *Rivista di Studi Sudasiatici*, Rome, no. 1, 2006, pp. 185-207.

"Two Wake a Sleeping Giant: Vālmīki's Account(s) of the Life and Death of Kumbhakarṇa." In Proceedings of the XIIth World Sanskrit Conference, Helsinki 2003: Epic Studies. Edited with Muneo Tokunaga. Delhi: Motilal Banarsidass, 2007.

The Rāmāyaṇa of Vālmīki*: An Epic of Ancient India, Vol. VI: Yuddhakāṇḍa.* Princeton: Princeton University Press, 2009. (Translated, annotated, and edited with Sally J. Sutherland Goldman.)

"Expert Nation: An Epic of Antiquity in the World of Modernity." In *Festschrift for Professor Sheldon I. Pollock*, Whitney Cox, Yigal Bronner, Gary Tubb, eds. (in Press).

Hermeneutical Glosses on Scholarly Work on the *Mahābhārata* and the Purāṇas

GREG BAILEY

Scholars generally hold the brahmins to have successfully utilized the *Mahābhārata* (*MBh*) and the Purāṇas as media for advancing their own cultural agenda as the central one for the society and polity they perceived to be normative. We then have to ask in what way the two genres differ and how they should be investigated as different historical sources, offering variant readings on a commonly perceived set of problems. My intuitive response to many years of reading the *MBh* and several Purāṇas is that the *MBh* is defining a problem from the perspective of an emergent self-conscious Brahmin class, as well as suggesting solutions to it, whereas the Purāṇas recognize no such problem and, instead, spread the same ideology throughout India, incorporating into it distinctive devotional trends and their conspicuously regional variant forms. Accepting these as two working propositions that need not elicit universal agreement we can ask: 1. Are the Purāṇas simply offering the logical ideological extension of what is initially developed in the *MBh*, albeit communicating this in a different generic structure? 2. Or are they responding to a totally different problematic to that perceived by those who participated in the early centuries of *MBh* adaptation, redaction and dissemination? Thus the intention of the present paper is to explore the relationships between two literary genres, their use as sources for historical data and the interpretative questions which arise out of these two foci.[1] Two forms of historical significance should be considered: firstly, one that rests in the description of particular historical events pertaining to material culture, society, politics, etc.; secondly, one that asserts there is an historical significance inherent in the emergence of separate literary genres, foregrounded in a particular set of historical constellations, such that in their initial redaction the epics reflect a different range of socio-political conditions than the Purāṇas.

Most scholarly work on the Purāṇas has unambiguously foregrounded them in the *MBh*. Not so much in the *MBh* as reconstructed in the various specific manuscript traditions that have come down to us, but in the broader generic tradition that has given rise to some overlapping in content, stylistic features and the ubiquitous use of *śloka*. For some early twentieth century European Indologists, the Purāṇas were somehow associated with a kind of a process, as when Winternitz used the word "puranizing" to refer to parts of the *MBh*, as did Blau with his "purāṇaartige" chapters in the Bālakāṇḍa (Lesny 1913) of the *Rāmāyaṇa*. This idea of process (Chakravarti 2001: 60) has been important in defining European approaches to Purāṇic study because it helped delimit the apparent unwieldiness and uncohesive quality of the purāṇic narrative and of parts of the two epics where the main narrative seems to be interrupted by what is sometimes regarded as extraneous matter. This is hardly surprising given the strong historicist tendency in Philology to focus on parallel contents (and plots) in tracing the evolution of a particular mythic or, occasionally, didactic motif. More often than not, as all the Kirfel-based studies have shown, such an evolution begins in Vedic literature, and the occurrence of many of the same myths in the *MBh* suggests it might have a special role to play in mediating Vedic culture (or the vestiges of it) to later cultural disseminators. But the fundamental difference remains: the *MBh* is defining foundational social and cultural problems and suggesting solutions to them, the Purāṇas assume these problems to be resolved and are responding to new ones. Yet if we read them as generic mirrors of each other, as seems a contemporary commonplace reading, this may produce a different interpretative response than if we were to assign interpretative priority to the separateness of intertextually related genres.

The problem I foresee is this: Both the *MBh* and the Purāṇas are emically regarded by their traditional audiences as historical texts, even if it is not always clear what their historicity might be. But they are also used etically as raw data by historians of ancient and medieval India. From the viewpoint of contemporary historians, two modes of interpretation are necessarily in operation here: firstly, that of the composers of the primary Sanskrit sources and especially of their subsequent redactors, and, secondly, the subsequent interpretative procedure applied to these sources by contemporary historians. Both interpreters utilize a variety of sources themselves and a decisive emplotment and narrative structure is evident in both cases. However, there is a difference: the generic structure of *itihāsa* and *purāṇa* is defined in the primary sources themselves, definitions, to some extent, respected by later historians.

The American historiographer Hayden White is especially concerned to investigate how narratives written by historians make sense in relation to the audiences of their own day (cf. Thapar 2002: 1–29), suggesting a kind of reader response theory for historical writing. His idea of the encoding of the historian's narrative in order to shape the resulting "scholarly text," implicitly meeting the expectations of contemporary readers, is especially pertinent to the problem I have set. Yet it is potentially more provocative than this in also inviting us take account of three sets of texts which might appear to be qualitatively different,[2] the two collections of primary sources themselves and the recent historical writings which have utilized them in constructing historical narratives. Each encodes in its own way, though we would anticipate, perhaps falsely, this to be more transparent in the case of contemporary historical writing. Here is White's understanding of 'emplotment' and what it specifically gives to the nature of historical writing:

> ... what the historian brings to his consideration of the historical record is a notion of the types of configurations of events that can be recognized as stories by the audience for which he is writing. ... The important point is that most historical sequences can be emplotted in a number of different ways, so as to provide different interpretations of those events and to endow them with different meanings.
>
> ... the historians shared with their audiences certain preconceptions about how the [French] revolution might be emplotted, in response to imperatives that were generally extra historical, ideological, aesthetic, or mythical. (White 1978: 84–85)

This requires us then to elaborate the historiographical and ideological 'emplotments' we can find in the writings of contemporary historians. But it is also surely applicable to the *MBh* and the Purāṇas to the extent these are foundational sources for writing the history of early historical India. What really marks them as foundational is that their period of composition and on-going redaction lies within the formative period of Hinduism, between 200 BCE and 400 CE, the *MBh* at the beginning and the Purāṇas at the end.

The *Mahābhārata*

Reading back from the present day there is a now widely held view that those who composed, revised (re-interpreted) and disseminated this text for the first six hundred years (let us say 200 BCE-400 CE) of its existence believed they were confronted with fundamental cultural and political problems. Such was the seriousness of these problems for those who had defined them that they demanded a response, involving the development and consolidation of a coherent and communicable cultural system that would also have perceptible political and social ramifications because it would enjoy legitimation from the cultural elites and persuasive value for those below. These problems were manifested above all in three areas:

1. A pre-occupation with the problem of dharma understood as a kind of universal ordering principle and the testing of its relevance in situations where adherence to it seems to produce unanticipated results.
2. An attempt to excavate the correct normative relationship between brahmins and kṣatriyas, a task involving the assertion and testing (in narrative form) of normative role models for each, with emphasis being placed on the delineation of the protective function of the king.
3. The repackaging of vestigial Vedic religious and social concepts into a new identity for the brahmin as a partial response to the emerging importance of devotional (and ascetic) tendencies in mainstream religion.

As an instrument for presenting resolutions to these problems—or, equally important, offering the possibility to people that there was a body of knowledge available for accessing responses to these problems—the Sanskrit *MBh* was used by the brahmins as a means of defining a new cultural mainstream. What had been developed and transmitted through Vedic literature was always restricted to a small component of the population, becoming smaller and smaller by the time of the early Upaniṣads as cultural possibilities expanded. Ascetic practices and associated concepts become well known from about 600 BCE. It is hardly of importance that large numbers of people chose not to adopt the rigorous lifestyle of asceticism, yet if not practised as part of the mainstream it was favourably acknowledged because of the highly conspicuous practices of its adherents who were educated and good communicators, producing a large volume of literature that has survived. Where it does become most significant is in its institutional ramifications, involving the formal development of monastic and lay orders, each required to fulfill obligations to the other. Buddhism was most successful here and its material success between 200 BCE and 200 CE must have made a huge impact.

The argument here (cf. Bailey 2004) is that the success of Buddhism was conspicuous and that there must have developed a perception amongst the cultural elite (usually brahmins) that Buddhist monks were offering a total life-style, successfully being sold over many parts of the Subcontinent. In response to this, but also out of a desire to define a normative form of monarchical government, the brahmins developed their own coherent vision of culture that would cohere different social classes and ethnic groups, one that did not need the formal institutional base of the Buddhists and the Jains. This was formalized in the Dharmasūtras and Dharmaśāstras (Bailey 2005), but these were texts having hardly any appeal to anyone beyond the most learned of the brahmins and were certainly well outside the comprehension of the great majority of the population. The advantage of the two epics is that they are able to encode their cultural vision within an extended plot easily accessible to people at all levels of society because of the ease with which they could be communicated in vernacular languages.

Judging from their success in redacting the *MBh*, the very anxiety presumably felt amongst certain brahmins that they needed to redefine their role is an index of the central position in cultural formation they believed they held. In my view this cultural position was well defined within the *MBh*, to the extent that even contested aspects of it are covered (Fitzgerald 2004: 100–42). Where the *MBh* is most significant is in presenting this picture within its own narrative context of an absolute crisis within the political and social culture of the area where it is set (Hiltebeitel 1976; Biardeau 2002). This crisis is used to bring out some of the most problematic elements associated with the definition of the king's role, definitions tested narratively speaking in the respective roles of many of the prominent characters in the *MBh*, and it highlights the theoretical exclusivity of the brahmin's role by developing characters (Droṇa, Bhīṣma, Viśvāmitra, Yudhiṣṭhira) who abrogate this role, introducing the possibility of *varṇasaṃkara* in their narrative roles. Such narratives either point to the actual (empirical) complexity of the brahmin's role—one strongly defined in contrast to the occupational categories of other classes—and/or portray an ideologically pure picture of how the brahmin should be seen by other classes in society. But this may be to present too much of a unidimensional reading of the text and one not paying sufficient attention to the kṣatriya, the other class so strongly highlighted.

In being traditionally recognized as the pre-eminent example of *itihāsa* or "the way things were," the *MBh* definitely drew upon multiple sources. Though we are unable definitely to locate precise narratives, it has long been known that the *Mahābhārata* draws upon *ākhyāna*, *purāṇa* and possibly *itihāsa* (Brockington 1998: 18-21) itself, using its own plot to reshape traditional material to serve its own ends, but we do not know where this plot came from. Yet it is not just the plot which tells us the prism through which the composers of the texts 'emplotted' the material available to them. The so-called didactic material in books five, twelve and thirteen is instructional and expository along the lines of the Dharmaśāstras and in its mode of instruction is intended to be such. It may be taken as performing a commentarial gloss on the issues raised in the narrative sections of the *MBh*, even if a full correlation has yet to be made between specific themes in the two different sections of the text. This in turn raises the question of the hermeneutical relationship between the two sections of the *MBh* and whether there is justification for even seeing two separate sections as many scholars have argued for and then assumed since the early part of the twentieth century. In an earlier paper (Bailey 1983) I argued that the didactic portions make explicit what is only implicit in the narrative parts of the epics, and we have to bear in mind that the narrative section runs throughout the entire length of the text and frames the didactic books, such that it inevitably gives a considerable lead in giving interpretative priority to one over the other (Thapar 1986: 363).

This has led to a tendency to read the *MBh* as a text composed of two different portions[3] and strikes at one of the hermeneutical problems lying at its heart (less so of the *Rāmāyaṇa*, where the śāstric component is much less): do these two sections bring with them two different 'emplotments' of whatever 'raw' data they have utilized and at what historic date should we cease to regard the *MBh* (in its two sections) as a product of the culture it reflects? The gist of this is well summarized by Fitzgerald:

> ... the more fundamental juxtaposition is between the regulating theme of the *RDhP* [*Rājadharmaparvan*], on the one hand, and the consummation of that theme in the *DDhP* [*Dānadharmaparvan*], on the other. The core of the *RDhP* promulgates a fundamental charter of brāhmaṇya kingship–one with various stipulations of brahmin authority and one that extends the status of dharma to variously apparently wicked practices of monarchical *nīti*—and the *DDhP* closes the arrangement with a set of texts that are concerned to specify the flow of wealth to brahmins in return for these blessings and their attendant services. The *Āpaddharmaparvan* (*ĀDhP*) and the *MDhP* play critically important auxiliary roles in establishing and clarifying the proper relationships among brahmins, their royal clients, and the larger society in which both the brahman and the kṣatriya must exist and survive. ... The *MDhP* provides a profound new rationale for society's privileging and supporting the brahmin elite (Fitzgerald 2006: 258).

As for the *Mokṣadharmaparvan*, the dating of the *MBh* (indeed, the status of the *MBh* as an ongoing process of dissemination until the present day) prevents scholars from tying it to a specific set of political and cultural conditions. It will never be able to be tied into a precise period, because the ideas contained in it are universal in their intent and could apply to any of the centuries after 200 BCE. Yet if we accept the widely held proposition that a fundamental redaction occurred in the *MBh* spurred on by the concerns of the brahmins then we must look for historical evidence indicative of brahmin self doubt beyond the text. The difficulty here is that it is the texts themselves—the *MBh* and the Dharmaśāstras—which project such a strong conviction of brahmanical pre-eminence.

A recent volume (Olivelle 2006) has posited the period between the Maurya and Gupta 'empires' as the period in which the development of the *MBh* occurred in conjunction with other foundational features of Indian civilization. The two outer limits (roughly 200 BCE and 400 CE) are often regarded as points of consolidation of prior periods where the institutions identified as existing around the time of these dates either did not exist, or represent points of greater cultural uniformity over the Subcontinent because of the larger area of geographical space consistent with control of a single group. Between the limits defined by these two 'empires' the situation is in every respect fluid with many different kingdoms rising and falling, the initial success of Buddhism becoming apparent and the perceived need amongst brahmins for Hinduism to be defined as a unitary cultural system. Plurality of a whole variety of forms is the defining characteristic of the time, at least to the external eye and from a great distance in time. The task of the historian is to try to reconstruct what cannot be known from the available sources, especially how the majority of the population viewed—if they did at all—the events of these six centuries and not just the literate (political) and artistic elite who seem to have been the principal agents in the production of our primary sources. What may seem like a period of great change, characterized by the input of many innovative cultural elements, may have seemed much more stable to the people living through it.

The Purāṇas

There is a commonly held view that the earliest Purāṇas date from the beginning of the Gupta period (Bhandare 2006: 72; Witzel 2006: 491; Brockington 1998: 286-87; Mylius 1988: 135; Rocher 1986: 100-01; O'Flaherty 1983; Thapar 1986: 376ff.; Renou and Filliozat 1985: 413), a dating which would chronologically dovetail with the end of the main period of the brahmanical revision of the *MBh*. This view partially relates to the listings in the Purāṇic genealogies, but also to other factors relating to date of composition. From a strict hermeneutical perspective it is surely the case that this is fortuitous given the strong overlap between the *MBh* and the Purāṇas, at least regarded as such by contemporary scholars.

Winternitz offers this highly influential opinion on the relationship—if not sheer identity—between the *MBh* and the Purāṇas:

> It is difficult to determine the exact position of the Purāṇas in the history of Indian literature, both according to contents and chronologically. Actually they belong to the *religious* literature, and are, for the later Indian religion, which is generally called "Hinduism," and which culminates in the worship of Viṣṇu and Śiva, approximately what the Veda is for the oldest religion or Brahmanism. On the other hand, how closely the Purāṇas are connected with the *epic* compositions can already be deduced sufficiently from the fact that in the preceding chapters we repeatedly had to speak of them. Indeed, the Mahābhārata for the greater part and the Harivaṃśa almost entirely, are nothing other than Purāṇas, and even the later books and sections of the Rāmāyaṇa partake of the character of Purāṇas. (Winternitz 1971: 1.517; cf. Mylius 1988: 133)

There is much to recommend in this assessment of the two genres even if the problem of generic difference is substantially glossed over. His historical distinction between Brahminism and Hinduism, simplistic as the use of such labels might seem today, takes seriously the fundamentally different entities represented by those names. Yet there is a narrowness here in the attribution simply of a religious element in the Purāṇas. This might have been imputed because Winternitz regarded the Vedas as being fundamentally religious—that is, that they capture a religious spirit above all else—for the period attributed to them and that if there was an equivalent for everything regarded as post-Vedic this would have to be the Purāṇas. However, Vedic literature is in many respects narrow in its range of content and certainly restricted in its target audience, not so the Purāṇas in either respect. Apart from the more technical contents of texts like the *Agni Purāṇa* where medicine, grammar and *alaṃkāraśāstra* are found, the Mahāpurāṇas include large sections on *varṇāśramadharma*, imposing upon the whole genre a strong social element, as if they were virtual substitutes for the Dharmaśāstras. More problematic is Winternitz's reading back from the Purāṇas to the *MBh* and the *Harivaṃśa*, the latter correspondence being more credible given the similarity of this text's contents with the *pañcalakṣaṇāni*. We might mount the counter-objection that if the *MBh* is virtually not different from a Purāṇa, why was it accorded a different generic name both in the *MBh* itself and in the more scholastic tradition of poetics? Since Winternitz's *History* (1978), if not since Wilson's *Viṣṇu Purāṇa* (1840), received opinion has virtually been that the Purāṇas and the *MBh* draw upon an older body of literature, simply called purāṇa, understood as 'old lore' (Renou and Filliozat 1985: 1.412; Winternitz 1971: 517 and 520). The very idea of new genres drawing upon what is considered old correlates perfectly with the indigenous belief that what is old/tradition is to be valued highly. Antiquity is a value in itself. Obviously this is going to account for some commonality of content, yet Winternitz's view that the *MBh* is a Purāṇa surely represents a failure to appreciate the connection between the narrative and didactic portions of the text in the way this has been done by Fitzgerald, for example, because it is the multiplication of material in the didactic books that so concerns Winternitz (1971: 1.459) and others. Most of the Purāṇa-like material in the *MBh* occurs in the first, third and twelfth books and is reflected in creation myths and lineages, as well as in the dharmaśāstric material in books twelve and thirteen. It is the extended narrative plot of the *MBh* that makes it so markedly different from the Purāṇas with their short myths and interspersed didactic sections.

Winternitz and many other Indologists seem troubled by the occurrence of these explicitly didactic sections because they would like the genres to be much more tightly defined in their content (narrative plot) and style (running narrative). In this they give insufficient recognition to the significance of eclecticism (or intertextuality, to use a more modern term) as one of the defining features of Purāṇic style. All scholars implicitly recognize this eclecticism but do not wish to elevate it to the status of a defining interpretative paradigm. In other publications (Bailey 1987: 106-14; 1995) I have criticized the desire of many European scholars to reshape Purāṇic contents into a frame easier for them to work with, the *pañcalakṣaṇa* frame being the one most desired, following the influential early work of Kirfel (1927). In part this reflects a philological obsession with the recovery of the original form of a text and a difficulty in assigning interpretative value with what has been added over time. It is to the credit of R.C. Hazra (1975) that in several pioneering works the historical transformations that occurred in the individual Mahāpurāṇas (less so in the Upapurāṇas) was firmly established and elevated into forming an integral part of the Purāṇic tradition, above all because it took seriously the eclecticism of the Purāṇas. That means one of the principal hermeneutical tasks of the Purāṇa scholar is to define that specific generic quality which enables the Purāṇas to be reshaped, where what was original or early is of no more importance to the genre than what is late.

If we distinguish between a Purāṇic process as a compositional strategy of integrating data into a body of established literature and as a set of texts deemed as having an original form continually subject to addition, then two different interpretative emphases are implied. The first method, represented best in the work of V. Narayana Rao (1993; 2004) extrapolates from the existing Purāṇas a mode of composition in which content undergoes the filter of a particular ideology to make it eligible to be called Purāṇic. Focussing on this requires us to consider the perceived needs of audiences and disseminators alike in privileging certain information and adding new material to an existing text. It is not so much a case of the Purāṇic audience knowing they will be witnessing a *known transformation* from *a known earlier version* of the text, as more of a vague recognition that what is included is there because it is of contemporary interest at the time of reception, yet is given the touch of antiquity merely by being found within the Purāṇa, such that it appears always to have been within the tradition.[4] But this begs the question of whether Purāṇic recitation was always perceived (received) like this. At some stage the tradition must have become popular (at a level outside of that of the educated brahmin) and have become so because of the status involved in something's being associated with the Purāṇa process.

The second is also historical. It ties the Purāṇas down to a body of content at the micro-level of specific myths and motifs, and focuses on the subsequent development of these contents. Changes in the contents are contrasted with the earliest and earlier forms of what that content might be. It focuses more on identifiable units of composition rather than on entire texts (as Hazra has extrapolated from the *Dānasāgara* and later *Nibandhas*), substantially ignoring the mode of combining such contents within an individual Purāṇa. Despite its strong historicism, it does take seriously the idea of the Purāṇic process, but only to the extent this can be reduced to a mechanical process.

Narayana Rao has been especially insightful in elucidating the first view of Purāṇa as a kind of 'civilizational process'. He describes what he calls a Purāṇic ideology, encompassing both creation and, above all, actual reception of the genre in respect of its individual texts, and extends the traditional scholarly understanding of *pañcalakṣaṇa* when he writes: "The five *lakṣaṇas* order the events of the Purāṇa. They provide the listeners with a view of time and space in which the events narrated in the Purāṇas occur. In other words, the *pañcalakṣaṇas* create a world and a worldview" (1993: 89). He further argues that the resulting ideological frame means that the individual Purāṇas "do not work in isolation; they are part of a totality of a text tradition with intertextual relationships and commentarial contexts. One could make sense of any of these texts only by listening to the texts as part of this tradition" (Narayana Rao 1993: 92). And it is in the oral transmission of this tradition that the sense of process becomes fundamental, for he argues that,

> Each Purāṇa has a different speaker. However, it is important to note that no speaker ever directly narrates. All the Purāṇa narratives are reported narratives. Each speaker has an earlier speaker. Each listener has an earlier listener. They look inward and backward drawing us into an ideologically closed environment. *But if the Purāṇas are ideologically closed texts, they are functionally open texts: they have accepted into their fold events, stories, legends and occurrences of many regions and communities, transforming them to conform to a fixed ideology.* (Narayana Rao 1993: 94, my italics)

This is immensely valuable in explaining the on-going co-existence of a set of generic characteristics in the face of a massive variance in the content of the texts allegedly possessing these characteristics. But shifting away from the subject of Purāṇa as cultural process to Purāṇa as historical document where does it leave an Indologist's assessment of the Purāṇas as historical sources? Probably not much beyond the advances Hazra had made in his path breaking *Purāṇic Records*, in which he consistently argues that the earliest Purāṇas are texts of a brahminical counter-reaction or revival against the Buddhists and the followers of an emerging Tantrism. Here White's idea of 'emplotment' emerges in Hazra's (1975:

Part 2)[5] explicit use of the Purāṇas as the central part of a narrative where the brahmins as a self-conscious class are portrayed countering any religious, social or ethnic movements seemingly threatening the hegemony of the culture they represent. This plot of resistance has also been applied (by Fitzgerald) to the *MBh* and arguably it could also be read into the period (roughly 1206–1707) between the Delhi Sultanate and the Mughals when the Nibandhas were being composed, texts re-codifying the fundamental principles of brahmanical society using the Purāṇas as the theoretical foundation for this codification. This 'emplotment' has become paradigmatic, especially for scholars from South Asia whether in the methodologically unsophisticated Purāṇa Studies (Bailey 2003: 157-59) or the theoretically informed work of Kunal Chakravarti. Whilst it has explanatory power for the role of the brahmins in redacting the *MBh*, this is not a continuity between *MBh* and Purāṇa, but an identical emplotment of their role in early historical India. One final point needs to be made about what might seem to be either a fundamental difference between the *MBh* and the Purāṇas or just another hidden form of continuity. Bhakti in all of its manifestations as the theory and practice of devotion is just emerging in the *MBh* and the *Rāmāyaṇa* and yet dominates the Purāṇas. It is arguable that the exposition of bhakti was not part of the brahmanical agenda in their socio-political theory presented in the *MBh*. Their agenda required the elevation of the group over the individual, a position according well with the social disposition associated with the Vedic sacrifice that had by and large become vestigial in the *MBh*. However, bhakti breaks through the distinction between community and individual as the deity can be approached collectively or singly by the devotee (cf. O'Flaherty 1983: 110). The Purāṇas are of course filled with examples of both, yet the principal example in the *MBh* is largely restricted to the *Bhagavadgītā*, unless the *Nārāyaṇīyaparvan* should be regarded as the text of a community of *vaiṣṇava bhaktas*. Given that both genres have been appropriated by the brahmins, the greater focus of the Purāṇas on bhakti in contrast with the focus on society and politics in the *MBh*, suggests obviously a different level of self-understanding and confidence on the part of the brahmins. To put it simplistically, the brahmins utilize the *MBh* to establish their socio-cultural hegemony, at least as standing at the top of four classes. Once this hegemony has been established, it must simply be communicated to others who do not accept it or are not sensitive to it. One attractive way to do this, as several scholars have argued, must have been to appropriate existing cults living on the fringes of 'metropolitan society' and to integrate these within a pre-existing theological framework, represented by the huge body of mythology growing ever larger since the Vedas, and to define this pragmatically in terms of *pūjā*, a basic ritual simple to perform and cheap as well (Renou and Filliozat 1985: 1.413; Witzel 2006: 491).

Genre, History and Ideology

Theories of interpretation are always difficult and tend to be formally eschewed by Indologists who rely substantially on the implicit and positivistic methodology favoured by classical philology. Ethnographers of contemporary India are less positivistic and utilize interpretative frameworks derived from social theory, all more easily testable on the basis of empirical data. The problem with classicists is that they too might like to function as ethnologists by working on texts of an alien culture (except for those from South Asia itself), whose level(s) of meaning they must unpack before entering into the observations an ethnologist can make. Yet the perpetual gap between the texts they use as artefacts of culture during a particular historical period and the actual culture of which those texts are an artefact remains yawning and disallows the kinds of verification procedures available in ethnology.

But are we talking in fantasies? At least three problems confront us:

(1) Dating the texts. (2) Defining the genre of the texts. (3) Tracing the relationship(s) between the text and its total historical context.

These questions already presuppose other questions:

(1) Can we define the genres? (2) Is there a connection between genre and history? (3) Is there a logical (= generic) and historical connection between the two genres, namely the *MBh* one and the Purāṇic one.

These are fundamental questions and cannot be answered easily. Their utility may only lie in the stimulus they provide in making us seek more clarification in the connection between genre and historical knowledge, because to date the embedding of a particular genre within a broader historical frame has not been investigated much in Indological scholarship. We are surely correct to assume there is an epistemological gap between the kind of knowledge extracted from literary sources and from all other sources in the ancient Indian context. This would scarcely be disputed by most scholars, yet most would be prepared implicitly to find major generic continuities between the *MBh* and the Purāṇas, but would struggle to propose an historical foundation for the continuity apart from the on-going role of brahmins in the expansion of a particular form of society beyond its metropolitan and existing brahminized areas. Even this seems to favour a particular form of 'emplotment', possibly corresponding to a particular brahminical self-consciousness in the twentieth century. As such it is rather too smooth to come to terms fully with what must have been a much more messy and complex set of historical conditions existing on the ground outside of these somewhat normative texts. In view of this complexity, as evidenced so demonstrably in twentieth century ethnographic studies, the task of the student of ancient India is to develop a hermeneutics of complexity and multiple readings as opposed to one of simplicity and distinctive emplotment.

Notes

1. It is not my intention here to take up the difficult hermeneutical question of the relationship between literary and non-literary sources in the study of early Indian history. An excellent survey of the problems is given in Bhandare 2006: 67-75.

2. The point being that a modern reader will expect different standards of transparency of sources and consistency of argument in contemporary works of history, but will not look for the same in the primary sources used by historians.

3. See Thapar 2002: 102, who prefers to talk about later interpolations, and Biardeau 2002, who does not deal with the didactic portions.

4. This is very eloquently paraphrased by Romila Thapar: "Purāṇic literature, in the sections other than the vaṅśānucarita, reflects facets of change which impinged upon the historical tradition. It comprises essentially assimilative texts where the Sanskritic tradition and the local tradition are sought to be intermeshed. This was inevitable in a situation where those of a Sanskritic cultural milieu received grants of land and settled in areas where the exposure to Sanskritic culture had been relatively sparse, if at all. ... The culture of the dominant and of the subordinate remained distinct, but proximity and some degree of absorption smoothened the edges of an otherwise angular relationship in many areas (1986: 372-73)."

5. O'Flaherty (1983: 108) reads the Purāṇas in an identical way but not the *MBh*.

Bibliography

Bailey, Greg. 1983. "Suffering in the Mahābhārata: Draupadī and Yudhiṣṭhira," *Collections Puruśārtha* 7: 109-29.

——. 1987. "On the Object of Study in Purāṇic Research: Three Recent Books on the Purāṇas," *Asian Studies Association of Australia* 10 (3): 106-14.

——. 1995. *The Gaṇeśa Purāṇa. Volume One: Upāsanā Khaṇḍa.* Otto Harrassowitz: Wiesbaden.

——. 2003. "The Purāṇas. A Study in the Development of Hinduism," in A. Sharma, ed., *The Study of Hinduism.* Columbia (S.C.): University of South Carolina Press.

——. 2004. "The Mahābhārata as Counterpoint to the Pāli Canon," *Orientalia Suecana* LIII: 37-48.

——. 2005. "Introduction. Epics, Khilas and Purāṇas. Continuities and Ruptures," in Koskikallio, P., ed., *Epics, Khilas and Purāṇas. Continuities and Ruptures.* Zagreb: Croatian Academy of Arts and Sciences.

Bhandare, S. 2006. "Numismatic Overview of the Maurya-Gupta Interlude," in P. Olivelle, ed.

Biardeau, M. 2002. *Le Mahābhārata: un récit fondateur du brahmanisme et son interpretation.* Paris: Seuil.

Brockington, J. L. 1998. *The Sanskrit Epics.* Leiden: Brill.

Chakravarti, K. 2001. *Religious Process: The Puranas and the Making of a Regional Tradition.* Delhi: Oxford University Press.

Fitzgerald, J.L. 2004. *The Mahābhārata, Volume 7.* Chicago: University of Chicago Press.

——. 2006. "Negotiating the Shape of 'Scripture': New Perspectives on the Development and Growth of the Mahābhārata between the Empires," in P. Olivelle, ed.

Hazra, R.C. 1975. *Studies in the Puranic Records on Hindu Rites and Customs.* Delhi: Motilal Banarsidass, original 1940.

Hiltebeitel, A. 1976. *The Ritual of Battle: Krishna in the Mahabharata.* Ithaca: Cornell University Press.

Kirfel, W. 1927. *Das Purāṇa Pañcalakṣaṇa.* Bonn: Schroeder.

Lesny, V. 1913. "Über das purāṇaartige Gepräge des Bālakāṇḍa," *Zeitschrift der Deutschen Morgenländischen Gesellschaft* 67: 497-500.

Mylius, K. 1988. *Geschichte der altindischen Literatur.* Bern: Scherz.

Narayana Rao, V. 1983. "Purāṇa as Brahminic Ideology," in Wendy Doniger, ed. *Purāṇa Perennis: Reciprocity and Transformation in Hindu and Jaina Texts.* Albany: SUNY Press.

——. 2004. "Purāṇa," in S. Mittal and G. Thursby, eds. *The Hindu World.* New York: Routledge.

O'Flaherty, W. D. 1983. "The Image of the Heretic in the Gupta Purāṇas," in B.L. Smith, ed., *Essays on Gupta Culture.* Delhi: Motilal Banarsidass.

Olivelle, P., ed. 2006. *Between The Empires. Society in India 300 BCE to 400 CE.* New York: Oxford University Press.

Renou, L. and J. Filliozat. 1985. *L'Inde Classique. Manuel des Études Indiennes.* Paris: Adrien Maisonneuve, original 1947-49.

Rocher, L. 1986. *The Purāṇas*, Wiesbaden: Otto Harrassowitz.

Thapar, R. 1986. "Society and Historical Consciousness: The Itihāsa-Purāṇa Tradition," in S. Bhattacharya and R. Thapar, eds. *Situating Indian History for Sarvapelli Gopal.* Delhi: Oxford University Press.

____. 2002. *Early India: From the Origins to AD 1300.* Berkeley: University of California Press.

White, H. 1978. *Tropics of Discourse: Essays in Cultural Criticism.* Baltimore: The Johns Hopkins University Press.

Winternitz, M. 1971. *A History of Indian Literature.* New York: Russell and Russell, original 1907.

Witzel, M. 2006. "Brahmanical Reactions to Foreign Influences and to Social and Religious Change," in P. Olivelle, ed.

Is the Script Relevant? Further Evidence from a Nevārī-script *Rāmāyaṇa* Manuscript

JOHN BROCKINGTON

If my memory serves me correctly, it is 36 years since Robert Goldman and I first met—in Pune, where we were each studying and researching—just months after he first became fascinated by the idea of translating the *Rāmāyaṇa*.[1] Although we were both by then publishing articles on the *Rāmāyaṇa*, this was over 15 years before the publication of his translation of the *Bālakāṇḍa* and my *Righteous Rāma*. Since then we have both continued to work on the *Rāmāyaṇa* (as well as on other topics) and so it seems fitting, in this volume celebrating Robert Goldman's achievements during his scholarly career, to contribute a further study on *Rāmāyaṇa* manuscripts, or more precisely on one particular manuscript, and thereby also fulfill an intention that I expressed a good many years ago. That intention was voiced in the context of earlier work on manuscripts of the *Ayodhyākāṇḍa* and I noted then that I was unable to locate any further Nevārī-script manuscripts of that book but that I did locate one of the *Araṇyakāṇḍa*.[2]

That manuscript is ms 4828 of the Government Collection held in the Asiatic Society, Calcutta, which is a palmleaf manuscript in Nevārī script but in poor condition; it is regarded as of seventeenth-century date in the Asiatic Society catalogue but the script suggests it could well be older.[3] Its fragmentary state may well be the reason that it was not utilised for the Critical Edition (for which other manuscripts in this collection were used), since it is certainly the case that most of the manuscripts selected are essentially complete, whereas many older manuscripts have lost parts of their text. The editors' tendency to choose complete texts may well have resulted in the use of younger manuscripts. Since very large numbers of *Rāmāyaṇa* manuscripts are preserved in various collections, most of which are extremely late in the overall history of the transmission of the text (ruling out the possibility of establishing a stemma codicum), the number of manuscripts used for the Critical Edition is actually quite small: the largest number was used for the Uttarakāṇḍa and the smallest—29—was used for the *Ayodhyā*, *Araṇya* and *Sundara kāṇḍas*, although admittedly a larger number was initially collated. Variant readings and new patterns of omission or addition can therefore be found in virtually every manuscript examined. Even more significantly, this evidence is crucial to drawing a truer picture of the complex relationships between the different recensions and versions. This is indeed vastly more complex than the picture presented in the introductions to the successive volumes of the Critical Edition, although it can to quite an extent be teased out by careful study of the Critical Apparatus, even before further manuscript evidence is adduced.

Essentially the point at issue is that the Critical Edition's system of assigning manuscripts to recensions or to script versions is almost as limiting as constructing a stemma codicum (which does have the merit of corresponding on the whole to the way that manuscripts are propagated). The drawback is that this still involves an either/or situation, where a particular manuscript is assigned to a particular recension or version, or else is casually dismissed as "contaminated" or a "Mischcodex". The reality is that script boundaries are by no means as rigid as this scheme of classification would suggest and that the only effective way of tracing alignments is by plotting the shared features of specific manuscripts.[4]

A particularly good example of this is indeed provided by the two manuscripts in Nevārī script used for both the *Ayodhyā* and *Araṇya kāṇḍas.* Although they are classified as representative of the NE recension, Divanji was constrained to remark in his introduction to the *Araṇyakāṇḍa* that "Ñ1 is leaning towards the NW Version while Ñ2 is leaning towards the NE Version."[5] What is particularly significant here is that Ñ1 is the oldest *Rāmāyaṇa* manuscript known by a considerable margin (it is dated saṃvat 1076 = CE 1020) and, if the alignments by script do not hold good in its case, why should they subsequently?

Still, let me continue by giving some particulars of this manuscript. It is written on palmleaf, measuring 15 inches by 2 inches, with 4 lines to the side and around 60 *akṣaras* to the full line; gaps in the second and third lines of text to allow room for the string hole (which is somewhat to the left of centre) reduce these lines by about 5 *akṣaras*. The writing is in general clear and careful. The line ends are marked by single and double *daṇḍas* but neither verses nor *sargas* are numbered (all my references are therefore to the numbering of the CE); sargas are, however, given names. The leaves bear a clear contemporary numbering in the right margin of the verso. The manuscript starts on f.1 with an invocation (*oṃ namo rāmabhadrāya || jitam bhagavatā tena hariṇā lokadhāriṇā | ajena viśvarūpeṇa nirguṇena guṇatmananā*), after which the text follows without a break, beginning at 2.108.1, since the manuscript follows the *kāṇḍa* division of the NE recension. Several leaves are missing throughout and the last leaf extant is numbered 144 but it is followed by a further six leaves (displaced from earlier because of loss of their numbers and several reversed),[6] which are damaged on the right and/or left margin, as are many within the main body of the manuscript.[7] In all there are some 24 leaves missing out of the total of 144—a sixth of the total. The final f.144 contains on its numbered verso the passage 3.52.3c-5c, including 1027*, well short of the end of the *Araṇyakāṇḍa*. The manuscript is thus doubly incomplete.

There are occasional *akṣaras* (probably in the same hand) in the left margin which are no doubt corrections to the text, although it is often not possible on the microfilm to ascertain with certainty where they relate to, since mostly erasures are not easily discernible. Features of the orthography include the doubling commonly of consonants after *r* (most consistently of *m*, whereas *y* is never doubled), lack of distinction between *b* and *v*, the use always of *cch* initially for *ch*, the not infrequent erroneous addition or omission of *visarga* or *anusvāra*, and the use quite generally of the homorganic nasal (and of *m* before *v*) but of *anusvāra* in pausa. There is frequent confusion between *s* and *ś* (for example *śaṃsitavratāḥ* for *saṃśita°* at 3.9.4b) and indeed Sītā's name is invariably spelt *śītā*, which even has repercussions for sandhi: for example, the manuscript has *katicic chīte* for *katicit sīte* at 2.2375*1 and *tasmāc śīteti* for *tasmāt sīteti* at 2.2389*3. Conversely, Śurpaṇakhā's name is regularly written as *sūrpanakhā*.[8] In addition, there is occasional substitution of *kṣ* for *kh* (e.g. at 2.109.16) or *ṣ* (e.g. 2.109.17b and 3.7.18b) and of *ṣ* for *kh* (e.g. 3.5.3a and 204*3) or *kh* for *ṣ* (e.g. 3.102*3 and 7.14a). These last clearly reflect regional pronunciation, as no doubt do such instances as *upajātaḥ* for *upayātaḥ* at 3.6.10c and conversely of *yuṣṭam* for *juṣṭam* at 3.164*.

Other features which may well reflect pronunciation, not simply orthography, are the fairly frequent retention of final *t* before initial *m* (e.g. at 3.1.9c, 3.19b, 53*1 post., 3.21c) and the occasional absence of voicing of *t* before an initial vowel (e.g. at 3.15*2), the spelling *rugma-* (e.g. at 3.40*2 and 4.9b) rather than *rukma-* (found, however, at 3.45*1), *rājena* for *rājyena* at 3.2.18a, *vālakhillāḥ* for *vālakhilyāḥ* at 3.5.2a, and possibly *prāpsyasepatyam* for *prāpsasy apatyam* at 2.2385*12. Occasional failure to write retroflex *ṇ* where required (e.g. *santvaramānayā* at 2.108.12b and *ramyāni* at 3.9.21d and 142*1) may simply betoken carelessness or may be the result of copying from an exemplar in a different script (*ṇ* in the Bengali script could easily be misread as *n*); other likely instances of misreadings arising in this way include *yāsyānadīnivāsānām* for *pampā°* at 3.5.16a, *bhāsām* for *tāsām* at 3.10.16c, *nīna-* for *nīla-* at 3 App.2.3 and *upamucyate* for *upabhujyate* at 3.10.80d.[9] Variant *sandhis* include the not uncommon use of *visarga* rather than *ṣ* before *k* (e.g. *niḥkrama* at 3.10.6c), a feature which it shares with the Maithilī manuscript of the *Araṇyakāṇḍa*, V1, and the use of *ardhacandra* rather than *anusvāra* on f.33v, covering 3 App.I.2 (where exceptionally there are also corrections in the top and bottom margins). The scribe also occasionally uses *l* for *ḍ* (e.g. *vilolitam* for *viloḍitam* at 3.144*1 and *balisa-* for *baḍiśa-* at 3.49.22c v.l.). One idiosyncratic wrong spelling is *śrārddha* for *śrāddha* (3.10.54d, 55d and 171*12), perhaps prompted by the doubled consonant. Such orthographic variants and trivial errors will be ignored in my subsequent analysis, unless they are relevant to the point being made (or I am quoting directly from the manuscript).

My remarks on this manuscript are based primarily on thirty leaves from the beginning (ff.1-37 in its numbering because of lost leaves, excluding f.<35>), which cover 25% of the total manuscript and form therefore an adequately representative sample.[10] The first eight of these leaves (ff.1-10) correspond to the end of the *Ayodhyākāṇḍa* in the Critical Edition; unfortunately, the transition to the CE *Araṇyakāṇḍa* must have been on the now lost f.11. The use of different manuscripts for the two *kāṇḍas* of the Critical Edition has meant that some of the material below needs to be presented in these two parts.

One feature that is relatively constant throughout the sample is the considerable proportion of unique readings, which constitute between a fifth and a quarter of the variants (nearly 22% in the *Ayodhyā* section and over 23% in the *Araṇya* section); unique variants also continue throughout the text. The manuscript shows very few unique additions or omissions. Indeed, the only addition within the sample is an expansion to the sententious 3.209* by adding an extra line between its two lines, which themselves show unique variants:

gṛhāgataṃ nātithiṃ yo yathāśaktyā prapūjayet ||
atithir yasya bhagnāśo gṛhāt pratinivarttate |
datvā svaṃ duḥkṛtaṃ tasya puṇyam ādāya gacchati ||

However, at a later point it adds an apparently unique line (*gṛhītvā vinatañ capi cāyaṃ hātakabhūṣaṇaṃ*) following 3.42.4ab (in which it follows the v.l. of V1 B4 D5.7) and it also continues the *sarga* from 28 to 29 by reading 558* without a break following 554*8 (although Ś1 D1-3 continue the *sarga* here too, their text is considerably different). Within the sample unique omissions are of 2.109.13ab, 2.110.24cd, 3.1.8 and 3.3.1-10 (apart from 33* after 2.13ab; however, all NE mss except Ñ1 omit 10), and there is a unique transposition of 3.97*1-2.

Most of the manuscript's unique readings are of course relatively minor variants without any appreciable impact on the sense (such as its second unique reading, *saumitrer* for *lakṣmaṇasya* at 2.108.6c), and some are clearly corruptions (such as its first unique reading, *(va)ḥ śītā* + + + *kṛtaṃ* at 2.108.5b, which—fragmentary as it is—clearly does not coincide with any recorded reading), but some are interesting in themselves for one reason or another. For example, its *yadi pāpo bhaved bharttā mamārye dharmmavarjjitaḥ* is stronger than the Critical Edition text at 2.110.3ab, *yady apy eṣa bhaved bhartā mamārye vṛttavarjitaḥ*, or any of its listed variants (but the fact that it shares the variant *upakartavyas* for *upavartavyas* in *c* only with Dm1 is no doubt purely coincidental). Again, its reading of *phālayann* at 3.2.9d (*cālayann iva medinīm*) uses a rarer verb to make the simile more vivid, suggesting either an ancient variant unattested elsewhere or a more literate scribe than the rest of the manuscript indicates, although its *gatāyor* for *gatāsor* just a few verses later at 3.2.22c might point in that direction (as might *satyapūrvaṃ* for *mṛdupūrvaṃ* later in the text, at 3.38.10b). The distribution of these unique readings is also rather variable, with as many as 53 in 3.10 (including 7 in App.I 2, included within this *sarga*) and 23 in 2.110 to as few as four in 3.4 and three in 3.7, but the variation appears to be random. An interesting instance from later in the text occurs at 3.38.4c, where this manuscript reads *adharmmaśīlasya* for *pāpaśīlasya* of the CE text and this hypermetric variant is closest to the reading of V B1.3, *dharmaśīlasya*, in form but to the reading of Ś1 Ñ2 B4 D2.3.5.7, *dharmahīnasya*, in meaning.

While the number and quality of these unique readings are relevant to an assessment of the significance of the manuscript as a whole, its alignments with the various groupings visible in the apparatus of the Critical Edition are more relevant to an assessment of the validity of the groupings by script which is my main focus in this article. The readings shared with all N manuscripts—28 (*c.* 10%) in the *Ayodhyā* section and 48 (*c.* 7.5%) in the *Araṇya* section—reveal more about the editorial policy of the CE editors than anything else and can be left out of account. The proportion of readings shared with both Ñ manuscripts and varying numbers of other manuscripts is similar in both sections (19, *c.* 7%, in the *Ayodhyā* section and 31, c. 5%, in the *Araṇya* section) but there is a striking difference in the proportions shared with only one of them: in the *Ayodhyā* section 50 (nearly 20%) are shared with Ñ1 but not Ñ2 and 79 (over 28%) with Ñ2 but not Ñ1, whereas in the *Araṇya* section 23 (under 4%) are shared with Ñ1 but not Ñ2 and 287 (45%) with Ñ2 but not Ñ1. Thus, the degree of commonality with Ñ1 is markedly lower in the second section than in the first.

But even this does not tell the whole story. The section of text from 2.110.22 to the end of *Ayodhyā* goes often (59 times) with a grouping Ñ2 V1 B2.3 but the only previous instance of this is at 2.109.6b (where, however, the reading of the other NE manuscripts is little different). Conversely, the section from 2.108.1 to 110.8 goes frequently (32 times) with the grouping Ś1 Ñ1 B1 D2.4-6 (plus or minus one D ms), but only at 110.34d after 110.21. The shift may well have been at the further colophon added after 110.20/2382* by all N mss (absent in this ms on the lost f.6). Both of these groupings are subsets of the Northern recension but they do not correspond to either the NE (Ñ1-2, V1 B1-4, D4) or the NW + W (Ś1 D6-7 + D1-3.5) groupings identified for the *Ayodhyā* manuscripts of the CE, not even by moving Ñ1 from NE to NW. In particular, not only do they separate the two Nevārī manuscripts but the Bengali manuscripts are also divided between them. By contrast, in the *Araṇya* section the largest number of shared readings (180, 28%) is with the grouping Ñ2 V B D5.7, which comprises all NE manuscripts except Ñ1.

More interesting still are the rather smaller proportion of instances where this manuscript shares readings with one or more other NE manuscripts, without the Ñ mss. There are 29 of these in the *Ayodhyā* section (nearly 11% of the total) and 79 (around 12%) in the *Araṇya* section. More specifically still, 9 of the 29 (over 3% of the total) are shared with V1 (the only Maithilī-script manuscript for the *Ayodhyā* section, where it is in fact V1 of the *Araṇyakāṇḍa*) and one or more other NE manuscripts (3 of them with V1 alone) and 42 of the 79 (over 6.5%) with one or both of the Maithilī-script manuscripts for the *Araṇya* section plus one or more other NE manuscripts (7 of them with V1 alone). A particularly striking example from outside the sample occurs within *sarga* 45 (on f.126), where not only does it not have 893* (the only exclusive *passage of Ñ2) but in 896* it has a variant recorded for V1 alone (for the record, in its next line, 45.35cd, it uniquely reads *bhuṃktvā* for *pītvā*, while a little earlier at 30c it has the variant of the NW manuscripts Ś1 D1-3). When we add to these agreements with the Maithilī-script manuscripts, the instances where the reading of this Nevārī manuscript is shared with just one of the Bengali manuscripts (8 in the *Ayodhyā* section and 14 in the *Araṇya* section, with another 4 shared with more than one Bengali manuscript but no others), it is clear that the alignment of this manuscript is not with an exclusively Nevārī version nor yet with Ñ2 alone (for it shares only 4 readings in the whole of the sample solely with one or both of the two CE Nevārī mss) but rather with the NE recension in a broad sense.

Instances of readings shared only with the Maithilī-script manuscripts or only with the Bengali ones continue throughout the text. Instances noted include *sthiraḥ* for *sthitaḥ* in 464*4 with V1 only, *dharmadārapradharṣaṇāt* with V1 only at 3.49.23b (in a v.l. common to Ñ2 V1 B1.3.4 D5.7, the others reading *°dharṣaṇaṃ*), *gamyate* for *gaccha tvaṃ* at 3.979*7 with V1 only, *aham* for *ayam* at 549*7 with V2 only, omission with V of 554*9-12 (the whole passage is inserted by Ñ2 V B1.3.4 D5.7) and of App.I.11.56-59 with V1 only, and *pātayiṣye* for *pātayeyaṃ* at 3.22.20b with B2.3 only. Sometimes the agreement is with some Maithilī and Bengali mss together against other NE mss, as when it reads 3.27.1 after 26.20 in common with Ñ2 V B1.3.4 D5.7 but not 514* (which V B1.3 also do not), reads *atipragalbhasya tathā* for 29.3c with V B4, has *upāyaṃ* with V1 B3 in the NE v.l. for 38.8c, and has the same transposition as V1 B1.4 at 793*.[11]

Another way in which this broader alignment can be seen is in the extent to which it follows the pattern of insertion typical of the NE recension: while in general terms this is the case, it has its own unique variants within several of these insertions and furthermore it does not insert 3.8* (read by Ñ2 V1 B D7—a clear majority of the NE mss), for example, and omits 2.109.1d-2367*2 pr. in common with B1 only and 2.110.22ab with B2 only. Again, as with other manuscripts that I have examined previously, there are occasional readings which it shares with Gorresio's edition only (*dharmyābhiḥ* at 2.2385*2 and *nakṣatragrahamaṇḍitā* at 2.111.9b), further confirming that the manuscript basis for that edition included some not used for the Critical Edition. There are also the instances where it shows varying alignments within a single verse; that is, in terms of the CE manuscripts its readings are shared with quite distinct manuscripts. Examples can be found at 2.2360* (*munayo rāmaṃ* with B1, *tatra* uniquely, *padmadalekṣanaṃ* with Ñ1 D4.5), 2.110.47 (*āropayatā* with Ñ1 B1-3 D2.4-6 M4, *tac ca* with Ñ2 B2.3, *hi tad* for *dvidhā* uniquely, *'bhavad ghoraḥ* with V1 B2) and 3.10.22 (readings in *a* and *c* shared with V1 only and D1 only). It would clearly be misguided to think of this in terms of eclecticism by the scribe of this manuscript. It is yet another demonstration of the fact that, while it makes sense to think of a NE recension in broad terms, there is no such thing as a single script tradition, even though manuscripts from one area (a deliberately geographical term) tend to have more in common. Elsewhere I have proposed that a better model than either the Critical Edition's system of script versions or a stemma codicum would be the Venn diagram, which with its overlapping circles or ovals can better indicate degrees of commonality between various manuscripts, as well as being capable of arrangement to a certain extent in a form reminiscent of geographical relationships.[12]

A further way in which the agreement with other manuscripts can be explored is through examination of the *sarga* names. These are as follows (standardly preceded by *āraṇyake*, here omitted, with a note of the manuscripts having identical or similar names):[13]

3.1	*āśramadarśano nāma*	cf. *āśramadarśanam* Ñ2 V1 B1.2
3	*virādhavadhaḥ*	as Ñ2 V B D1-3.5.7
4	*śarabhaṅgabrahmalokagamanaṃ*	none at all close
5	*sutīkṣṇāśramagamanaṃ*	none at all close (but cf. D3 for *sarga* 6)
7	*sutīkṣṇāśramanivāsaḥ*	as Ś1 Ñ V B D3.5.7
8	*daṇḍakāraṇyapraveśe śītavākyaṃ*	as V2 B3 D3 (cf. B2.4 D2)
9	*<daṇḍa>kāraṇyapraveśe rāmavākyaṃ*	as B2-4
after 10.41	*<aga>styakīrtanaṃ*	as B2
after 10.68	*agastyabhrātṛdarśanaṃ*	as V B
10	*agastyāśramavarṇṇanā*	as B2-4 (°*ṇaṃ* in Ñ V B1 D3.5.7)
11	*dhanuḥpradānaṃ*	as V B
12	*agastyopadeśaḥ*	as Ñ2 V B2-4 D5.7
14	*pañcavaṭyāśramaniveśaḥ*	most N have °*nivāsaḥ*
15	*hemantasamayavarṇṇanā*	most N have *hemantavarṇanaṃ*

16	*<sūrpana>khādarśanaṃ*	as all N (°*khī*° in D3)
17	*sūrpanakhāvirūpaṇaṃ*	as Ñ1 V2 B2-4
18	*kharaprahitarākṣasaprayāṇaṃ*	as B1.3 (cf. V B2.4)
19	*kharaprahitarākṣasacaturddaśavadhaḥ*	as V1 B1
20	*kharoddīpaṇaṃ*	as Ñ2 V B D5.7
21	*kharaniryāṇaṃ*	as Ñ V2 B D1.5.7 (°*ṇaḥ* in D2.3)
22	*kharanidarśanaṃ*	none close
23	*kharasainyadarśanaṃ*	as V B
24	*kharasainyavināśaṃ*	none close
25	*dūṣaṇavadhaḥ*	as all N (except Ñ1 and B2)
26	*triśiraso vadhaḥ*	cf. *triśirovadhaḥ* in Ś1 Ñ V B1.3.4 D5.7
27	*kharavirathīkaraṇaṃ*	as all N (except absent from B2)
30	*rāvaṇavarṇṇanā*	as B1.4 (°*naṃ* in Ñ2 V1 D5.7)
31	*rāvaṇoddīpaṇaṃ*	as Ñ2 V B1.3.4 D5.7
32	*sūrppanakhāvākyaṃ*	as Ñ2 V B1.3.4 D1.3.5.7
33	*mārīcāśramapraveśaḥ*	as V B1.3.4
34	*rāvaṇavākyaṃ*	as all N that name the *sarga*
35	*mārīca<vākyam>*	as all N that name the *sarga*
36	*mārīcavākyaṃ*	as all N that name the *sarga*
37	*mārīcavākyaṃ*	as Ñ2 V2 B1.3 D3.7
39	*mārīcavākyaṃ*	as Ñ B1.3 D1.3.5.7
App.11.45	*mārīcābhyupapattiḥ*	cf. V1 B1.4
41	*lakṣmaṇasamādeśaḥ*	cf. V1 B1.3.4
43	*lakṣmaṇaprayāṇaṃ*	as all N except Ñ1 D2
44	*rāvaṇagamanaṃ*	as V1 B3
45	*rāmāyaṇe śītāra* + ... + (no *āraṇyake*)	cf. *sītārāvaṇasaṃvādaḥ* of B3
46	*śītāharaṇasamvādaḥ*	as V1
47	*śītapahāraḥ*	unique
in 966*	*jaṭāyuvadhaḥ* (reading not certain)[14]	unique
49	*jaṭāyuvadhaḥ*	cf. *jaṭāyurvadhaḥ* Ñ V1 B1.3.4 D5.7
51	*śītāvākyaṃ*	as Ñ V B1.3.4 D1.3.5.7

It is noteworthy that many of these *sarga* names are shared with all or some of the Maithilī and Bengali manuscripts against the rest of the NE recension and that none are shared with either Ñ manuscript without also a majority of the Maithilī and Bengali manuscripts.

The details noted above with regard to the readings of this Nevārī-script manuscript are yet another indication of the incompleteness of the manuscript evidence assembled in the Critical Edition, which, though based on a wider number of manuscripts than older editions and organized along critical lines, still did not take as full account as it might have done of the wealth of available material. In terms of its closest relationships, first and foremost this manuscript does of course share many readings with a grouping that includes Ñ2, except in the section from 2.108.1 to 110.8 where it goes with a grouping that includes Ñ1. However, it is abundantly clear that it is not particularly closely related to either of the Nevārī-script manuscripts used for the Critical Edition, as its substantial proportion of unique readings is enough to demonstrate, quite apart from the small number of readings shared only with one (or both) of the Ñ manuscripts. Instead it has quite a close relationship to the Maithilī and Bengali manuscripts, in which respect it is surely significant that the area of use of the Maithilī script is the closest to Nepal and the two areas share many cultural features.

After analysing in a previous article the readings of an Oriya-script manuscript for the *Ayodhyākāṇḍa,* which showed most similarity with the Maithilī-script manuscript V1, I remarked that

> It is not, of course, surprising that manuscripts written in areas either side of Bengal should show similarities with Bengali manuscripts, but their agreement with each other could point to the derivation of all three from a common ancestor rather than by spread from Bengal, although it will probably prove closer to the truth that both mechanisms were involved. In the same way, links of a manuscript in Oriya script both with Bengali manuscripts and with S manuscripts are not unexpected and to that extent this new Oriya manuscript produces no surprises. On the other hand, it is not just an offshoot from the Bengali version, as the convergences with V1 and with the S recension demonstrate.[15]

In the case of this Nevārī-script manuscript, its links with either Ñ manuscript of the Critical Edition are more tenuous than with the Maithilī manuscript(s) and this fact, together with its shared readings with other smaller groupings within the NE recension, tends to reinforce my suggestion of derivation from a common ancestor rather than spread from Bengal. Indeed its evidence, taken with that of the Oriya-script manuscript, may suggest assigning greater importance to the Maithilī manuscripts. The material from this Nevārī-script manuscript thus provides yet another item in the steadily accumulating data, which indicate not just that the simple opposition between N and S recensions—however useful it may once have been as a heuristic device—does not adequately represent the complexities of the chain of transmission involved, but also that within the N recension, the NE and NW (or NW + W) recensions, have less solid reality than is generally assigned to them. The realities are often the smaller groupings that recur repeatedly in the Critical Apparatus of the Critical Edition, such as Ñ2 V1 B2.3, with which this manuscript shares 59 readings (21%) in the *Ayodhyā* section of its text.

Ultimately, only further work on the relationships between particular manuscripts or small groups of manuscripts can make the picture more accurate. It must be accepted that this will probably not so much produce a clear portrait as obscure a situation that has so far been drawn too simply; increased detail will nonetheless result in a truer portrait of its complexities. We cannot airbrush out of existence the marks of age arising from the long history of the *Rāmāyaṇa* manuscript transmission—marks that reflect the true character of the text.

Notes

1. "The idea of preparing a scholarly, readable, and densely annotated translation of the *Vālmīki Rāmāyana* has fascinated me since the summer of 1969," The *Rāmāyaṇa of Vālmīki, an epic of ancient India*, vol. 1: *Bālakāṇḍa*, tr. Robert P. Goldman, Princeton University Press, Princeton, New Jersey, p. xiii.

2. In a paper presented at the 7th World Sanskrit Conference at Leiden in 1987, I stated that I hoped in due course to undertake some study of this manuscript from microfilm (see "The text of the Rāmāyaṇa", reprinted in *Epic Threads: John Brockington on the Sanskrit Epics*, ed. Greg Bailey and Mary Brockington, Oxford University Press, New Delhi, 2000, pp. 207-17, esp. p. 214); I must stress that I now have access only to this microfilm, with the attendant limitations that this imposes.

3. *Descriptive Catalogue of Sanskrit Manuscripts in the Government Collection, under the care of the Asiatic Society, Bengal*, Calcutta, 1928.

4. The point that script boundaries are less significant than assumed by the editors of the Critical Edition is one that is valid for the *Mahābhārata* also, as research being done in Cambridge under John Smith by a former student of mine is demonstrating by the rather different technique of applying cladistics (see Wendy J. Phillips-Rodriguez, "The Evolution of a Sanskrit Epic: some genetic considerations about scripts", in *The Evolution of Texts: Confronting*

Stemmatological and Genetical Methods, ed. C. Macé, P. Baret, A Bozzi, L. Cignoni, *Linguistica Computazionale* 24-25, 2005 (IEPI, Pisa-Roma).

5. *The Vālmīki-Rāmāyaṇa*, vol. III: *The Araṇyakāṇḍa*, critically edited by P. C. Divanji, Oriental Institute, Baroda, 1963, p. xxv. P. L. Vaidya does not comment in his introduction to the *Ayodhyākāṇḍa*.

6. The first of these leaves (recto below f.144v on the microfilm and the upper half of the next exposure) can be identified as f.61 containing 3.400*-22.27ab, the second as f.104 containing 3.38.4-17, the third as f.9 containing 2.2398*8-110.49ab, the fourth as f.138 containing 3.49.21cd-980*, the fifth as f.28 containing 3.10.10d-24b and the sixth as f.43 containing 3.14.1-266*5. The lower half of the final exposure contains a poorly written standard conclusion (beginning *vede rāmāyane caiva purāṇe bhārate tathā ādāv ante ca madhye ca hairiḥ sarvarta gīyate ||*, cf. 6.3707*1-2) in a hand which is rather closer to devanāgarī and appears substantially later than that of the manuscript to which it is appended; this leaf is not the recto of f.1, and may even not belong to this manuscript.

7. The folios extant are (basically in the sequence of the microfilm, with angled brackets round numbers absent but inferable with certainty from the text sequence): 1, <5> (displaced), 3-4, (<5> displaced to follow f.1), <7>, 8, (<9> displaced to the end), 10, 12-16, 18-21, 23, 25-27, (<28> displaced to the end), 29-34, (<35> displaced to follow f.134), <36>, 37-8, 40-41, (<43> displaced to the end) <44>, 45-49, <50>, 51-55, (56 displaced to follow 65), <57>, 58-60, (<61> displaced to the end), 62-65, 56 (displaced), <66>, 67-8, <69>, 70-71, <72> 73-79, <80>, 81, <83>, 85, <86>, 87-89, <90>, 91, <92>, 93-4, <95-97>, 98, 100-03, 107-08, <109>, 110, 112, <114>, <117>, 115, <127>, 118-19, <121>, 122-23, <124>, (126 displaced till later), 128-31, (132 displaced till later), <133>, 134, <35> (misplaced), 126, 132, 135-36, <138>, 139-41, <143>, 144, then the six listed in the previous footnote.

8. Another name that is consistently spelt differently is *anusūyā* for Anasūyā. Agastya is also occasionally spelt Agasti (e.g. at 3.10.31c and 11.15b).

9. A good example from other manuscripts is *mārīca* at 2.2354* substituted by Ś1 and D6 for 2.108.19ab, where *śārīra* occurs and is presumably a misreading, giving rise to expansion into the two lines of 2.2354* for clarification of the supposed allusion.

10. The collation of these thirty folios had been completed before I identified f.<35> during further sampling of the text to establish the correct sequence of the leaves lacking numbers. Examples noticed during this sampling will also be given, where appropriate, but not of course included in the figures for proportions.

11. One might also add here *baddhāsiś ca dhanvī ca* with V1 B4 D5.7 at 3.42.4a and *tat syāt* for *'dharmyaṃ* with D5.7 at 3.49.26c. It should also be noted that there are a small number of instances where this manuscript shares readings with Ś1 but neither Ñ ms: 15 in the *Ayodhyā* section (10 of these with Ś1 B1 D2.4-6) but just 11 in the *Araṇya* section. Also of interest is its reading at 3.28.26c, *bhagnān tu gulmāṃś ca vṛkṣāṃś ca*, where the transposition of *gulmāṃś* and *vṛkṣāṃś* is shared with all NE mss but *bhagnān* (for *bhasma*) is read only by Dg1 T3, and *tu* is added uniquely (giving a hypermetric line). This shared reading with two S manuscripts appears significant but in general its rare convergences with S manuscripts only are most probably coincidental (and trivial, such as *ko sau* for *kvāsau* with Dt1 D6 at 3.11.13c); there are 9 instances in total within the sample of agreement only or mainly with S manuscripts. There are just occasional instances subsequently (for example, *sopamardaṃ* for *savamardaṃ* at 3.38.11a with Dg1 Dm1 D8 G3 M1).

12. See "Textual studies in Vālmīki's *Rāmāyaṇa*" (reprinted in *Epic Threads: John Brockington on the Sanskrit Epics*, ed. Greg Bailey and Mary Brockington, Oxford University Press, New Delhi, 2000, pp. 195-206), p. 204.

13. Apart from one on f.8 (verso ll. 2-3) following 2.2397* which divides 2.110, where only *ma sargaḥ* is legible because of leaf breakage, all those in the *Ayodhyā* section are lost. The sarga names are given exactly as in the manuscript, with missing *akṣaras* supplied within angled brackets, but mere orthographic variants are ignored in noting the parallels.

14. This colophon occurs at the end of the first line of the verso of f.136, where breakage of the leaf has removed the upper part of the line; however, the remaining portion is most plausibly read as given and corresponds exactly with the equivalent part of the next colophon.

15. "The text of the *Rāmāyaṇa*" (reprinted in *Epic Threads: John Brockington on the Sanskrit Epics*, ed. Greg Bailey and Mary Brockington, Oxford University Press, New Delhi, 2000, pp. 207-17), p. 217.

The Boy 'Slowpoke' as Deep Thinker: In Defense of 'Straying' Wives against Father's Uxoricidal Rage

JAMES L. FITZGERALD

More than any other scholar in recent memory, Robert Goldman has focused our attention on some of the central, universally human elements of Sanskrit literature. During a time in American humanistic scholarship when French structuralism became all the rage and homegrown 'ethno-science' seemed to many an appropriate countermeasure to the arrogant excesses of some insouciantly ethnocentric cultural and social sciences, Robert Goldman challenged the fashionable scholarly isolationism with a strong demonstration of the presence and relevance of trans-cultural psychological dynamics.[1] With one swing of a gleaming *sarvaśaikyāyasī gadā*[2]—his "Fathers, Sons, and Gurus: Oedipal Conflict in the Sanskrit Epics" in 1978—Robert Goldman smashed through a curtain of darkness obscuring the reading of many Indian epic myths and stories. In that paper and several companion pieces, he convincingly demonstrated the presence of 'oedipal' or oedipal-like themes in Sanskrit epic literature. That fundamental insight and a number of accompanying explorations of related themes were followed in later years by several other deft analyses of Sanskrit epic material,[3] to say nothing of his mounting and editing the monumental and finely executed *Rāmāyaṇa* Translation Project, for which all of us stand deeply in his debt.

My contribution here examines a curious episode found in the *Mokṣadharmaparvan* of the *Mahābhārata* (*MBh*), an episode that traverses some of the kinds of topics and themes Bob Goldman helped open up. Among the 63 items anthologized in the *Mokṣadharmaparvan*[4] there is a set of seven texts (extending across thirteen *adhyāyas*) that are all concerned to criticize *hiṃsā* (causing pain or harm in thought, word, or deed)—especially, but not only, the *hiṃsā* involved in the ancient Vedic sacrifice (*MBh* 12.252-64). The third text in this series, *MBh* 12.258, "The Cirakārikopākhyāna," is an interesting little piece that has nothing to do with the ethics of the *paśubandha* (animal sacrifice), at least not on its surface.[5] It is instead a sermonizing parable arguing against an enraged husband's sentencing his wife to death for infidelity. "The Story of Cirakārin" is a transparent use of a deliberately contrived fusion of the two old patriarchal myths[6] that are hardest on 'unfaithful' wives—the myths of Ahalyā's seduction by Indra and Reṇukā's execution by her obedient son Rāma Jāmadagnya for 'lusting in her heart' for a man not her husband, and there is a strongly implied rebuttal of the irascible boy Śvetaketu's pronouncement on these matters as well.[7] At the very heart of this narrative contrivance its author publishes a striking brief defending—against their husbands' punishments—women who 'stray' in various ways. The arguments in this brief are subsequently ratified in the parable by the enraged husband's change of heart and his withdrawing the sentence of death he had pronounced against his wife. The story thus contains a sort of 'minority report' of the woman's side of various sorts of infidelity,[8] one that was put on the record in a parable that had a happy outcome all around. Some of what is said in this 'brief' (258.35 and 37) applies equally well to the plight of Sītā in the *Rāmāyaṇa*.

The "Story of Cirakārin" also comments, by narrative implication, on the subject of sons' abjuring their own egos and wills in favor of their fathers', an issue that Bob Goldman has treated at length and with insight in the works mentioned earlier. In this one complex 'metamyth'[9] some voice within the epic narrative tradition simultaneously repudiated not only the behavior of Ahalyā's husband Gautama and Reṇukā's husband Jamadagni, but also the unthinking obedience of Jamadagni's son Rāma in beheading his mother at his father's command and Śvetaketu's rejection of women's sexual liberty.[10] While having many marks of the 'oedipal' conflict of wills, there are in this story several striking inversions of that (or of the versions of it identified by Robert Goldman in those earlier essays): here a father orders his son to kill his wife, the boy's mother, because she had sex with another male; the son strongly resists the father's will even as he wishes to comply with it; the son offers a number of statements arguing against the unjust punishment of women such as his mother; the husband and father comes deeply to regret his command; the husband and father deconstructs the adulterous relationship, absolves the parties involved of guilt, and holds himself responsible for causing great harm because of his jealousy. Instances of sons defending mothers against aggressors are hardly unknown in Sanskrit epic literature,[11] but I can think of no other instance in which a man's sovereign will is shown to reverse itself on its own.[12] I do not undertake here a psychological interpretation of the story of Cirakārin, though it is rife with terrifying emotional charges coming from deep within interpersonal familial psychodynamics. All I shall do here is map the text, resolve a number of statements in it that are as difficult to construe confidently as they are unexpected, and register this text in the dossier of narratives on which we might base a broader, cross-cultural depth-psychology of family relations along the lines called for by Obeyesekere in his intriguing and important book *The Work of Culture.*[13]

This story of Cirakārin is a very striking confection. As I said, it deliberately fuses the critical elements of two famous stories of a wife's 'straying' from sexual exclusiveness and her enraged husband's punishment of her: Ahalyā's seduction by Indra and her husband Gautama's subsequent punishment of them both;[14] and Reṇukā's being aroused by the sight of a king flirting with his wives while on an outing along a river and her subsequent beheading by her own youngest son Rāma at the command of her husband Jamadagni, who had divined her state of mind.[15] The author's selection of these two stories for comment and discussion is interesting in itself. And while it may seem obvious to us that the two myths have much in common, the two stories are also very different: The Reṇukā story is about imagined infidelity—'the lust in her heart', that was, in turn, divined telepathically by her husband—but the punishment for Reṇukā's 'straying' was the very real physical decapitation of her by her youngest son, Rāma, son of Jamadagni. The Ahalyā story is about actual physical intercourse that took place in the home as Ahalyā was seduced by the God Indra, who was disguised as a brahmin guest (he was disguised as her own husband in some versions of the myth).[16] But this woman is not sentenced to death, though her husband punishes her and Indra both, severely. The Ahalyā story has no children in it. Furthermore, the psychological centers of gravity in each are radically different: the Ahalyā story turns upon the interactions between paramour and wife, husband and wife, and husband and paramour, while the Reṇukā story centers upon the monumental rage of the father, his commanding his sons to kill their mother, and the horror of his sons when ordered to turn his rage into their mother's death. The combined version of the Cirakārin parable sets up a very different dynamic from either of the original tales, one which the fictitiously concocted sleepy boy, 'Slowpoke', fits very well. And the whole of this artifice creates a narratively plausible stage from which to argue a general defense of 'straying' women. The 'crime' in the contrived Cirakārin parable is Ahalyā's actual adultery, but the punishment is the sentence of death which her son (likely also to be the youngest of several) was ordered to carry out by the enraged husband and father. After considering his father's direct command, the boy Cirakārin moves on to the topic of wifely infidelity and ends up arguing that the women involved commit no wrong and the husband is wrong to punish them, and he does so as coolly as Śvetaketu angrily argues the opposite.

The narrative structure of the Cirakārikopākhyāna is also interesting. As can be seen from a glance at the summary just below, the center of the text consists of two soliloquies. The first is the son's weighing the father's command to kill his mother against his senses both of a more fundamental connection to his mother than his father and of the injustice of the command. The second is the father's soliloquy re-examining the originating event, repenting his harsh punishment, and then his prayers that his son shall have lived up to his name Cirakārin, that is 'Slowpoke'. These two soliloquies work in the linear order narrated. The son's soliloquy establishes the boy's fundamental loyalty to the father, his deeper sense of loyalty to his mother, and then presents the brief defending women generally against charges of culpable infidelity (*ślokas* 258.34-38). The boy's reflections provide a narrative, emotional, and logical basis for the narration of the father's change of heart (which is said to have occurred when Vedic recitation 'tamed his savage breast'[17]) and his revising his understanding of the inappropriate sex (it was simply the result of misunderstanding). On the other hand, we are told that the two soliloquies took place simultaneously in real time, in what might be one primitive anticipation of the exquisite shadow scene in the third act of Bhavabhūti's *Uttararāmacarita*.[18] On the one hand, the asserted simultaneity focuses more attention on the here paradoxically resolved tension between son and father, and on the other hand it makes the reconciliation of father and disobedient son all the more powerful. Nonetheless, the father's change of heart would be much less plausible did it not rest on the linearly anterior argumentation provided by the son's soliloquy.

My reading of this text and my interpretation of its difficulties are fundamentally informed by Bob Goldman's pioneering works on these themes of infra-familial desire, will, and violence. It is a great pleasure to offer some striking comments of the *Mahābhārata* on uxoriousness and filiality in a volume honoring him and his work.

The Story of Cirakārin, Slowpoke

Here is a brief synopsis of this story:

> 258 (267[6]; 9481). Yudhiṣṭhira asks Bhīṣma whether one should examine one's responsibilities at length or not. Bhīṣma relates The Story of Cirakārin, "Slowpoke." A scion of Gautama named Medhātithi ordered his son Cirakārin to kill his wife, the boy's mother, because she was unfaithful (1-5). Cirakārin accepted his father's command, but the boy then thought the whole matter over carefully. At length he weighed the unhesitating obedience one owes his father against the absolute protection one owes his mother. He concluded the latter is more important than the former (5-30). Turning to the subject of adultery, he judged men, both husbands and paramours, responsible for all the wrong in such incidents (30-40). At the same time, Medhātithi reconsidered the matter and he concluded his wife was innocent of wrongdoing and that he was wrong to have ordered her execution. Shedding copious tears, he fervently hoped his son would live up to his name (40-45). He was relieved to find his son had not yet obeyed his command and the father praised his son and the value of acting with due deliberation (45-65). Bhīṣma repeats the general moral to Yudhiṣṭhira at rather fulsome length (65-75).

Slowpoke the Boy

Interestingly the dissent from the conventional wisdom about 'straying women' that this story presents turns upon the issue of intellectual slowness. Had the son here been quick-witted and zealous, like Rāma Jāmadagnya, Gautama's wife would have been dead like Reṇukā before the man came to his senses. The author of the text has made this important point with the transparently editorial name Cirakārin, "Slow-acting", which is clearly meant to be taken as somewhat ironically humorous. Thus it is quite justifiable to translate it in English as "Slowpoke". The name is meant not as criticism, but as a gambit intended to give the parable's author some initial space in which to deploy his, or her (?) out of the ordinary arguments.

> 'Slowpoke' was the very wise son of a descendent of Gautama. He scrutinized everything he was supposed to do thoroughly and at great length before he started on it. [4] He was called Slowpoke because everything he did became a long, drawn-out affair—he thought about matters at length, he stayed awake long, and he slept long too. [5][19]

But this tongue-in-cheek introduction of the boy ends with an earnest point that anticipates the deadly serious exhortation to 'go slow' that will soon be dramatized.

> *alasagrahaṇaṃ prāpto durmedhāvī tathocyate /*
> *buddhilāghavayuktena janenādīrghadarśinā //6 //*

> A person who takes hold of things in a leisurely way is called stupid only by someone who has a shallow mind and is shortsighted. [6]

Having introduced the boy in this one dimensional way the author sets the dilemma that provokes the dilatory boy's remarkable reflections.

> Once, when his mother strayed somehow, his enraged father—passing over his other sons—told Slowpoke, "Kill this mother of yours!" [7][20] Slowpoke naturally said "Yes" after a while. Reflecting carefully, he thought about it for a long time, because he really was slow to act. [8]

Though not stated initially, the sequel makes clear that the fault here involves actual intercourse, as did Ahalyā's case, but while the Ahalyā story typically focuses particularly upon the varied interactions between Gautama and Ahalyā after he discovers her and her divine lover,[21] the reaction of Slowpoke's father here is the same as Jamadagni's to Reṇukā's arousal.[22] Though no siblings of Slowpoke are ever again explicitly mentioned in this story, it is said that Medhātithi ordered Slowpoke to kill his mother after "passing over his other sons".[23] This element was significant in the story of Rāma's killing his mother, for, as Goldman, pointed out in "Fathers, Sons, and Gurus", this element gives the Rāma-Reṇukā story important psychological parallelism to Yayāti's extravagant demands that his five sons trade their youth for his old age—a demand to which only the youngest, Pūru, acquiesced.[24] In the case of Rāma's elder brothers, their refusal of their father's command cost them their sanity.

The Boy's Soliloquy

A. Obedience to Father's Will is of the Highest Importance

The boy's long reflections were a careful weighing of the countervailing claims of obeying his father and protecting his mother.

> A father's command is a son's highest obligation *(para dharma)*, but protecting his mother is a son's particular obligation *(svadharma)*. [10ab]

> Deeply anxious, he asked,

> Being a son means being subordinate *(asvatantra)*—how can I possibly avoid being crushed in this? [10cd] ... It is not right to disrespect one's father, yet protecting one's mother is a fixed rule°—both of these are appropriate and fit; how can I avoid violating either (obligation)?[12][25]

The conflict led him to question whether his father's command was actually obligatory, or only had the appearance of an obligation *(dharmacchala*, in 9), but he set that question aside with a series of thoughts that reflect the Freudian theme of self-castration Goldman discussed with regard to the epics.[26]

> A son exists merely to please his father; his father is everything for a boy [17ab] ... what a father says must be done, and done without any thought whatsoever. Sons are cleansed of even the gravest sins when they do what their fathers say. [18] ... When one's father rejoices, all one's evil actions are acquitted. [21]

B. But Mother's Love is More Fundamental and Weightier

But then the boy gives voice to another theme heard frequently in the written versions of both Sanskrit epics, that the mother's authority outweighs the father's.[27] Affirming this at length, the dilatory boy says,

> But though I have considered a father's importance to his son to be this great, fatherhood is really the lower status.[28] I will now consider my mother. [23] The very conglomeration of the five elements that makes up what is mortal in me has my mother as its cause ... [24abc] When a man can return home and say 'Mother,' he never grieves ... [25a,d] Even a man with a liberal sprinkling of sons and grandsons acts like a two-year old when he comes to his mother—even after a hundred years! [26] A mother protects her child whether he is capable or inept, whether he is robust or scrawny—no one else nurtures him just as a matter of course. [27] When separated from his mother a man grows old, he is pained,[29] the world is empty for him. [28] There is no shade like one's mother, no place to go like one's mother; no safety is the equal of mother, no oasis on the road is the same as one's mother. [29]

He comes to an intermediate conclusion expressed as a rhetorical question:

> What man with any sense, whose head is not as empty as a gourd, would kill her? [31cd][30]

Cirakārin is no Rāma.[31]

C. The Different Roles of Men and Women in Procreation

And then the boy changes his tack. He considers the relations between mothers and fathers, pointing to the complexities inherent in reproduction requiring two unequally involved mates and a long gestation period. He not only affirms the relative superiority of mothers again, a tone mildly critical of fathers is heard.

> Both the mother and the father are aware of the intention *(abhisaṃdhi)* that is formed when husband and wife mingle their life-energies; but the realization of that intention depends upon the mother. [32] The mother knows the *gotra* of the child and the mother knows whose he is. From just bearing a child a mother feels delight and affection whereas the father just has progeny.[32] [33]

D. Wives Cannot be Blamed or Punished for Having Sex with Other Men

From the complexities of joint parenthood—a topic that bears upon the boy's connection to each parent—Cirakārin goes on to a direct consideration of the relations of husbands and wives which moves to the general and abstract question whether husbands even have the right to punish their wives for intercourse with another man. Unlike the preceding parts of Cirakārin's soliloquy, the text of the five stanzas of this portion of it (258.34-38) present a number of difficulties, partly because what they are saying trends in a direction quite different from most contemporaneous texts on the subject. Additionally, these five *ślokas* are difficult to construe because they are framed as general pronouncements that range beyond the details of the story and do not explicitly address it. But the reflections in these stanzas seem to lie at the heart of the general intention behind the entire construction of this parable, so clarifying their meaning with some care is critically important. What follows is my best reading of these five stanzas as an interdependent series of reflections in the context of this artificially constructed corrective tale. We have to assume that these five stanzas form a connected set of points pertinent to this narrative setting. That is to say, with regard to the narrative frame of this parable, we must assume the author has imputed to Cirakārin a full awareness of the incident that enraged his father, even though we are not explicitly informed that the boy has such awareness.[33] On the basis of that assumption it is possible to infer plausible connections between each *śloka* and the salient theme of a husband's rights, or lack of them, and his responsibilities in connection with a woman's having sexual intercourse with a man not her husband. A meaningful, if not necessary, progression from one *śloka* to the next is discernible. Nonetheless, even then it is not the case that they are all able to be interpreted with absolute certainty in all details.

Exhibiting the same striking authority Śvetaketu did, Cirakārin speaks here about the position of women in marriage and the relative culpabilities of husbands, wives, and the paramours of wives. Perhaps it is the displacement from the usual voice of adult male authority (or that of a woman such as Pañcacūḍā, speaking at the behest of such a male at *MBh* 13.38; see note 39) to the voice of a slow-witted son that allows the unusual ideas asserted in these five *ślokas* to be expressed. Whatever the source of his insights, in each of the following five statements, Cirakārin defends wives against the charges of wrongdoing that are made against them when they engage in sex with a man other than their husband. Though his points do not pass feminist muster in twenty-first century America, he does argue—if I read him correctly—that women are essentially condign with men (37), in spite of the subordination to their husbands imposed upon them by tradition. Thus women are not inherently sinful or offensive.[34] He adds to that claim two other claims that are pertinent to this situation: husbands commit a serious wrong (*adharma*) if they fail to bear in mind that there is no Vedic law restricting women's pursuit of their sexual gratification (38) and a husband's status as "husband" depends in part on his keeping other men away from his wife (35). In sum, women are guilty of no offense when they are raped or seduced or even go outside the marriage on their own (36-38) and husbands cannot expel them from marriage (and thus, *a fortiori*, cannot execute them; 34).

It is conceivable that the five stanzas 12.258.34-38 constituted a pre-existing set of statements compiled around the theme of the culpability of wives, or the lack thereof, when they were involved in infidelity (something of an 'Answering Śvetaketu' piece). Were that the case, it would be further conceivable that this 'metamyth' was composed around these stanzas to provide a vehicle for proclaiming them. Supporting this conjecture is the fact that these *ślokas* follow *ślokas* 32 and 33, which, as we saw, move away from Cirakārin's earlier professions of loyalty to his mother onto 'theoretical' territory of which a boy would presumably have little to say, normally. Also supporting that conjecture is the fact that these stanzas are not as plainly and smoothly connected to the context as are the preceding passages of Cirakārin's soliloquy. There is not enough evidence, however, to argue that this suggestion is actually the case. The stanzas can be construed as germane to Cirakārin's theme, and, apart from their allusiveness, they do share other stylistic features with the preceding—for example, the generally paratactic movement with which the whole proceeds and the occasional reliance upon etymologies to define relationships.

As I present these five stanzas I will proceed differently from the earlier presentation of Cirakārin's reflections, because these stanza are both more important and more difficult than the rest. I will first present the Sanskrit text as a continuous passage. I will then offer paraphrases of the point of each *śloka* with bracketed statements of its pertinence to Cirakārin's larger argument. Finally I offer a full translation of each verse and discuss the salient issues.

The Text of 12.258.34-38

pāṇibandhaṃ svayaṃ kṛtvā sahadharmam upetya ca /
yadi yāpyanti puruṣāḥ striyo nārhanti yāpyatām //34//
bharaṇād dhi striyo bhartā pātyāc caiva striyāḥ patiḥ /
guṇasyāsya nivṛttau tu na bhartā na patiḥ patiḥ //35//

evaṃ strī nāparādhnoti nara evāparādhyati /
vyuccaraṃś ca mahādoṣaṃ nara evāparādhyati //36//
striyā hi paramo bhartā daivataṃ paramaṃ smṛtam /
tasyātmanā tu sadṛśam ātmānaṃ paramaṃ dadau /
sarvakāryāparādhyatvān nāparādhyanti cāṅganāḥ //37//
yaś ca nokto hi nirdeśaḥ striyā maithunatṛptaye /
tasyāsmārayato[35] *vyaktam adharmo nātra saṃśayaḥ //38//*

Paraphrase and Application of *Ślokas* 34-38

34. A properly married woman is not to be dismissed (divorced [or, *a fortiori*, executed]). [So Medhātithi's sentence upon Cirakārin's mother was wrong.]

35. A husband who ceases to support or protect his wife loses husband-status and has no standing to sanction his wife. [So Medhātithi's command is not valid for lack of *adhikāra* (standing, authority).]

36. It is the man who sins in cases of adultery, not the woman. [So Cirakārin's mother is innocent of any "crime."]

37. Though a woman is subordinate to her husband, she has a sovereign soul that is the same as her husband's. Women commit no wrong by virtue simply of being women; all the sinfulness comes from whatever she was forced to do by her male seducer or rapist. [Again, Cirakārin's mother is faultless.]

38. No rule for [the limiting of] women's sexual gratification has ever been proclaimed, and husbands must respect that fact. [No rule of *dharma* forbade Cirakārin's mother's enjoyment of sex with the guest; Medhātithi did violate *dharma* by failing to remember that.]

Full Translation and Discussion

34

pāṇibandhaṃ svayaṃ kṛtvā sahadharmam upetya ca /
yadi yāpyanti puruṣāḥ striyo nārhanti yāpyatām //34//

If men dismiss their wives after they have voluntarily joined hands and undertaken the Meritorious Lawful Deeds of Marriage, those wives ought not be dismissed.[34]

With Thieme[36] I take *yāpyanti* as a syncopated form of *yāpayanti*, "cause to go, expel, dismiss". I believe Jamison is correct to see the expulsion as generally "divorce".[37] The boy invokes the concept of marriage to declare his father's 'rejection' of his mother's wrong. As I noted above, I presume this generalization is meant to be construed in the context of the current crisis: a wife's, his mother's, sexual congress with a paramour. Such 'straying' (*vyabhicāra*) on her part is actually his father's fault (as the next *śloka* will imply) for failing to provide the protection (*pātya*) of her that his status as 'lord-husband', *pati*, is based upon.

35

> *bharaṇād dhi striyo bhartā pātyāc caiva striyāḥ patiḥ /*
> *guṇasyāsya nivṛttau tu na bhartā na patiḥ patiḥ* //35//
>
> A husband is the 'lord-supporter' (*bhartṛ*) of his wife because he supports her (*bharaṇāt*); he is the 'lord-husband' (*pati*) of his wife because he "rules over and guards" her (*pātyāt*); but when he ceases to have those traits, that lord-husband is her lord-supporter no longer, no longer her lord-husband. [35]

If his mother engaged in an adulterous liaison, then the father had failed to guard her adequately (*pātya*) and he no longer has the standing as *pati* to sanction her. It is worth noting, however, that according to Śvetaketu's father Uddālaka at *MBh* 1.113.14, women were not at that time sequestered by their husbands.[38] Obviously, in the current narrative context, Gautama did not regard his wife to be sexually at liberty, but he failed to take sufficient precautions against the wily paramour, Indra. In a clear permutation of the basic Ahalyā tale, Devaśarman seemed to have learned from Gautama's failings. He commanded his student Vipula to guard his beautiful wife Ruci, who, Bhīṣma says, is a good example of the inherent sexual voraciousness and promiscuity of women. Vipula defended Ruci from Indra by penetrating and controlling her body with *yoga* power (by way of the eyes).[39] It is not clear, however, whether the principle of *patitva* Cirakārin invokes here by etymology (*nirukti*) would forbid a husband's offering his well-guarded wife to guests, as Sudarśana did Oghavatī at *MBh* 13.2.[40] Upon reflection, however, these latter two stories, which turn upon a husband's exaggerated control of his wife, and Pañcacūḍā's nearby testimony justifying the need for such control, seem closer to salacious fantasy than earnest *dharmaśāstra*.

Nīlakaṇṭha interprets the burden of these etymological characterizations of the husband as disqualifying a husband from ordering his wife's death, rather than disqualifying him from all punishment for adultery because of his own failure. He writes:

> The intention [of *śloka* 258.35] is "I will not kill my mother at the command of one who seems to be out of his mind (*unmatta*) and has none of the qualities of a husband (*bhartṛ* 'or the like'), who wishes to end his wife's life."[41]
>
> Nīlakaṇṭha's argument is circular: Pronouncing the death sentence is too extreme and makes Medhātithi not a husband, and not worthy of being obeyed as a father. While the issue of *bharaṇa* (support) may be seen as lending itself to this more general interpretation of Medhātithi's loss of husband-status (but we might ask how that status has any bearing upon Cirakārin's obligation to obey him), the issue of *pātya* (protection, warding off others) clearly is cited to get at the heart of the issue of infidelity.

36

> *evaṃ strī nāparādhnoti nara evāparādhyati /*
> *vyuccaraṃś ca mahādoṣaṃ nara evāparādhyati //36//*
>
> In this way, the woman does not sin, only the man sins. When a man strays (in adultery)—he alone commits a great offense. [36]

The adverb "in this way" (*evam*) connects the claim here to the preceding statement in some consequential way. Nīlakaṇṭha reduces it to a simple conjunction, "also", which removes the requirement of finding a serious connection. As the previous *śloka* says the husband who is careless about sequestering his wife loses the standing required to punish her adulterous liaisons, the *evam* here seems to extend that condition. The sense would be "And under these circumstances [the husband's failure to exercise *pātya*], the woman involved in adultery does nothing wrong." That Cirakārin must mean just this, and mean it in just this straightforward a way, is shown by the principle he cites below in *śloka* 38, which refers to the anti-Śvetaketu position that there is no binding prohibition limiting women's enjoyment of sex.

Not seeing the two *ślokas* connected in this way, Nīlakaṇṭha says Cirakārin here rejects his mother's guilt on the grounds that she was seduced, and women seduced are not guilty. Nīlakaṇṭha writes:

> [Cirakārin] wondered, "Now should not an adulterous woman be killed, because otherwise [her adultery] would effect a confusing intermixture of families?" and then he said ... "If she has been seduced, then she would not [deserve killing]. In that case this sin would not attach [to her]. Therefore this sin would attach only to the man, who took the initiative." That's the meaning of it [*śloka* 12.258.36].[42]

So, according to Cirakārin his mother has incurred no blame in spite of having sex with the guest. The boy makes the same point again in 37, stressing both the wife's general subordination to her husband and her essential equality at the highest level of human being (the similarity of her *paramātman* to his *paramātman*).

37

> *striyā hi paramo bhartā daivataṃ paramaṃ smṛtam /*
> *tasyātmanā tu sadṛśam ātmānaṃ paramaṃ dadau /*
> *sarvakāryāparādhyatvān nāparādhyanti cāṅganāḥ* //37//

> Certainly a woman's husband is taught by tradition to be her supreme lord, her highest God. But she gave to him her highest Self, which is the like of his own Self. Women do not sin (just) because of the sinfulness in any of the things they may be forced to do. [37]

The first two lines of this *śloka* make a critically important point: even though women are subordinate to men by traditional teaching (*smṛta*), their essential self is the same as that of men. One implication of this statement would seem to be that "sinfulness" is not inherently in women any more than in men (a wife's *ātman* is *tadātmasadṛśa*). Leaving that possible implication unspoken, the extra half *śloka* that follows seems to assume something like this when it emphasizes that in situations such as the one at hand for Cirakārin's parents (or perhaps even more generally, this half *śloka* can certainly be read to absolve women from all kinds of *aparādha* arising from obligations or duties, *kārya-s*), women do not "sin", the "sinfulness" arises from all, that is anything, that is forced upon them. Such coercion may refer to rape or a woman's being ordered by her husband to accommodate a guest sexually (see n. 40) and perhaps other things as well.

38

In 38 I amend Belvalkar's *tasya smārayataḥ* in c to *tasyāsmārayataḥ*, which is read by $Ś_1$ and $K_{1.2.6}$ against all other manuscripts. In my experience with the Bhandarkar edition of the *Śāntiparvan*, the first three of these manuscripts frequently offer readings superior to most other manuscripts (in spite of Grünendahl's telling criticism of Sukthankar's so-called Kaśmirī tradition of the written Sanskrit *MBh*[43]).

yaś ca nokto hi nirdeśaḥ striyā maithunatṛptaye /
tasyāsmārayato vyaktam adharmo nātra saṃśayaḥ //38//

> As no restriction has ever been declared for women's sexual gratification, clearly he who does not keep that [absent restriction] in mind commits a Serious Wrong *(adharma)*, no doubt of that. [38]

This *śloka* is somewhat vexed on its face. What *nirdeśa*, "rule, specification", regarding women's sexual satisfaction might be its subject? And how should we read the first four syllables? Is it *yaś ca na-uktaḥ* ... *(nirdeśaḥ)*, "That (stipulation) not declared"? Or is it *yaś cana-uktaḥ* ... *(nirdeśaḥ)*, "Some declared (stipulation)"? Nīlakaṇṭha adopted the latter, followed by Belvalkar. Arjunamiśra the former, as did by Deussen and Strauss. I believe Arjunamiśra to be right and also read and translate *ca na-uktaḥ*. Reading *yaś cana* here, thereby eliminating the particle of negation, would create the only instance of *cana* not following an interrogative word that has been recognized by any of the editors of any *parvan* of the entire Pune *MBh*, star passages and appendices included. (It may be that some such instances of "*ca na*" in the constituted Pune text or apparatus should be read as *cana*, but I have pointedly looked at many and did not find even one where I think an editor was mistaken in refusing to adopt that most unusual construction. Belvalkar's reading here stands alone.) For this reason, as well as reasons of sense and context (see below), I think we must reject Nīlakaṇṭha's reading, restore the negation, and construe the relative clause as describing some *nirdeśa*, rule, that has *not* been enjoined *(na-ukta)*, rather than one that has been enjoined.

But Nīlakaṇṭha's understanding of the *śloka* is interesting and pertinent. Regarding the statement to be about a rule, specification or stipulation that *has* been enjoined, Nīlakaṇṭha (followed by Belvalkar) understands that stipulation to be the concession allowing women to have sex at will after giving birth, not merely in their fertile season (*ṛtu*).[44] This concession is said to have been granted to women by Indra in exchange for women accepting a portion of the evil that attached to that God from his killing the God Tvaṣṭṛ's three-headed son Viśvarūpa (an act identified as brahmin-murder by the *MBh* at 5.10.42). Nīlakaṇṭha quotes the episode from *Taittirīya Saṃhitā* 2.5.1.5:

> They [the women, responding to Indra's command that they take a one-third portion of the negative consequences of his brahmin murder] said: "We would like you to grant us a wish: Let us get pregnant as a result of our fertile period; let us enjoy sex at will after giving birth."[45]

Nīlakaṇṭha (reading *tasya smārayatas* in 38c) goes on to say that Indra (the seducer of Cirakārin's mother) clearly committed serious wrong by reminding the woman of this ancient exchange in order to seduce her. In the earliest full version of the Ahalyā story that we have, in the *Bālakāṇḍa* of the *Rāmāyaṇa,* Indra, disguised as Ahalyā's husband urged her on, saying "Those who want it don't pay any attention to the fertile period,"[46] and Nīlakaṇṭha has this in mind.

Seeing the line to be about some kind of *nirdeśa* that has *not* been declared, Arjunamiśra says the missing *nirdeśa* is a[n] [absent] restriction on women's pursuing their own sexual gratification. He construes 258.38ab to say,

> No [limiting] rule has been declared regarding (women's's) sexual satisfaction; on the contrary, that [sex or sexual gratification, *maithuna*] is ordained for them *(āsāṃ vihitam)* in accordance with their desires. Thus [she, that is, Cirakārin's mother] was just following the inclination of her desires and there was no fault in it.[47]

Arjunamiśra's understanding of the *nirdeśa* here implicitly imagines Cirakārin to be living in that era of women's complete sexual freedom that Śvetaketu is supposed to have brought to an end, though, very interestingly with regard to the question of the authorship of this parable, Cirakārin is untroubled by his mother's encounter with Indra. Arjunamiśra's explanation of 258.38ab addresses the context directly and is, I think, the most economical way to interpret the stanza.[48] Unfortunately, Belvalkar did not quote what Arjunamiśra had to say, if anything, about 38cd.

So both Nīlakaṇṭha and Arjunamiśra see the *nirdeśa* as a general rule giving women either complete freedom (Arjunamiśra, as no restricting *nirdeśa* was ever declared) or greater freedom within marriage (Nīlakaṇṭha, as a concessive *nirdeśa* allowing a greater range of times of sexual indulgence once a wife has produced a child).

Nīlakaṇṭha—and evidently most of the tradition, which reads *smārayatas* in c—understands Ahalyā's seducer, Indra, to be bringing this concession up to the woman in order to seduce her, and so he has "clearly committed a Great Wrong (*adharma*)." This understanding would be something of a follow-up to the point regarding the wife's innocence in situations of coercion mentioned in 37; but while 37 was concerned with coercion, this understanding of 38 is only about persuasion, reminding the woman of her freedom. And such persuasion seems less than pertinent to the progression of Cirakārin's points, it rejects their tenor, if I read Cirakārin correctly. Even if her paramour's reminding Ahalyā of her actual sexual freedom is wrong (*adharma*) of him, that wrong of his has no real bearing on the actions or guilt of either Ahalyā or Medhātithi. So the statement in cd "it is clearly wrong (*adharma*) for him ... " must necessarily apply to Medhātithi. And the only conceivable wrong on his part would be his overlooking (*asmārayatas*, failing to remind himself, failing to bear in mind) the fact that his wife was free to enjoy sex as she would (either because of the concession-*nirdeśa* or because no restriction-*nirdeśa* on female sexuality was ever uttered in *śruti*).[49]

We need not see Cirakārin here as advocating the idea of 'free-love' for women. His invocation of the principle of *pātya* (male domination, 'protection', sequestration) in 35 implies that in his view husbands have the right to restrain women and bar access to them by other men. But if a husband's restrictions to that end, his 'protection' of his wife, breaks down, he cannot lay any responsibility for what happens on his wife. This understanding of female psychology agrees with Śvetaketu's views and those of Pañcacūḍā and Bhīṣma, as he introduces (at *MBh* 13.40) the need for Devaśarman to keep Ruci sequestered; but Cirakārin uses this understanding of women to accuse his father of serious wrong (*adharma*) here for failing to bear it in mind and ordering the punishment of his wife. The *Rāmāyaṇa* account of Ahalyā's seduction has Indra coming to Ahalyā disguised as her husband, but she saw through the disguise and welcomed his advances "because she had the hots for the king of the Gods".[50] Cirakārin here is saying she did nothing wrong in doing so; having failed to prevent this happening, Medhātithi has no justification in *dharma* (in addition to having no standing) to punish his wife.

E. Conclusion: A Boy Cannot Kill His Mother

And now Cirakārin is done. He sums up nicely, going back to his practical conclusion that he should not kill his mother, and the scene then shifts from him to his father.

> *yāvan nārīṃ mātaraṃ ca gaurave cādhike sthitām /*
> *avadhyāṃ tu vijānīyuḥ paśavo 'py avicakṣaṇāḥ //39//*
> *devatānāṃ samāvāyam ekasthaṃ pitaraṃ viduḥ /*
> *martyānāṃ devatānāṃ ca snehād abhyeti mātaram //40//*

> Even thoughtless beasts seem to understand the extent to which the female and mother is of greater importance and is not to be killed. [39] They say a father is a fusion of divinities; but one goes to his mother out of affection, for she is a fusion of divinities and mortalities. [40]

The Father's Soliloquy

At the same time, Slowpoke's father, the Gautama seer Medhātithi, came to regret his harsh command.

> As he [Cirakārin] deliberated this way at length, being very slow to act, a long time went by, and then his father came back. [41] Medhātithi, wise scion of Gautama, had been engaged in asceticism, and during that time he reflected on his wife's transgression of the rule. [42] He had become remorseful in the soothing calm of his habitual recitation of the Veda.[51] So, miserably tormented, copiously shedding tears, he said ... [43][52]

He reviewed the incident and concluded that no one—not Indra, not his wife, nor himself—had been at fault in the occurrence of Indra's having sex with his wife. A verbal misunderstanding had occurred at some point in the course of the woman's offering normal hospitality to an apparent brahmin guest (this version of the Ahalyā tale knows nothing of Indra's being disguised as Ahalyā's husband). Given that this story is in fact a variant of the Ahalyā tale, we should presume the misunderstanding arose after the disguised Indra had proposed sex to his hostess. Her answer was ambiguous. When she said to him "*paravatī asmi*" ("I am '*paravatī*', [literally, "I am of another [under the control of, I belong to, someone other than myself]"), what she intended to say was "I am another man's wife;" what Indra took her to say was "I am at your disposal."

Medhātithi recapitulates:

> *āśramaṃ mama saṃprāptas trilokeśaḥ puraṃdaraḥ /*
> *atithivratam āsthāya brāhmaṇaṃ rūpam āsthitaḥ* //44//
> *samayā sāntvito vāgbhiḥ svāgatenābhipūjitaḥ /*
> *arghyaṃ pādyaṃ ca nyāyena tayābhipratipāditaḥ* //45//
> *paravaty asmi cāpy uktaḥ praṇayiṣye nayena ca /*
> *atra cākuśale jāte striyo nāsti vyatikramaḥ* //46//
> *evaṃ na strī na caivāhaṃ nādhvagas tridaśeśvaraḥ /*
> *aparādhyati dharmasya pramādas tv aparādhyati* //47//

The Lord of the Three Worlds (Indra), the Smasher of Cities, arrived at my hermitage in the guise of a brahmin and acting like a guest. [44] With a proper reserve[53] she spoke kind words to him, honored him with a welcome, and appropriately presented him with water to drink and water for his feet. [45] When she said to him, "I belong to another," what he heard was, "I am at your disposal,"[54] and he replied, "It is permissible then that I make love to you."[55] So when evil arose, it was not my wife's transgression. [46] Not my wife, nor I, nor the journeying Lord of the Thirty Gods fell short of Lawful Norms. Rather, emotional transport (*pramāda*) is to blame. [47]

The "emotional transport", *pramāda,* that is at fault here can be seen as referring to Indra's taking the wife's words as he did and then acting upon them as a result of his lust. Perhaps there is also a hint that Ahalyā's lust was operative too; perhaps she spoke ambiguously on purpose. The idea could also embrace Medhātithi's own reaction, in which his jealousy and rage led him to dole out harsh punishments (though how Indra was dealt with in this instance is not addressed in our parable) rather than ask exactly what happened and how. Seeing the idea extending to Medhātithi's response makes sense in light of the seer's lament of his jealousy that follows immediately.

Had Medhātithi been in sufficient control of his emotions, he thinks, he would have understood immediately what he has now come to understand: neither his wife nor Indra had committed a culpable sin of adultery. By his reasoning now, their sex was inadvertent. But he had been transported by jealous rage and lacked sufficient presence of mind to deal with the situation properly.

īrṣyājaṃ vyasanaṃ prāhus tena caivordhvaretasaḥ /
īrṣyayā tv aham ākṣipto magno duṣkṛtasāgare //48//
hatvā sādhvīṃ ca nārīṃ ca vyasanitvāc ca śāsitām /
bhartavyatvena bhāryāṃ ca ko nu māṃ tārayiṣyati //49//

Celibate men[56] say catastrophe arises from jealousy at this; but overcome with jealousy I was, and I am drowning in the ocean of an evil deed. [48] Who is going to save me now that I have killed a good woman, my "wife" (*bharyā*)—as she was mine to support (*bhartavyatva*)—whom I punished in this catastrophe of mine? [49]

The Denoument

The real evil here arose after the incident and this was Medhātithi's responsibility. He failed to control his emotions, he allowed jealously to fuel his rage and that led to the catastrophe of his command to Cirakārin to kill the woman. He pins all hope of salvation now on the desired possibility that Cirakārin will live up to his name, and he prays to the heavens for that as he makes his way back.

> If the noble Slowpoke, whom I ordered to do this in a momentary lapse, really were slow to act today, he would save me from sin. [50] O please, Slowpoke! Please! If today you have been slow to act, then you really are a slowpoke. [51] Save me and your mother and yourself as well from mortal sins, and save too whatever ascetic power I have accumulated. Be a slowpoke today! [52]
>
> Being slow to act is innate in you, because you have long-lasting wisdom; let your slowness to act be fruitful today—be slow to act today! [53] Long hoped for by your mother, long carried in her womb, let your slowness to act be fruitful today—be slow to act today! [54]
>
> I hope grief slows him down. I hope he considered our grief, and I hope that gave him such pause that he is now taking a long nap. O Slowpoke! [55]

And of course the seer got this wish.

> Then, king, that great seer of Gautama's line who was so miserable saw his son nearby. [56] Now Slowpoke was extremely unhappy when he saw his father. He let go of his blade and approached him, bowing down his head to seek his father's favor. [57] But when the Gautama seer saw his son with his head bowed to the ground, and saw his wife standing there without expression,[57] he thrilled with joy. [58]

What follows is a capsule summary of all that 'happened' after the father gave his command and left:

> *na hi sā tena saṃbhedaṃ patnī nītā mahātmanā /*
> *vijane cāśramasthena putraś cāpi samāhitaḥ //59//*
> *hanyāt tv anapavādena śastrapāṇau sute sthite /*
> *vinītaṃ praśnayitvā ca vyavasyed ātmakarmasu //60//*
>
> Indeed, though the exalted boy stayed behind in the hermitage, he had not chopped the seer's wife apart. He had been off by himself, trans-

fixed in thought. [59] But as her son stood there weapon in hand, he was supposed to kill her without demurring. Instead, he was to decide on his own actions after posing questions in a nuanced way. [60]

As he saw his son bowed down at his feet, this is what the father thought: "Out of fear he checked my fickleness in resorting to the blade." [61] Then the father praised the boy for a long while, buried his face in the boy's head a long while, as he embraced him a long while between his two arms. And then he said, "Live long!" [62]

So the very wise scion of Gautama, filled with excitement and delight, saluted his son and said: [63] "Blessings upon you, Slowpoke! Be slow to act for a long time! With you being dilatory, I will be annoyed, but very well so, for a long time." [64] And the learned Gautama, the most excellent of hermits, uttered these verses that have as their import to point out the virtues of the wise Slowpoke. [65]

Final Observations and Questions

Bhīṣma draws out the general moral of this story in great detail for almost ten more *ślokas,* a coda that conveys a message distinctly different from that of the central parable. But this coda does match up well with the general question Yudhiṣṭhira asked at the outset, and it may have been appended to a pre-existing Cirakārin parable defending Ahalyā (and by extension, Reṇukā). At the same time, it is not hard to imagine that the parable and the coda were composed as part of a single effort by a single author. But if we see the parable and the coda as a compositional whole, then the legalistic brief exonerating Ahalyā from guilt in *ślokas* 34-38 stands out from its context even more dramatically. And again, if we see the parable and the coda as an integral composition, we are led to ask where the center of gravity of the text actually lies. Is it a sermon against rashness, one that uses the Ahalyā and Reṇukā stories as a cautionary illustration? Or was Cirakārin's brief for Ahalyā the principal focus of its author's compositional effort? If the defense of Ahalyā and women in her position was the principal point, perhaps the dilatory sermon on being slow and careful in all matters was composed to camouflage a social doctrine that might not sit well with some important members of the author's society. Whatever the actual history of this *adhyāya* may be, the brief for Ahalyā is remarkable in its own right and worthy of more attention than it has received before now. The picture of women and female agency that informs it is hardly flattering to women, but its arguments about women were made in the interest of defusing male rage and jealousy, which seldom feel the need to justify themselves in Sanskrit epic literature.

Notes

1. See my discussion of these general issues and of William Sax's and Gananath Obeyesekere's challenges to Goldman in Fitzgerald 2007.

2. Bhīmasena's club made entirely of molten steel (see Fitzgerald 2000).

3. I mention only three of these: his "Karma, Guilt, and Buried Memories: Public Reality and Private Fantasy in Ancient India" (Goldman 1985), "A City of the Heart: Epic Mathurā and the Indian Imagination" (Goldman 1986) and "Transsexualism, Gender, and Anxiety in Traditional India" (Goldman 1993).

4. Chapters 168 through 353 of Book 12 of the *Mahābhārata.* All references to the *Mahābhārata* are to Sukthankar, Belvalkar et al. 1933-66.

5. But see Jamison 1996: 172ff. for reflections upon the ways in which women, that is wives, are interconnected with the animal victims of Vedic sacrifices and are sometimes, anxiously and ambivalently, imagined in the role of sacrificial victim. Interestingly, the Cirakārikopākhyāna does follow immediately upon a general condemnation of the *paśubandha* and the endorsement of a blessing to be pronounced upon cattle in lieu of their actually being sacrificed, "The Song of King Vicaknhu", *MBh* 12.257.

6. I mean by "myth" a narrative intended to imply general norms of behavior or thought. The ultimate authority of a myth depends upon who tells it, where, and under what circumstances. I do not intend to indicate anything regarding the truth or falsity of the narrative.

7. Śvetaketu is said, at *MBh* 1.113.9ff. to enjoin monogamy on wives. Whether 1.113.18 enjoins it on husbands is not clear. See Robert Goldman's comments on the boy's reaction to witnessing his mother's exercise of sexual freedom (Goldman 1985: 417-18). Patrick Olivelle (Olivelle 1999) has shown that Śvetaketu has long been associated with the matter of sexual intercourse.

8. Various types of sexual infidelity come within the purview of Cirakārin's 'brief' in *ślokas* 34-38 of the parable: seduction of a wife, seduction of her with trickery, arousal at the sight of a man other than the husband, rape, and even, if I read 258.38 correctly, deliberate adultery initiated by the wife. These are all serious offenses from the husband's point of view, but this

story does not make theoretical distinctions among them. The central focus of this story is to rebut the husband's outrage and turn it. Brief arguments of exoneration are made addressing each type of extra-marital sex by a woman, and in each case the point is that the woman has not really done wrong and the husband has no right to punish her.

9. Robert Goldman used the concept of 'metamyth' extensively in his early book on the Bhārgava stories of the *MBh*, Goldman 1977. A 'metamyth' describes a narrative in the epic that comments on some narrative presented previously in the epic.

10. In making this argument I mean to say that I believe the Cirakārikopākhyāna is a composition that is later in time and later in its inclusion within the *MBh* than is the history of Śvetaketu's pronouncement which is put in the mouth of Pāṇḍu in 1.113 as he tries to persuade Kuntī to accept his charge to conceive sons for him by other men. While some (like the *MBh* commentator Arjunamiśra, see below in connection with the discussion of *śloka* 38 of our parable) may imagine that Cirakārin lived in the time of women's liberty, before Śvetaketu's law (*maryādā ... dharmyā*, 1.113.20), I believe the author of the parable intended to convey that sense, but for the purpose of combating Śvetaketu's law. What we have here are rival histories being told for sexual political purposes, and the Cirakārikopākhyāna seems clearly the later.

11. See the stories of Cyavana (*MBh* 1.6.1-4) and Aurva (*MBh* 1.169.20ff.) and my revisionist discussion of Rāma Jāmadagnya in the Appendix to Fitzgerald 2002: 130-31.

12. The undermining of male rage or will is usually accomplished only as a result of external intervention as with Parāśara's attempt to kill all the world's Rākṣasas (*MBh* 1.172) and Janamejaya's attempt to kill all the world's snakes with the inimical sacrifice at which the *Mahābhārata* was first narrated in public (see *MBh* 1.47-53). Such rage is typically a matter of male sex and not age: the essential point is not changed by the fact that the boy Aurva must be stopped as he vengefully heats himself up to destroy the universe (*MBh* 1.170-71); and the initially youthful Rāma Jāmadagnya's repeated genocidal slaughters of the world's kṣatriyas (see *MBh* 3.117.10ff. and 14.29-30) must be halted by his ancestors.

13. Obeyesekere 1990. See Fitzgerald 2007.

14. The story of Ahalyā is not told in any ancient sources prior to the *Bālakāṇḍa* of the *Rāmāyaṇa* (*Rāmāyaṇa* 1.47; see Bhatt and Shah 1960-75). And contrary to the *MBh's* boast that nothing occurs anywhere that is not also found in the *MBh*, the *MBh* does not tell the basic story, though it is well aware of it. For a discussion of the various forms this story takes in old Indian literature

see Söhnen-Thieme 1996. The story of Cirakārin does not turn up as a variant in Söhnen-Thieme's review, presumably because it is a fundamentally different tale, even if based on the Ahalyā theme, and the name Ahalyā does not occur in the Cirakārin story.

15. Though there are a number of retellings in the *MBh* of Rāma Jāmadagnya's famous slaughter of the world's kṣatriyas, his killing of his mother Reṇukā is narrated just once, at 3.116. For a presentation and discussion of this story see Goldman 1982.

16. See Söhnen-Thieme 1996.

17. 12.258.43c.

18. For Sanskrit text and English translation see Pollock 2007

19. *cirakārī mahāprājño gautamasyābhavat sutaḥ / ciraṃ hi sarvakāryāṇi samekṣāvān prapadyate //4// ciraṃ saṃcintayann arthāṃś ciraṃ jāgrac ciraṃ svapan / cirakāryābhisaṃpatteś cirakārī tathocyate //5//*

20. *vyabhicāre tu kasmiṃś cid vyatikramyāparān sutān / pitroktaḥ kupitenātha jahīmāṃ jananīm iti //7//*

21. See Renate Söhnen-Thieme's survey "The Ahalyā Story through the Ages", Söhnen-Thieme 1996. As Söhnen-Thieme's discussion shows, the Ahalyā story, in its various forms, turns upon certain ambiguities: Indra often has taken the form of Ahalyā's husband, the woman sometimes sees through the disguise, and sometimes verbal ambiguity plays an important role in Gautama's dealing with his wife. As we shall soon see, the last element turns up in this episode in a critical way.

22. See *MBh* 3.116. As those familiar with the Ahalyā story know, Gautama does not condemn Ahalyā to death.

23. 12.258.7: *vyabhicāre tu kasmiṃś cid vyatikramyāparān sutān / pitroktaḥ kupitenātha jahīmāṃ jananīm iti.* There are no children involved in the base-stories of Ahalyā and Gautama.

24. See Goldman 1978: 346-47.

25. *asvatantraṃ ca putratvaṃ kiṃ nu māṃ nātra pīḍayet //10cd// ... anavajñā pitur yuktā dhāraṇaṃ mātṛrakṣaṇam / yuktakṣamāv ubhāv etau nātivartetamāṃ katham //12//.* The standard lexica have previously recorded the sense of "fixed rule" not for *dhāraṇa* but only for its cognate *dhāraṇā;* there can, however, be no doubt of that meaning here. Regarding the suffix *-tamām* in 12d, Nīlakaṇṭha cites Pāṇini (5.4.11) to point out that we have here the suffix-

combination -*tama*- and -*ām* added to the finite verb *ativarte* to express intensity. This instance seems to be the only occurrence of this form in the constituted Pune text and its apparatus.

26. See Goldman 1978: 343-48.

27. E.g., see *MBh* 12.109.15-16; see Meyer 1953: 199ff.

28. *pitā hy alpataraṃ sthānaṃ*, 23c.

29. Text note: See the endnote at 258.28.

30. *cetanāvān naro hanyād yasya nāsuṣiraṃ śiraḥ //31cd//.*

31. Goldman 1982 argued that matricide was a necessary preparation for both Rāma Jāmadagnya and Rāma Dāśarathi to become mighty warriors.

32. *dampatyoḥ prāṇasaṃśleṣe yo 'bhisaṃdhiḥ kṛtaḥ kila / taṃ mātā vā pitā veda bhūtārtho mātari sthitaḥ //32// mātā jānāti yad gotraṃ mātā jānāti yasya saḥ / mātur bharaṇamātreṇa prītiḥ snehaḥ pituḥ prajāḥ //33//*

33. A fundamental feature of Śvetaketu's angry pronouncement was that his mother's willingly going with another man happened before his own eyes: *śvetaketoḥ kila purā samakṣaṃ mātaraṃ pituḥ / jagrāha brāhmaṇaḥ pāṇau gacchāva iti cābravīt //11// ṛṣiputras tataḥ kopaṃ cakārāmarṣitas tadā / mātaraṃ tāṃ tathā dṛṣṭvā nīyamānāṃ balād iva //12//.* The significance of the *balād iva*, of course, is that she was not forced, but away she went all the same.

34. For a strikingly misogynistic statement to the opposite effect see Bhīṣma's comments at *MBh* 13.40.4-14.

35. The reading *tasyāsmāryatas* amends Belvalkar's *tasya smārayatas.* See the discussion below.

36. Thieme 1977: 513-14. In his Critical Notes to his edition of the *Śāntiparvan* Belvalkar takes the *yāpyanti* in a medial sense and as a denominative from *yāpya:* men, bringing disgrace upon themselves, "deserve to be dismissed". Though it is not unusual for the *MBh* to use active endings where middle ones are prescribed, there is a very strong sense that if this verb was to describe men "bringing themselves into a state demanding dismissal", we would have the middle here. And well we could: Though Belvalkar does not discuss it, one could postulate that the text reads *yāpyanti* for *yāpyante* here for the sake of the meter. The ending -e of the middle form here is disallowed in this *vipulā* form of the *śloka.* But while Belvalkar's interpretation can easily be read in light of the next two stanzas, it does not seem to fit the context exactly.

37. Jamison 1996: 298, n. 26.

38. *anāvṛtā hi sarveṣāṃ varṇānām aṅganā bhuvi / yathā gāvaḥ sthitās tāta sve sve varṇe tathā prajāḥ //14//* Manu's strictures regarding the continuous *rakṣaṇa* ("protecting guarding, keeping [as desired by the keepers]") of women by males and their never being autonomous, *svatantra*, were not part of the picture described here by Uddālaka. The most relevant passages in Manu are 5.148 and 9.03.

39. *MBh* 13.39-43. Vipula's method caused Devaśarman some initial discomfort, when he learned of it. But it worked and Devaśarman was reconciled to it when assured of Vipula's having had pure intentions. (As with Sulabhā's taking over Janaka in this way at *MBh* 12.308, one must always wonder how ironically such stories were meant to be heard. See Fitzgerald 2002.) Perhaps the *MBh's* most famous rehearsal of women's sexual appetites is cleverly put into the mouth of a beautiful *Apsaras* (a young woman who sings and dances for the Gods in the heavens), Pañcacūḍā, speaking at the behest of Nārada, just prior to the story of Vipula's remarkable 'protection' of Ruci, at *MBh* 13.38.

40. This story lionizes a Brahmin for sharing his wife with a guest completely. Regarding this form of hospitality see Jamison 1996: 153-57 and Meyer 1953: 512-17, esp. the notes to 516-17.

41. *bhāryaṃ patnīṃ ca prāṇair viyojayitum icchanto 'sya bhartṛtvādiguṇaśūnyas yonmattasyeva vacanān mātaraṃ na hiṃsiṣye—ityāśayaḥ.* All citations from Nīlakaṇṭha are from Kinjawadekar 1929-36.

42. *nanu vyabhicāriṇī strī hantavyaiva, anyathā kulasaṅkarāpatter ity āśaṅkhyāha | ... yadi prārthayitaiva, na syāt [hantavyā] | tarhi nāyaṃ doṣaḥ prasajjyeta | ataḥ prathamapravṛtte puṃsy evāyaṃ doṣaḥ | ity arthaḥ* (Nīlakaṇṭha at 12.258.36).

43. Grünendahl 1993

44. Regarding the calculation and specification of the *ṛtu*, see the helpful notes of Patrick Olivelle to his translation of Manu 3.45ff.

45. *sá strīṣaṃsādám upāsīdad asyái brahmahatyā́yai tṛ́tīyaṃ práti gṛhṇītéti | tā́ abruván váraṃ vṛṇāmahā ṛ́tviyāt prajā́ṃ vindāmahāi, kā́mam ā́ víjanitoḥ sáṃ bhavāméti | tásmād ṛ́tviyāt stríyaḥ prajā́ṃ vindante kā́mam ā́ víjanitoḥ sáṃ bhavanti / vā́revṛtam* (Nīlakaṇṭha, quoting *Taittirīya Saṃhitā* 2.5.1.5 at *MBh* 12.258.38; full text from Taḷekara, Kāḷe et al. 1959-78).

46. *Rāmāyaṇa* 1.47.18ab: *ṛtukālaṃ pratīkṣante nārthinaḥ susamāhite.*

47. *maithunatṛptaye nokto nirdeśaḥ pratyuta yāthākāmyam evāsāṃ vihitam | tena*

kāmapravaraṇatvam api nāsya doṣaḥ. Arjunamiśra at *MBh* 12.258.38ab, as cited in the apparatus of Belvalkar to this half-*śloka*.

48. Deussen and Strauss 1906 *ad loc*. also read *ca na*. They take the *nirdeśa* to be a wife's invitation to her husband to intercourse (or, as here, her not issuing one). While the interpretation of Deussen and Strauss renders the whole *śloka* more or less adequately (reading 38c as *tasya smārayataḥ*, and taking that phrase as "bringing the subject up"), their reading does not really address the context very well at all. *(Er, an den keine Aufforderung auf Seiten des Weibes zum Geschlechtsgenusse erging, der vielmehr seinerseits offen darauf die Rede brachte, er ist der schuldige Teil, daran ist kein Zweifel.)* Meyer 1953: 206) follows Deussen and Strauss.

49. Of course if we do take the word *ukta* in 38 to refer to *śruti*, Vedic injunctions, then 38 could be read as a direct rejection of the authority of Śvetaketu's *maryādā*.

50. *Rāmāyaṇa* 1.47.19: *munaveṣaṃ sahasrākṣaṃ vijñāya raghunandana / matiṃ cakāra durmedhā devarājakutūhalāt.*

51. "Habitual recitation of the Veda" seems the best way to understand *śrutadhairya* here.

52. *evaṃ vimṛśatas tasya cirakāritayā bahu / dīrghaḥ kālo vyatikrāntas tatas tasyāgamat pitā //41// medhātithir mahāprājño gautamas tapasi sthitaḥ / vimṛśya tena kālena patnyāḥ saṃsthāvyatikramam //42// so 'bravīd duḥkhasaṃtapto bhṛśam aśrūṇi vartayan / śrutadhairyaprasādena paścāttāpam upāgataḥ //43//*

53. *samayā ... tayā ...* Belvalkar greatly improved upon the vulgate by reading *samayā* for *sa mayā*, but he took it as an adverb meaning "entirely". I take it rather as an adjective modifying *tayā* (referring to Medhātithi's wife) and signifying "of flat demeanor, of even temperament, etc.", which I think is best rendered here in terms of being "reserved" (rather than using the flatter "equably" or the ambiguous "demurely"). Medhātithi thus informs us that his wife was not flirtatious, did nothing to encourage Indra's sexual advances.

54. The woman's words, *paravatī-asmi*, can be construed both ways.

55. *praṇayiṣye nayena*, with *nayena* used in the sense of *nyāyena*, "fitly, properly, rightly", a sense recorded in the Sanskrit lexica.

56. Who exactly are these celibates at the time this text is being composed?

57. *nirākāra*. We might think that her lack of expression is an ironic editorial registration by the author of the story of the woman's complete lack of voice

and standing in these proceedings (the only words of hers in all of this are Medhātithi's quotation of her ill-chosen expression of *pātivratya* to the brahmin guest). And we may well be right to think that. Within the frame of the narrative the word would signify that she was impassively watching her son, waiting for him to carry out the father's command. I think it is more likely that her lack of expression is meant here to signify that she had no inkling of her husband's command or the son's inner struggle. But whatever be the significance on the surface of the narrative, this label does point directly to her complete objectification in this weighty (and long!) deliberation.

Bibliography

Primary Sources

Mahābhārata. Edited by R.S. Kinjawadekar. *Śrīmanmahābhāratam with the Bhāratabhāvadīpa of Nīlakaṇṭha.* Pune: Citrashala Press, 1929-36.

Mahābhārata. Edited by V.S. Sukthankar, et al. *The Mahābhārata for the First Time Critically Edited.* Pune: Bhandarkar Oriental Research Institute, 1933-66.

Mahābhārata. Translated by P. Deussen and O. Strauss. *Vier Philosophische Texte des Mahābhāratam.* Leipzig: F. A. Brockhaus, 1906.

Mānavadharmaśāstra. Edited by P. Olivelle. *Manu's Code of Law: A Critical Edition and Translation of the Mānava-Dharmaśāstra.* New York: Oxford University Press, 2005.

Rāmāyaṇa. Edited by G.H. Bhatt and U.P. Shah. *The Vālmīki Rāmāyaṇa: Critical Edition.* 7 vols. Baroda: Oriental Institute, 1960-75.

Taittirīya Saṃhitā. Edited by N. Taḷekara, et al. *Kṛṣṇayajurvedīyataittirīyasaṃhitā, Śrīmatsāyaṇācāryaviracitabhāṣyasametā.* Pune: Anandasrama Sanskrit Series, 1959-78.

Uttararāmacarita of Bhavabhūti. Edited and translated by S. Pollock. *Rāma's Last Act by Bhavabhuti.* New York: New York University Press, 2007.

Secondary Sources

Fitzgerald, J.L. 2000. "*pīta* and *śaikya*: Two Terms of Iron and Steel Technology in the *Mahābhārata.*" *Journal of the American Oriental Society* 120 (1): 44-61.

____. 2002. "Nun Befuddles King, Shows *karmayoga* does not Work: Sulabhā's Refutation of King Janaka at *MBh* 12.308." *Journal of Indian Philosophy* 30 (6): 641-77.

____. 2002. "The Rāma Jāmadagnya Thread of the *Mahābhārata:* A New Survey of Rāma Jāmadagnya in the Pune Text," in M. Brockington, ed. *Stages and Transitions: Temporal and Historical Frameworks in Epic and Purāṇic Literature.* Zagreb: Croatian Academy of Sciences and Arts.

____. 2007. "Bhīṣma beyond Freud: The Fall of the Sky, Bhīṣma in the Mahābhārata, 1," in B. Black and S. Brodbeck, eds. *Epic Constructions: Gender, Myth, and Society in the Mahābhārata*. London: Routledge.

Goldman, R.P. 1977. *Gods, Priests, and Warriors: The Bhṛgus of the Mahābhārata*. New York: Columbia University Press.

____. 1978. "Fathers, Sons, and Gurus: Oedipal Conflict in the Sanskrit Epics." *Journal of Indian Philosophy* 6: 325-93.

____. 1980. "Rāmaḥ Sahalakṣmaṇaḥ: Psychological and Literary Aspects of the Composite Hero of Vālmīki's *Rāmāyaṇa*." *Journal of Indian Philosophy* 8: 149-89.

____. 1982. "Matricide, Renunciation, and Compensation in the Legends of Two Warrior-Heroes of the Sanskrit Epics." *Indologica Taurinensia* 10: 117-31.

____. 1985. "Karma, Guilt, and Buried Memories: Public Fantasy and Private Reality in Traditional India." *Journal of the American Oriental Society* 105 (3): 413-25.

____. 1986. "A City of the Heart: Epic Mathurā and the Indian Imagination." *Journal of the American Oriental Society* 106 (3): 471-83.

____. 1993. "Transsexualism, Gender, and Anxiety in Traditional India." *Journal of the American Oriental Society* 113 (3): 374-401.

Grünendahl, R. 1993. "Zur Klassifizierung von Mahābhārata-Handschriften." *Indica et Tibetica* 22 (Studien zur Indologie und Buddhismuskunde): 101-30.

Jamison, S.W. 1996. *Sacrificed Wife/Sacrificer's Wife*. New York: Oxford University Press.

Meyer, J.J. 1953. *Sexual Life in Ancient India: A Study in the Comparative History of Indian Culture*. New York: Barnes & Noble, Inc.

Obeyesekere, G. 1990. *The Work of Culture: Symbolic Transformation in Psychoanalysis and Anthropology*. Chicago: University of Chicago Press.

Olivelle, P. 1999. "Young Śvetaketu: A Literary Study of an Upaniṣadic Story." *Journal of the American Oriental Society* 119 (1): 46-70.

Söhnen-Thieme, R. 1996. "The Ahalyā Story through the Ages," in J. Leslie, ed. *Myth and Mythmaking*. Richmond, Surrey: Curzon Press.

Thieme, P. 1977. "Bhartṛhari's Allegorie von Schicksalwürfelspiel," in *Beiträge zur Indienforschung, Ernst Waldschmidt zum 80. Geburtstag gewidmet*. Berlin: Museum für indische Kunst.

Time in the *Mahābhārata* and the Time of the *Mahābhārata*[1]

LUIS GONZÁLEZ-REIMANN

According to tradition, the story told in the *Mahābhārata* takes place at the end of the Dvāpara Yuga and the beginning of the terrible Kali Yuga, our current age. This refers, of course, to the well-known theory of the yugas or eras of the world, according to which society goes through four ages that bring about a gradual decay in morals and respect for dharma. The first yuga, Kṛta (later called Satya), is a time when everyone follows dharma and society functions perfectly. Throughout the second and third yugas—Tretā and Dvāpara—respect for dharma declines until it reaches its lowest point in the fourth and last yuga, Kali. This degeneration of dharma follows a 4-3-2-1 numerical pattern that forms an integral part of the system of yugas and is often illustrated by envisioning dharma as a cow that stands firmly on its four legs in the Kṛta Yuga, while it stands on only three, two, and one in the subsequent ages. Both the names of the yugas and their descending 4-3-2-1 sequence are derived from the Indian game of dice as it was played in the last centuries BCE and the first centuries CE, and as it appears in the *Mahābhārata*, where a game of dice plays a crucial role in the narrative.

The Kali Yuga

That the action of the *Mahābhārata* occurs at the beginning of the Kali Yuga, or indeed, that it inaugurates it, is taken for granted not only by traditional commentators and Purāṇic composers, but also by a large number of modern scholars.[2] There is an obvious hermeneutic benefit to this assumption in that it serves to explain—and therefore understand—some troubling elements in the epic's narrative, mainly the adharmic behavior of its heroes and the nearly total destruction of all the parties to the conflict, especially the Bhāratas. Whether one takes the Bhārata war as a traditional historical event or as a mythological narrative—or some combination of the two—the yuga theory, as an interpretive tool, can help make sense of different negative or questionable aspects of the story. It accomplishes this by neatly placing the story in a cosmic-historical framework that justifies these happenings as inevitable consequences of the arrival of the darkest yuga. Things happened as they did, the explanation goes, because the Dvāpara Yuga was ending and the negative Kali Yuga was quickly making its presence felt. The unseemly behavior of the heroes—and of the god Kṛṣṇa himself—was merely the result of cosmic influence. The times were changing, and the epic's players had to act accordingly. This notion of an important cosmically-determined negative "turning point" in mythic-historical time that opens the worst of the yugas is, thus, assumed to inform the narrative and to be present throughout the epic.

But is this assumption warranted? Is it clear from the narrative of the *Mahābhārata* that the Kali Yuga is about to begin, and that this should explain the conduct of the heroes and other aspects of the story? The fact is that the text itself makes the connection very few times (only nine) and, with only one exception, they are outside of the main narrative. Most of these instances are very brief, which makes their scarcity even more remarkable considering that the poem is 75,000 verses long. Of these nine instances, two are found in the Nārāyaṇīya part of Book Twelve,[3] while a third comes from Book Six, in a section closely connected to the Nārāyaṇīya.[4] The fourth instance is also in Book Six, in a section on cosmography;[5] and the fifth is in Book Thirteen, when the wise Bhīṣma, on his dying bed of arrows, exalts Kṛṣṇa as the Supreme God and states that he is born in the Kali Yuga as adharma.[6] Instances six and seven come from Book Three, when the Pāṇḍava brothers are living in exile in the forest. One occurs during Bhīma's encounter with Hanumān,[7] and the other in the discourse that the learned Bhārgava sage Mārkaṇḍeya delivers to Yudhiṣṭhira.[8] Instance eight is to be found in Book One, in the introductory survey of the story.[9] Finally, our last instance, and the only one that is embedded in the narrative, appears in Book Nine, at the time of the death of Duryodhana at the hands of the Pāṇḍava hero Bhīma. It is a passing remark made by Kṛṣṇa that takes up merely half a verse.[10]

To be sure, the yugas—or simply the word yuga—are mentioned at other points in the poem, but without any explicit link to the story. It is significant that the verses that do make the connection are heavily concentrated in books three and twelve—which include much extraneous material—while there is no mention whatsoever of the yugas in the last three books. It is these last books that describe the death of Kṛṣṇa as well as Yudhiṣṭhira's handing over of the kingdom to Parikṣit and the death of the Pāṇḍavas during their journey to the Himalayas. If these events marked the arrival of the Kali Yuga, that fact surely deserved at least a passing mention.

It is unusual then, one would think, that something as important as the placement of the action of the *Mahābhārata* at the beginning of the Kali Yuga would not be referred to more often and in unambiguous terms in the text itself. But this is only surprising if such a placement were really fundamental to the narrative, and if it was meant by the authors to be the background cause of events, and a basis for symbolical connections of different sorts. It is not unusual or surprising if we consider such a placement of the epic's events in the yuga scheme as a late addition to the story. The nine instances just mentioned, in which the connection is clearly made, belong for the most part in sections of the epic generally considered to have been added later, as is the case with the Nārāyaṇīya of Book Twelve and the Mārkaṇḍeya section of Book Three. Likewise, the mention in the introductory summary to the poem is surely later than the main story itself. Furthermore, most of these instances have little or nothing to do with the main story and are, rather, linked to proclamations of Kṛṣṇa's status as Supreme God and/or as *avatāra* of Viṣṇu.

A close look at the yuga passages in the *Mahābhārata* reveals that the connection between the start of the Kali Yuga and the conflict portrayed in the Epic is only superficial. It appears to have been superimposed on the poem at a late phase in the text's history, although for later tradition it became an inseparable part of the story. By the time of the Guptas (4th–5th centuries), the connection was firmly established and never seriously questioned. It is taken for granted in the Purāṇas, the Dharmaśāstras, the astronomical Siddhāntas, and by later commentators and most modern scholars.

Dice and Yugas

In contrast to the peripheral role played in the epic narrative by the transition from the Dvāpara Yuga to the Kali Yuga, the game of dice in which Duryodh-ana defeats Yudhiṣṭhira with the help of Śakuni is a central event. And it is to a large extent the importance of the game of dice—along with the fact that Śakuni and Duryodhana were considered to be incarnations of the two worst throws, Dvāpara and Kali—that made it easy for the change of yuga theme to be incorporated into the story, because the yuga theory took its nomenclature and its descending numerical pattern from the dice game. This has allowed for passages that clearly refer to dice to be construed as references to the yugas, even though the text says nothing to that effect. The best example is probably Kṛṣṇa's admonition to Karṇa shortly before the war, when he repeatedly warns the hero that as soon as the war breaks out "there will ... be no Tretā, no Kṛta and no Dvāpara," *na tadā bhavitā tretā na kṛtaṃ dvāparaṃ na ca,*[11] in what seems an obvious reference to the dicing match won by the Kauravas that had sent the Pāṇḍavas into exile. Kṛṣṇa appears to be telling Karṇa that this time around the confrontation will not be settled by throwing dice (Tretā, Kṛta or Dvāpara). Instead, it will have to be resolved in real combat. It is noteworthy that although the word "yuga" does not appear in this passage, modern translators have routinely added it, thus turning Kṛṣṇa's words about the difference between a game of dice and a real life battle into an ominous announcement of the arrival of the terrible Kali Yuga. The contrast between a dice match and real combat had been stated explicitly by Āśvatthāman earlier in the story, when he sarcastically declared that Śakuni—who had won the dice game by means of trickery—could not win in a real battle because Arjuna's bow, Gāṇḍīva, "...does not throw dice, whether Kṛta or Dvāpara. Gāṇḍīva throws blazing, sharp, hard arrows".[12] Along the same lines, Bhīma, after striking down Duryodhana at the end of the war, declares, "We do not use humiliation, fire, dice games and cheating; we destroy our enemies with the strength of our arms."[13]

A good illustration of how contemporary scholars can be tempted to see references to the Kali Yuga when the term *kali* is mentioned, or when a great crisis is described, can be found in an article by Madeleine Biardeau (1984). In an essay about the story of King Nala and its connection to the epic, Biardeau discusses the negative role of Kali (the personified worst dice throw) vis-à-vis Nala, and then states "Who wouldn't think ... of identifying Kali with the sinister Kaliyuga ... ?"[14] This statement illustrates the problem very well, for only someone familiar with the theory's supposed intimate connection to the *Mahābhārata* would immediately find a parallel between a negative character called Kali and the Kali Yuga in the story of Nala, a story that makes no such connection and never even mentions the yugas. This points to a predisposition to read the yugas into the text in places where there is no reason for doing so.

It must be borne in mind that when the *Mahābhārata* was composed the yuga theory was at a formative stage and was most likely being shaped within the later strata of the Epic itself. This means that in order to understand the possible role played by the yugas in the story we need to look mainly at literature that is earlier than, or contemporaneous with the *Mahābhārata*, instead of texts that came later. When we do so, we discover that the yuga theory is conspicuously absent from Vedic literature and makes its first appearances in the *Mahābhārata* itself, in the *Yuga Purāṇa* (a chapter of the *Gārgīya Jyotiṣa*), and in the *Mānava Dharma Śāstra*, all of which are roughly contemporaneous and date from the last centuries BCE or the early centuries CE. These texts reflect differing versions of the yuga theory, as would be expected at a time when the system was still taking shape. Also from this period is the Buddhist Pali Canon, in which the terms *kali*, *dvāpara*, *tretā* and *kṛta* appear many times, but always with reference to the names of the dice throws or the negative or positive—*kali* or *kṛta*—qualities of something. They are not applied to the yugas. This indicates that it was more common at the time to associate these names with dice throws or with things deemed good or bad, than with yugas. The connection between the names of the dice throws and those of the yugas made it easy to incorporate the yuga theory into the *Mahābhārata* and, eventually, superimpose its cosmic-historical blueprint onto the epic story.

Kāla

There is another, very significant element that we must take into account: the importance throughout the *Mahābhārata* of time, *kāla*, as a powerful, unstoppable force that drives everything to its conclusion. In sharp contrast to the very few references to the beginning of the Kali Yuga, time is repeatedly blamed for the events of the epic. Dhṛtarāṣṭra frequently complains about it, and Vyāsa, the purported author of the poem, invokes it to account for the way in which events unfold. What's more, Vyāsa himself is on one occasion referred to as a *kālavādin*, a believer in the doctrine of *kāla* as the supreme principle.[15] In the epic, *kāla* is an irresistible, inscrutable force. It is the equivalent of destiny, and the actors of the epic narrative are bound by its dictates. This is forcefully portrayed in Dhṛtarāṣṭra's despair over the events on the battlefield, when he exclaims that "an action is intended one way, but it is controlled [so as to result] another way. Alas, destiny is powerful, and time is unconquerable!"[16]

It is not surprising that an epic story that graphically describes the death of countless heroes should resort to the notion of destiny or the cosmic force of time as an explanation for such tragic events. This is not unusual in epic traditions. But, beyond this, we must point out that the idea that time is a supreme power that eventually leads everyone and everything to their destruction was already an old and familiar one by the time of the composition of the *Mahābhārata*, and this is in marked contrast with the absence of the yuga theory in pre-epic literature. Although the word *kāla* itself does not appear in the *Ṛgveda*,[17] the notion of the passage of time as an unstoppable force that draws us nearer to death is present in the Ṛgvedic hymns to Uṣas, the goddess Dawn. These hymns often refer to the way in which she shortens our life span with her daily return.[18] The *Atharvaveda*,[19] on the other hand, devotes two hymns to *kāla* as the supreme principle while, in the Brāhmaṇas, time had to be conquered through ritual activity in order to achieve immortality.[20] In fact, by the end of the Vedic period and the time of the composition of the *Mahābhārata* the importance of time as a destructive force had reached new heights, and the word *kāla* had practically become synonymous with death.

That notions of time and destiny played a prominent role among ideas that were popular at the end of the Vedic period is underscored, for instance, by the mention of *kāla* in the *Śvetāśvatara Upaniṣad* as one of the current explanations for the cause of things,[21] and by the central role played by destiny in the doctrines of the Ājīvikas, one of the so-called heterodox movements.[22] Ultimately, it is also reflected in the then emerging notion that life is suffering or sorrow, *duḥkha*, and that the only escape is to go beyond time and into liberation (*mokṣa*) or *nirvāṇa*.

The importance of time, *kāla*, in the *Mahābhārata*, then, is consistent not only with its epic character, but also—and more importantly—with the philosophical and religious currents of the period in which it was composed. The yuga theory, on the other hand, was a newcomer to the scene, and it is precisely the embedded importance of *kāla* in the *Mahābhārata* that made it easy for the yugas to be incorporated into its story. Therefore, when the epic players blame *kāla* for their misfortune we cannot assume that this implies a reference to the yuga theory, as has been done on many occasions.

It is later, in the Purāṇas, that the yugas were explicitly considered to be one of the major manifestations of time. They represent—together with two other newcomers, the kalpas and the manvantaras—the macrocosmic, large-scale projection of time. Vedic literature is not particularly concerned with time on a large scale, but this became a crucial element of post-Vedic cosmogony and ideas about history. *Kāla*, which had first been applied mainly to time as the destroyer of human life, was now projected onto the macrocosm to also represent the force responsible for the destruction of the world. Just as humans go through a cycle of birth, life, old age, death and rebirth, the universe was understood to go through a parallel process: the periodic death and rebirth of the cosmos.[23] The rising god Śiva now presided over the death of the cosmos and was known as Mahākāla, "Great Time". Likewise, the epic goddess Kālarātrī, whose name means "the night of time", became the Purāṇic goddess of the night of cosmic destruction.

The yugas, as a cycle mainly concerned with the periodic rise and fall of dharma—with human history one might say—became part of this new system of cosmic time and they were easily associated with the story of the *Mahābhārata*. From being blamed on an inscrutable, mysterious, general force know as *kāla*; the events of the epic could now be understood, even predicted, by framing them within a newly formed theory that provided history with a structure, a well-known pattern of transformation and, most significantly, with meaning.

More specifically, in terms of the narrative of the epic the incorporation of the yuga scheme served three main purposes. Firstly, it provided a rationale—a cosmic explanation—for the adharmic behavior of the epic heroes and for the devastating consequences of the fratricidal fight for succession that is at the core of the poem. Secondly, it made it possible to turn an existing story about a struggle for royal succession into a cosmic drama that required the intervention of Viṣṇu—in his emerging role of Supreme God—in human affairs in order to restore a decadent dharma. And finally, in what was probably a separate addition to the text (the Mārkaṇḍeya section, discussed below), it reflected the historical reality faced by some members of the brahminical establishment at some point in the last centuries BCE and the first centuries CE, as their dharma seemed to be on the verge of collapse due to the presence of foreign rulers and the growing influence of native movements that challenged the authority of the Vedas, the validity of the *varṇa* system of social classes, and the existence of a creator god.

Metaphors, Comparisons and Yugānta

There is one last aspect of the process that deserves mention. In the Sanskrit epics it is very common to use metaphors and to make comparisons to powerful, awe-inspiring images when trying to convey the greatness of events, characters, or objects such as divine weapons. In these cases, the image of the yugas is employed frequently. To give an example, the interim rule of Bhīṣma while the Pāṇḍava and Kaurava princes were growing up is said to have been the Kṛta Yuga.[24] If we were to take this statement at face value, the traditional connection between the yugas and the events of the *Mahābhārata* would be upset because, among other things, Bhīṣma's "Kṛta Yuga" would have lasted no more than a few years, and the subsequent yugas would have been even shorter. Comparisons to the yugas are best illustrated by discussing a word that has probably contributed significantly to identifications, and even confusions, between the events of the epic and the yuga theory. I am referring to the term *yugānta*—a word often used in the epics and in many Purāṇas—the literal meaning of which is "the end of the yuga".

Yugānta actually has two distinct meanings in the *Mahābhārata*. The first one refers to a catastrophic event, an "end of the world" marked by natural disasters such as intense heat and fires, flooding, strong winds and earthquakes. In Purāṇic cosmogony, this would become the *kalpānta*, the end of the kalpa.[25] *Yugānta* is sometimes used in the poem for drawing comparisons between the tragic events of the story and a mythological end of the world. Take the following comment by Saṃjaya while he describes the battle to the blind King Dhṛtarāṣṭra, "When the fierce ... battle was going on ... it was like the end of the yuga (*yugānta iva*), when a violent destruction of the world takes place."[26] Or consider the description of the distraught Kaurava women when they receive news of the passing of their warriors, "Holding arms they mourned their sons, brothers and fathers, as if displaying (*darśayantīva*) the destruction of the world at the end of the yuga."[27] Such comparisons to *yugānta* are more frequently made to warriors and their weapons. During the battle, these are often said to be like the intense fire, the scorching sun, or the great clouds at *yugānta*. Heroes are as destructive in battle as *kāla* is at *yugānta*.

It is clear, then, that these mentions of *yugānta* are not intended to place the action in any particular phase of the yuga cycle. They are simply comparisons.[28] We can probably talk of a progression, a gradual change from comparison to identification that ended up equating the events of the *Mahābhārata* with the beginning of the Kali Yuga. This served to explain the nature of the narrative, as discussed above, but it also eventually established the purported events of the epic as the definite anchor for dating traditional history.[29] This process of identification was already at work in the late strata of the poem, but it was fully developed and sanctioned in the Purāṇas, the Dharmaśāstras, and the astronomical Siddhāntas.

The second meaning of *yugānta* refers to a social crisis in which the established stratified structure of the social classes is turned upside down, morality is at its lowest point, and two social evils become increasingly threatening to the brahmanical social order. These two evils are the presence of foreigners, *mlecchas*, more specifically *mleccha* rulers; and the growing influence of *nāstikas*, the heterodox movements that do not recognize the Vedas as revealed texts. This second meaning of *yugānta* as a social crisis refers to the end of the full cycle of the four yugas, when dharma has reached its lowest point. By definition, it has to do with the end of the Kali Yuga, not its beginning. In the *Mahābhārata*, this usage is restricted to the Mārkaṇḍeya section of Book Three, in a conversation between King Yudhiṣṭhira and the sage Mārkaṇḍeya.[30] The Pāṇḍava king questions the sage about the conditions of society at the end of the Kali Yuga instead of at its beginning, as would be expected if the start of the worst yuga were a central concern of the *Mahābhārata*'s narrative. Yudhiṣṭhira learns from Mārkaṇḍeya that a Brahmin called Kalkin will be born at the end of the Kali Yuga and will inaugurate a new Kṛta Yuga. This interest in the end of the Kali Yuga probably indicates that the author of this passage was expecting it to end soon and a new Kṛta to begin immediately after that.[31]

Conclusions

If we want to assume that a new theory like that of the yugas is deeply embedded in the *Mahābhārata*, and that it is fundamental to its understanding, there needs to be a solid basis for doing so, and that is not the case.[32] It is not enough to find general statements regarding the theory and a few scattered explicit mentions of a direct connection between it and the story, especially when some of these statements and mentions contradict each other.[33] In the absence of any solid basis, we are left with little more than speculation and a search for hidden meanings and implicit references for which there is no reasonable evidence.[34]

Interpreting the *Mahābhārata* in terms of the yuga theory often says more about the interpreter and his/her need to make sense of certain elements of the story than about the text and its authors. A modern interpretation that follows this path can easily resemble a Purāṇic reading. Such an approach tends to take for granted unwarranted assumptions, not only about the supposed relevance of the yuga theory in the *Mahābhārata*, but also about the poem's unity and its supposed underlying symbolism. It implies largely ignoring the evidence of textual layers, and brushing aside contradictions as merely superficial elements that will dissipate once a hypothetical cohesive, primordial, hidden meaning is finally exposed.

Notes

1. An early version of this article was presented at the 32nd Annual Conference on South Asia, in Madison, Wisconsin, in October of 2003. Many of the issues dealt with in this article are treated at length in González-Reimann 2002.

2. For several examples in modern scholarship, see González-Reimann 2002: 104–06; and 115–16, nn. 70–72.

3. 12.326.82, 12.337.42-44. All *Mahābhārata* references are to the Critical Edition. Translations are mine.

4. 6.62.39.

5. 6.11.14.

6. 13.143.9. Note that this contradicts Kṛṣṇa's role as upholder of dharma.

7. 3.148.37.

8. 3.188.3-7.

9. 1.2.9-10.

10. 9.59.21. For a detailed discussion of each instance see Chapter Three of González-Reimann 2002.

11. 5.140.6-15.

12. 4.45.23.

13. 9.58.8. See González-Reimann 2002: 58-60.

14. Biardeau 1984: 270.

15. 6.4.2.

16. 8.5.45, González-Reimann 2002: 29.

17. With one exception at *Ṛg Veda* 10.42.9.

18. *Ṛg Veda* 1.92.10, 1.179.1.

19. *Atharva Veda* 19.53-54.

20. See González-Reimann 2009.

21. *Śvetāśvatara Upaniṣad* 1.2.

22. For the Ājīvikas see Basham [1951] 1981. The term used by the movement is *niyati*.

23. See González-Reimann 2009.

24. 1.102.5. The same is said of the condition of the world after Rāma Jāmadagnya—known in later literature as Paraśurāma—had killed off the kṣatriyas 21 times (1.58.4-24).

25. The Mārkaṇḍeya section places these disasters at the end of one thousand cycles of four yugas (*yugasahasrānta*, 3.186.56), and these thousand cycles are said to be a day for Brahmā (3.186.22-3). In the Purāṇas, a day of Brahmā is the same as a kalpa, but not according to *MBh* 12.291.14, which states that a kalpa is only one cycle of the four yugas, instead of one thousand.

26. 7.102.8.

27. 11.9.13.

28. In a similar vein, the *Rāmāyaṇa* of Vālmīki (1.1.73) compares Rāma's rule after he had rescued Sītā to the Kṛta Yuga. At that time, things were "like in the Kṛta yuga", *yathā kṛtayuge tathā*.

29. The date for the beginning of the Kali Yuga was established as 3102 BCE, probably by astronomers of the Gupta period. See González-Reimann 2002: 169, 189.

30. 3.186-89.

31. 3.188.5-8. For a detailed study see González-Reimann 2002: 92-99.

32. Therefore, statements like the following one by Hiltebeitel (2001: 158) are more a reflection of later, traditional assumptions about the text than of what its authors might have intended. He writes that "... it would appear that the *Mahābhārata* is designed to set in motion the entire history of the universe down to and just past the *Mahābhārata* war, to the 'dawn' (*saṃdhyā*) of 'our times', the Kali yuga ..." Fitzgerald's remark concerning Hiltebeitel's suggestion about Vyāsa as a largely hidden author could also be applied to his ideas about a supposed implied presence of the yuga theory. Fitzgerald (2003: 815) writes of "the danger of invoking deliberate authorial concealment or silence as a hermeneutic principle".

33. An example of a relevant contradiction is the following: Rāma Jāmadagnya (Paraśurāma) is said at 1.2.3-8 to have appeared in the transition between Tretā and Dvāpara. But in 12.326.77-78 it is Rāma Dāśarathi (the hero of the *Rāmāyaṇa*) who is born at this juncture, while Rāma Jāmadagnya appears in the Tretā. In another example, at 3.148.16-33, the correspondence between colors and yugas is Kṛta, white; Tretā, red; Dvāpara, yellow; and Kali, black. In 3.187.31 (only a few chapters later), the colors for Tretā and Dvāpara are reversed. Hiltebeitel (2001: 164) writes that the authors "are not averse" to, among other things, "intriguing contradictions". But it seems more reasonable—and consistent with what we know about the text—to say that later interpolators or redactors (or even contemporary compilers) did not go through the trouble of working out every single contradiction when conflating versions and adding to their received text, or when reinterpreting it from their own perspective.

34. The following description by Lopez (1996: 240-41) of the attitude of traditional commentators of Buddhist texts is relevant: "... commentators ... are not concerned to say anything new; innovation is one of the great sins of Buddhist letters. Instead, they are concerned to reveal its hidden meaning ... The commentator's task is the discovery, the identification, the elaboration, even the manufacture, of allusion."

Bibliography

Primary Sources

Atharva-Veda-Saṃhitā: Text With English Translation, Mantra Index and Names of Ṛṣis and Devatās. Edited by Nag Sharan Singh. 2 vols. Delhi: Nag Publishers, 1987. The translation is by W.D. Whitney and R. Griffith (Book 20).

The Early Upaniṣads: Annotated Text and Translation. Edited and translated by Patrick Olivelle. New York: Oxford University Press, 1998.

The Mahābhārata: For the First Time Critically Edited. Edited by V.S. Sukthankar et al.

19 vols. Poona: Bhandarkar Oriental Research Institute, 1933-59.

Rig Veda: A Metrically Restored Text with an Introduction and Notes. Edited by Barend A. van Nooten and Gary B. Holland. Cambridge, MA: Harvard University Press, 1994.

The Vālmīki Rāmāyaṇa: Critical Edition. General editors G.H. Bhatt and U.P. Shah. 7 vols. Baroda: Oriental Institute, 1960-75.

Secondary Sources

Basham, A.L. [1951] 1981. *History and Doctrines of the Ājīvikas: A Vanished Indian Religion.* Delhi: Motilal Banarsidass.

Biardeau, Madeleine. 1984. "Nala et Damayantī, héros Épiques I." *Indo-Iranian Journal* 27: 247-74.

Fitzgerald, James L. 2003. "The Many Voices of the Mahābhārata." *Journal of the American Oriental Society* 123 (4): 803-18. Review article of Alf Hiltebeitel, *Rethinking the Mahābhārata: A Reader's Guide to the Education of the Dharma King*, 2001.

González-Reimann, Luis. 2002. *The Mahābhārata and the Yugas: India's Great Epic Poem and the Hindu System of World Ages.* New York: Peter Lang.

____. 2009. "Cosmic Cycles, Cosmology and Cosmography." In *Brill's Encyclopedia of Hinduism*, ed. in chief Knut A. Jacobsen. Vol. 1. Leiden: Brill, 411-28.

Hiltebeitel, Alf. 2001. *Rethinking the Mahābhārata: A Reader's Guide to the Education of the Dharma King.* Chicago and London: University of Chicago Press.

Lopez Jr., Donald S. 1996. *Elaborations on Emptiness: Uses of the* Heart Sūtra. Princeton: Princeton University Press.

Karma, Curse, or Divine Illusion: The Destruction of the Buddha's Clan and the Slaughter of the Yādavas

PHYLLIS GRANOFF

The early Indian story tradition knows several accounts of what we might call genocide: the total destruction of a group of people united by a common ethnic background. Buddhists told the story of the destruction of the Buddha's own clan, the Śākyas, and early Hindus told of the destruction of the Yādavas, the kinsmen of the god Kṛṣṇa. The slaughter of the Yādavas was followed by the inundation of Dvārakā, Kṛṣṇa's capital. The Jains also preserve a version of the account of the flooding of Dvārakā. It would seem that accounts of a genocide of an important clan were transmitted by different religious groups in early and medieval India. This paper explores several of these accounts, from Buddhist sources and from the *Mahābhārata* and the *Bhāgavata Purāṇa*.

While we cannot know how old the story of the destruction of the Śākya clan is, that it figures in so many of the different monastic codes or *vinayas* may well suggest an early origin, although even this is difficult to argue given the great rate at which the texts borrowed from each other.[1] At the very least, the appearance of the account of the demise of the Śākyas in so many texts indicates that the story was broadly known. André Bareau (1981) collected different versions of the account of the Śākya genocide. He noted that it can be found in the Pāli *Jātaka* as the *Bhaddasāla Jātaka* (465), the *Dhammapada* commentary, *Viḍūḍabhavatthu* (4.3), the *Ekottarāgama*, and the *vinayas* of the Mahīśāsaka, Dharmaguptaka and Mūlasarvāstivādins. It is also known to other texts preserved in the Chinese Buddhist canon, such as the *Ṣatpāramitāsaṃgraha sūtra* and the *Arthavargīyasūtra*. A vivid account of the attack on the Śākyas even found a place in Kṣemendra's eleventh century collection of *Avadānas*, the *Avadānakalpalatā*, as chapter eleven, the *Virūḍhakāvadāna*. This text, written by a non-Buddhist, attests amply to the popularity of certain Buddhist tales in medieval Kashmir, among which figured an account of the destruction of the Śākyas.

Bareau concluded that in its many versions the story of the slaughter of the Śākyas was a legend that was invented by pilgrims to explain the dilapidated condition in which they found the Buddha's city of origin, Kapilavastu. He suggests that the miserable ruins they encountered were a far cry from the glorious Kapilavastu that they had heard about in the texts and so they devised this story to explain its decline. This seems to me a hypothesis that is difficult either to prove or disprove. It also ignores the crucial ethical questions that this troubling story raises and obscures its relationship with that other early and famous story of genocide, the destruction of Kṛṣṇa's relatives, the Yādavas.

In the versions found in the *Jātaka* and *Dhammapada* commentary, the story of the destruction of the Śākyas is one of many intertwining plots in a larger complex narrative. It asks what must have been for the storyteller and audience some painful questions. Briefly, the story recounts how Viḍūḍabha, son of a Śākya king and a slave girl, is insulted by the Śākyas and takes revenge on them by slaughtering them. The Buddha saves his relatives three times, but eventually abandons them to their own fate. In the course of telling the story, we will see that different versions to a different extent raise these two questions: What was the Buddha's reaction to the slaughter of his relatives? Could he have prevented the slaughter, and if so, why did he not do so? In raising these questions, the story of the Śākya genocide, perpetrated by one of their own, very closely recalls the account of the destruction of Kṛṣṇa's clan that was told in the *Mausalaparvan* of the *Mahābhārata*. That slaughter, too, was brought about from within the clan. And it too became the occasion to explore the limits and nature of divine power and to examine the possibly hidden causes of such untrammeled violence. I would argue that if the *Mahābhārata* story did not actually form the basis of the Buddhist story, which I think it may well have done, it certainly influenced some of its versions. For example, in the *Dhammapada* commentary, the land-locked Śākyas must be carried to their death by rivers so that they may drown in the ocean. This cannot fail to remind us of the much more coherent account of the destruction of Kṛṣṇa's clan and the inundation of his seaside city, Dvārakā, which, being located on the ocean, was far more likely to be naturally flooded by the rising tide.

The story of the destruction of the Yādavas appears for the first time in Hindu sources in the *Mahābhārata* and would have a long life. It was retold in the eleventh book of the *Bhāgavata Purāṇa* and in the many subsequent renderings of the *Mahābhārata*, in Sanskrit poetic texts and in India's many vernacular languages. I have written about a selection of these accounts in some detail in another essay, and by necessity some of my comments here can also be found in this longer study (Granoff 2008). In many ways the later retellings of the Sanskrit *Mahābhārata* act as commentaries on the root text. As the story of the destruction of the Yādavas was retold, the questions about Kṛṣṇa's own role in the slaughter and why he could not have stopped it became increasingly important. In fact attempts to answer these questions would come to shape the very plot of the story. The *Mahābhārata* and its retellings are more explicit than are any of the Buddhist stories about this one particular aspect of the genocide. If the Buddhist accounts emphasize what the Śākyas themselves did to merit such a fate, the epic account and its successors are far more interested in knowing what Kṛṣṇa did or might have done during the course of these terrible events. The epic retellings focus clearly on whether Kṛṣṇa could have stopped the slaughter and if so then why he did not. The epic and particularly its sequels also confront the implications that answers to these questions have for a broader understanding of the nature of God and divine power.

The Buddhist stories examined here by no means ignore the issue of the Buddha's power and its limits, but I would like to propose here that they address this question less openly. To some extent they preempt the question by saying that the Buddha knew that the Śākyas had committed a bad deed in their previous life and so after three successful attempts at warding off the slaughter, the Buddha simply did not go out a fourth time to protect them. This is the approach taken by both of the Pāli texts, the *Bhaddasāla Jātaka* and *Dhammapada* commentary. Both the *Bhaddasāla Jātaka* (152) and the *Dhammapada* commentary (357) use the same sentence to describe what transpired, "The teacher knew what the Sākas had done in a previous life, that they had thrown poison into a river. And knowing that this karma could not be prevented from ripening, he did not go forth (to protect them) a fourth time."[2] The *Dhammapada* commentary returns at the conclusion of the story to the question of whether or not the slaughter of the Sākas was justified. I would emphasize that the text never asks the question that plagues the *Mahābhārata* and its retellings. It never asks whether the Buddha was justified in allowing the slaughter to happen or whether he might have prevented it entirely. The Buddha merely explains that while the slaughter may have seemed unjust in terms of the behavior of the Śākyas in this life, it was justified in terms of what they had done in a previous life: "O monks, if the slaughter of the Sākas seems somehow unjustified in terms of their present life, it was justified by what they had done in a past life."[3]

In the much later Sanskrit *Avadānakalpalatā*, the monk Mahāmaudgalyāyana is actually ready to leap into the fray and rescue the Buddha's clansmen, but the Buddha stops him and explains "This is the ripening of the Śākya's karma. To try to protect them makes no more sense than to try to construct a bridge in the sky."[4] After the slaughter, the monks ask the Blessed One what deed the Śākyas had committed to merit this fate, and he explains, "This slaughter of the Śākyas was due to the ripening of their own karma."[5]

Looking at these passages, we might even be tempted to say that these Buddhist stories of the extermination of the Buddha's kinsmen are told in such a way as to minimize the role of the Buddha and avoid the question of whether or not the Buddha could have ultimately prevented the slaughter. While Bareau noted that in some versions the Buddha does not even appear, I would add that in the versions discussed here, the role of the Buddha in the actual course of events is, at best, slight. His emotional reaction to the slaughter is also minimal, if it is mentioned at all. It is only in the late *Avadānakalpalatā*, which, we should keep in mind, was written by a non-Buddhist author (who also wrote a version of the *Mahābhārata*), that we even hear that the Buddha was emotionally affected by seeing his relatives slaughtered. In the language of the text, "The Blessed one, seeing the destruction of the Śākyas at the hand of their enemy, knowing that it was connected to their karma, was momentarily distressed."[6] Before that, knowing of their impending death, his main act had been to teach them the dharma, "for the welfare of those pure and good people" (*śreyase śuddhasattvānāṃ vidadhe dharmadeśanām*, verse 98). There seems to be no question in this case of the Buddha's even considering an attempt to save his relatives from the destruction awaiting them.

The Buddhist stories of the extermination of the Śākyas imply that the law of karma is so tightly constructed that ultimately no intervention in its workings is possible. Neither the gifted monk Mahāmaudgalyāyana nor the Buddha himself should intervene to save the Śākyas. The apparently meaningless and unjustified slaughter of an entire ethnic group is viewed as the just reward for past crimes. There are nonetheless indications within the different stories that the events being described were troubling to their audience. The very fact that all versions of the story make an effort to underscore the perfidy of the Śākyas suggests that the storyteller felt the need to justify both the slaughter itself and the Buddha's withdrawal from any active role in it. The *Dhammapada*, as we have seen, concludes with an explicit question about how the slaughter could be justified; the *Avadānakalpalatā* adds a second karma story to explain more directly the peculiar animosity that Virūḍhaka feels for the Śākyas. In all the other versions Virūḍhaka's hatred for the Śākyas has to do with the fact that they insult him since he is the son of a slave-girl. The author of the *Avadānakalpalatā* (and the story-telling tradition upon which he draws), seems to have found this an inadequate explanation for such a terrible consequence. Kṣemendra tells us that in addition to the insult he had received in his life as Virūḍhaka, there were strong reasons from his past life that made Virūḍhaka so determined to kill the Śākyas. Virūḍhaka and his priest were once fish, and the Śākyas were fishermen who caught them and tormented them; in the next birth Virūḍhaka and his priest were simply ordinary householders who were killed by the Śākyas, who were thieves (129-31). The monks are at once convinced that karma is inescapable. We have in this version of the story an explanation for not only the terrible fate of the Śākyas, but also for why it had to be Virūḍhaka who was the agent of their demise.

If these Buddhist stories focus on causal connections and karma, making the connections increasingly tighter and more specific, we have seen that there are other stories within the Indian religious tradition that deal with the same general issues and ask, Can genocide ever be justified? If so, how? Is it possible for powerful figures to intervene in a genocide? And what do the answers imply about human/divine agency? To gain a better sense of the range of answers to these questions in the Indian tradition in what follows I begin with the Buddhist stories and then examine the *Mahābhārata* and *Bhāgavata Purāṇa* accounts of the destruction of the Yādavas. Eventually one vernacular *Mahābhārata* version, the Oriya *Mahābhārata* of Sāralā Dās, will return to the Buddhist preoccupation with karma, the karma of the victims and the agents, to describe a universe with its own relentless, compulsive logic, but this is not necessarily the answer of the Sanskrit *Mahābhārata* itself or its other medieval interpreters. Nonetheless, it would seem that in the final analysis, the explanation offered by the Buddhists for the slaughter of the Śākyas remained one of many viable and compelling interpretations of genocide. In such an interpretation, questions about the cruelty of Kṛṣṇa or the Buddha or at best their indifference could be answered by reference to a cosmic law to which even the gods or the Buddha are subject. But coming to this conclusion was by no means a straightforward process nor was it the only possible conclusion. Different texts offer glimpses of both the seriousness of the questions and the difficulty of answering them. I begin with some more detailed discussion of the Buddhist story as it appears in the *Bhaddasāla Jātaka* and the *Avadānakalpalatā*.

The *Bhaddasāla Jātaka* and the *Avadānakalpalatā*

The *Bhaddasāla Jātaka* in many ways more clearly outlines the moral dilemma of the Buddha at the death of his clansmen than its parallel version in the commentary to the *Dhammapada*. The destruction of the Śākyas is really nothing more than the frame story for the *jātaka* itself, which is set in the time of the king Brahmadatta. The frame story begins when King Pasenadi wants the Buddha and the monks to dine at his invitation. Koichi Shinohara has written about the importance of taking a meal in a lay donor's home and this story underscores his point (Shinohara forthcoming). The Buddha explains to the king that the monks prefer to go where they feel safe and confident that they will be treated properly, and they feel safest among their relatives. As the text tells us, "Blessed One, what makes a meal the most excellent of all meals?" "O great king, trust is the best spice. Even simple rice gruel tastes like honey when it is offered by a person one trusts."[7] The king proceeds to ask, "Blessed One! Who is it whom the monks trust?", with the response "O great king, they trust their relatives, the Sākas."[8] This sparks in the king the desire to marry a Śākya princess. The Śākyas are afraid to refuse the king's demand for a bride, but they trick the king into accepting a woman born of Śākya royal blood on her father's side and a slave girl as her mother. The son of this union, Viḍūḍhabha, only learns of his lowly origins when he pays a visit to his mother's relatives. He sees one of the Śākya servants washing down the seat he has just vacated with milk and water to purify it. He vows one day to wash the seats of the Śākyas in their own blood. Time passes and one day Viḍūḍhabha recalls his vow and sets out to kill the Śākyas. The Buddha realizes that his clan is about to perish (*ñātisaṃghassa vināsaṃ disvā* 152) and flies to Kapilavastu, where he stations himself under a tree with little shade. Viḍūḍhabha finds it odd that the Buddha has chosen such a pathetic tree when there is a big nigrodha tree right there, offering an abundance of cool shade. The Buddha replies that the shadow of his relatives is cooling enough, *ñātakānaṃ chāyā nāma sītalā* (152). Viḍūḍhabha suspects correctly that the Buddha has come to protect his clansman and he is unable to slaughter them in the Buddha's presence. He returns to Sāvatthi. The Buddha does this two more times, before he accepts, in the passage quoted above, that the Śākyas cannot be saved and leaves them to their fate.

This entire story of Viḍūḍhabha forms the frame story to the actual *Bhaddasāla Jātaka*. The *jātaka* that follows illustrates how the Buddha performed this praiseworthy act of protecting his own group in the past as well. The *jātaka* describes how once the Buddha was a tree-spirit or *yakkha*, Bhaddasāla, who resided in a tree that King Brahmadatta wanted to cut down to make his marvelous one-pillared palace. The *yakkha* was worried that the tree would fall and kill his fellow-trees growing around him. He asked for it to be cut down in a way that would prevent their destruction, even though this would be a much more painful death for him. King Brahmadatta was so impressed by the *yakkha's* compassion and concern for his relatives that he decided to spare the tree in which the *yakkha* was residing.

This is in many ways an odd story with which to follow the account of the Buddha and the Śākyas, for after the Buddha protects his clan three times, he does in fact eventually abandon them to their death. As we have seen, when Viḍūḍhabha comes the fourth time to slay the Śākyas, the Buddha realizes that they had done a very wicked deed in the past and deliberately chooses not to go to protect them.

The two stories juxtaposed together seem to be giving us a double message or at least a complicated message: both praise the bond of trust between relatives and single out for particular emphasis the virtue of protecting one's relatives. It is among one's relatives that a person feels the safest, and the Buddha is the example of someone who in a past life and his present life had saved his kin. But this is, of course, only partly true in the frame story of Viḍūḍhabha. There, although the Buddha postponed the slaughter of his relatives, in the end he did not save them from a painful death. As a rationale for this, the story tells us that even the Buddha cannot or will not stand in the way of the law of karma. And here, I would suggest, is the reason if not for the story's origin, then at least for its undeniable longevity. The story deals with a very important question: can the Buddha, or anyone, for that matter, stop horrible things from happening, and if so why does he not? The story of Viḍūḍabha is curiously ambiguous: It suggests both that the Buddha could stop the slaughter, and that he also could not. Ultimately karma must take its course. The story further seems to tell us that the Buddha made a deliberate choice not to protect his relatives. The Buddha may not have been incapable of protecting the Śākyas, in so far as his presence under the tree did spare them three times, but in the end he withdrew from the scene. It is, then, not merely or not even a question of power, but of knowledge, knowledge of the inevitability of certain events. We shall see that in the *Mahābhārata* the questions will focus on both what Kṛṣṇa knew and what he had the power to do, with the second part of this question becoming increasingly central. But before I engage those texts I would like to comment further on the version of the story of the destruction of the Buddha's kinsmen that is found in the *Avadānakalpalatā* of Kṣemendra. As were many of the stories in Kṣemendra's text, this one was closely modeled on the much earlier account in the *Mūlasarvāstivādavinaya*, in a section of the text that is now preserved in Chinese (Taisho 1451: 234a-244a).

The account in the *Avadānakalpalatā*, called the *Virūḍhakāvadāna*, differs in several telling ways from the Pāli accounts. The *Avadānakalpalatā* version deals primarily with the destruction of the Śakyas and eliminates many of the other competing plots. It also emphasizes karma and not the virtue of protecting one's kin. Everything in the story is karmically determined and carefully explained by reference to past deeds. In this version, King Prasenajit dies of diarrhea and we learn that this was because in a past life he had resented his mother's giving food to a Pratyekabuddha and cursed the Pratyekabuddha to have diarrhea. In addition, as we have seen above, the connection between Virūḍhaka and the Śākyas is much more intimate, and Virūḍhaka's hatred of the Śākyas is directly motivated by incidents in their past births. In Kṣemendra's account Virūḍhaka is egged on in his evil deeds by his house priest or *purohita*. We have seen how in a past life the pair, Virūḍhaka and priest, were tortured and murdered by the Śākyas. The karmic stories are further multiplied. After he has killed their men-folk, Virūḍhaka torments the Śākya women, cutting off their hands. This, too, was the consequence of past karma, in this instance, the past karma of the women. In a previous life they had tried to seduce a Pratyekabuddha by making amorous gestures with their hands. And so in a direct reflection of their sin, the offending hands are now cut off by Virūḍhaka. The world of the *Virūḍhakāvadāna* is a tightly controlled universe in which nothing is left to chance. And as if to emphasize this, the Buddha in this story makes only one attempt to stop Virūḍhaka from killing the Śākyas, instead of the three attempts in the Pāli texts. If the *Pāli* texts raised questions about the justice of the genocide, the *Avadānakalpalatā* leaves little room for such questions, where everything that happens, even the most painful of deaths or tortures, is a result of previous deeds.

When we turn to stories told about the slaughter of the Yādavas, we see perhaps a wider range of responses to the problem of genocide. The accounts focus more closely on the role of the god Kṛṣṇa than did any of the Buddhist texts on the role of the Buddha, and yet their conclusions are remarkably similar.

The Destruction of the Yādavas: The Sanskrit *Mahābhārata*

The story of the destruction of the Yādavas occupies an entire, if short, book of the Sanskrit *Mahābhārata*, book sixteen, the *Mausalaparvan.* I will argue that in this early account although there are passages suggesting that there may well be factors beyond the control even of the god Kṛṣṇa that determined the death of Kṛṣṇa's clansmen, these passages are overshadowed by others that emphasize both Kṛṣṇa's power to save his kin and his deliberate choice not to do so.

In most of the accounts of the death of the Yādavas the proximate cause of their destruction is a curse leveled by one or more angry sages. Some Yādava youths try to trick the sages by dressing the boy Sāmba up as a woman and pretending that "she" is pregnant. They ask the sages whether the child will be a girl or a boy. Omniscient, the sages see through the trick and angrily proclaim that Sāmba will give birth to an iron club that will be the cause of their destruction. In some accounts Kṛṣṇa is included in the curse; in others, the curse extends to the entire Yādava clan with the exclusion of Kṛṣṇa and his brother, Balarāma, as is the case in the Sanskrit *Mahābhārata*, 16.2.9. In the Sanskrit *Mahābhārata*, the death of the Yādavas is what I would call "over-determined", or at least multiply determined. The Yādavas also die because of an earlier curse by Gāndhārī, who accused Kṛṣṇa of having stood by and done nothing to avert the slaughter of the Kurus and Pāṇḍavas when they were being butchered in the great Mahābhārata war (11.25.40-41). Goldman has aptly described these curses in the *Mahābhārata* as a "dramatic personalization of the idea of karma" (Goldman 1985: 421). There is no question that the curses in the *Mausalaparvan* play the same role as karma in the Buddhist stories of the destruction of the Śākya clan.

The curses work in tandem with a more abstract force. We are also told repeatedly that the Yādavas were brought down by Fate or Time. Kṛṣṇa is often described as "knowing that Time had turned against them" *jānan kālasya paryayam*, or "not wishing to change the course of Fate, although he was Lord of the World" *kṛtāntam anyathā naicchat kartum sa jagataḥ prabhuḥ* (16.2.14 ; 16.4.30; 16.4.42). In other verses we see this Fate made apparent in terrible omens, the significance of which was clear to Kṛṣṇa (11.25.43-46; 16.2.14; 16.3.21). Such verses leave no doubt that Kṛṣṇa knew beforehand what was going to happen to the Yādavas. Whether the proximate cause of the destruction of Yādavas is described as the curses or Time/Fate, it is abundantly clear from the text that Kṛṣṇa both knew that the Vṛṣṇis would be destroyed and that he did not wish to prevent their destruction. The text tells us this explicitly, "Knowing that the destruction of the Vṛṣṇis was at hand, Hari did not want to prevent it," *jānan vināśaṃ vṛṣṇīnām naicchad vārayituṃ hariḥ* (16.4.11). In fact, what is perhaps even more surprising, is that Kṛṣṇa positively wants to work with the curse and make the curse of the sages come true. Thus we learn that Kṛṣṇa ordered the Yādavas to make their ill-fated pilgrimage, during which they will slaughter each other, because he wanted "to make that curse come true", *cikīrṣan satyam eva tat* (16.3.21). The pilgrimage itself raised many questions for the later tradition that I have discussed elsewhere (Granoff, 2008). But Kṛṣṇa does more than just order the pilgrimage; once the Yādavas begin to fight, he takes an active role in the mayhem and kills many of his relatives himself (16.4.34-35). This would cause later tellers of the story even more difficulty than the ironic or disingenuous comment at the conclusion of the *Mausalaparvan* that Kṛṣṇa was capable of averting the slaughter, but "chose to look the other way" (16.9.26).

While there are some hints in the text that Kṛṣṇa may not have been able to stop what Time had ordained, passages like those cited here predominate. Kṛṣṇa not only knew what was going to happen; he did not wish to stop the events and moreover actively conspired in them. If there is any ambiguity in the *Mausalaparvan*, the redactors of the text are clear about what they wish us to think about Kṛṣṇa's role in the events. Vyāsa, at the conclusion to the *Mausalaparvan*, insists that Kṛṣṇa was indeed capable of stopping the slaughter; he is in fact capable of turning the world into its very opposite if he chose do to so. Here is what Vyāsa tells us, "Kṛṣṇa could transform the entire universe of movable and immovable creatures into something else; changing a curse of the sages is nothing for him."[9] What is important is that Kṛṣṇa did not choose to change the curse, and his reasons resemble the reasons given in the

Buddhist story for the Buddha's ultimate withdrawal. Kṛṣṇa knew that there was some force, some power, that determined that the Yādavas had to die. Vyāsa tells us that Kṛṣṇa did not stop the slaughter because he knew that the Yādavas were fated to die, "This was the fate ordained for those great ones," *bhavitavyaṃ tathā taddhi diṣṭam etan mahātmanām* (16.9.26). In addition, Vyāsa says that the Yādavas had been burnt up by the force of the Brahmins' curse *brahmaśāpanirdagdhā* (16.9. 25). Kṛṣṇa in the end allows Fate and the curse to take their course.

In this reading of the text, there is very little difference between this Kṛṣṇa and the Buddha; both bow to the power of some law outside themselves, whether by choice or by necessity. We are told explicitly that Kṛṣṇa was capable of averting the catastrophe, but instead remained aloof or ignored it (*upekṣitaṃ ca kṛṣṇena śaktenāpi vyapohitum* 16.9.26). In this Kṛṣṇa resembles the Buddha, whose presence under the tree was all that was required to make Viḍūḍhabha turn back, and yet who in the end stayed away from Kapilavastu, realizing that his clansmen had committed a terrible deed in the past. Vyāsa goes on to explain that the slaughter of the Yādavas was part of some larger plan; after the Yādavas have killed each other, Kṛṣṇa, realizing that his task of lightening the burden of the world has been accomplished, has returned to heaven. Any sense of such a larger scheme into which the genocide fits was lacking in the Buddhist versions. Karma, even the shared karma of the Śākyas, lacks such an overarching telos.

This reading of the *Mausalaparvan*, then, leads to the conclusions that Kṛṣṇa knew about the impending death of the Yādavas, was capable of stopping it, and deliberately chose not to do so. The question that is less easy to answer is why. In some cases the text seems to say that this was because Kṛṣṇa simply bowed to the force of Time or Fate, raising doubts about his actual power to do otherwise. In other, albeit fewer cases, the text suggests that Kṛṣṇa himself was the controlling force behind everything, from the curses to the slaughter, and that it was indeed a part of his larger plan that his clansmen die. In one very telling verse, not in the *Mausalaparvan* but in the *Strīparvan*, when Kṛṣṇa responds to Gāndhārī's curse, Kṛṣṇa seems to say that only he can kill his clansmen, "Oh Lovely one," he says, "I alone and no one else will bring destruction on the Vṛṣṇi clan," *saṃhartā vṛṣṇicakrasya nānyo mad vidyate śubhe* (11.25.4). This will be the starting point for the next major version of the story in the *Bhāgavata Purāṇa*, but within the *Mausalaparvan*, even in Vyāsa's concluding speech just mentioned, Kṛṣṇa seems to be more subject to a law that exists independently of him than the author of any governing plan. Vyāsa's concluding speech, addressed to the despondent

Arjuna, after all ends with a bleak statement of the inexorable workings of Time, casting down those on high and raising up the lowly, *yadṛcchayā*, as if without any reason at all (16.9.33). One cannot help wondering if behind all the assertions that Kṛṣṇa had the power to avert the curse or Fate there are not fears that just the opposite might be true.

To a great extent the *Mausalaparvan* echoes questions that reverberate throughout the whole of the *Mahābhārata* about the efficacy of human effort in the face of Fate. The *Mausalaparvan* merely substitutes God for mere mortals as it asks about the power of Fate or Time, and in so doing raises questions that must have been uncomfortable for the devotees of the nascent Kṛṣṇa cult. It contains the seeds of later developments, in which Kṛṣṇa will be the agent of everything that happens in the universe, even events as horrifying as the destruction of the Yādavas. This is indeed what we find in the most important retelling of the *Mahābhārata*, the *Bhāgavata Purāṇa*, to which I now briefly turn.

The *Bhāgavata Purāṇa*

The *Bhāgavata Purāṇa* introduces a new factor into the discussion. The Yādavas are not only struck down by Fate in the form of the curse of the sages; they are also deluded by the *māyā* of Kṛṣṇa (*kṛṣṇamāyāvimūḍhānām*, 11.30.13). They strike each other, having been deprived of their reason by Kṛṣṇa (*mukundena vimohitā*, 11.30.17). Mention of the curse is repeatedly coupled with mention of Kṛṣṇa's deluding power (11.30.24). It is also made much more explicit that the destruction of the Yādavas was part of Kṛṣṇa's larger plan to rid the earth of its unwanted burden (11.30.25), an idea to which Vyāsa had only briefly alluded in his final speech in the *Mausalaparvan*. In the *Bhāgavata Purāṇa* Kṛṣṇa's power lies behind the curse and works in concert with it. This is also the case when we come to the treatment of Kṛṣṇa's own death. In the Sanskrit epic, when the hunter who shot Kṛṣṇa had realized his error and fallen at Kṛṣṇa's feet, the text tells us only that Kṛṣṇa consoled him (16.5.21). In the *Bhāgavata Purāṇa* Kṛṣṇa frees the hunter from any taint of sin by telling him that he was actually the author of his own death. Thus he tells the despondent hunter, "Do not be afraid, Jarā. Get up. This was my doing" *mā bhāir jare tvam uttiṣtha eṣa kṛto hi me* (11.30.39). And to Dāruka, his charioteer, he explains that everything that has happened, from the destruction of the Yādavas to his own impending death, was simply a creation of his own creative/illusionary power, his *māyā*.[10]

Unlike the Buddha and unlike the Kṛṣṇa of the *Mausalaparvan*, this Kṛṣṇa is unambiguously the active agent of the events that transpire. Moreover, those events are not quite what they seem. By introducing the concept of *māyā*, the author(s) of the *Bhāgavata Purāṇa* also provide an answer to Gāndhārī's accusations. Kṛṣṇa is not intentionally cruel, nor is he morally reprehensible when he seems to stand by and watch people die or even kills them himself. In fact, he acts in a way that is beyond our understanding and that places him outside the standards of ordinary behavior. It is the very nature of God to create and destroy, remaining himself aloof from the process. We are reminded here of the word Vyāsa had used at the end of the *Mausalaparvan*, *upekṣita*, which implies an indifference to the course of events. It remained for the *Bhāgavata Purāṇa* to develop ideas nascent in the earlier text. For the *Bhāgavata Purāṇa*, unlike both the Buddhist stories we have examined and the Sanskrit epic, karma and curses, mechanical forces, are no longer a satisfactory answer to the question why the genocide occurred, and being capable but refusing to stop it is also no longer a valid understanding of God's role in events that affect mortals. In the *Bhāgavata Purāṇa* responsibility is removed from the victim or from some impersonal force and placed squarely on the shoulders of the god Kṛṣṇa, and we are told both that his motives are beyond our understanding, and that everything that we think is transpiring may not turn out to be quite what we think it is. God's *māyā* is, after all, also the ultimate illusion-making power, and the text subscribes to a kind of theistic Vedānta in which much of what is available to the senses is not ultimately real.

That this was not the final word on god, moral responsibility and tragedy, is clear from the many vernacular versions of the destruction of the Yādavas in which the discussion continued (Granoff 2008). I stop here, however, and offer some brief conclusions.

Conclusion

As these texts show, the debate over genocide and the search for answers as to why such terrible events can happen, appeared early in Indian religious literature and crossed sectarian boundaries. The Buddhist texts were not the only ones to propose that there are laws of the universe that operate beyond compassion; even the Buddha could do nothing against the law of karma. The Sanskrit *Mahābhārata* seemed largely to concur with the Buddhist verdict. There, too, Kṛṣṇa chooses not to defy the mechanical laws of curses, Time or Fate. If there is a difference between the Kṛṣṇa of the Sanskrit epic and the Buddha of the stories examined here, it is that the Sanskrit epic is more concerned about whether or not Kṛṣṇa could have done anything to avert the curse/Fate/Time. The answer is not always a resounding yes, but it is nonetheless a yes. Kṛṣṇa was capable of averting the slaughter but chose not to do so. But this, too, seems not to have been an entirely satisfactory solution; the *Mahābhārata* stands at the beginning of new theistic movements, in which the presence of a God who was capable of stopping a genocide but chose not to intervene raised unsettling questions. The *Bhāgavata Purāṇa* picks up where the epic left off. It emphasizes again and again that its God is an omniscient and omnipotent God. The limits that it places are on human understanding and not God's power. Kṛṣṇa certainly knew what was to happen; he was not by any means subject to any outside force like a curse or Time or Fate, as the *Mausalaparvan* can at times hint. And he was not indifferent. He had motives that we cannot fathom for letting the slaughter take place. The later tradition would revisit these questions again and again, apparently not satisfied with God (or Buddha) who could but would not act, or a God who actively brought about such mayhem, and with a theory of karma or Fate that could condemn an entire ethnic group. The difficulties with the various answers our texts propose suggest what we scarcely need to be told, that there are events so overpoweringly devastating that they cannot help but call into question all our deepest assumptions. And it is in this context, I would argue, that the Buddhist story should be read. The story of the destruction of the Buddha's clan is a Buddhist response to important religious questions that were being asked by many different groups, and most pressingly by the growing devotional movement centering around the god Kṛṣṇa.

Notes

1. Bareau (1981: 70) argued for a date of second century BCE for the introduction of this story into the Buddhist corpus. His article compares in detail the different versions. I deal here with only three representative versions, two from the Pāli tradition and one from the Mūlasarvāstivādin tradition as it appears in the *Avadānakalpalatā.*

2. *Satthā Sākiyānaṃ pubbakammam oloketvā tesāṃ nadiyaṃ visapakkhepana-pāpakammassa appaṭibāhiyabhāvaṃ ñātvā catutthavāraṃ na agamāsi.*

3. *Bhikkhave imasmin attabhāve kiñcāpi Sākiyānam evam maraṇam ayuttaṃ pubbe katakammavasena pana yuttam eva* (*Dhammapada* 360).

4. *śākyānāṃ karmadoṣo 'yaṃ sarvathā samupasthitaḥ / tatra rakṣāvidhānaṃ te gagane setubandhanam* (v. 106).

5. *nijakarmavipākena śākyānām eṣa saṃkṣayaḥ* (v. 128).

6. *bhagavān api śākyānāṃ śatrūṇā bhedanaṃ kṛtam/ karmānubaddhaṃ vijñāya babhūva vimanāḥ kṣaṇam* (v. 126). Bareau (1981: 61) notes that in three versions, the *Ekottarāgama, Vinaya* of the Mūlasarvāstivādins and *Ṣatpāramitāsaṃgrahasūtra*, the Blessed One has a terrible headache as the slaughter takes place.

7. *Bhante bhojanaṃ nāma kiṃparaman ti pucchi. Vissāsaparamaṃ mahārāja, kañjinkamattaṃpi hi vissāsikena dinnaṃ madhuraṃ hotịti* (p. 144).

8. *bhante kena pana saddhiṃ bhikkhūnṃ vissāso hotīti ñātīhi vā sakyakulehi vā mahārājā ti* (p. 144)

9. *trailokyam api kṛṣṇo hi kṛtsnam sthāvarajaṅgamam / prasahed anyathā kartuṃ kim u śāpaṃ manīṣiṇām* (6.9.27).

10. *manmāyāracanāṃ etāṃ vijñāyopaśamaṃ vraja* (11.30.49).

Bibliography

Primary Sources

Avadānakalpalatā of Kṣemendra. Edited by P.L. Vaidya. Buddhist Sanskrit Texts Series no. 22. Darbhanga: Mithila Institute of Postgraduate Studies and Research in Sanskrit Learning, 1959.

The Commentary on the Dhammapada. Edited by H.C. Norman. Vol. 1. London: Pali Text Society, 1970.

The Jātaka with its Commentary. Edited by V. Fausboll. Vol. 4. London: Pali Text Society, 1963.

Mūlasarvāstivāda vinaya, Taisho 1451, 234a-244a.

Secondary Sources

Bareau, André. 1981. "Le Massacre des Śākya: Essai d'interpretation." *Bulletin de l'École Francaise d'Extreme Orient* 69: 45-73.

Goldman, Robert. 1985. "Karma, Guilt and Buried Memories: Public Fantasy and Private Reality in Traditional India." *Journal of the American Oriental Society* 105 (3): 413-25.

Granoff, Phyllis. 2008. "The Mausala Parvan: Between Story and Theology." *Asiatische Studien* LXII (2): 545-62.

Shinohara, Koichi. Forthcoming. "Taking a Meal at a Lay Supporter's Residence: The Evolution of the Practice in Chinese *Vinaya* Commentaries." In James Robson and James Benn, eds. *Neither Too Far, Nor Too Near: The Historical and Cultural Contexts of Buddhist Monasteries in Asia.*

Mapping *Bhakti* through Friendship in the Sanskrit Epics

ALF HILTEBEITEL

> Oh friends, there is no friend.

This ever-so-brief apostrophe is attributed to Aristotle, his audience unknown, and untraceable in his writings. Jacques Derrida opens his book *Politics of Friendship* with it as his touchstone.

> ... no one is really anyone's friend—interests just coincide with other interests like elephants in the forests. (*MBh* 12.136.104)

So says a mouse to a cat who wants to befriend the mouse to repay a debt—in a fable told in the twelfth book of the *Mahābhārata*.

From different worlds, the question: What is a friend? Both Western and Indian literatures suggest it is a subject full of enigmas. Derrida's book is altogether a meditation on the West, drawing almost entirely from

Greek, Latin, French, and German sources and, as regards religious texts, attentive mainly to Christianity, but it is nonetheless an overture to the study of friendship in other cultures and religions, beginning, as he says, with "Judaism and Islam *at the very least.*"[1] As is typical of Derrida, it is a tour of aporias: friendship as defined and grounded in fraternity, brotherhood, and with the questions that grounding raises regarding friendship with and among women;[2] the earth as mother, and thus brotherhood as autochthonous and partisan—with no friendship with the father;[3] paternal/royal friendship due to the slave; we and they, the *socius* and the foreigner;[4] fratricide—what Benedict Anderson trenchantly calls "the reassurance of fratricide";[5] betrayal, the enemy as the true friend, exemplary and primary friendship;[6] friendship and number: one cannot have very many friends, and two is the ideal—friendship and love;[7] self-friendship and self-enmity; the notion of one soul in two bodies, and the wish to die together (both as per Aristotle); the third friend as odd one out or mysterious presence;[8] friendship and secrecy;[9] friendship and equality; steadfast, reliable, and faithful friendship as exclusively human;[10] or is it possible with God and/or animals;[11] friendship and time, outliving friends, and the interminable work of mourning.[12] Needless to say, I have mentioned aporias that are pertinent to India's epics.

Friendship seems a good topic to take up in a felicitation for Bob Goldman, who has been a good friend since we met in Pune in 1974. Recalling especially our good time among the langurs of Mahabaleshwar, I offer this piece in the spirit of what Buddhists call good friendship (*kalyāṇamittatā*) and helpful conversation (*sappayākathā*).[13] Also behind this piece is a larger "mapping" project that extends this discussion of friendship into areas of gender and hospitality, again with reference to *bhakti*.[14]

Bhakti and Friendship

Mapping *bhakti* in the Sanskrit epics is something I have long felt the need for, but with a special diffidence that has arisen from thirty years putting the task off. Why such diffidence? Because I have always known that no matter how many dots one connects—no matter how many "dark" Kṛṣṇas might be linked with "dark" Rāmas and Bharatas, for instance—it will not convince those who prefer to dwell on the spaces between the dots. Indeed, one can foresee that textual atomists will only see the dots as grist for their interpolationist mills.

It has indeed been difficult to have a meaningful discussion about *bhakti* in the Sanskrit epics. The conventional scholarly view is that it may be something one finds in "late" portions of the conflated "pseudo-epic" (to use E.W. Hopkins' term),[15] and that it is not what the epics are "really" about. Moreover, as exemplified by Friedhelm Hardy's *Viraha Bhakti*, there is the corollary notion, one that I believe is colored by the view that real *bhakti* grows out of the vernacular-based *bhakti* movement, that *bhakti* in the epics is not only superficial but "intellectual" and thus barely worthy of the name.[16] From this vantage point it is argued that where the epics use the term *bhakti*, they mean primarily "loyalty," and that *bhakti* is not the right term for framing a discussion of the epics when dealing with their treatment of divinity's interactions with humanity. Whatever its variants, the negative position on the originality of *bhakti* in the epics has been hard to challenge, since passages where it is evident look rather easy to select out, making it tempting to hold that the rest is about whatever the given scholar finds more interesting. *Mahābhārata* scholarship remains divided on these issues, but there has been some unsettling of this negative position in *Rāmāyaṇa* studies: implicitly but also to my mind decisively, if one takes his findings in that direction, in Sheldon Pollock's groundbreaking article on "the divinity of Rāma"; and explicitly in Robert Goldman and Sally Sutherland Goldman's encouraging introduction to the *Sundarakāṇḍa*, where they hold that *bhakti* is often "assured" by "conventions" even without being "foregrounded."[17]

According to James L. Fitzgerald, however, there was once, prior to what we now know as the "main story," a "main *Mahābhārata*", a first written redaction composed fairly early in post-Mauryan times, that was "concerned to provide ideological and narrative grounding for a Brahminical conception of kingly rule and hierarchical society in the wake of the Mauryan Empire and that government's cosmopolitanism and its insufficient recognition of the uniqueness of Brahminic authority."[18] To get the flavor of this quickly, let me quote Fitzgerald's short list of passages that this "main *Mahābhārata*" would *not* have included because they "probably came later": "[m]ost of the material in Bhīṣma's instructions to Yudhiṣṭhira," the *Bhagavad Gītā*, and "all episodes that elaborate some theme of devotion to Viṣṇu, Śiva, or Kṛṣṇa"—"such as" the killing of Śiśupāla, "Arjuna's and Duryodhana's attending upon Kṛṣṇa and choosing, respectively, for aid in the war, Kṛṣṇa and his Nārāyaṇa warriors at *Udyoga Parvan* 7, and several highly polished expressions of Kṛṣṇa bhakti in the narrative wake of Yudhiṣṭhira's *abhiṣeka*" between 12.40 and 12.56.[19] *Bhakti* appendectomies on the Indian epics are an old and continuing practice, and people have performed them for over a century of different reasons. But Fitzgerald's reasons are distinctive and challenging.

Fitzgerald makes a good point that the epic poets have a political agenda that is intelligible in a post-Mauryan setting, but, at least to my mind, this political agenda does not gain in intelligibility by divorcing it from *bhakti*; rather, it loses an intelligibility by which *bhakti* nuances and deepens the political agendas of these texts. To borrow Fitzgerald's phrasing, both Sanskrit epics"provide [their] ideological and narrative grounding for a Brahminical conception of kingly rule and hierarchical society" in *bhakti*, in a politics of *bhakti itself*, but one that is mapped differently in each epic. The question then becomes, how? And the answer is strikingly simple. Whereas the *Mahābhārata* grounds its politics of *bhakti* in a politics of friendship centered on the divine friend—or, more exactly, since it concerns not only Kṛṣṇa's relation to Arjuna but to Karṇa, a politics of friendship and the enemy,[20] the *Rāmāyaṇa* grounds its politics of *bhakti* in a master-slave dialectic[21] centered on an exaltation of the figure of the divine king.[22] A little Derrida, a little Hegel. Or in Gauḍīya Vaiṣṇava terms, an early validation of *sākhya bhāva* and *dāsya bhāva*.

Such a comparison must raise the question of the historical relation between the two texts, and for reasons I cannot go into here, I regard the *Rāmāyaṇa* to be the slightly later of the two.[23] But two reasons for taking this view are pertinent here. The first reason is that I believe the *Rāmāyaṇa* poet is familiar with the *Mahābhārata*'s archetypal *parvan* design.[24] That is, the two epics can be aligned in parallel from Books 1-5: Book 1: Origins; Book 2: Court Intrigue; Book 3: Forest; Book 4: Inversions; Book 5: Divine Messengers; and then traced through further parallel unfoldings in the War Books (*Rāmāyaṇa* 6 paralleling *Mahābhārata* 6-11) and the Denouements (*Rām* 7 paralleling *MBh* 12-18). That is, of course, a very rough blueprint, but the point is that such designs do not grow on trees: if it *is* a design, one epic must be replicating the use of it by the other. Arguments still can go either way, but I favor the priority of the *Mahābhārata*. Why? One reason is that it is easier to imagine Vālmīki refining *kāvya* out of the *Mahābhārata* than Vyāsa deconstructing it out of the *Rāmāyaṇa*. And the second reason is my suspicion that a *bhakti* politics of friendship and the enemy would have logical priority over a *bhakti* politics exalting the master-servant underpinnings of kingship. Why? One reason is that it draws upon and theorizes older concerns of hospitality: the *atithi* relation between hosts and guests. I believe there is something yet to be made of the fact that Viṣṇu is "the 'guest' par excellence" in the *ātithya* rites used in the Brahmanical sacrifice to "call the gods to mind", indeed, to "attain *dharma*";[25] and that this bears on the frequency with which the *Mahābhārata* pauses over scenes of Kṛṣṇa's arrivals and departures among the Kurus. Rāma never gets to be a guest in the ways that Kṛṣṇa does.

As something of a preliminary report on such matters, let me then attempt to bring together the early results of three interrelated lines of inquiry. First, I will mention some of the main Vedic and Upaniṣadic themes that the epics—and here especially the *Mahābhārata*, which I believe does the foundational work on friendship in Sanskrit (Pāli would be another interesting matter)—had at hand to draw from in constructing a *bhakti* politics of friendship. Second, I will attempt to differentiate the basic senses of the primary epic terms for friendship and their relation to terms of kinship. And third, I will attempt to show how each epic develops these vocabularies, focusing, necessarily very selectively, on the five pre-war books in each epic. Here, I will stress how the *Rāmāyaṇa* poet persistently defines relationships of friendship as relationships of servitude, and indeed in some cases could be said to redefine or transform them from the one to the other. I must also ask that one keep in mind some further unfoldings of *sakhi/sakhya* in the *Mahābhārata* that I will not have space for: Arjuna's declaring himself not just Kṛṣṇa's *sakhi* but his *bhakta* in the *Bhagavad Gītā*; the fact that Kṛṣṇa puts in a lot of work and a little dance of joy at the death of Ghaṭotkaca all to bring about the death of Karṇa; the nearly interminable mourning of Yudhiṣṭhira that the killing of this unknown brother brings about; Arjuna's poignant survival of his friend, God;[26] likewise, for the *Rāmāyaṇa*, there is not space here to discuss the way that Rāma most fully becomes a slave of his people in his explanation for the banishment of Sītā.

Vedic Sources for the Epics' *Bhakti* Politics of Friendship

First, then, regarding Vedic sources, let me say that this is a matter that has interested me for some time: in two early articles where I discuss chariot imagery and the friend relation of warriors and charioteers,[27] and in the treatment of *sakhi* and *sakhya* in the broken friendship/pact between Indra and Namuci or Vṛtra, in which Indra defeats Vṛtra with the help of his own "intimate friend" Viṣṇu (*índrasya yújyaḥ sákhā*; *ṚV* 1.22.19) in Vedic texts, and similarly defeats Namuci in the *Mahābhārata*.[28] Georges Dumézil's commentary remains interesting here: "The translation 'friendship' is inadequate, but it is difficult to establish with precision the variety of social relationship which the word *sakhi*—probably from the same root as the Latin *socius*—signifies."[29] In discussing variants of these myths, Dumézil goes on to translate *sakhi* by *socius* three times.[30]

The terms *sakhi/sakhya* provide the main friendship vocabulary that the epics have to conjure with, and already we notice two meanings that seem to be in tension: one defining a social bond, pact, or alliance that can be applied to varied relations, not the least of them god and demon, and which it can be expedient both to form and to break; and the other, the relation of "intimate friend" (*yújyaḥ sákhā*) exemplified by Indra and Viṣṇu. In the latter case, much the same terms (*dvā suparṇā sayujā sakhāyā ...*) define the relation of the two birds who nestle in the same tree in *Ṛgveda* 1.164.20—a riddle[31] that gets reinterpreted as a *bhakti* parable about the soul and the Lord in the *Śvetāśvatara* (4.6-7) and *Muṇḍaka* (3.1.1.2) *Upaniṣads*.

It has been argued that the *Mahābhārata* makes allusion to both of these meanings of *sakhi/sakhya*. As I have pointed out,[32] when the nexus of kept and broken friendships results in the death of Karṇa, Kṛṣṇa jubilantly tells Arjuna, "Vṛtra was slain by the destroyer of Bala [Indra]; Karṇa by you, Dhanaṁjaya. People will tell the death of Vṛtra and Karṇa as a doublet (*vadhaṃ vai karṇavṛtrābhyāṃ kathayiṣyanti mānavāḥ*)" (8.69.2cd). This is the most decisive of several comparisons, all but one of them made by Kṛṣṇa himself, between the killings of Karṇa and those of Vṛtra *and* Namuci.[33] Meanwhile, Biardeau sees the parable of the two birds behind Kṛṣṇa's story of the two allies of Jarāsandha, Haṃsa ("Gander") and Ḍimbhaka ("fool").[34] First, after another Haṃsa is killed in battle, Ḍimbhaka drowns having thought it was the real Haṃsa; then the real Haṃsa drowns having learned of the drowning of Ḍimbhaka (2.13.11, 30-42). For Biardeau, their double drowning parodies the Upaniṣadic two birds as friends, the *ātman* and *jīva*. No term for friendship is actually used in this bizarre story, but from the fact that Ḍimbhaka died "deciding, 'I am unable to live in this world without Haṃsa (*vinā haṃsena loke 'smin nāhaṃ jīvitum utsahe*)'" (13.41ab), it is clear that it is a friendship of excessive closeness different from the assured and reliable friendship of Arjuna and Kṛṣṇa. But what I would like to pause over here is this: Whether it is "pact friendship" or "intimate friendship", all these "exemplary" friendships that draw on Vedic models are male friendships. In particular, where it is the intimate friendship of the two birds, the Upaniṣadic *bhakti* twist introduces the feminine as "her who is not the Lord", the "tasty fig" that deludes the one friend who eats while "the other, not eating looks on".[35] To put it briefly, the exemplary *sakhi* friendship of the two birds passes entirely over "her" head.[36] I will suggest that the *Mahābhārata*'s *bhakti* politics of friendship does something to go beyond this.

Finally, as one more Vedic resource, or if one prefers, roughly contemporary parallel, since the relative dating of the late *Śvetāśvatara*

Upaniṣad and the *Mahābhārata* is perhaps too close to call,[37] it is worth quoting from this Upaniṣad's last three verses:

> By the power of his austerities and by the grace of God (*devaprasādād*), the wise Śvetāśvatara first came to know *brahman* and then proclaimed it to those who had passed beyond their order of life as the highest means of purification that brings delight (*juṣṭam*) to the company of seers (*ṛṣisaṅgha*).
> ...
> Only in a man who has the deepest love for god (*yasya deve parābhaktir*), and who shows the same love for his teacher as towards God, do these points (*arthāḥ*) declared by the Noble One shine forth (*prakāśante mahātmanaḥ*, which is repeated). (*Śvet. Up.* 6.21 and 23) [38]

What is interesting here is how this *bhakti* text does something we all know that *bhakti* is famous for: constructing community, and with it audience. We learn about those eligible to receive this explicitly "bhakti" teaching that comes from the grace of God: males are certainly singled out, but with no doubt a larger human audience in mind as well among those who show the same love for the teacher as for God. Indeed, with attendant passages in this and the *Kaṭha Upaniṣad* that locate the human heart as the hidden place where divine grace operates to reveal the self,[39] we see that one of the ways these late *bhakti* Upaniṣads, or, if one prefers, theistic-yogic Upaniṣads, create community is by extending to "people" at large the earlier Upaniṣadic teachings on the human heart as the seat of the self:[40]

> That God, the maker of all, the immense self, is always residing in the hearts of people (*sadā janānāṃ hṛdaye saṃniviṣṭaḥ*). With the heart, with insight, with thought has he been contemplated (*hṛdā manīṣā manasābhiklṛpto*). Those who know this become immortal." (*Śvet. Up.* 4.17)[41]

One audience for such new teachings is thus the hearts of people. But above and beyond that, we learn more specifically about those who first received *Śvetāśvatara*'s teaching with delight (*juṣṭam*)—the Ṛṣisaṅgha, the company of seers. Here we are very close to the way the *Mahābhārata* creates its widest, grandest, and most elevated *bhakti* audience and community among the delighted and wonder-filled Ṛṣis of the Naimiṣa Forest. Indeed, in a usage that suggests encapsulation for the transmission of a new "secret teaching," Yama reveals to Naciketas that the self that lies "hidden in the impenetrable cave" is a "subtle doctrine (*dharma*)" (*Kaṭha Upaniṣad* 1.21 and 2.13-14).[42]

Primary Vocabularies of Friendship and Kinship

Second, then, I turn to the primary epic vocabularies of friendship and kinship. I believe it is helpful and plausible as a preliminary move to divide the Sanskrit epics' vocabularies for what I am calling their politics of friendship into two broad groups—those having primarily to do with friendship and those having primarily to do with kinship—with *bhakti* in its three basic meanings of loyalty, partisanship, and devotion as a kind of floater moving between the two groups. I find that there are three basic terms for friend and friendship—*sakhi/sakhya*, *suhṛd/sauhṛda*, and *mitra/maitra*—and at least two additional terms that adumbrate friendship but in more specialized senses—*sahāya*, usually translated as "companion", and *vayasya/vayasyatva*, which Pollock and Rosalind Lefeber tend to translate as either "friend" or "comrade" and J.A.B. van Buitenen as either "friend" or "contemporary".[43] On the kinship side, most important are the basic "brother" terms, especially *saubhrātra*, "good brotherhood" or "brotherly love", and *sodara/sodarya*, born from the same womb, co-uterine.[44] That is when the men talk. When the women talk, the main term for friendship is certainly *sakhī*, with some different ranges: most notably, that whereas men have single friends, women tend to have *sakhīs*, plural. Draupadī, however, is an exception.

There are two general points to be made about this vocabulary. First, I think it is possible to speak of a main sense of each of the three main friendship words. *Sakhi* keeps its Vedic double specificity of "pact friend"/*socius* and "intimate friend" in tension. It is, I will venture, the main and basic term to keep in mind as "friend" in both these senses. *Mitra*, along with its opposite *amitra*, likewise keeps a Ṛgvedic range of meanings to convey the opposition of friend/ally and foe, especially in epithets, personal names, maxims, and proverbs. For differential purposes, it thus usually connotes "ally". Finally, *suhṛd*, literally "good-hearted", "one with a good heart", is a term whose main usages imply a plurality of friends, and could best, I suggest, most often be translated as "well-wisher", with all the ambiguity that the term suggests. It is to be noted that unlike *sakhi* and *mitra*, *suhṛd* has no Ṛgvedic usage,[45] and I do not find it either in the Upaniṣads. It would seem that it is a new epic term for "friends" that builds upon Upaniṣadic teachings about the heart and widens the narrative and audience range of what can be told about *sakhis*.

The second matter to take into account is the narrative centrality of these terms. While all of them are repeatedly and forcefully run together to heighten the richness of the multiple cliques and clusters who meet together, fight together, and die together, I would say that with one important pair of exceptions it is *sakhi*, not surprisingly, that provides the underlying narrative thread, or double thread, in both epics.[46] The exceptions occur in the second books of both epics, in which the terms *suhṛd* and *saubhrātra* take on temporary narrative centrality. Regarding *suhṛd*, the *Mahābhārata* makes this the driving friendship term when Dhṛtarāṣṭra invites the Pāṇḍavas to a *suhṛddyūta* (2.45.54c). Van Buitenen, going over (I think mistakenly) to the kinship side of things, renders *suhṛddyūta* as "family game of dice" while C.V. Narasimhan, I think more correctly, renders it as "friendly dice match".[47] But it is really a game played not only among family and friends but among all the supposed wellwishers of both parties assembled in the Kaurava assembly hall or *sabhā*. Meanwhile, the *Rāmāyaṇa* gives the same term centrality in describing the responses of the *suhṛds* of Rāma, Lakṣmaṇa, and Bharata to the early events surrounding Rāma's banishment. Likewise, among kinship terms the main one to have narrative centrality is *saubhrātra*, which, in each epic, is used for the first time in the second book: in the one case by Dhṛtarāṣṭra just as he has tried to sort things out after the first dice match (the only one called "friendly"), to Yudhiṣṭhira: "Ajātaśatru, good luck to you! Return to Khāṇḍavaprastha. Let there be good brotherhood with your brothers (*bhrātṛbhis te astu saubhrātram*) ..." (2.65.15); and in the *Rāmāyaṇa*, at the corresponding nodal point when Mantharā, urging the banishment of Rāma, tells Kaikeyī how she will suffer under Rāma and Lakṣmaṇa with their "good brotherhood as celebrated as that of the Aśvins" (2.8.20)—adding that Bharata is Rāma's "natural enemy (*sahajo ripuḥ*)" (24b).[48]

The Pre-war Books

Finally, let us then take a synoptic look, albeit a much too uneven and skeletal one, at how these vocabularies are used in the pre-war books, following mainly what I have called the double thread of *sakhi/sakhya* as "pact friendship" and "intimate friendship", and looking more closely at the *suhṛd* variations in the second books—but observing as well, where we can, how our other friendship and kinship terms intertwine with these threads.

Book 1: In each epic, one of the tasks of the first book is to delineate a network of "pact friendships" either as they lie behind the story, sometimes intergenerationally, or in anticipation of later developments. The *Rāmāyaṇa*, however, leaves most such matters for later books and restricts the *Bālakāṇḍa* to three such usages. First, Rāma's friendship with Sugrīva (1.3.15cd), which will of course grow into an intimate friendship, is anticipated. Then we hear of Daśaratha's friendship with the Aṅga king Romapāda (1.10.3a; 16c; 17c)[49] and Vasiṣṭha's long-deferred friendship with Viśvāmitra (64.16cd): the first providing background to the intervention of Ṛśyaśṛṅga that makes possible the birth of Daśaratha's four sons as portions of Viṣṇu; the second as background to the formation of the group of great Ṛṣis who, beginning with Viśvāmitra, will set Rāma's life agenda.[50]

In contrast, pact friendship in the *Mahābhārata* has a kind of overture that begins in earnest with the sequential stories of Garuḍa and Śeṣa, which unfold out of the sister-rivalry between Vinatā, mother of birds, and Kadrū, mother of snakes. After Garuḍa agrees to be the mount and flagstaff-emblem of Viṣṇu, who is also called Nārāyaṇa and Kṛṣṇa here (1.29.12-16) and is *not* called a friend, Garuḍa immediately overwhelms Indra, who then desires and is granted "eternal friendship (*sakhyam ... anantam*)" with Garuḍa (1.29.33-30.1, 3). This soon comes in handy when Indra, invoking this new friendship (30.7), gets Garuḍa to arrange for him to receive the Soma elixir Garuḍa has stolen from the snakes who had won it temporarily, and Garuḍa gets Indra's permission to be a devourer of snakes (8-13). This leads to the story of Śeṣa, an exception among the snakes dissatisfied with the dimwittedness and quarrelsomeness of his "nest-brothers."[51] After performing austerity (*tapas*) at Badarī and other places, Śeṣa gets Brahmā to give him the boon that his "intellect (*buddhi*) may delight in *dharma*, tranquility, and austerity" (1.32.17cd), and Brahmā additionally assigns Śeṣa the charge of encompassing the earth and bearing her on his head (19-24), and gives him Garuḍa "as a *sakhi*" (*suparṇaṃ ca sakhāya*; 25). Clearly one of the points of this sequence is to establish "friendship" between Viṣṇu-Kṛṣṇa-Nārāyaṇa's diurnal and nocturnal mounts, who would otherwise be enemies, and to link this friendship further with that between Garuḍa and Indra who, as one knows from elsewhere, is a friend of Viṣṇu even if the latter's two mounts are apparently not so. The *Ādiparvan* also brings other pact-friendships to our attention: the Pāñcāla king Pṛṣata and the Ṛṣi Bharadvāja (121.8; 154.6); Arjuna and the Gandharva Citraratha (158.53-55); Pāṇḍu and Drupada (185.18b); Takṣaka and Indra (215.7a; 219.13a), etc.

Meanwhile, intimate friendships are also forming, all with fateful outcomes. These begin when Śūra, as "a friend in great-spirited friendship" (*sakhā sakhye mahātmane*),[52] gives his daughter-child Pṛthā/Kuntī to Kuntibhoja, who had asked the favor of Śūra's firstborn (1.104.3). It is in this household that Kuntī secretly gives birth to Karṇa, whom we might just as well call the Pāṇḍavas' and Kṛṣṇa's secret and third friend. For hiding behind this friendship and all its narrative consequences is Kṛṣṇa, who will be Śūra's grandson, Kuntī's nephew, the Pāṇḍavas' friend and cousin, and—the biggest secret of all because the *Mahābhārata* never mentions it—the cousin of Karṇa (though as we shall see, the epic will give us grounds to say Kṛṣṇa and Karṇa are friends). Then comes the centerpiece of the *Ādiparvan*'s treatment of *sakhi* friendship (there are thirty uses of *sakhi/sakhya/sakhitva* from 1.121 to 1.128): the run from the childhood friendship between Drupada and Droṇa (sons respectively of the Pāñcāla king Pṛṣata and the Ṛṣi Bharadvāja, themselves friends, as we have seen) to Duryodhana's friendship with Karṇa (126.15 and 38). It is not only the Pāṇḍavas, Kauravas, Karṇa, and Aśvatthāman who train with Droṇa, in each case with outcomes that have narrative development and are thus well enough known. "Other princes also gathered there, Bharata bull, and approached Droṇa the best of Brahmans to learn about weapons, such as the Vṛṣṇis and Andhakas ..." (1.122.46). *Which* Vṛṣṇis and Andhakas come to study with Droṇa!?[53] Something mysterious, dropped in almost as if to be overlooked, or better, half-remembered. In any case, the two most prominent Vṛṣṇis, Kṛṣṇa and Baladeva, soon show up along with other Andhakas and Vṛṣṇis to recognize the Pāṇḍavas at Draupadī's *svayaṃvara*. And finally, Arjuna and Kṛṣṇa meet for a picnic just before they burn down the Khāṇḍava Forest—a picnic where they are joined in drinking and strolling about by Draupadī, Subhadrā and the latter's *sakhīs* (211.14c)—these could well be Gopīs, counterparts of the Gopā-Nārāyaṇas Kṛṣṇa will give to Duryodhana (5.7.16), if she brought any with her from Dvārakā. It is here that we finally learn about Arjuna and Kṛṣṇa that "these two dear friends were the Ṛṣis Nara and Nārāyaṇa (*āstām priyasakhāyau tau naranārāyaṇāv ṛṣī*)" (1.210.5). As Biardeau, having come to these passages, indicates,[54] the *Mahābhārata* introduces Kṛṣṇa slowly, now for the first time emphasizing his name Govinda (212.30; 214.17) and reminding us of his and his sister's cowherder connections by having Subhadrā dress in the "clothes of a cow-keeper (*gopālikā*)" when she first meets Draupadī (213.17). Cumulative hints, cumulative mysteries: enough to suggest that the *Mahābhārata* has set in motion a burst of *sakhi* friendships of both the pact and intimate varieties that often enough have something to do with Viṣṇu and/or Kṛṣṇa.

Book 2: In the *Rāmāyaṇa*, with no sustained problematic of friendship preceding it in Book 1, as far as pact friendship relations go the main development in Book 2 is the first articulation of *sakhi* as a "friend to master" (*sakhi* to *bhartā*) relation specifically focussed on Rāma in his dealings with the low caste Niṣāda Guha.[55]

Otherwise, as Rāma emerges into view in his court and palace life as he is about to be made *yuvarāja*, *sakhi* is never prominently used for any relation he has with anyone else in this book. In departing Ayodhyā, Rāma leaves no close *sakhi* friends behind. What he leaves behind most prominently are *suhṛds*. While *suhṛd* is used fairly frequently, what is noteworthy is that although Rāma has *suhṛds*, when they are around him they are impersonal, never named.[56] For example, 2.36.16: "As for Rāma's wellwishers, they were all bewildered: crushed by the weight of their grief, they could not rise from where they had fallen." Note that the *suhṛds* are last in the run of those bidding Rāma adieu, with the *suhṛds* mentioned just before "Ayodhyā, with all its hosts of soldiers and herds and horses and elephants..." (36.17)—after which Rāma disappears from the sight (37.1-2) of those remaining in the capital. Shortly after this, "the class or multitude of his well-wishers" (*suhṛdvarga*) who now stay behind like his father are distinguished from those more "loyal men" (*anuraktā ... mānavāḥ*) who continue to follow Rāma (2.40.1-2). Nonetheless, once the exile has begun, there is a hint that the poet has names for some of Rāma's *suhṛds*. When Vasiṣṭha names messengers to go to fetch Bharata in Kekaya, he addresses four men to undertake this role: "Come, Siddhārtha, Vijaya, Jayanta, Aśokanandana" (2.62.5ab: *ehi siddhārtha vijaya jayantāśokanandana*). This is certainly a curiously named group of Kṣatriyas ready to carry out the services of the Ikṣvāku line![57] Here, the seeming wellwishers are ready to go as messengers (*dūtas*), a role that, as we know from various texts including the *Mahābhārata*, implies service and can sometimes imply a lowering of a higher person's status, but can be taken on by the high no less than the low—as when Kṛṣṇa visits the Kuru court in Book 5. When the messengers arrive, it is clarified further that they are among the *suhṛj-jana* of Bharata when he greets them, now unnamed (2.64.5b).

Lakṣmaṇa likewise has his *suhṛjjana*, a depersonalized throng of wellwishers (28.11cd and 15ab), whom Rāma bids him say adieu to once Lakṣmaṇa has pleased Rāma with his detailed promise of services to him and Sītā in the forest.

With Bharata, however, things are a little different. At least in Rājagṛha among his mother's people of Kekaya he has *sakhis* who can speak to him as his *suhṛds* (2.63.5-7). This is no doubt to nuance the fact that these "friends of Bharata" are potential rivals of Rāma, for Bharata's own loyalty to (and *saubhrātra* with) Rāma is being at this point still held up to question. Yet once he is back in Ayodhyā and readying to seek Rāma out in his early exile at Citrakūṭa, Bharata addresses no *sakhi*-"friends" among those who will accompany him, but only *suhṛds* (2.76.29d).[58]

As the *kāṇḍa* ends, there is some coordination of this theme, most notably where Bharata, now back in Ayodhyā, is advised by Vasiṣṭha and his other ministers on how to rule—"always zealous for your kinsmen (*bandhu*), steadfast in your brotherly love (*tiṣṭhato bhrātṛsauhṛde*), keeping the noble way (*āryamārgam prapannasya*)" (2.107.6a-c; see also 2.96.29cd, 2.99.19). *Bhrātṛsauhṛda* certainly calls to mind the *saubhrātra* that has now been tested through the whole second book, and affirms that it is now safely assured for all four brothers in the loving relation of the two foremost among them.

The *Mahābhārata* also makes occasional references in the *Sabhāparvan* to surrounding pact friendships.[59] But the narrative focus, as mentioned, is on the *suhṛddyūta*, and in some ways the situation is a striking contrast to that in the *Rāmāyaṇa*. When the Pāṇḍavas depart for the forest after the *suhṛddyūta*, we know who all these well-wishers are—Karṇa among them—and what they have had to say in the Kaurava *sabhā* on the treatment of Draupadī. Moreover, we also know what has been said in the Pāṇḍava *sabhā* about Kṛṣṇa when he received Bhīṣma's acknowledgment as the foremost person present at Yudhiṣṭhira's Rājasūya and was berated by Śiśupāla—the key figure to illustrate "devotion through hatred" (*dveṣabhakti*) in the *Mahābhārata* and also, like Karṇa and Arjuna, a son of one of Kṛṣṇa's paternal aunts.[60] But these scenes have been discussed enough elsewhere, as has the killing of Jarāsandha. They have their well-known *bhakti* moments, but carry on, with one exception, without the term *sakhi*. That exception occurs when Draupadī says, "How can I, wife of the Pāṇḍus, sister of Pārṣata, a good woman (*satī*), and the friend of Vāsudeva (*vāsudevasya ca sakhī*) enter the hall of kings? Is the wife of King Dharma whose birth matches his a slave or not a slave (*dāsīm adāsīṃ vā*)? Speak, Kauravas, I shall abide by your answer" (62.10-11). This is the first time we learn that Draupadī is Kṛṣṇa's *sakhī*: just before she calls on him, if she does call on *him*,[61] as her last resort. This friendship between Draupadī and Kṛṣṇa is, from the start, set apart from any relation of "slavery." It is, moreover, richly developed in subsequent *bhakti* scenes,[62] and is clearly the *Mahābhārata*'s answer to the question we left with the two birds in the same tree. Moreover, in mentioning Kṛṣṇa's friendship here in connection with the question of her "slavery". Draupadī positions her "friend" Kṛṣṇa directly opposite Karṇa. For it is Karṇa who has risen, both just before her words (60.27cd; 61.81d) and again just after them (63.1c, 4c), to argue that she *is* a slave now that she has been won at dice.

Book 3. The third or Forest Books need not much detain us. In the *Mahābhārata* the main *sakhi* event is Kṛṣṇa's first meeting with Draupadī since the dice match. In this powerful *bhakti* passage that culminates in Kṛṣṇa's promise to vindicate her, she says to him, "Here am I, she who tells you her grief (*duḥkham*) out of love (*praṇayāt*), Madhusūdana[63]—for are you not the lord of all beings, both human and divine?—how was it that a woman like me, wife to the Pārthas, your friend (*tava ... sakhī*), O Kṛṣṇa, Lord, the sister of Dhṛṣṭadyumna, came to be dragged into the hall" (3.13.52-53). As indicated, Kṛṣṇa's *sakhi* friendship with Draupadī is singular and special for opening, entirely on the intimate side of the term *sakhi*, new possibilities for *bhakti*.[64] For this paper I can develop it no further other than to observe that the *Mahābhārata* continues to unfold it, and that it is without parallel in the *Rāmāyaṇa*.

Meanwhile, in the *Rāmāyaṇa*, Jaṭāyus makes his appearance as a former *sakhi* (3.13.4a; also *vayasya*: 4.13.3d) of Daśaratha, thus widening the strange net of Rāma's low status pact friendships, this one inherited, like that with Jaṭāyus's brother Sampāti (4.55.20; 56 9 and 12), but unlike those to come with Sugrīva and Vibhīṣaṇa. Rāma thus extends *sakhi* relations to animals. And especially with Sugrīva, the pact friendship becomes an intimate friendship as well. This latter process is set in motion toward the end of the *Araṇyakāṇḍa* when the erstwhile monster Kabandha reveals that for Rāma to find Rāvaṇa, and thus the whereabouts of Sītā, he must form a friendship with Sugrīva. Let us note the order of terms by which Kabandha instructs Rāma as to how this should come about.

First, before his cremation, Kabandha says:

1. "Now I will give you some good advice, bull among men, and make known to you an ally (*mitram*) once the two of you have purified me with fire" (67.17).

2. "You will do well to form a friendship (*sakhyam*) with him, Rāghava. He adheres to established usage, and he will be pleased and straightaway render you assistance" (67.30).[65]

Then, once he is cremated and a redeemed being, Kabandha continues, giving the further instruction that matters most:

3. "Quickly make him a *vayasya*, having gone there now, Rāghava, sealing your compact in the presence of blazing fire to shun all trickery" (68.13; again at 68.17d).

And finally:

4. "Do not be disdainful of the lord of monkeys. Sugrīva is very powerful and can take on any form at will. He now finds himself seeking a companion (*sahāya*) and always honors claims of gratitude" (68.14).

Obviously Sugrīva and Rāma cannot yet be *suhṛds*, which, it seems, requires some acquaintance. So we are ready for *Rāmāyaṇa* Book 4 and a look at this new term, *vayasya*.

Book 4: But before we get to that, let us note how Hanumān in his *bhikṣurūpam* or mendicant guise defines the discourse on friendship from the beginning as emerging out of a mutual desire for *sakhya*: to Rāma he says, "Righteous Sugrīva desires friendship (*sakhyam icchati*) with you" (*Rām* 4.3.20); and to Sugrīva he says, "These brothers, Rāma and Lakṣmaṇa, are desirous of friendship (*sakhyakāmau*) with you" (4.5.7). It is by these words that he transacts the pact aspect of their friendship, which Sugrīva soon confirms with the words, "For me it is indeed an honor and also a great advantage, lord, that you desire friendship (*sauhārdam*) with me, a monkey. And if such a friendship (*sakhya*) is agreeable to you, here is my outstretched arm. Take my hand in yours and let us make a firm pact (*maryādā*)" (11cd-12)—to which Rāma responds by embracing Sugrīva tightly (*paryāṣvajata pīḍitam*), "having accepted cordial friendship (*hṛdyaṁ sauhṛdam ālambya*)" (13).

Now that we have seen how Rāma and Sugrīva add the well-wishing or heartfelt *suhṛd* variety of friendship to fill out Kabandha's prologue to their alliance, we may back up and consider how Vālmīki develops their friendship through the term *vayasya* and its derivatives.

First, as Kabandha had specifically instructed, Sugrīva and Rāghava entered into *vayasya* (*vayasyatvam upāgatau*) by reverently circling the blazing fire (4.5.16cd). That is, their bonding is reminiscent of a marriage. Then comes an exchange in which *vayasya* is used four times before it widens into other bonding terms. In this passage, Sugrīva offers some advice to Rāma about not giving way to grief, and what is beginning to come across is that they are each now drawing from parallel or similar experiences. With that in mind, I suggest that *vayasya*, which is built on the term *vayas*, "age", conveys something more here than comradeship or contemporaneity. It suggests that the best translation of *vayasya*, in this seemingly special context, would be "sympathizer", or even better, "comforter" or "commiserator". Using the latter, here is what Sugrīva says: "It is out of being a commiserator (*vayasyabhāvena*) that I offer this counsel. I am not telling you what to do. But if you honor my commiseration (*vayasyatām*), you should not grieve." To which Rāma replies, "You have done what is right and proper for a loving and helpful commiserator (*vayasyena snighdhena ca hitena*) to do, Sugrīva. Oh friend (*sakhe*), I am comforted here by you and restored to my normal state. Such a *bandhu* is indeed hard to find, particularly in a time like this" (4.7.13-17).

Lefeber translates everything here as friend or friendship.[66] But what is to be appreciated is that Sugrīva mentions *vayasyatā* and *vayasyabhāva* as appropriate to his giving advice on grief from his own parallel experience to Rāma's of exile and wife-abduction. Still, it is *sakhi/sakhya* friendship that drives the narrative, with Rāma not only addressing Sugrīva in the vocative "*sakhe*" but Sugrīva grounding what follows in the same term (4.8.2d and 39cd).

It thus seems that it is the surcharge of the new term *vayasya* as "commiserator-friend" to give grounds to explore the parallels in the careers of Rāma and the monkey Sugrīva. This is Rāma's central friendship. Rāma leaves it to Sugrīva to express all the mawkishness of their common predicaments. Moreover, there is in this *vayasya*-friendship a one-sided willingness—by Sugrīva, of course (4.8.9b; 4.8.26a)—to give up his own life for it. Yet although this *vayasya* is articulated as one of Sugrīva's subordination to Rāma, Rāma also becomes a kind of slave to his servant Sugrīva in his willingness to kill Sugrīva's brother and rival Vāli. Rāma makes fairly clear why his *vayasya* with Sugrīva is pertinent to his allegedly "righteous" killing of Vāli, to whom he says: "Your chastisement must be viewed as righteous in every way. One who keeps *dharma* clearly in view must be of assistance to a *vayasya* (*vayasyasya upakartavyam*)" (4.18.29). But the relevance is most fully developed when Lakṣmaṇa finally brings closure on the matter of Sugrīva's rousting himself to look for Sītā at the end of the rainy season, during which, after Vāli's death has brought an end to one of the parallels between Rāma and Sugrīva's lives, their pact friendship is left in doubt. Says Lakṣmaṇa, reminding us of the other parallel between them, "Nevertheless, hero, you must leave this place at once with me. Console your commiserator (*sāntvayasva vayasyam*), who is suffering because of his wife's abduction" (4.35.19). That is the last usage of *vayasya* in the *Kiṣkindhākāṇḍa*, and there is not another one until two in Book 6, both again with Rāma addressing Sugrīva.[67] And that is just about all there is of *vayasya* in the *Rāmāyaṇa*.[68] More than this, it never has this sense of "comforter" or "commiserator" in the *Mahābhārata* and, more specifically, it is not used at all in the *Rāmopākhyāna*: that is, it is in particular absent in descriptions of the *sakhya* relation between Rāma and Sugrīva, which the *Rāmopākhyāna* knows well enough to cite three times (*MBh* 3.264.11 and 57; 266.62). I would suggest that we have here a signal that its *Rāmāyaṇa* usage is the twist of a master poet who has set himself the challenge of deepening the story—the one that is *his* story—of this extraordinary man-monkey friendship by exploring "the feeling of commiseration"—indeed, *vayasyabhāva*—as an "ancillary feeling" (*vyabhicāri-bhāva*) to grief.[69]

Meanwhile, for the *Mahābhārata*, let it suffice to say that the chief *sakhya* event of the *Virāṭaparvan* is the friendship Virāṭa grants to the disguised Yudhiṣṭhira: "As my friend (*sakhā*) you shall ride on the same conveyance and have plentiful clothing and food and drink" (*MBh* 4.5.14ab).

Book 5: Finally, I turn to the two fifth books: the books of the divine messengers. The main *sakhya* event in the *Sundarakāṇḍa* is Hanumān's bringing the news of the friendship of Rāma and Sugrīva, mentioned four times (*Rām* 5.32.34; 49.29; 57.14; 63.16), to Sītā. As far as I can see, Hanumān himself is never described as a *sakhi* of Rāma or anyone else, although he can recall his father Vāyu's friendship (*sakhya*) with Agni to account for his (Hanumān's) not being burnt when he has set fire to Laṅkā (5.51.33). I would tentatively suggest that Hanumān bears a similarity here to Garuḍa and Śeṣa, likewise not identified as friends of Viṣṇu, who, like Hanumān, are literally emblems of *bhakti* and occasional carriers of the deity.

Once again it is the *Mahābhārata*'s turn to have the richer *sakhya* dossier. I pass over the decisive but well-enough discussed scene of Arjuna and Duryodhana coming to Kṛṣṇa's bedside, which results in Kṛṣṇa's playing host for a change and in his becoming Arjuna's charioteer, to concentrate by way of conclusion on Kṛṣṇa's meeting with Karṇa toward the end of his embassy to the Kurus.

Recounting Karṇa's true origins, Kṛṣṇa tells him he is legally a Pāṇḍava—on his father's side related to the Pāṇḍavas, on his mother's to the Andhakas and Vṛṣṇis—and offers him the kingship (*MBh* 5.138.9-10). The Pāṇḍavas and the Andhakas and Vṛṣṇis will clasp his feet (12). Draupadī will make him her sixth (15cd). Kṛṣṇa himself will consecrate him; as Karṇa rides the royal chariot, Yudhiṣṭhira as *yuvarāja* (his junior in the line of succession) will fan him (18-19). Arjuna will drive his chariot (21). Karṇa will have a whole new nexus of allies, about whom Kṛṣṇa concludes: "Your allies (*mitrāṇi*) shall shudder with joy, your enemies (*ripavas*) with fear. Today let there be good brotherhood (*saubhrātram*) between you and your Pāṇḍava brothers!" (138.28). Both Kṛṣṇa and Karṇa would know how these changes for Karṇa would also change things entirely for Karṇa's real friend, Duryodhana, and for the larger Pāṇḍava-Kaurava *saubhrātra*-"brotherhood", of whom Kṛṣṇa says nothing here.[70]

Karṇa shows that he takes these words as coming from the heart: "I have no doubt at all, Keśava, that you are speaking to me out of good-heartedness (*sauhṛdāt*) and affection (*praṇayāt*) and with friendship (*sakhyena*), Vārṣṇeya, as to my best interests" (139.1). Karṇa does not doubt that Kṛṣṇa is a *suhṛd* speaking from love or affection, and further, that he speaks "with *sakhya*" to Karṇa's best interests. I believe Karṇa is registering here the maternal ties that link him with Kṛṣṇa, which Kṛṣṇa has just spoken of to him: No less than Kṛṣṇa and Arjuna, Kṛṣṇa and Karṇa are, as we have noted, cousins through Kuntī.

The theme of these words being heartfelt is then carried through to the parting words of their meeting, where Kṛṣṇa responds to Karṇa's explanation of why he must refuse: "Kṛṣṇa said, 'Of a certainty the destruction of the earth is now near, for my words do not touch your heart, Karṇa (*tathā hi me vacaḥ karṇa nopaiti hṛdayaṁ tava*). When the destruction of all creatures is at hand, bad policy disguised as good does not stir from the heart (*anayo nayasaṃkāśo hṛdayān nāpasarpati*)" (141.43-44).[71] As they part, Karṇa "clasped Mādhava tightly (*pariṣvajya ca pīḍitam*)".[72]

But most interesting is the narrative setting for this meeting. Dhṛtarāṣṭra said, "Before he rode out amidst princes and councillors, O Saṁjaya, Madhusūdana had Karṇa mount his chariot" (5.138.1). Dhṛtarāṣṭra asks, "What consolations (*kāni sāntvāni*)"[73] did Kṛṣṇa-Govinda offer with his "voice roaring like a flood or a cloud" to the Sūta's son, "whether gently or sharply" (*mṛdu vā yadi vā tīkṣṇam*)" (3). Saṁjaya replies, "Hear from me, Bhārata, what Madhusūdana of boundless self (*ameyātmā*) said to Rādheya in the course of their conversing, in words that were smooth (*ślakṣṇāni*) and gentle (*mṛdūni*), dear (*priyāṇi*), joined with *dharma* (*dharmayuktāni*), truthful (*satyāni*), helpful (*hitāni*), and *to be cherished in the heart* (*hṛdayagrahaṇīyāni*)" (138.4-5). How often are someone's *words* so extensively glossed? And to be cherished in *whose* heart? Karṇa's? Dhṛtarāṣṭra's? The hearts of Janamejaya and the *sadasyas* at Janamejaya's snake sacrifice? The hearts of the Ṛṣis of the Naimiṣa Forest? All listeners and readers? The phrase puts a big asterisk to these words of Kṛṣṇa's, which provide one of those points where we can feel that the notion of the *suhṛd* as "well-wisher" ultimately extends to the *bhakti* community of readers that the *Mahābhārata* seeks to create as its audience of aficionados: that is, its *sahṛdayas*.

Notes

1. Derrida 1997: 103, my emphasis; cf. 289.

2. Derrida 1997, 101, 155-57, 164-86, 191 n. 6, 201, 238-39, 273-74, 281-83, 291, 293.

3. Derrida 1997: 90,143,761.

4. Derrida 1997: 184, 231, 251, 297-98.

5. Derrida 1997: 148, 150-51, 267; Anderson 1991: 202.

6. Derrida 1997: 2, 17-19, 72, 272.

7. Derrida 1997: 21-22, 101, 220-21.

8. Derrida 1997: 177 and 190 (regarding Aristotle); 260, 176-77, 293.

9. Derrida 1997: 20, 257; Kant's black swan, 276.

10. Derrida 1997: 16-17, 253, 261.

11. Derrida 1997: 17, 19,198, 206-07, 211, 222-24, 294.

12. Derrida 1997: 13-14, 289 ff.

13. Walshe 1995: 593.

14. See Hiltebeitel 2007a; forthcoming-a, b, and c.

15. See Hopkins [1901] 1969.

16. See Hardy 1983: 20-29.

17. See Pollock 1984; Goldman and Sutherland Goldman 1996: 19, 43.

18. Fitzgerald 2003: 11. This "main *Mahābhārata*" centers on Dharmarāja Yudhiṣṭhira as a grim and somber extension of his father Dharmarāja Yama, the god of death. Yudhiṣṭhira must preside over a divine raiding party of the gods that descends to earth to restore Brahmans to privileges denied them by the pro-Buddhist Mauryan emperor Aśoka, projecting "a deep and bitter political rage at the center of the *Mahābhārata*" (Fitzgerald 2001, 85; cf. Fitzgerald 2006, 269 n. 14).

19. Fitzgerald 2006: 271-72.

20. See especially the discussion of the theories of Carl Schmidt in Derrida 1997: chapters 4 and 5. Cf. Hiltebeitel 2007a.

21. I have in mind the master-slave dialectic described by F.G.H. Hegel. See Miller 1997: 111-19.

22. The basic elements of this point were appreciated by Sheldon Pollock, who I believe nonetheless made the mistake of chronologically prioritizing the politics over the *bhakti*, even though he admitted that no evidence supported it; see Pollock 1991: 6, 52; Hiltebeitel 1994: 36-53; 2003: 123-24.

23. See now Hiltebeitel 2005 and forthcoming-a for some further discussion. I am persuaded here by Biardeau 1999: xxxv, li-lii; 2002, 1: 701.

24. See further Hiltebeitel 2004 and forthcoming-a, and, with important groundwork on this point, Pollock 1986: 38-42; Biardeau 1997: 77-79

25. Patton 2005: 9, 171-73, quoting 272.

26. My thanks to Andrea Custodi for reminding me that, contrary to the usual order of things, in this case God actually predeceases his human friend.

27. Hiltebeitel 1982, 1984.

28. Hiltebeitel [1976] 1990: 254-66.

29. Dumézil 1969: 28. Whether or not *sakhi* and *socius* are related etymologically, Dumézil's translation is apt, as is evident from the fourth meaning given *socius* by the *Oxford Latin Dictionary*: "a. One pledged by treaty to give support in war, etc., an ally (esp. plural) b. applied, often in conjunction with *amicus*, to extra-Italian allies of Rome" (Glare 1992: 1799).

30. For example, "*Maitrāyaṇi Saṃhitā* 4.3.4 says that at first the two had fought, or rather that Indra had tried to trap Namuci without succeeding, and that Namuci had proposed: *sakhāyā asāvā*, 'let us both be *socii*!' In response to this, Indra promised: 'I will not kill you [*nā'haṃ haniṣyāmi*]!' And he added, 'I am going to agree to an agreement with you [*saṃdhāṃ te saṃdadhai*]; that I will kill you neither by day nor by night, with neither the dry nor the wet"; Dumézil 1969: 30.

31. See most recently Houben 2000: 520-22.

32. Hiltebeitel [1976] 1990: 262-64.

33. For Vṛtra, 8.68.52; for Namuci, 8.65.19, with Kṛṣṇa speaking. There is also a second "interpolated" reference to Namuci (again, Kṛṣṇa speaking) at 8.88.36-App. 1, No. 41. See Hiltebeitel 2007b: 57, 72-73 n. 211.

34. Biardeau 2002, 2: 756.

35. Indeed, given the preceding verse that contextualizes this parable in the *Śvetāśvatara Upaniṣad*, she is, as one of the three "unborn" or *aja*/*ajās*, none other than tri-colored primal matter whom the one unborn male "burning

with passion, covers" while the other "unborn male leaves her after he has finished enjoying her pleasures"; see Olivelle 1998: 259.

36. On these passages, see further Hiltebeitel 2007a.

37. I would not go as far as Oberlies, who argues that the *Śvetāśvatara* is from around CE 0-200 (1997: 86; 1988: 57-59), though he may be right (even if I doubt it) that it is younger than the *Gītā*. Cf. Olivelle 1998: 252: "Its thought and vocabulary are close to that other theistic document, the *Bhagavad Gītā*."

38. Olivelle trans. 1998: 265.

39. *Kaṭha Up.* 2.20: "Finer than the finest, larger than the largest, is the self (*ātman*) that lies here hidden in the heart of a living being. Without desires and free from sorrow, a man perceives by the creator's grace the grandeur of the self" (Olivelle trans. 1998: 387); cf. the similar *Śvet. Up.* 3.20. Cf. *Muṇḍaka Up.* 3.2.3 in which the "choosing self" is not explicitly divine or gracious.

40. See Olivelle 1998: 23.

41. Olivelle 1998: 426-27; the second line repeats the second line of *Kaṭha Up.* 6.9, which occurs in a *bhakti*/yogic-theistic context that develops the chariot image and focuses on Viṣṇu: see *Kaṭha Up.* 3.3-17 (noting the last verse on audience: "... in a gathering of Brahmins, or during a meal for the dead ..." [Olivelle 1998: 390-91]), which is that Upaniṣad's precedent for understanding 6.6-9. Cf. also *Śvet. Up.* 4.20; 5.14; 6.5-6.

42. Olivelle trans. 1998: 379, 385; cf. Horsch 2004: 437; Bowles 2007: 102-03.

43. See Pollock 1991; Lefeber 1994; van Buitenen 1973, 1975, 1978.

44. There is also some suggestion, at least in Monier-Williams [1899] 1964, 425, that *jñātis*, near- and especially paternal relations, can be differentiated from *sambandhins*, those connected by marriage, as agnates are distinguished from affines. And finally, the terms *bandhu* and *bandhava* seem to refer to kinsmen or relations in general, but also to friends and allies.

45. On these matters, see Lubotsky 1997, 1: 105 on *amítra*, etc.; 2: 1071-75 on *mitrá-*, etc.; and 2: 1456-59 on *sákhi-*, etc.; 2: 1560 mentions *ṚV* 8.2.5c as a single usage of *suhārdam*.

46. As to *mitra*, although it is used extensively amid the insults between Karṇa and Śalya at the beginning of the *Karṇaparvan*, I can think of no case where it really governs the narrative in the way that *sakhi* does—indeed, even there, Karṇa undercuts the whole squabble by reminding Śalya, "I am the dear friend (*priyaḥ sakhā*) of the intelligent son of Dhṛtarāṣṭra" (*MBh* 8.27.94ab).

47. See van Buitenen 1975: 114, etc; Narasimhan 1965: 49. With three uses occurring right after this first one to describe the event (51.21d, 52.81b, 53.21d). On the other hand, the blind Dhṛtarāṣṭra's post-*anudyūta* explanation for the invitation to the dice match includes that he wanted to see his *mitras* (2.65.12).

48. *Saubhrātra* is thus used at the point where the "good brotherhood" of all four brothers is first held in narrative suspension. But after that, the term drops from view, I think because it is never again seriously in question, until the *Uttarakāṇḍa*, where it is used twice not in connection with Rāma and his brothers but with reference to the breakdown in brotherly relations between Rāvaṇa and Kubera (7.11.12c; 13.13a)—the first time when Prahasta ridicules *saubhrātra* as something that Rāvaṇa can ignore just as it was ignored in the brotherly battles between the Gods and Asuras (12-17).

49. They are also *suhṛds* (*Rām* 1.10.23a).

50. See Hiltebeitel forthcoming-a.

51. As van Buitenen 1973: 92 nicely translates *sodaryas* at *MBh* 1.32.8a.

52. We do not know much about the pact that preceded it, which may suggest a problematic confusion.

53. And did they only stay for the military training? When Droṇa assembles his disciples to tell them what he wants for his *dakṣiṇā*, it says he "exhorted them all, without remainder (*sarvān aśeṣeṇa*)" (128.1). Presumably just those who were still there at and after the tournament, after the Vṛṣṇis and Andhakas quietly went home.

54. Biardeau 2002, 1: 300; cf. 293.

55. See 2.44.9b and 14a*; 2.78.5ab* and 11cd; 79.2b, 80.7a, 81.16b: Guha is friend and Rāma master in the starred passages. Another *sakhi* of Lakṣmaṇa and Rāma mentioned briefly is the Ayodhyā priest Suyajña (*Rām* 2.29.1 and 7).

56. See *Rām* 2.3.29ab; 2.5.12ab; 2.15.1, 4ab and 9ab; 2.16.55 and 61; 2.31.4 (he has taken leave here of "all his *suhṛds*").

57. For whatever it may be worth, I have in mind the claim that the Buddha is a descendant of Okkāka (Ikṣvāku); see *Majjhima Nikāya* 1.3.1.15-16.

58. After the leading subjects and the army and just before mentioning the people in every family and in the four castes (2.76.29-30).

59. 2.4.30 (Arjuna and Tumburu), 2.10.22 (Śiva-Paśupati and Kubera), 13.14ff. (Pāṇḍu and Bhagadatta), 13.20 and 28.40-41 (Indra and King Rukmin Bhīṣmaka of Bhojakaṭa), and 48.42 (the Pāñcālas' *sakhya* by marriage with the Pāṇḍavas). It is also curious that as the Pāṇḍavas leave for the forest, Droṇa tells the four gloating chief Kauravas how he unseated Drupada from his kingdom "in a contest of *sakhis* (*sakhivigrahe*)" (71.38b)—as if foreshadowing the *suhṛddyūta* to the extent that this prior "contest" is also, as he says, fated to result in disaster.

60. See Dumézil 1971: 63, 65-66.

61. That is, as she does at least in most Sanskrit texts prior to the Critical Edition. See Hiltebeitel 2001: 249-57.

62. See Hiltebeitel 2007a; forthcoming-c.

63. This is one of those context-sensitive names of Kṛṣṇa with strong *bhakti* overtones that needs attention, notably in relation to *MBh* 12.335.21-66, the Madhu and Kaiṭabha myth in the *Nārāyaṇīya*; see Hiltebeitel 2006.

64. See Hiltebeitel 2007a; forthcoming-c.

65. This is reiterated in closing the theme for the whole *kāṇḍa* at 69.35d.

66. See Lefeber 1994: 67.

67. Both occur with Rāma addressing Sugrīva as a *vayasya* and *suhṛd* who has done all he could and bidding him return to Kiṣkindhā: in the first while Rāma is swooning at what he thinks are fatal injuries (6.39.28), and the second when he is ready to part with Sītā for Ayodhyā (6.110.13a).

68. Of the few usages prior to this episode, one is remakable, where Rāma's motherly and fatherly-like embrace gives all who have come with Bharata to see him at Mount Citrakūṭa the sense that he is "their one true kinsman or one true friend" (*cakāra sarvān savayasyabāndhavān*)" (2.95.46a; Pollock trans., 1986: 287). Cf. 2.63.3; and 7.37.1 and 5, where it is used twice to describe the Kāśi king Pratardana in relation to Rāma.

69. See Chari 1993, 52 ff.

70. Kuntī too says to Karṇa, just after this: "Let the Kurus today witness the meeting of Karṇa and Arjuna in a spirt of brotherhood (*saubhrātreṇa*)" (5.143.9).

71. Kṛṣṇa would seem to be commending Karṇa for sticking to a good policy in a bad situation. Cf. Hiltebeitel 2007b: 30-33.

72. Thus with basically the same terms as when Rāma embraces Sugrīva in establishing their "cordial friendship"—each epic thus describing an embrace between Viṣṇu's incarnation and a son of the Sun.

73. Conciliations, mild words? Van Buitenen has "blandishments" (1978: 444).

Bibliography

Anderson, Benedict. 1991. *Imagined Communities: Reflections on the Origin and Spread of Nationalism*. Revised edition. London: Verso.

Biardeau, Madeleine. 1997. "Some Remarks on the Links between the Epics, the Purāṇas and their Vedic Sources." In Gerhard Oberhammer, ed. *Studies in Hinduism: Vedism and Hinduism*. Vienna: Verlag der Österreichischen Akademie der Wissenschaften.

_____. 1999. *Le Rāmāyaṇa de Vālmīki*. Paris: Gallimard.

_____. 2002. *Le Mahābhārata: Un récit fondateur du brahmanisme et son interprétation*. 2 vols. Paris: Éditions du Seuil.

Bowles, Adam. 2007. *Dharma, Disorder and the Political in Ancient India: The Āpaddharmaparvan of the Mahābhārata*. Leiden: Brill.

Chari, V.K. 1993. *Sanskrit Criticism*. Delhi: Motilal Banarsidass.

Derrida, Jacques. 1997. *Politics of Friendship*, George Collins trans. London: Verso.

Dumézil, Georges. 1969. *The Destiny of the Warrior*. Trans. Alf Hiltebeitel. Chicago: University of Chicago Press.

_____. 1971. *Mythe et épopée 2: Types épiques indo-européens: un héros, un sorcier, un roi*. Paris: Éditions Gallimard.

Fitzgerald, James L. 2001. "Making Yudhiṣṭhira the King: The Dialectics and the Politics of Violence in the *Mahābhārata*." *Rocznik Orientalistyczny* 54 (1): 63-92.

_____. 2003. "The Many Voices of the *Mahābhārata*." Review of Hiltebeitel 2001. *Journal of the American Oriental Society* 123 (4): 803-18.

_____. 2006. "Negotiating the Shape of 'Scripture': New Perspectives on the Development and Growth of the *Mahābhārata* between the Empires." In Patrick Olivelle, ed. *Between the Empires: Society in India 300 BCE to 400 CE*. New York: Oxford University Press.

Glare, P.G.W. 1982. *Oxford Latin Dictionary*. Oxford: Clarendon Press.

Goldman, Robert P. and Sally J. Sutherland Goldman, trans. 1996. *The Rāmāyaṇa of Vālmīki*, vol. 5: *Sundarakāṇḍa*. Princeton: Princeton University Press.

Hardy, Friedhelm. 1983. *Viraha Bhakti*. Delhi: Oxford University Press.

Hiltebeitel, Alf. [1976] 1990. *The Ritual of Battle: Krishna in the Mahābhārata*. Albany: State University of New York Press.

_____. 1982. "Brothers, Friends, and Charioteers: Parallel Episodes in the Irish and Indian Epics." In Edgar C. Polomé, ed. *Homage to Georges Dumézil*. *Journal of Indo-European Studies* Monograph, No. 3: 85-112.

____. 1984. "The Two Kṛṣṇas on One Chariot: Upaniṣadic Imagery and Epic Mythology." *History of Religions* 24: 1-26.
____. 1994. "Epic Studies: Classical Hinduism in the *Mahābhārata* and the *Rāmāyaṇa*." *Annals of the Bhandarkar Oriental Research Institute* 74: 1-62.
____. 2001. *Rethinking the Mahābhārata: A Reader's Guide to the Education of the Dharma King*. Chicago: University of Chicago Press.
____. 2003. "India's Epics: Writing, Orality, and Divinity." In Arvind Sharma, ed., *The Study of Hinduism*. Columbia, SC: University of South Carolina Press.
____. 2004. "More Rethinking the *Mahābhārata*: Toward a Politics of *Bhakti*." *Indo-Iranian Journal* 47: 203-27.
____. 2005. "Not Without Subtales: Telling Laws and Truths in the Sanskrit Epics." *Journal of Indian Philosophy* 33: 455-511.
____. 2006. "The *Nārāyaṇīya* and the Early Reading Communities of the *Mahābhārata*." In Patrick Olivelle, ed. *Between the Empires: Society in India 300 BCE to 400 CE*. New York: Oxford University Press.
____. 2007a. "Among Friends: Marriage, Women, and Some Little Birds." In Simon Brodbeck and Brian Black, eds. *Gender and Narrative in the Mahābhārata*. London: Routledge.
____. 2007b. "Krishna in the *Mahabharata*: The Death of Karna." In Edwin F. Bryant, ed. *Krishna: A Sourcebook*. Oxford: Oxford University Press.
____. Forthcoming-a. "Authorial Paths Through the Two Sanskrit Epics, Via the *Rāmopākhyāna*." In Robert P. Goldman and Muneo Tokunaga eds., *Epic Undertakings*, vol. 2 of Petteri Koskikallio and Asko Parpola gen. eds., *Papers of the 12th World Sanskrit Conference, Helsinki, 13-18 July 2003*, pp. 1-46. Delhi: Motilal Banarsidass.
____. Forthcoming-b. "Mapping *Bhakti* through Friendship and Hospitality in the Sanskrit Epics." In John Brockington, ed., *Battles, Bards, Brāhmans, Papers from Epics Section of the 13th World Sanskrit Conference, Edinburgh, 10-14 July 2006*, pp. 113-38.
____. Forthcoming-c. "Epic Asvamedhas." In Joel Brereton ed. Proceedings of the 4th International Veda Conference, Austin TX. Under consideration by Motilal Banarsidass, Delhi.

Hopkins, Edward Washburn. [1901] 1969. *The Great Epic of India: Its Character and Origin*. Calcutta: Punthi Pustak.

Horsch, Paul. 2004. "From Creation Myth to World Law: The Early History of *Dharma*." Jarrod L. Whitaker, trans. *Journal of Indian Philosophy* 32 (5-6): 423-48.

Houben, Jan. 2000. "The Ritual Pragmatics of a Vedic Hymn: The 'Riddle Hymn' and the Pravargya Ritual." *Journal of the American Oriental Society* 120 (4): 499-536.

Lefeber, Rosalind, trans. 1994. *The Rāmāyaṇa of Vālmīki*, vol. 4: *Kiṣkindhākāṇḍa*. Princeton: Princeton University Press.

Lubotsky, Alexander. 1997. *A Ṛgvedic Word Concordance*. 2 vols. New Haven: American Oriental Society.

Miller, A.V. trans. 1997. *Hegel's Phenomenology of Spirit*. Oxford: Oxford University Press.

Monier-Williams, Monier. [1899] 1964. *A Sanskrit-English Dictionary*. Oxford: Clarendon Press.

Narasimhan, Chakravarthi, trans. 1965. *The Mahābhārata: An English Version Based on Selected Verses*. New York: Columbia University Press.

Oberlies, Thomas. 1988. "Die Śvetāśvatara-Upaniṣad: eine Studie ihrer Gotteslehre (Studien zu den 'mittleren' Upaniṣads I)." *Wiener Zeitschrift für die Kunde Südasiens* 32: 57-59.

———. 1997. "Die Textgeschichte der Śvetadvīpa-Episode des *Nārāyaṇīya* (*MBh.* 12.321-326)." In Peter Schreiner, ed. *Nārāyaṇīya Studien*. Purāṇa Research Publications—Tubingen, vol. 6. Wiesbaden: Harrassowitz Verlag.

Olivelle, Patrick, trans. 1998. *The Upaniṣads*. New York: Oxford University Press.

Patton, Laurie L. 2005. *Bringing the Gods to Mind: Mantra and Ritual in Early Indian Sacrifice*. Berkeley: University of California Press.

Pollock, Sheldon. 1984. "Ātmānam mānuṣam manye: Dharmākūtam on the Divinity of Rāma." *Journal of the Oriental Institute of Baroda* 33: 505-28.

———, trans. 1986. *The Rāmāyaṇa of Vālmīki: An Epic of Ancient India*, vol. 2: *Ayodhyākāṇḍa*. Princeton: Princeton University Press.

———, trans. 1991. *The Rāmāyaṇa of Vālmīki: An Epic of Ancient India*, vol. 3: *Araṇyakāṇḍa*. Princeton: Princeton University Press.

van Buitenen, J.A.B. 1973, 1975, 1978. *The Mahābhārata*, vols. I: 1. *The Book of Beginnings;* II: 2. *The Book of the Assembly Hall;* 3. *The Book of the Forest;* III: 4. *The Book of Virāṭa;* 5. *The Book of the Effort*. Chicago: University of Chicago Press.

Walshe, Maurice, trans. [1987] 1995. *The Long Discourses of the Buddha: A Translation of the Dīgha Nikāya*. Boston: Wisdom Publications.

I'll Wash Out Your Mouth With My Boot: A Guide to Philological Argument in Mughal-era Banaras

CHRISTOPHER MINKOWSKI

> *iha jagati khalānāṃ kaṇṭakānāṃ dvidhaiva*
> *pratikṛtir atiramyā proditā paṇḍitendraiḥ* |
> *nikaṭam upagatānām āsyabhaṅgo 'ṅghrirakṣair*
> *vyavahitavasatīnāṃ sarvathopekṣaṇaiva* ||
> (conclusion, *Durjanamukhapadmapādukā*)

> The wise have declared that there are two good ways to respond to the vile and obnoxious of this world: complete indifference provided they keep clear; but when they get too close—a smack in the mouth with one's shoes.

Who would have guessed that intellectual discord could be fun? Clearly the śāstrīs did. Śāstrīs, after all, have always been philologists. That is, to use a broad definition, they have been intellectuals whose chief activity has been to take texts seriously and to work at making sense of them.[1] Now philologists everywhere have enjoyed the reputation of being contentious, even belligerent, over their own patch of ground. Occasionally the philologist has even been justified in this *Streitbarigkeit.* There can be weighty matters at stake. The old joke notwithstanding, the competition has sometimes been so fierce because the stakes were so high.

The śāstrī has been no exception in this. Although, according to the Dharmaśāstras, a learned Brahmin was not to be violent, but rather mild, a source of refinement and improvement for others, nevertheless, when it came to arguing about the truth of a text, especially an important one, other, fiercer manners could come to the fore.

And yet, judging from the literature that survives there must always have been limits to what could and could not be said in Sanskrit to an opponent in the setting of a debate or in polemical writing. A scholar's forcefulness could be balanced with good humor or propriety. Or at least, there must once have been limits. As the energies of India's early-modern world overtook the śāstrīs, however, those unexpressed limits appear in some notorious cases to have been obliterated.

This seems to be the place to bring up one of those notorious cases. Bob Goldman has never shied from controversy. In his work he has been willing to read Sanskrit texts against the grain, in order to uncover contentious meanings—psychological, social and political. And he has been interested in how śāstrīs read texts with or against the grain, as commentators.

The case that is brought up here concerns a long-running controversy over the canonical status of the Vaiṣṇava *Bhāgavata Purāṇa*, which became a hugely powerful text in the world of Sanskrit discourse over the course of the second millennium CE.[2] I wish to consider the discord that the Vaiṣṇava *Bhāgavata* generated, as it appears always to have done, at a particular moment in Banaras—in the late sixteenth and early seventeeth centuries, and the way that the śāstrīs who were involved used philological arguments in order to settle more than philological matters.

In considering this fracas there is no need to work at exposing or unmasking a subtext, for here the terms of the debate and what was at stake in it are not concealed from view.

In what follows, I will present the background of the controversy, which began much earlier, and outline the terms of the argument. Then I will look at four texts, three of which were composed in Banaras during this period, one somewhat later.

The Controversial *Bhāgavata*

The three short texts from the period have rude titles, which indicate that each one knew and responded to the preceding one(s). They are, in the order in which they were composed, the "Smack on the Mouth of the Wicked" (*Durjana-mukha-capeṭikā*), then in reply the "Big Smack on the Mouth of the Wicked" (*Durjana-mukha-mahācapeṭikā*), and then the "Shoe in the Lotus-Mouth of the Wicked" (*Durjana-mukhapadma-pādukā*), at once more insulting and yet somewhat more decorous, for its reference to the opponent's lotus-mouth.[3] The fourth work, perhaps from the mid-eighteenth century, has by comparison a tellingly, though perhaps disappointingly, bland title, the "Ornament of the [Vaiṣṇava] *Bhāgavata*" (*Bhāgavatabhūṣaṇa*). Part of the later story to be told is one of recoiling from the vehemence that dominated the three works, though not recoiling too far, as we shall see.

The first three texts, which are not composed in terribly dense academic Sanskrit, were noticed even in the earliest stages of European research into the history of the Vaiṣṇava *Bhāgavata* as part of purāṇic literature. They attracted the attention of Thomas Colebrooke and H.H. Wilson.[4] It was Eugène Burnouf who included complete translations of all three, along with extensive annotations, in the *Préface* to the first volume of his edition and translation of the Vaiṣṇava *Bhāgavata*, in 1840.[5]

Burnouf gave careful consideration to these works because the literary history of all of the Purāṇas, including the Vaiṣṇava *Bhāgavata*, had until then proved difficult to establish. Burnouf recognized that the three texts included information relevant to that literary history. Furthermore, and more directly pertinent to our interest here, they were representative to his mind "de curieux exemples de la méthode proper à la polémique orthodoxe",[6] affording a way to "constater l'état actuel de la méthode et de l'argumentation brâhmanique".[7]

The three polemical texts were, as Burnouf knew, part of a brahminical controversy of much longer standing about whether the Vaiṣṇava *Bhāgavata* should be considered to belong in the same category with the other Purāṇas; to be more specific, whether it should be considered to be, as it claimed, a work composed by Vyāsa.

A great deal more is known about the history of the Purāṇas now than was known in Burnouf's day, and yet the exact history of the Vaiṣṇava *Bhāgavata* is still unclear.[8] It is clear that this text is strikingly different from the other Purāṇas in formal terms: its language, style, and metrical structures are much more polished and elaborate than those of the other Purāṇas enumerated in the canonical lists. It includes conscious archaisms, most conspicuously the use of forms of Sanskrit morphology not seen since the days of the Vedas, and the use of forms of apparent antiquity which are however found nowhere in the extant Vedas.[9] At the same time it makes use of syntactical structures peculiar to rather daring developments in Sanskrit kāvya.

The best guess as to the date of the Vaiṣṇava *Bhāgavata* was offered by F. Hardy, who concluded that it was composed in the ninth century or perhaps the early tenth.[10] Nevertheless the text continues to elude scholarly agreement about the date of its composition. This is not an accident. It is rather a byproduct of the text's design. The text was designed to pass for being much older than it was, intended as a sort of theological Trojan horse. The Vaiṣṇava *Bhāgavata* was composed as a proselytizing treatise, with a provocative, double agenda contained throughout: to show that the theology and practice of emotional Kṛṣṇa worship were in fact the central current of the mainstream of Vedic brahminical tradition, and at the same time to assert that emotional Kṛṣṇaite theology and practice constituted a new dispensation, a supersession of the Vedic tradition.

Of course, the Vaiṣṇava *Bhāgavata* was not alone among purāṇic texts in having an insinuating intention of this sort. The legacy of just such cultural efforts, made in India's medieval period by a variety of religious and ritual movements with diverse theologies, modes of worship and yogic practices, dominates the purāṇic corpus as we have it today. Nevertheless, the Vaiṣṇava *Bhāgavata* was an exceptional effort, and not just for staying more consistently "on message". What was unique was the form that the effort took. In the case of this text the exceptional formal characteristics constituted the chief means of advancing its aims. Kṛṣṇa bhaktas considered their *Bhāgavata Purāṇa* to surpass the other Purāṇas and indeed to surpass the Vedic literature as a whole because of this form, which they argued generates a special experience of more than aesthetic rasa. In an important sense for them this made the text more true.[11]

Because of the extraordinary qualities of the text, the controversy that Burnouf discovered in his three polemical texts had been going on well before those works were produced, probably from the time when the Vaiṣṇava *Bhāgavata* entered the public sphere of śāstric philological discussion. A knowledge of the controversy is found already in one of the earliest surviving commentaries on the text, that of Śrīdhara, produced in about 1400. In his discussion of the first verse, Śrīdhara responds to what he knows to have been ongoing doubts about whether the Vaiṣṇava *Bhāgavata* was one of the canonical Purāṇas attributed to Vyāsa. He offers proofs that it is, citing passages from three Purāṇas: the *Matsya*, the *Padma*, and 'another' (purāṇāntara).[12]

We need not revisit all of the details of the controversy here, as most of these have been reported by Sanyal and Rocher.[13] It is worth mentioning here only that in the early modern period the controversy developed into a topic for regular independent discussion, the short polemical treatise about it becoming almost a genre of text in its own right. Among other works that appeared after our three were the *Durjanarasanārgala* "A Gag on the Tongue of the Wicked" produced in response to the *Durjanakapolacapeṭikā* "A Smack on the Cheek of the Wicked." There was eventually a *Durjanamukhacapeṭikādi-saṃgraha*, a "Compendium of Works Beginning with the *Smack on the Mouth of the Wicked*."[14] Rāmāśrama gave a smack heard round the world.

The question around which the polemical efforts of these pamphlets revolve was whether the Vaiṣṇava *Bhāgavata* was composed by Vyāsa, that is, whether it was *ārṣa*, and as a corollary whether it was therefore one of the canonical eighteen Purāṇas. Needless to say, from the outset devotees of Kṛṣṇa, whether affiliated to one of the Vaiṣṇava sampradāyas or not, maintained that it was. Others argued that it was not. Some of those arguing against claimed that it was a forgery by Bopadeva, the thirteenth century grammarian.[15] Some of those arguing against, whether or not they accepted the attribution to Bopadeva, proposed that in fact the real *Bhāgavata Purāṇa* was the *Devī Purāṇa*, also called the *Devī Bhāgavata Purāṇa*.[16]

Those who argued on all sides of this controversy focused on a limited number of topics, which included primarily the following:

- Passages in other Purāṇas that describe some of the contents of the "*Bhāgavata*". Mentioned here are passages that refer to a lengthy discussion of dharma based on the meaning of the Gāyatrī mantra; the slaying of the asura Vṛtra; the men and gods who lived in the Sārasvata kalpa; and the Hayagrīva Brahmavidyā.
- Passages in other Purāṇas that describe the form of the "*Bhāgavata*". Here passages are cited which assert that the "*Bhāgavata*" begins with the Gāyatrī mantra; or that it consists of two parts, or of 18,000 verses, or of twelve skandhas, or is uttered by Śuka.[17]
- Canonical lists in other Purāṇas of the eighteen Mahāpurāṇas and Upapurāṇas, and the inclusion of a "*Bhāgavata*" therein.
- The correct etymology and meaning of the adjective *bhāgavata*—whether it refers to a worshipper of *bhagavān*, i.e. Kṛṣṇa, or on the other hand to a worshipper of *bhagavatī*, i.e. the goddess.
- Whether the Vaiṣṇava *Bhāgavata Purāṇa* conforms to the canonical shape of a Mahāpurāṇa as regularly stated in the purāṇic enumeration of the genre's five distinctive characteristics (*pañcalakṣaṇa*).

The mode in which the śāstrīs approached all of these topics was properly philological. They drew on passages from texts generally available, or for which they could claim there existed verifiable evidence; concerned themselves with the reliability of the exact wording of their sources, and discussed ways of assessing it; made use of the work of scholars who intervened in time between the texts and themselves, and in general assumed the possibility of historical change.

Four New Ways to Argue

In the three texts from early modern Banaras that were introduced above we find a number of arguments that appear to be new developments, and that are perhaps characteristic of the energies of the city in its śāstric heyday. I shall discuss four of the more interesting new forms of argument here: relative and absolute chronologies; the invocation of contemporary authorities; the idea of a developing Vyāsa; and second-guessing the personal motives of others.

We should begin, however, with a few words about what is known of the authors of the three works. The first text, the *Durjanamukhacapeṭikā*, was composed by Rāmāśrama, whom P.K. Gode has persuasively shown to be the same as the son of Bhaṭṭoji Dīkṣita, Bhānuji Dīkṣita, who went on to take sannyāsa and a monastic name.[18] Rāmāśrama / Bhānuji is best known as the author of the *Vyākhyāsudhā*, a commentary on the *Amarakośa*. Rāmāśrama belonged to one of the most prominent and well-remembered families of Deccani Brahmins in Banaras of the sixteenth and seventeenth centuries.[19] Aside from their celebrated work in grammar and philosophy of language, this was a family of Advaitins and Śaivas. Bhānuji after all had become a dasnāmī sannyāsī. Nevertheless in the *Durjanamukhacapeṭikā* he accepts the authenticity and value of the Vaiṣṇava *Bhāgavata*. I think that it is this development that touched off the controversy, viz., that it was a member of the Banarsī establishment, as it were, and not simply a member of a Vaiṣṇava sampradāya, who championed the cause of the Vaiṣṇava *Bhāgavata*.

The *Durjanamukha(mahā)capeṭikā* was written by Kāśīnātha Bhaṭṭa Bhaḍa, son of Jayarāma Bhaṭṭa.[20] The colophon of the work indicates that he was born in Banaras, and was a guru in the 'right-hand' tradition of the Śaiva Siddhānta. The family name Bhaḍa suggests that the family was from the town of that name in the Lātūr district of Maharashtra. Kāśīnātha was the author of about seventy-five other works, including a number of other polemical treatises.[21] He appears to have been a close contemporary of Rāmāśrama. In his *Durjanamukha(mahā)capeṭikā* he argues that the true *Bhāgavata* is the *Devībhāgavata*, and not the Vaiṣṇava *Bhāgavata*.

The third work, the *Durjanamukhapadmapādukā*, mentions no author, and has no maṅgala verse from which one could learn anything of the author's background.[22] In a similar way the text concludes only with the verse cited above about the most agreeable way to treat the vile and obnoxious of this world. It appears to mention a work by Nāgoji Bhaṭṭa, and if that is correct it was composed slightly later in the seventeenth century. All indications from the arguments, however, and how tightly connected they are to Rāmāśrama's, along with direct citation of Kāśīnātha's work by name, suggest that this essay is nearly contemporary with the other two, especially given the text's direct address of Rāmāśrama and mention of 'your father', i.e. Bhaṭṭoji.[23] This text argues that the Vaiṣṇava *Bhāgavata* was a forgery by Bopadeva.

Relative and Absolute Chronology

In reading Rāmāśrama's essay we jump into the middle of things, for his arguments in favor of the text's ārṣatva are organized as a series of rejoinders to some antagonist whose work is not preserved as far as we know. Rāmāśrama takes up the question of the attribution of the Vaiṣṇava *Bhāgavata* to Bopadeva. He offers two arguments that depend on an appeal to the relative chronology of various works, as well as an appeal to the absolute chronology of two authors. He argues first that it is not possible for Citsukha (who Rāmāśrama thinks was prior to Bopadeva) to have written a commentary on the Vaiṣṇava *Bhāgavata*, if Bopadeva were the *Bhāgavata*'s author.[24] Furthermore, he points out that Vijayadhvaja Tīrtha mentions at the beginning of his Dvaitin commentary on the Vaiṣṇava *Bhāgavata* that he read eight commentaries, one of which was by Śaṅkarācārya, and this too would be impossible if Bopadeva were the author, since Bopadeva lived five centuries ago, while Śaṅkara lived seventeen centuries ago.[25]

Kāśīnātha does not address these arguments, but the anonymous author of the *Durjanamukhapadmapādukā* (henceforth *DMPP*) points out that there is no proof that Śaṅkara wrote such a commentary, and indeed one can be certain that he did not.[26] Burnouf was unable to confirm or deny this claim, but the author of the *DMPP* is probably correct in this. The assertion that this commentary does not exist because it no longer survives is anticipated by Rāmāśrama, who argues that it did not survive because it was difficult, and too few were competent to read it.[27] He likens it to Citsukha's commentary on the *Bhāgavata* in that respect, but

Citsukha's putative commentary was no more available than Śaṅkara's, and the third author points out the problems with likening one missing piece of evidence to another known to be missing.

Of greater interest than the introduction of references to past texts that perhaps never existed, however, is the argument by way of the relative chronology of authors who are not part of the same textual tradition. That is, it would not necessarily be a simple matter for a student only of the Advaitin textual tradition to know whether Citsukha and Śaṅkarācārya were prior to or subsequent to Bopadeva. Even more interesting than this more comprehensive awareness of the history of authors in various śāstras is Rāmāśrama's certainty about the absolute dates of both Bopadeva and Śaṅkara, placing the former in the twelfth century and the latter in the first century BCE. Neither of these dates is particularly correct from what we know today, (though the date of Bopadeva is not wildly off), but it is noteworthy that already in the seventeenth century there was a sense current in Banaras of the great antiquity of Śaṅkara.

Contemporary Authorities

At the same time, the argument that appears to carry even more weight for Rāmāśrama is the appeal to the acceptance of the Vaiṣṇava *Bhāgavata* by authorities who do not belong to the distant past, but who are figures more or less contemporary to him. Especially remarkable is that he invokes prominent authorities of the Banaras of his own day. As a way of casting doubt on the learning of his antagonist, he points out that

> the [Vaiṣṇava] *Bhāgavata* has been accepted by Appayya Dīkṣita who cited it as a proof text in the *Śivatattvaviveka* and others of his works. Madhusūdana Sarasvatī has commented on the [Vaiṣṇava] *Bhāgavata* in his *Bhaktirasāyana*. The [Vaiṣṇava] *Bhāgavata* is praised by Pūrṇendra Sarasvatī and Brahmendra Sarasvatī, our contemporaries (vidyamāna). And Bhaṭṭoji Dīkṣita has accepted the [Vaiṣṇava] *Bhāgavata*. By comparison to them, what greater scholar could there be who would presume to criticize the [Vaiṣṇava] *Bhāgavata*?[28]

The work of both Appayya and Madhusūdana, figures of a generation or two earlier than Rāmāśrama, is well known. Here I will mention only that they were hugely prominent in the world of Advaita Vedānta in seventeenth century Banaras. Madhusūdana had lived in Banaras, of course, while Appayya had many influential disciples and students in the city, among them Bhaṭṭoji, who was Rāmāśrama's father.

Much of the public life of śāstric learning in Banaras in that era was conducted within the ambit of prominent sannyāsīs. The two sannyāsīs mentioned by Rāmāśrama, Pūrṇendra Sarasvatī and Brahmendra Sarasvatī, are known to us from texts and documents that survive from those days. Brahmendra was the author of three texts that survive: the *Advaitāmṛta*, the *Prabodhacandrikā* commentary on the *Bhagavad Gītā*, and a *Vedāntaparibhāṣā*.[29] There are two works attributed to Pūrṇendra Sarasvatī, the *Praṇavārthaprakāśikā* and the *Brahmabhāvanānirṇaya*.[30] Brahmendra contributed to the *Kavīndracandrodaya*, an anthology of praśastis composed in prose or poetry by about sixty learned Brahmins and sannyāsīs, which was created to felicitate another prominent sannyāsī in Banaras, Kavīndrācārya Sarasvatī, for persuading Shāh Jahān to abolish the *jizya* tax on pilgrims to Kāśī and Prayāga.[31] Brahmendra and Pūrṇendra are mentioned both individually and as a pair by the other contributors to the *Kavīndracandrodaya*, and it is clear from these references that the two were looked upon as in some important sense the leaders of the community of the learned and wise in the city.[32]

What is more, we know that in 1657 both sannyāsīs appeared at a meeting of about seventy pandits and sannyāsīs in the Muktimaṇḍapa of the Viśvanāth temple—the principal venue for paṇḍitasabhās in the city, where they jointly signed a judgement (nirṇayapattra) concerning the caste status of Devrukh Brahmins.[33] Since in that document Brahmendra appears to be given the alternative name of Nṛsiṃhāśrama, P.K. Gode has suggested that Brahmendra / Nṛsiṃha received letters from the Mughal prince Dārā Shukoh, the son of Shāh Jahān, who famously commissioned the translation of fifty Upaniṣads and of other Sanskrit texts.[34]

Thus in invoking this list of names Rāmāśrama was connecting his stand in the controversy to the highest circle of authority and prestige in the world of śāstric learning of his day, the circle in which he had grown up, and the circle with direct connections to the imperial court in Agra and Delhi. It is worthwhile remarking, by the way, that the śāstric public sphere that this circle dominated was a decidedly Advaitin one.[35]

Elsewhere in his text Rāmāśrama narrates a story "from the days of Mādhava Sarasvatī," to which we will return below, but the Mādhava Sarasvatī he means is surely the charismatic figure of Banaras of the previous century, who was the guru of Madhusūdana.[36]

Again, Kāśīnātha has nothing to say in reply to this argument of Rāmāśrama's. The author of the *DMPP*, on the other hand, points out that in the *Śabdakaustubha* of Bhaṭṭoji and in the *(Paribhāṣendu)śekhara* of Nāgoji Bhaṭṭa there are a number of works that are spoken of as if they were ārṣa, and yet which we know are not, such as the commentary of Kaiyyaṭa.[37] At the same time, he also points out that there are men far more learned than Appayya, such as Vardhamāna Upādhyāya and (Jagannātha) Paṇḍitarāja, who are willing to enter into the question of the Bhāgavata's ārṣatva with a pure and detached mind.[38] The former of these figures was an author of works on Dharmaśāstra in Mithilā in the late fifteenth century, and so was not a contemporary, but the poet and literary theorist Jagannātha Paṇḍitarāja was very much a figure of Banaras in the first half of the seventeenth century, and a darling of the Mughal court.[39] Our author does not claim that Jagannātha rejected the Vaiṣṇava *Bhāgavata*, only that he is a better man than Appayya, for being beloved of Kṛṣṇa and pure of heart. What he does not mention is that Jagannātha and Bhaṭṭoji had engaged in a very public quarrel over what Jagannātha saw as Bhaṭṭoji's betrayal of his teacher, Śeṣa Kṛṣṇa.[40] For a long time Jagannātha was not a figure of the establishment in Banaras, perhaps for insulting his guru, or for consorting too closely with the Mughal court. Legend has it that Bhaṭṭoji went so far as to call him a mleccha. Thus mentioning Jagannātha is a well-aimed jab by the author of the *DMPP*, but apparently he does not have that much that he can say in response to Rāmāśrama's appeal to the Banārasī culture of prestige and living institutional authority.

The Developing Vyāsa

The obvious question for the philologist about the Vaiṣṇava *Bhāgavata*, however, is why its language and style are different from those of all other Purāṇas. This must have been an argument made early on by those who were dubious of its status as a proper Purāṇa, and Kāśīnātha states the objection in what was probably its ordinary form: the language (*vāṇī*) found in all of the eighteen Purāṇas and in the *Mahābhārata* is one thing, the glorious language (stavyarūpa-vāṇī) of the Vaiṣṇava *Bhāgavata* is another. Therefore the Vaiṣṇava *Bhāgavata* is not one of the Purāṇas.[41]

Careful analysis of what exactly that difference consists in is not offered by our authors, but Rāmāśrama offers a novel argument to explain it: Vyāsa developed his abilities as an author as he went along, and wrote the Vaiṣṇava *Bhāgavata* only after completing all of his other works, at the height of his powers. Vyāsa was, moreover, fond of the subject of Kṛṣṇa, but did not really care about the other works he wrote. Thus he put more of himself into the Vaiṣṇava *Bhāgavata*. It is for this reason that the text is different from the other Purāṇas.[42]

The author of the *DMPP* rejects these arguments by pointing out that the Purāṇas tell us that Vyāsa was born a perfectly learned man. Furthermore the undesirable consequence of positing a developing Vyāsa would be that the other Purāṇas and the *Mahābhārata* were somehow imperfect, since they were composed by a less than perfected author. As for the suggestion of Vyāsa's favoritism, the author of the *DMPP* declares that this contradicts what we know of that sage's dispassionate view of all things.[43] Most interesting here, however, is that this author points out that no one has made the argument before, that is, that Rāmāśrama has made an innovative argument.

Second-guessing Motives

The last topic that we will consider here has to do with the motives of the author(s) of the Vaiṣṇava *Bhāgavata*, and it is on this topic that the rudeness comes in. The topic must have been around from earlier periods, for once it has been claimed that the Vaiṣṇava *Bhāgavata* was a forgery by Bopadeva, apologists for the text are free to ask why. What, after all, would motivate someone to compose a text of this length and then attribute it to someone else? It cannot be wealth or fame or intellectual credit, the usual motivations. These arguments come up at the beginning of Rāmāśrama's work, and are responded to in the other two, but here instead let us consider the more invidious form that this argument takes on.

Under the second topic above, I cited a passage from Rāmāśrama, in which he ended with a question—what greater scholar could there be who would presume to criticize the [Vaiṣṇava] *Bhāgavata*? The answer Rāmāśrama offers is that it is the tāntrikas of the dangerous or left-side path who would so presume. This is because they hate the Vaiṣṇava *Bhāgavata*, since it criticizes them. The leftists hate Viṣṇu and the Veda too, as their texts show. And they hate the Vaiṣṇava *Bhāgavata* because it does not support their eating of meat.[44] Dualists come in for similar treatment. They hate the Vaiṣṇava *Bhāgavata* and the Vedas because dualists maintain views that are contrary to the Vedas' and the *Bhāgavata*'s teaching. Thus they are heretics (*pākhaṇḍa*), really.[45]

What is more, Kāśīnātha narrates the story of something that happened in the days of Mādhava Sarasvatī, a prominent sannyāsī of Banaras of several generations earlier, and the guru of Madhusūdana

Sarasvatī. Mādhava Sarasvatī was looked upon as having the powers of insight into people and situations that are attributed to some sādhus. The story goes that there was a pandit of those days (there in Banaras, presumably,) who said that the Vaiṣṇava *Bhāgavata* was not authoritative. Then the master (i.e. Mādhava Sarasvatī) said, "look into the matter, and you'll discover that this man is a bastard (*jāraja*)". When it was looked into by the pandits, it was found that the man was indeed the bastard son of a Brahmin widow (*golaka*).[46]

Kāśīnātha reverses these arguments and says that it is the Vaiṣṇavas who hate the *Devī Bhāgavata* and the Goddess in her highest form as Parāśakti, because the Śākta Purāṇas criticize Vaiṣṇavas. What is more, he in turn calls the Vaiṣṇavas dualists, and says that it is their hatred of the *Devī Bhāgavata* which brings them to call the Śāktas bastards.[47] He cites the *Vāyavīyasaṃhitā*, a section of the *Śiva Purāṇa*, at some length, the upshot of the passage being that followers of the [Vaiṣṇava] Pāñcarātra tantric path lack the slightest bit of religious merit (*puṇyaleśavivarjita*), are the result of caste intermixture (*utpattisāṃkarya*), can't distinguish Vedic from non-Vedic (*vaidikāvaidikācārā-dvibhāga-jñānavivarjita*), are the lowest of men (*puruṣādhama*), and are the most sinful sort of pseudo-Vedic poseurs (*pāpiṣṭhavaidikābhāsa*).

The author of our third text the *DMPP* spends a significant amount of time on the general logic of the motives of Vyāsa or of any pseudo-Vyāsa. As to the story of Mādhava Sarasvatī, he rejects the very idea of using such a story as a legitimate argument, but having done so then offers a counter-story. This counter-story does not come from recent days in Banaras, but from the days of Śaṅkara himself. The story our third author tells is that once when Śaṅkara was lecturing on the *Devī Bhāgavata* a Vaiṣṇava who thought himself learned interrupted to say that the *Devī Bhāgavata* was not a work of inspiration and was therefore non-canonical. Śaṅkara called him a *vaideha*, that is, a half-breed against the grain, the son of Brahmin woman from a Vaiśya father. He diagnosed the man as no doubt leprous in nature, and destined to lose his entire nose. This loss of nose then happened to him, at the hands of the king of Kerala, Sudhanvan.[48]

Aside from this swipe at the background and inner nature of his opponents, however, the author of the *DMPP* takes a different tack through the invidious waters of this part of the discussion. He argues that the fact of doubt does not logically require hatred as its cause, but can, rather, come simply from an interest in knowing the truth.[49]

In general this is the note the third author sounds. It is Rāmāśrama who speaks of hatred as the explanatory cause of arguments, and of a Vyāsa who is partisan to some of his work and not attracted to other parts. Kāśīnātha falls into this way of speaking as well, but the third author returns to claims about dispassionate interest in the truth and a dispassionate Vyāsa. The third author in general appears to value arguments that make sense and are not special pleading or based on imaginary data, or dependent on prestige and current opinion.

Bhāgavatabhūṣaṇa

Of course, the *Durjanamukhapadmapādukā* was not the end of the debate. As we have seen, texts continued to appear, and the argument has gone on in other forms even in the modern period. What, however, became of the four ways of arguing that we identified in the three texts from Banaras? Let us look at a Sanskrit work of perhaps a century later, the *Bhāgavatabhūṣaṇa*, to see.

The *Bhāgavatabhūṣaṇa* was composed by Gopālācārya, the son of Nārāyaṇācārya and Gaṅgā, and grandson of Vāsudevācārya, a Vaiṣṇava who lived on the bank of the Kṛṣṇā River in Karhāḍa in Mahārāṣṭra.[50] Gopāla was a Dvaitin, and cites Madhva's commentary on the *Brahmasūtra* respectfully and approvingly. He is of course a defender of the canonical status of the Vaiṣṇava *Bhāgavata*. Among many Sanskrit authors he cites Bhāskararāya Makhin, who flourished in 1728. He appears to be a figure of the later eighteenth century.[51]

The text is not designed as a polemical treatise in the same way that the earlier three were, but the controversies surrounding the Vaiṣṇava *Bhāgavata* dominate its contents. It is divided into four sections (*ullāsa*), the first on the good effects that come from reading the Vaiṣṇava *Bhāgavata* (*paramānandada*), the second on settling the controversy about its canonical status (*durjana-dhikkāra*), the third on resolving minor problems that have been raised (*kṣudropadrava-nivāraṇa*), and the fourth on the proper procedure for a complete reading of the *Bhāgavata* in the course of a week (*saptāhavidhāna-kathana*). While in general the text has backed away from the sort of nastiness that characterized the works of Rāmāśrama and Kāśīnātha, it nevertheless summons up the memory of their work, in the title to its chapter on the main controversy—the damning (*dhikkāra*) of the wicked (*durjana*).

What is most striking about the *Bhāgavatabhūṣaṇa* by comparison with the earlier texts is that its main polemical strategy appears to be to argue by amassing a preponderance of evidence, which is achieved by heaping up citations of vast numbers of authorities.[52] This is made clearest in the argument that, the opponents' claims notwithstanding, the Vaiṣṇava *Bhāgavata* is indeed treated as an authoritative work by the standard treatises on dharma (*nibandha*). In this argument forty-seven authorities, together with the text of the relevant passages, are cited in one colossal sentence that stretches over two pages.[53]

Another distinctive feature of the work is its regular insistence on the indisputability of the material concreteness of the evidence of the texts. Perhaps this is a response to insinuations by opponents that Vaiṣṇavas since Madhva had been forgers, or perhaps it is in response to assertions that specific words in documents had been altered, either intentionally or unintentionally, in ways that suited the Vaiṣṇava view.[54] In the *Bhāgavatabhūṣaṇa* what we see is regular reference to the locations where manuscript copies of texts can be consulted. For example, in referring to a passage in the *Gaurītantra*, Gopāla says that this text can be found in Kāśī, Mathurā, Jhānsī, Puṇe, and other places.[55] In a number of other places the author argues that a section of a text is not an interpolation because it is found in copies available all over India.[56] Although these are properly philological arguments, and properly empirical ones, in this form they appear to be something new in the realm of śāstric argument.

There is, however, no appeal in the *Bhāgavatabhūṣaṇa* to any living authority, nor to any figure or institution of prestige, as we had seen in Rāmāśrama's work. All of the authorities are cited as literary figures. Nevertheless, in his amassing of authoritative evidence Gopāla, though himself a dualist, emphasizes the evidence from texts by Advaitins. Śaṅkara, Citsukha, Appayya, and Madhusūdana come in for regular mention, along with Nāgoji and Bhaṭṭoji, as do Banārasī dharmaśāstrīs of the sixteenth and seventeenth century such as Ananta Deva, Kamalākara Bhaṭṭa, and Dinakara Bhaṭṭa.

As to the question of the Vaiṣṇava *Bhāgavata*'s style, there is no suggestion that Vyāsa developed during the course of his career, nor is there an argument against that idea. Instead what we find is Gopāla asserting that the charm of the language (*padalālitya*) is no reason not to consider it a proper locus of religious authority (*prāmāṇya*), since one finds similar artfulness in the *Sundarakāṇḍa* of the *Rāmāyaṇa*, in the *Puṣkaraprādurbhāva* section of the *Harivaṃśa*, and so on.[57] There is an acknowledgement that the verses of Vaiṣṇava *Bhāgavata* have contradictions and difficulties that require commentary.[58]

The *Bhāgavatabhūṣaṇa* has none of the reasoning about the motives of authors or forgers that was found earlier in the history of the controversy. Nor does it spend much time on the nastier form of that discussion that had appeared in the earlier three texts. In one of Gopāla's pūrvapakṣas the denunciation of the Vaiṣṇava *Bhāgavata* as Bopadeva's forgery comes up. It is attributed to the Śaivas and Tantrikas, because they could not bear to be told that they were following the wrong path. Having brought this up in a pūrvapakṣa, Gopāla, quickly brings the discussion back to the quality of their reasoning rather than of their morality or of their origins, and proceeds along those lines.[59]

With the vastly increased numbers of authorities that he cites, Gopāla makes a much more complex argument about relative chronology as well. He also has new sources to offer when it comes to the absolute chronology of Bopadeva. After establishing the chronological relationship of Bopadeva and Hemādri, the minister at the Yādava court in Devagiri, Gopāla then invokes Marāṭhī works by Vaiṣṇava devotees of Viṭṭhala in Pandharpur which place "Hemāḍ Pant" soon after Jñāneśvara who, Gopāla asserts , was born in 1212 Śaka or 1290 CE.[60] These dates are coordinated with the dates given in Madhvācārya's works.

In general, then, Gopāla is a milder writer, the principal force of whose argument is to overwhelm by the weight of the evidence he presents. Despite the ideological variety of the sources he cites he is not at all "ecumenical" in his approach, even though he is aware of something like that possibility from reading Nīlakaṇṭha Caturdhara's commentary on the *Mahābhārata*. Gopāla paraphrases a passage from the beginning of Nīlakaṇṭha's commentary to the effect that there are many ways of looking at things, for example that Vedāntins consider the *Gītā* to be about knowledge, while devotionalists consider the *Gītā* to be about devotion, just as Vaiṣṇavas consider Banaras to be a Vaiṣṇava town and Śaivas consider Banaras to be a Śaiva town depending on the texts they read. In this way, out of a hatred for Viṣṇu some say that the Vaiṣṇava *Bhāgavata* is a human fabrication and full of negativity (*tāmasa*).[61]

In fact, this paraphrase, with its non sequitur at the end, is a paraphrase of Nīlakaṇṭha and not a direct citation. Gopāla has turned Nīlakaṇṭha's more neutral and pluralist position to a more partisan purpose.

Nīlakaṇṭha was active in Banaras in the second half of the seventeenth century, and it is most likely that he knew the authors of the three texts or their cohorts personally. In his commentary he shows that he is aware of the dispute, and denounces as far too limited those who engage in it. As he puts it,

> Criticism of the [Vaiṣṇava] *Bhāgavata* or the [Śaiva] *Sutasaṃhitā* as being demonic forgeries because they set out a hierarchy of Viṣṇu and other deities, using the obstinate claims of worshippers that Viṣṇu is the ultimate while Śiva is a mere unliberated soul or vice versa, are based on not understanding the parameters of śāstric interpretation.[62]

And yet Nīlakaṇṭha does not seem particularly averse to the idea of controversy itself, for he then goes on a little later in the same comment to denounce the participants in it using some of the abuse that so dominated the language of the polemicists themselves.

> These mangey lowlife Vaiṣṇavas and Śaivas do not understand the language of variety used in the Purāṇas. The (lowlifes) are unaware of the Vedic statements about non-difference which point out the fault that lies in seeing difference between Śiva and Viṣṇu and that is described in the Smṛti literature as follows, "Those who have been misled by Hindu imposters are bewildered by the impression of difference when they see Brahmā, Kṛṣṇa and Rudra, and do not see them as one." They do not know the truth of the Śāstra that the one root cause gives rise to all effects, just as an actor takes on different forms. And accepting only one or other of the forms they criticize each other, making a great mutual ruckus, and hence as a result of the injury they do to the masters they are readying themselves only for hell.[63]

Conclusion

Arguments continued to be made that the Vaiṣṇava *Bhāgavata* was a forgery, but after Rāmāśrama's essay the text came increasingly to be accepted as a proper part of the literature of the Brahminical literary establishment. It is not that the pro-Vaiṣṇava arguments were necessarily better ones, so much as that they went on being made more relentlessly and more consistently, and took eventually a self-fulfilling form. The interest of the controversy here in retrospect has to do with the terms of the debate, in which the views and acceptance of prominent Advaitins in seventeenth century Banaras played such a role. Nīlakaṇṭha's criticism even of the very idea of partisanship was couched entirely in non-dualist terms. Śaṅkara's variety of non-dualism, as reformulated by Madhusūdana and others in the city, retained its position at the top of a notional hierarchy of views, and it is that philosophy or the prestige of the promoters of it that was invoked even by the Dvaitins and sectarians who participated in the argument.

As for the vehemence of the language in which it was transacted, we might try to put that down to how hard the feelings were. Even today there are incidents of shoes being thrown at the face, in a recent one the face of a US president. In the end, however, the vehement language appears to have been part of the stakes for which śāstrīs in Banaras played at that moment, for the best of praise (as in the *Kavīndracandrodaya*) while risking the rudest of abuse. Nīlakaṇṭha, even as he attempted to rise above what he saw as unenlightened bickering, could not avoid the idiom in which that bickering had been conducted. That perhaps is one more reason why one shouldn't attempt to avoid the philology.

List of some independent works in Sanskrit on the *Bhāgavata* controversy[64]

1. *Bhāgavataviṣayasvarūpaśaṅkānirāsatrayodaśa* of Puruṣottama Tīṛtha. Also called *Bhāgavatasvarūpaśaṅkānirāsatrayodaśa*. [V]*
2. *Durjanamukhacapeṭikā* of Bhānuji Dīkṣita, son of Bhaṭṭojī Dīkṣita, (Sannyāsi name: Rāmāśrama) Banaras, first half of the seventeenth century. Also called *Durjanacapeṭikā, Bhāgavatārṣānarṣatvavicāra,* and *Bhāgavatamaṇḍana*. [V]*
3. *Durjanamukha(mahā)capeṭikā* of Kāśīnātha Bhaṭṭa, son of Jayarāma Bhaṭṭa, son of Śivarāma, Banaras, mid-seventeenth century, author of more than fifty works. Also called *Bhāgavatadvayavyavasthā*. [D]*
4. *Durjanamukhapadmapāduka* anonymous, probably Banaras, mid-seventeenth century. [D]*
5. *Durjanakapolacapeṭikā* mentioned in next work. [D]
6. *Durjanarasanārgala* of Raghunātha, son of Bālakṛṣṇa, pupil of Bhāskara Rāya, eighteenth century. Ākhaṇḍalakheṭa, court of Rāma, in response to *Durjanakapolacapeṭikā* [V]
7. *Siddhāntadarpaṇa* of Baladeva Vidyābhūṣaṇa, early eighteenth century, Jaipur. [V]*
8. *Devībhāgavatasthiti* of Śaiva Nīlakaṇṭha, eighteenth century. Also called *Bhāgavatavyavasthiti*. [D]*
9. *Devībhāgavatavyavasthā* of Vidyātīrtha, eighteenth century. Also called *Devībhāgavatasthiti*. [D]*
10. *Pāṣaṇḍadhvaṃsanabhāskara* of Viśvanātha Siṃhadeva a prince who served Bāhādur Sītārāma Candra, Rewah, early nineteenth century. [V]
11. *Bhāgavatabhūṣaṇa* of Gopālācārya, Gopālācārya, son of Nārāyaṇācārya and Gaṅgā, grandson of Vāsudevācārya, Karahāṭaka, (Kṛṣṇā river, Sātāra district). [V]

Works of unconfirmed date[65]

Durjanamukhacapeṭikādisaṃgraha
Devībhāgavatakhaṇḍanapūrvakaviṣṇubhāgavatasthāpana
Bhāgavataprāmāṇyavicāra by Viśveśvaranātha. Also called *Durjanamukha-capeṭikā.*
Bhāgavatavāditoṣiṇī of Gaṇeśa [V]
Bhāgavatavyavasthākroḍapatra
Bhāgavataśaṅkānirāsa
Bhāgavataśaṅkānivāraṇamañjarī of Śivasahāya.
Bhāgavatasvarūpaśaṅkānirāsatrayodaśa by Śrīnātha.
Bhāgavatārṣānarṣatvavicāra of Vopadeva, son of Keśava Bhiṣak.
Bhāgavatārṣānarṣatvasaṃśaya
Śrīmadbhāgavatadevībhāgavatayor madhye kataradvyāsakṛtam iti vicāraḥ

Notes

1. For a fresh consideration of the definition of philology, Pollock 2009: 4.

2. In what follows all dates are given according to the Common Era. I refer to the Vaiṣnava *Bhāgavata* as such because as we shall see it is only one of two texts claiming to be the real or canonical *Bhāgavata Purāṇa.*

3. MSS: *Durjanamukhacapeṭikā* IO 3545 (accn. no. 846d), UPenn 2815 (Poleman 1387); *Durjanamukhamahācapeṭikā* IO 3367 (accn. no. 1301a), UPenn 2814 (Poleman 1386), UPenn 749.2 (Poleman 1385); IO 3546 (accn. no. 846c). More manuscripts are listed in NCC. The *Durjanamukhamahācapeṭikā* is called simply the *Durjanamukhacapeṭikā* in the colophons of the four manuscripts that are listed here. NCC notes an alternative title: the *Bhāgavatavyavasthā* or *Bhāgavatadvayavyavasthā*. But since the third work, the *Durjanamukhapadmapādukā* refers to Kāśīnatha's work as the *-mahācapeṭikā*, i.e. the "big smack" not just the "smack," I will use that name here, in order to avoid confusion. Note also that Burnouf has put the *-mahācapeṭikā* last in the sequence of his translations, even though, as he points out, it is cited by the (historically) third work, the *-pādukā*. This is because the *-pādukā* responds much more directly and completely to the first work.

4. Manuscripts of all three were acquired, probably commissioned, by H.T. Colebrooke, who read and annotated them. It was the manuscripts from Colebrooke's collection that ended up in the India Office library, and were used by Burnouf later. See also Colebrooke 1805: 467. Wilson 1840 : xxvii-xxx.

5. Burnouf 1840: LIX-XCVI.

6. Burnouf 1840: LVI.

7. Burnouf 1840: LIX.

8. For a survey of the bibliography on the history and distinctive characteristics of the Vaiṣṇava *Bhāgavata*, see Rocher 1986: 138-51.

9. Meier 1931.

10. Hardy 1983, where he demonstrates the influence on the text of the Tamil devotional poetry of the Ālvārs.

11. In a similar way, Muslims say that while Muhammad performed no miracles, the *Qur'ān* itself—in its unique language and form—constitutes the miracle.

12. The discussion comes at the end of the commentary to the first verse, beginning *gāyatryā prārambhena ca ...* and ending ... *ata eva bhāgavataṃ nāmānyad ity api na śaṅkanīyam*.

13. Rocher 1986: 144-49; Sanyal 1969.

14. See Appendix 1 for a partial list of independent works from the early modern period and later that treat the problem.

15. This was the view accepted by Colebrooke, and after him Burnouf. On the other hand, Winternitz, and R.C. Hazra among others accepted the claim of the Vaiṣṇava *Bhāgavata*. Sanyal 1969: 158.

16. For a contemporary assessment of the controversy that finds in favor of the *Devī Bhāgavata*, see Sanyal 1969.

17. It should be noted here that the three proofs offered by Śrīdhara all fall under the first two of these headings: that according to the *Matsya Purāṇa* the true *Bhāgavata* begins with the gāyatrī and consists in brahmavidyā; that another Purāṇa says it consists of 18,000 verses and twelve skandhas, and contains the slaying of Vṛtra and the Hayagrīva Brahmavidyā; and that the *Padma Purāṇa* describes it as uttered by Śuka.

18. Colophon: *iti śrīrāmāśramaviracitā durjanamukhacapeṭikā samāptā*. In some texts his name appears as Rāmacandrāśrama or Rāmāśramayati. Gode 1944.

19. For a study of Bhaṭṭoji and his family, together with a compendious and recent bibliography, see Bronkhorst 2005.

20. Colophon: *iti śrīmad-bhaḍopanāmaka-jayarāmabhaṭṭasuta-vārāṇasīgarbhasambhava-dakṣiṇācāramatapravartaka-kāśīnāthabhaṭṭa-viracitā durjanamukhacapeṭikā samāptā*. All citations of this text are from UPenn 2814 (Poleman 1386). Some passages in this manuscript are not translated by Burnouf, and it would of course be worthwhile to establish proper editions of all of these texts.

21. NCC 4: 129-32. Titles include the *Aṣṭādaśapurāṇavyavasthā*, *Vāmācāramatakhaṇḍana*, and the *Śaivasiddhāntamaṇḍana*.

22. Colophon (cited from IO catalogue): *iti durjanamukhapadmapādukā samāptā.*

23. See Burnouf 1840: LXXXI. Citations from this text will unfortunately have to be drawn from Burnouf's translation.

24. *kiṃ ca cirakālair bopadevādibhyaḥ prāktanaiś citśukācāryaiḥ* <sic> *ṭīkāpraṇayanaṃ na sambhavati* (ff.1v-2r.) Note that the text offers a peculiar spelling of Citsukha's name as Citśuka, though no author with that name is known to us. Presumably the connection with Śuka the narrator of the Vaiṣṇava *Bhāgavata* is intended. A further point to remark here is that there is no extant manuscript of a commentary on the *Bhāgavata* attributed to Citsukha the Advaitin author of the thirteenth century, who was an approximate contemporary of Bopadeva.

25. *kiṃ ca mādhvena vijayadhvajena bhāgavate ṭīkā kṛtā tatrādāv "aṣṭau ṭīkā avalokye"ty uktaṃ "hanumaṭṭīkāṃ śaṃkarācāryaṭīkāṃ ce"ty uktaṃ. tat kathaṃ saṃgacchatāṃ? bopadevasya pañcaśatī saṃvatsarāṇāṃ vyatītā śaṃkarācāryāṇāṃ saptadaśaśatī vyatikrāntā* (f. 2r). Burnouf was unaware of the work of Vijayadhvaja Tīrtha, who was indeed a Mādhva who wrote a *Padaratnāvalī* on the Vaiṣṇava *Bhāgavata*. However it should be noted that the passages of Vijayadhvaja's commentary directly cited by Rāmāśrama are not to be found in the published version of the Padaratnāvalī's lengthy comment on verse one.

26. Burnouf 1840: LXXVI.

27. *ācāryādiṭīkā kuto na pravartata iti cet kaṭhinatvād adhikārābhāvāt citśukīvat* <sic> (f. 2r).

28. *apayya*<sic>*dīkṣitaiḥ śivatattvavivekādau saṃmatitvena bhāgavataṃ svīkṛtaṃ. madhusūdanasarasvatībhir bhaktirasāyane bhāgavataṃ vyākhyātaṃ. vidyamānaiḥ pūrṇendrabrahmendrādisarasvatyādibhir*<sic> *bhāgavataṃ stūyate. bhaṭṭojidīkṣītair bhāgavataṃ svīkṛtaṃ. tadapekṣayā ko 'yam adhikaḥ paṇḍito yo nindet bhāgavataṃ?* (ff. 2r-2v.)

29. Potter 1983: 378. The last title is not to be confused with the more successful *Vedāntaparibhāṣā* of Dharmarāja.

30. NCC XII: 180. Brahmendra was the disciple of Devendra Sarasvatī, but also went by the sobriquet Vāṇīgīr. Raghavan 1940: 163.

31. Sharma and Patkar 1939: ix. This must have occurred in the 1630s or 1640s. Brahmendra praised Kavīndrācārya among other things for being the delight of all the princes and even the (Mughal) emperor through his many accomplishments: *sārvabhauma-prabhṛti-sakalamahīpāla-saṃtoṣāvaha-sakalakalāvirājamāneṣu.*

32. Raghavan 1940: 163. For example in verses 178 and 189, that is in the fifth verse of the *Kavīndrāṣṭaka* that was produced by a collective of residents of Banaras, *brahmendra-pūrṇendra-yatīndravṛndamukhyair aśeṣair abhinandyamānaḥ*, etc., or again in the seventh verse of that same contribution, *amunā kavīndranāmnā śrībrahmendrasvāmyanugṛhītena*, etc. Sharma and Patkar 1939: 24-25. See also verse 12. No other figure receives the same sort of treatment in this anthology, except of course for Kavīndrācārya. Kavīndrācārya meanwhile composed verses in praise of Brahmendra in his *Kavīndrakalpadruma*. Raghavan 1940: 163.

33. O'Hanlon forthcoming.

34. Gode 1942. This Nṛsiṃhāśrama is not to be confused with the Advaitin author of the previous century, however, whom incidentally Brahmendra invokes among others in the line of Advaitin teachers at the beginning of his *Advaitāmṛta.*

35. Aside from the works of Appayya and Madhusūdana, note the titles of the works of Brahmendra and Pūrṇendra mentioned above. There is no hint of interest on Rāmāśrama's part in appealing to those who belonged to one of the Vaiṣṇava or Śaiva sampradāyas.

36. Tangasvāmiśarmā 1980: 282-88.

37. Burnouf 1840: LXXVIII.

38. Burnouf 1840: LXXVIII.

39. There was also of course another Vardhamāna Upādhyāya, a logician and son of Gaṅgeśa, who flourished in the thirteenth century. On the later Vardhamāna, the author of the *Smṛtitattvaviveka* among other works, see Kane 1975: 1218-19.

40. Bronkhorst 2005: 11-15.

41. *anyac ca. aṣṭādaśapurāṇakāriṇī vedasaṃmitā bhāratakāriṇī vāṇī bhinnā. vaiṣṇavabhāgavatasya stavyarūpavāṇī bhinnā. ataḥ vaiṣṇavabhāgavataṃ*

purāṇāntargataṃ na. aṣṭādaśapurāṇakāriṇī yā vāṇī saiva devībhāgavatasya vāṇī. ataḥ purāṇāntargataṃ devībhāgavataṃ (f. 4v).

42. *yat tu "vyāsakṛtapurāṇāntarastha-ślokānupūrvīsādṛśyam bhāgavataślokeṣu na dṛśyate" ity uktam atrāpy ucyate, sakaladharmaśāstretihāsādyanantaraṃ vyutpattidaśāyāṃ parama-premnā bhāgavataṃ kṛtam. atas teṣu purāṇāntar<a?> vailakṣaṇyam anumīyate. yathā śaṅkarācāryakṛtaṣoḍaśabhāṣyeṣu anyabhāṣya-sādṛśyaṃ śārīrakabhāṣye na dṛśyate. tat kiṃ śaṅkarācāryakṛtaṃ na bhavati? tathā bhāgavatam api. karmaṇaś ca nādarāt prītyabhāvān na tatra sauṣṭhavam.* (f. 3r-3v).

43. Burnouf 1840: LXXXII-LXXXIII.

44. *vāmamārgagāḥ bhāgavataṃ dviṣanti. "viśantu śīvadīkṣāyāṃ yatra daivaṃ surāsavam" ityādivāmamārgagasya bhāgavate ninditatvāt. kiṃ ca vāmamārgagā viṣṇum api nindanti. "viṣṇor nāma na gṛhṇīyān na spṛśet tulasīdalam" ityādinā. vedam api nindanti. "trayo vedasya kartāro munibhaṇḍaniśācarā" iti vadantaḥ. māṃsāśino bhāgavataṃ nindanti. "na dadyād āmiṣaṃ śrāddhe na cādyād dharmatattvavid" ityādinā māṃsabhakṣaṇasya bhāgavate niṣiddhatvāt* (f. 2v).

45. *dvaitavādino 'pi bhāgavataṃ dviṣanti. ... kiṃ ca te vedam api dviṣanti. ... ityādivedaviru-ddhārthapratipādakatvāt pākhaṇḍaviśeṣā eva te* (f. 2v).

46. *kiṃ ca mādhavasarasvatīsamaye kena cit paṇḍitena "bhāgavatam apramāṇam" ity uktam. tadā svā<mi>bhir uktam "ayam jārajo bhaviṣyatīti vicāraṇīyam." tadā paṇḍitair vicārite "sa golaka" iti niścitam* (f. 3r).

47. *'vaiṣṇikās* <sic - read *'vaidikās* or *vaiṣṇavās*> *tu śrīmaddevībhāgataṃ dviṣanti ... kiṃ ca pāñcarātrādimantramārgagāḥ parāśaktiṃ api nindanti. dvaitavādino 'pi śrīmaddevībhāgavatam dviṣanti "te jārajā" iti* (f. 4v).

48. Burnouf 1840: LXXX.

49. Burnouf 1840: LXXXIII.

50. colophon: *iti śrīnārāyaṇapārāyaṇa-śrīkṛṣṇātīra-śrīkarahāṭavāsi-vāsudevācārya-suta-nārāyaṇācāryāṅgaja-gaṅgāgarbhaja-gopālācāryaviracite śrībhāgavatabhūṣaṇe* etc. *Bhāgavatabhūṣaṇa*: 28r. The location suggests that the family were Karhāḍa Brahmins.

51. NCC knows of four, perhaps eight manuscripts of the *Bhāgavatabhūṣaṇa*, two of which are south Indian, but only one is dated (SB 71253), and this date is Saṃvat 1935. It is therefore possible that he is a figure of the next century, and perhaps the same person as the Gopālācārya who is the author of the *Kuladevatābhūṣaṇa* and the *Viṭṭhalabhūṣaṇa*, both published in Bombay in 1887.

52. See the description of RASB 3681 (Shāstrī 1928: 385-86), where Haraprasad Shastri counted more than eighty authors and texts cited.

53. It begins *dvitīyas tv asiddhaḥ* on page 7v and continues to *lakṣaśaḥ koṭiśo 'nyanibandheṣu ca purāṇatvenodāhṛteḥ*, on p. 8v.

54. For example see the third author on "bhārgava" transcribed as "bhāgavata" Burnouf 1840: LXXVII-LXXVIII.

55. "*grantho 'ṣṭādaśasāhasraḥ śrīmadbhāgavatābhidhaḥ | pañcatriṃśottarādhyāyatr iśatīyukta īśvarī"ti kāśīmathurājhāśīpuṇyagrāmādāv upalabhyamāne gaurītantre ca spaṣṭam uktatvāc ca. Bhāgavatabhūṣaṇa* 13v.

56. e.g. *na cedaṃ bhāgavatamāhātmyam pādmanāmnā kalpitam iti vācyam. ākāśī-rāmeśvarīyeṣu padmapurāṇapustakeṣu sarveṣūpalaMBhāt. Bhāgavatabhūṣaṇa* 3r.

57. *Bhāgavatabhūṣaṇa* 9v.

58. "*kṛṣṇas tu bhagavān svayaṃ sitakṛṣṇakeśāv" ityādibhāgavatīyapadyeṣu parasparaviruddheṣu "gaṅgāyamunājalasvāminav" ityādikliṣṭavyākhyāna-* etc. *Bhāgavatabhūṣaṇa* 9r.

59. *pauruṣeyatve niścite pāṣaṇḍaśaivavāmādyair vedamārgagāḥ kalau yuge iti vijaya-dhvajasaṃmata-daśamaskandhīyaśrīmadbhāgavatavacanabodhita-durmārgatvam asahamānaiḥ pāṣaṇḍajaṅgamādiśaivatāntrikavāmādibhir utprekṣitasya bopa-devakṛtam iti pralāpasya prāmāṇikatvād iti cen na. Bhāgavatabhūṣaṇa* 6r-6v.

60. *sa cāyaṃ hemādrir dvādaśādhikadvādaśaśata 1212 śakodbhava-dākṣiṇātyālandī-grāmastha-jñāneśvarasaṃjñaka-bhagavadbhakta-kṛtagītāvyākhyānottarakāliko hemāḍapantanāmnā prākṛtabhāṣayā prasiddhas ....* . Hemādri was a Karhāḍa Brahmin and our author is from a family from Karhāda, so perhaps mention of this Maharashtrian evidence is not surprising.

61. *ke cit tu ... gītā tu yathā kāśīkṣetraṃ vāmanapurāṇa-lakṣmīsaṃhitā-tristhalīsetu-paryālocanayā vaiṣṇavam iti vaiṣṇavā vadanti, skandapurāṇa-śivarahasyādi-paryālocanayā śaivam iti śaivā vadanti, tathā jñānapradhāneti jñānavādino bhaktipradhāneti bhaktā iti tadudāhṛtir ity āhuḥ. ata eva śrīmatbhāgavatam upak-ramya viṣṇudveṣāt pauruṣeyaṃ tāmasaṃ ceti ke cana vadantīty ādiparvādau vili-lekha caturdharaḥ. Bhāgavatabhūṣaṇa* 10v.

62. *tena "viṣṇuḥ sarvottamaḥ śivo jīvaḥ. śivaḥ sarvottamo viṣṇur jīvaḥ" ity upāsakānām āgraho viṣṇvādy-utkramapratipādaka-śrībhāgavata-sutasaṃhitādīnām anārṣatvāsuratvādivacanair dūṣaṇaṃ ca śāstramaryādānavabodhamūlam eva | Bhāratabhāvadīpa* on Ādiparvan 1.23.

63. *tam imaṃ paurāṇaṃ bhāṣābhedam ajānantaḥ pāmarāḥ śaivavaiṣṇavāpasadā "brahmāṇaṃ keśavaṃ rudraṃ bhedabhāvena mohitāḥ | paśyanty ekaṃ na jānanti pākhaṇḍopahatā janā" iti tatraiva smaryamāṇaṃ śivaviṣṇvor bhedadarśane doṣam udāhṛtyābhedaśrutīś cāpaśyanto mūlakāraṇam evāntyāt* <sic> *kāryān naṭa iva tattadrūpeṇa bhāsata iti śāstratattvam ajānanto 'nyatararūpaparigraheṇetaraṃ nindantaḥ parasparakalahāyamāṇāḥ svāmidrohān narakāyaiva sajjante ity alaṃ. Bhāratabhāvadīpa* on Ādiparvan 1.23.

64. The mark * indicates that the text is discussed in Sanyal 1969. A [D] indicates that it argues for the *Devī Bhāgavata* as the "true" *Bhāgavata*, while a [V] indicates that it supports the *Vaiṣṇava Bhāgavata*. There are also longer works in which the controversy comes up as a topic, but those works are not listed here. Aside from Sanyal the list relies on NCC and on some of the descriptive catalogues of manuscripts mentioned there.

65. Some of these may be alternative titles to works already listed.

Bibliography

Bhāgavatabhūṣaṇa of Gopālācārya. 2nd edn. Banaras: Vidyodaya Publishers, 1874.

Bhāratabhāvadīpa of Nīlakaṇṭha Caturdhara. Edited by Ramachandrashastri Kimjavadekar. Poona: Chitrashala Press, 1929.

Bronkhorst, Johannes. 2005. "Bhaṭṭoji Dīkṣita on Sphoṭa." *Journal of Indian Philosophy* 33: 3-41.

Burnouf, M. Eugène. 1840. *Le Bhâgavata Purâna, ou Histoire poétique de Krichna traduit et publié par M. Eugène Burnouf.* Vol. 1. Collection orientale. Manuscrits inédits de la Bibliothèque nationale. Paris: Imprimerie royale.

Chandler, James, and Arnold Davidson, eds. 2009. *The Fate of the Disciplines.* Special number, *Critical Inquiry* 35 (4).

Colebrooke, H.T. 1805. "On the Védas, or Sacred Writings of the Hindus." *Asiatick Researches* 8: 369-476.

Gode, P.K. 1942. "The Identification of Gosvāmi Nṛsiṃhāśrama of Dara Shukoh's Sanskrit Letter with Brahmendra Sarasvatī of the Kavīndracandrodaya (between 1628 and 1658)." *Adyar Library Bulletin* 6 (3): 172-77.

____. 1944. "A critical Survey of the Name-sakes of Rāmāśrama, the Author of Durjanamukha-capeṭikā between 1600 and 1677." *Pracyavāṇī* 1: 2-8.

Hardy, Friedhelm. 1983. *Viraha-bhakti: The Early History of Kṛṣṇa Devotion in South India.* Delhi: Oxford University Press.

Kane, P.V. 1975. *History of Dharmaśāstra*, vol. 1, pt. 2. 2nd edn. Poona: Bhandarkar Oriental Research Institute.

Law, Bimala Churn, ed. 1940. *D.R. Bhandarkar Felicitation Volume.* Calcutta: Indian Research Institute.

Meier, F.J. 1931. "Der Archaismus in der Sprache des Bhāgavata-Purāṇa." *Zeitschrift für Indologie und Iranistik* 8: 33-79.

O'Hanlon, Rosalind. Forthcoming. "Letters Home: Banaras Pundits and the Maratha Regions in Early Modern India." *Modern Asian Studies.*

Pollock, Sheldon. 2009. "Future Philology? The Fate of a Soft Science in a Hard World." In Chandler and Davidson.

Potter, Karl. 1983. *Encyclopedia of Indian Philosophies*: Bibliography. 2nd edn. Delhi: Motilal Banarsidass.

Raghavan, V. 1940. "Kavindracarya Sarasvati." In Law 1940: 159-65.

Rocher, Ludo. 1986. *The Purāṇas*. Wiesbaden.

Sanyal, Nirmal Chandra. 1969. "The Devī-Bhāgavata as the Real Bhāgavata." *Purāṇa* 11 (1): 127-58.

Sharma, Har Dutt, and M.M. Patkar. 1939, eds. *Kavīndracandrodaya*. Poona: Oriental Book Agency.

Shāstrī, Haraprasād. 1928. *A Descriptive Catalogue of Sanskrit Manuscripts in the Government Collection under the care of the Asiatic Society*, Volume Five, Purāṇa Manuscripts. Calcutta: Asiatic Society.

Tangasvāmiśarmā, R. 1980. *Advaitavedāntasāhityetihāsakośaḥ*. Madras: Madras University.

Wilson, H.H., tr. 1840. *The Vishńu Puráṇa, a System of Hindu Mythology and Tradition.* London: Oriental Translation Fund Committee.

What was Bhaṭṭa Nāyaka Saying? The Hermeneutical Transformation of Indian Aesthetics

SHELDON POLLOCK

Undoubtedly the greatest loss to the student of Indian aesthetics is Bhaṭṭa Nāyaka's *Hṛdayadarpaṇa* (*HD*), the "Heart's Mirror." Long thought to be a commentary on the *Nāṭyaśāstra*, the *HD* was more likely an independent treatise at once modeled on and critical of Ānandavardhana's mid-ninth century *Sahṛdayāloka*, "Light for the Lover of Literature" (some have plausibly suggested that the actual name of Bhaṭṭa Nāyaka's treatise was *Sahṛdayadarpaṇa*, "Mirror for the Lover of Literature").[1] The text seems to have disappeared by the twelfth or even eleventh century; the great literary theorist Mahima Bhaṭṭa (*c.* 1025) regrets he had been unable "to look into the *Mirror*" before undertaking his critique of *dhvani*. Thereafter no one appears to have had direct access to the book.[2] Our principal guide to its argument is the exposition of Dhanaṃjaya and Dhanika (in the fourth chapter of their works, the *Daśarūpaka* and *Avaloka*, respectively, both *c.* 975), who while never naming Bhaṭṭa Nāyaka offer virtually a systematic restatement of his doctrines, as I try to demonstrate here.[3] Aside from these two works, we must piece together his thought from the scattered citations preserved by his critics—and if there is a fate worse than this, for a paradigm-shifting scholar, it is hard to imagine what it would be. But the fragments and criticisms are enough to suggest that, however tired may be the idiom of paradigm shift, it is also hard to imagine a more appropriate description for Bhaṭṭa Nāyaka's role in the 1500-year-long tradition of Sanskrit aesthetics.

Beyond the fact that Bhaṭṭa Nāyaka wrote in Kashmir sometime between Ānandavardhana (*c.* 850), whom he critiques, and Abhinavagupta (*c.* 1000), who critiques him, we know little about him. Unlike some earlier scholars I believe it certain that the *Rājataraṅgiṇī* makes reference to our author, given the date (the reign of Śaṅkaravarman, 883-902) and the rarity of the name Nāyaka, but also especially in view of the combination of talents Kalhaṇa takes pains to emphasize: "The king put in charge of his two new Śiva temples a Brahman named Nāyaka, who was at once learned in the four Vedas and himself a veritable temple for poets, the tribe of Sarasvatī."[4] Not only was Bhaṭṭa Nāyaka's a stunningly original voice on literary matters, he was also a remarkably inventive scholar of Vedic hermeneutics: stray references in later critics confirm what the surviving fragments clearly suggest, that he had close affiliations with the tradition of Mīmāṃsā, which had begun to powerfully transform Indian literary theory by the middle of the ninth century.[5] Bhaṭṭa Nāyaka did not just borrow a term here or there from Mīmāṃsā, however, as scholars like Ānandavardhana did; he borrowed, and in doing so rethought, an entire conceptual scheme.

In order to grasp the extent of Bhaṭṭa Nāyaka's intellectual revolution in aesthetics in general and in the theory of rasa in particular, we need to have some picture of the aesthetic system he inherited. While most of its essentials are well known to students of the field, since they are tirelessly rehearsed in the scholarly literature (largely on the basis of Mammaṭa's mid-eleventh-century summation in *Kāvyaprakāśa* 4), two closely related points that condition our understanding of Bhaṭṭa Nāyaka's orientation toward this system are rarely made in the way they ought to be. The first addresses the seemingly minor question of the locus or substratum of rasa (*rasāśraya*), but actually concerns the whole analytical focus of aesthetics. As I tried to show on the basis of Bhoja's *Śṛṅgāraprakāśa* (*c.* 1050), which offers a grand synthesis of the "classical" system or normal science,[6] all writers prior to the tenth century conceived of rasa in the first (and often in the last) instance as a phenomenon pertaining to the characters, not the spectators (their attention to the actor and the poet are less consequential). In this conception, rasa meant the emotional response in the hero or heroine, and accordingly, the task of rasa analysis from the time of the *Nāṭyaśāstra* up to and including Ānandavardhana, was to understand the components into which the complex phenomena of literature could be analyzed as contributing to this emotional reality effect. The question to which their aesthetic treatises were in part answers was, How is it even possible that an emotion can come to inhabit the literary work?

Intimately connected with this formalist orientation toward textual procedures was the second question, How do we come to know about this emotion? For the earliest thinkers like Bhaṭṭa Lollaṭa (early ninth century?)—and this is undoubtedly the way the core of Bharata's *Nāṭyaśāstra* understands things[7]—rasa is something that "comes into being" in the characters (the *utpattivāda*); how the audience perceives this aesthetic emotion was too obvious a question even to place on the discursive table. The ninth-century *Nāṭyaśāstra* commentator Śrī Śaṅkuka (fl. 840) was the first to argue from the spectators' point of view but his doctrine, too, remains essentially text-centered and not reader-centered: rasa (i.e. in the character) cannot be directly perceived but can only be inferred from the imitation that is drama (*anumitipakṣa*), and it is with this imitation, and not with the viewer's inference, that Śrī Śaṅkuka was preoccupied. Ānandavardhana, too, is completely silent on how the reader knows of rasa or experiences it. He is concerned only with textual, even formalistic, processes when arguing that rasa is something that can never be directly expressed but only suggested or implied (*vyañjanāpakṣa*).

All these epistemological arguments, it seems to me, presuppose the ontology of rasa just indicated, namely, that it is, in the first instance, a phenomenon internal to the literary work, whether textual or performative, a position that seems to have maintained itself into the late tenth century, as Kuntaka's *Vakroktijīvita* shows.[8] The postulate that rasa is "inferred", for example, makes sense only if we think of both its ontological locus and its epistemological focus as being external to the audience doing the inferring (you do not "infer" that you as spectator are feeling rasa).[9] As for rasa's being something "suggested" (*vyañjanā*), Dhanaṃjaya and Dhanika, who under Bhaṭṭa Nāyaka's influence adopted a radically different viewpoint, leave no doubt that the very idea of suggestion becomes impossible if rasa is located—as they insist on locating it—in the reader and not in the character:

> (Dhanaṃjaya) Rasa belongs to the spectator experiencing the rasa, and to him alone, because he is alive and present. It does not belong to the character.
>
> (Dhanika) ... All this being the case, the view that rasas can be the object of "manifestation" stands refuted. For an entity can only be manifested by something after it has been brought into being by something else: a pot, for example, can only be manifested by a light when it has already been produced by the clay. It is certainly not possible for an entity to be brought into existence by the very things that are supposed to manifest it, and this at one and the same moment.

All this indicates, they conclude, that, since rasa is something that must be seen as pertaining to the *spectators*, we need a new epistemology appropriate to that new ontology.[10]

Such, in brief, was the conceptual field of rasa when Bhaṭṭa Nāyaka entered onto it, and which he proceeded to reshape in every particular. At the heart of his critique of traditional aesthetics was the concern with redirecting attention away from the process by which emotion is engendered in and made accessible through the literary work, and toward the spectator's or reader's own subjective experience of this emotion.[11] And just as, by this move, answers to superseded questions were themselves superseded, so new answers were required for new, completely unanticipated questions (foremost among them, as we will see, the moral status of the *ālambanavibhāva*, or foundational factor, when the locus of rasa is shifted from the character to the spectator). And it was to make better sense of what actually occurs in this experience that he turned to Mīmāṃsā theory, and transformed it into a literary hermeneutics.

2.

Such, at least, is the story of Bhaṭṭa Nāyaka I believe I can tell. But certainty is elusive when the full citation record of his work is so pitiably small (I count twelve authentic verses, two dubious, three very brief prose passages, and one more extended; see appendix), and often so obscure, even when we supplement this with exegeses that bear the full impress of Bhaṭṭa Nāyaka's influence like the *Daśarūpaka* and *Avaloka*. How difficult it has proven to reconstruct his thinking with any real coherence is abundantly in evidence in both modern and premodern accounts, as one example from each should suffice to demonstrate.[12] The most accomplished recent translation of a work on Sanskrit aesthetics, which also offers an account of the early tradition as a whole, summarizes Bhaṭṭa Nāyaka's central literary-hermeneutical concept, *bhāvanā*, as follows: "Bhaṭṭanāyaka then applied the [Mīmāṃsā] term to poetry as the *aesthetic efficacy* of a particular combination of determinants and consequents. This aesthetic *bhāvanā*, he claimed, has the effect of universalizing the determinants and other factors, so that they may bring about or realize a *rasa*. Upon the realization of the *rasa*, a third stage of the aesthetic process begins, namely enjoyment (*bhoga*), which Bhaṭṭanāyaka regarded as springing from a third semantic power, *bhogakṛttva* [*sic*] (enjoyment-efficacy)."[13] While there be little entirely wrong here (aside from the curious notion that *bhoga/bhogīkṛttva* constitutes a "semantic power"), there is also nothing that makes much sense (why just those two aesthetic elements? how do they exert efficacy? what is the connection of "efficacy" with "universalizing" the elements?). But consider now the assessment of Jagannātha Paṇḍitarāja, the greatest literary theorist of early-modern India. When he claims that rasa arises for Bhaṭṭa Nāyaka only when the power of *abhidhā* (which Jagannātha takes to mean denotation) has been "crippled" and the various narrated entities (e.g., Duḥṣyanta, Śakuntalā, place, time, their ages, and concrete situations) thereby "commonalized" (*sādhāraṇīkṛta-*);[14] when he proclaims, "The only difference between Bhaṭṭa Nāyaka's thought and that of Abhinavagupta is that the former accepts 'reproductive capacity' (*bhāvakatva*); 'experientialization' (*bhogakṛttva* [*sic*]), however, is no different from manifestation (*vyañjanā*), and the rest of their doctrine is completely identical,"[15] his account, so far as I can judge, is astonishingly wrong in every particular.

It will become clear that for Bhaṭṭa Nāyaka, *abhidhā* does not have its usual sense of direct denotation, but signifies a language function far more comprehensive and by no means transcended ("crippled") in the aesthetic process but continuously essential to it. Furthermore, given that Bhaṭṭa Nāyaka redirected attention to rasa reception, that mysterious process by which the reader experiences the emotions of the literary work, the idea of *vyañjanā* as a mechanism for rasa was rendered irrelevant. He states his position unequivocally: "As for the other process called 'implicature' (*dhvani*), which consists of manifestation, even were it proven to be different from the other two [i.e. *abhidhā* and *lakṣaṇā*], it would only be a component of literature, not its essential form" (appendix #9).[16] Then, too, not only did Abhinavagupta fully accept *bhāvakatva*, taking it from Bhaṭṭa Nāyaka's work as he took so much else, but he placed the concept at the forefront of his reconstruction of aesthetics. In fact, by a curious fate, it is only through the appropriation of his critic, I want to suggest, that we are finally able to get to the heart of Bhaṭṭa Nāyaka's aesthetic insight. This will become clear once we have some sense of the basic ideas of his theory, beginning with his reexamination of the ontology and epistemology of rasa.

3.

Bhaṭṭa Nāyaka's critique of earlier views on where rasa exists and how we know it is preserved in Abhinavagupta's two literary-theoretical works and commentators on the brief précis offered in Mammaṭa's *Kāvyaprakāśa* (especially the oldest, Māṇikyacandra). Because of the celebrity of these sources, much of the critique is reasonably well known, but it is still worth recapitulating. First, Bhaṭṭa Nāyaka argues, rasa can neither actually come into being nor be the content of a normal perceptual experience whether direct or indirect (that is, through inference).[17] If rasa were actually produced and hence perceptible, it would have to be perceived as being in someone else or in oneself. If it were perceived as external to the perceiving subject, as present in, say, the actor, then it could not be a "taste" (that is, something experienced); it would be an object, like a pot, about which one would be emotionally indifferent. Again, if the spectator perceived the rasa externally (let alone if it actually came into being), he would be expected to be absorbed in one or another state of mind—shame, disgust, yearning—that one would feel on glimpsing with one's own eyes the love-making of the actual people involved, Rāma and Sītā say, and this could not possibly be a rasa experience.

If, on the other hand, rasa were perceived as internal to oneself, a range of additional problems arises. First, in the case of the tragic rasa, one would feel actual pain, and never again go to the theater to see sad plays. Second, it makes no sense that a character like Sītā could be a foundational factor (*ālambanavibhāva*) for the spectator enabling him to perceive the rasa in himself; she is a factor of that sort only for another character, Rāma. To be sure, her being loved is a property shared in common with the spectator's own wife, but the fact that the particular character per se cannot be what stimulates the spectator's own latent disposition of desire in order to function as a foundational factor is demonstrated precisely in the case of Sītā, who is a royal (or divine) being: the spectator surely has no awareness of remembering his own beloved in the midst of a description of the queen (or deity), since sexual love for her is entirely inappropriate. In the case of some other rasas, however, such as the heroic (Rāma's building the bridge to cross the ocean, for example), even the possibility of perceiving the rasa in oneself through the functioning of a commonly shared property is ruled out: there is no stable emotion the spectator shares in common with Rāma. And one cannot have any memory of Rāma's energy (the stable emotion of the heroic rasa) empowering him to cross the ocean, because one never had a perception of him in the first place to ground that memory; nor can one be said to have "perceived" Rāma by some other means of valid knowledge, say testimony or inference, in order to provide a basis for one's memory, since such a mediated perception would not provide any experience of rasa. Dhanaṃjaya summarizes the whole critique and reconstruction in two *kārikās*:

> That same entity [the stable emotion] is called rasa, because it is something that is savored. Rasa belongs to the spectator experiencing the rasa (*rasika*), and to him alone, because he is alive and present. It does not belong to the character, because (1) he is no longer alive and present; (2) the ultimate aim of literature cannot pertain to the character; (3) we would otherwise have the absurd situation of the spectator being overcome with shame, jealousy, passion, or hatred—just as if he had seen a man in everyday life in the embrace of his beloved—or else have a mere indifferent apprehension.[18]

Bhaṭṭa Nāyaka's reconstruction, it is clear, starts from foundational, if previously unacknowledged, problems of the process by which emotion in the literary text was thought to be engendered and known. All the old epistemologies and their associated ontologies fail to escape basic contradictions; an entirely new conceptualization is needed of how literary emotion is experienced and, more importantly, by whom. The core of this reconceptualization is equally basic. It is to a large degree a function of the method by which we understand textuality as such, and literary textuality in particular, to produce its effects. And for Bhaṭṭa Nāyaka, this method was Mīmāṃsā.

We have already seen that Bhaṭṭa Nāyaka was known as an adherent of the school of scriptural hermeneutics, a fact that his critics sometimes used to dismiss his views (*jaiminir anusṛtaḥ* "He is simply following the founder of Mīmāṃsā here," says Abhinavagupta as a retort in one such dispute).[19] Mīmāṃsā's views on the nature of discourse were the most sophisticated of any in the premodern world; only recently have Western scholars begun to make real sense of its complexity, and many aspects await serious clarification. But there are some principles central to Bhaṭṭa Nāyaka's transformation of aesthetic thought that we can grasp without too much difficulty.

For Mīmāṃsā, all language, a fortiori scriptural language, is action-oriented, but the idea that language use as such consists not only of speech that embodies action but speech that produces action was widely accepted outside the domain of Vedic discourse analysis as well. Dhanika is no doubt again following Bhaṭṭa Nāyaka (and standard Mīmāṃsā thinking) when he states, "Every sentence, whether human or divine, is directed toward action; otherwise it would be utterly worthless, like the babble of a madman."[20] But Bhoja, too, argues even more explicitly that all sentences eventuate in commands or prohibitions, whether or not imperatives are used: "A sentence like 'It is noon' means one should have lunch; 'There are stones in the river' means do not bathe there."[21] According to Mīmāṃsā, Vedic statements will thus always resolve into a command to perform (or avoid) some act, and it developed a general theory of this sort of language behavior that they called *bhāvanā*, "production".

No concept is more central to Mīmāṃsā than *bhāvanā*, and perhaps no concept has been worse served by modern Indological scholarship.[22] This is the case in part because of the very magnitude and complexity of the traditional analyses and in part because of Mīmāṃsā's own remarkable disagreements about precisely what *bhāvanā* is and how it works, not just among Kumārila, Prabhākara, and Maṇḍana Miśra, but among the Bhāṭṭas themselves over a very long period (Khaṇḍadeva [fl. 1650] shows that the internal dispute lasted a thousand years). The set of questions here is large and complex because the issue, the relationship between knowledge (or linguistic conceptualization) and action, goes to the heart of scriptural understanding.

When action is not spontaneous but compelled it requires instigation (*pravartanā* or *preraṇā*), which is the intention of a conscious being. In the case of the authorless Veda, this intention is something unique; it is called "expression" (*abhidhā*) and is inherent in language. That "expression" is enunciated by the verbal mood, paradigmatically the optative or imperative, and is called *śābdī* (or *śabda-* or *śābda-*) *bhāvanā* (or *abhidhābhāvanā*), "modal production". *Ārthī* (or *artha-* or *ārtha-*) *bhāvanā*, on the other hand, is enunciated by the verb stem and consists of the meaning or action of the verb; we might call it semantic production (and it is ultimately, therefore, said to be located in the agent himself). Reduced to the essentials, thus, in the commandment, "One who desires heaven should sacrifice", the "should" is modal *bhāvanā*, and "sacrifice" is semantic *bhāvanā*. Modal production is therefore said to produce semantic production, whereas semantic production (e.g. "sacrificing") for its part produces some real outcome, heaven and the like.[23]

As for *śābdī bhāvanā*, which will concern us in the first instance here, it is in the practice of mīmāṃsakas basically an analytic tool for understanding the quasi-illocutionary force of a discourse as a whole, what precisely the injunction is prompting the agent to do. It functions according to a very formal set of procedures. To correctly analyze a scriptural commandment we must understand it as indicating (1) *what* is to be produced by the action, (2) *whereby* it is to be produced, and (3) *how* it is to be produced (*sādhya, sādhana, itikartavyatā*), which together constitute the *tryaṃśa* or three components of *śābdī bhāvanā*.[24] This analytic procedure presupposes a more general axiom, namely, that the Veda is concerned with human ends; "Whatever portion of the actual Veda were not to present itself as a human end would cease to have authority. ... No enjoined activity can therefore come to an end until some human end is achieved."[25]

Consider a standard example of *śābdī bhāvanā* analysis. When we hear the sentence, "One who desires heaven should sacrifice with the Jyotiṣṭoma", we cannot take this mean "one should *produce* the *sacrifice*", since sacrifice in itself serves no human end. What we must interpret the sentence to mean is that "One should *produce [the attainment of] heaven* by means of the Jyotiṣṭoma sacrifice."[26] Furthermore, while a sentence like the above thus tells us what should be produced and by what means, the actual procedures for producing it may often, as in this case, need to be understood from other sentences in the large discourse unit in which the particular sentence is embedded (in this case, the sentences describing the ritual mantras to be recited and so on).[27] It is, moreover, in satisfying this *how* portion that the narrative sections of the Veda, the *arthavāda*, or "description of the purpose" of a rite—which as we shall see are of paradigmatic interest to literary hermeneutics—are said to execute their specific function.

Insofar as literature is a subset of discourse as such, a real science of literature, as Bhaṭṭa Nāyaka appears to have understood it, will necessarily accord with *bhāvanā* analysis and therefore explain what literature is "producing", and whereby and how. In one surviving fragment he puts the matter this way: "[In literature] the 'three components' are literary expression (*abhidhā*), a special type of reproduction (*anyā bhāvanā*), and its experientialization (*tadbhogīkṛti*)."[28] As the fragment shows, and as will become clear in what follows, the term *bhāvanā* itself bears two different meanings in his system: it designates on the one hand the aesthetic process over all and on the other the second component of the process (which in stricter usage is referred to as *bhāvakatva*).[29] Before explaining these particular components, we need to note two further general adaptations Bhaṭṭa Nāyaka has made of Mīmāṃsā doctrine.

First, the *action* involved in *bhāvanā* as a *literary* (rather than sentential or discursive) phenomenon is *experiencing* rasa, which is a very special kind of action. Dhanika brings out the full force of Bhaṭṭa Nāyaka's fragment:

> In the case of the language of literature, positive and negative evidence shows that its performance-oriented purpose, both for its message and for those who receive that, lies exclusively in savoring its incomparable pleasure. By this argument, we determine the "action" (*kārya*) of the language of literature to lie precisely in the genesis of the bliss proper to it. The cause of that genesis, as we come to understand, resides in the stable emotion "syntactically construed" (*-saṃsṛṣṭasya*) with the aesthetic elements.[30]

It is because the action to be produced in *bhāvanā* as an aesthetic process is the experience of pleasure that neither knowledge nor moral action (judgment), while not excluded as an outcome of literature, can be its primary focus for Bhaṭṭa Nāyaka (appendix #6). In a differentiation among discursive genres that he was almost certainly the first to draw, probably in the context of this very argument, worldly knowledge is in the province of historical discourse, which can thus be likened to a friend who advises; moral precepts in the province of scripture, which can thus be likened to a master who commands; and literature in the province of rasa, which can thus be likened to a beloved who seduces.[31]

Second, as Dhanika intimates in his comment here (and elaborates later), in the same way that a scriptural passage unifies its parts into a discursive whole that generates action, so rasa itself can be thought of as a "unit of discourse" (*vākyārtha*) in which the aesthetic elements (the foundational and stimulant factors, the reactions, the transitory emotions) are like the individual words (*padārtha*) "syntactically construed" into a unified whole that generates aesthetic experience: "Just as in the Veda," says Bhaṭṭa Nāyaka in a crucial fragment, "where syntactic construal and the other linguistic operations constitute sentence meaning—since sentence meaning is a unity and must bear a relation to some outcome of action—so here in literature does the erotic and every other rasa constitute a kind of sentence meaning" (appendix #12 and note). Again, the correct explication of this idea is found in Dhanika:

> In everyday sentences, the verb enhanced by oblique case forms constitutes the meaning of a sentence. ... In just the same way, in literature ... the aesthetic elements may be taken to stand for words, whereas the stable emotion, desire for example, when syntactically construed with them forms a sentence meaning. Thus, literature as

> such is a "Vākyapadīya", or a work concerned at once with word and sentence, the "words" and "sentences" being the ones just indicated.[32]

With this rich analogy of literary discourse—of aesthetic elements to words, of stable emotion to sentence meaning, and the experience of rasa to "action" to be "produced" by the discourse—the stage is set for a full-scale hermeneutical analysis of the literary phenomenon.

Bhaṭṭa Nāyaka explains literary *bhāvanā* as a three-part process precisely modeled on scriptural *bhāvanā*, but its components are identified by entirely new, or newly interpreted terms. The first is *abhidhā*. Normally this refers to primary or direct denotation in contrast to secondary forms of signification, such as figures of speech. For Bhaṭṭa Nāyaka, *abhidhā* is extended far beyond its narrow meaning to embrace literary expression as such, including the phonic language qualities (*guṇas*) and the figures: "To the abode of 'expression' belong the figures of sound and sense" (appendix #11); according to Ruyyaka's gloss, "The language process (*śabdavyāpāra*) is two-fold, distinguishing between primary and secondary meaning, that is, whether an unmediated or mediated sense is at issue" (appendix #3a).

In fact, *abhidhā* in Bhaṭṭa Nāyaka's usage is best understood or even translated as "literary language"; something "completely different" from the language of scripture and everyday discourse, as Abhinavagupta describes it.[33] It is crucially this kind of language that transforms objects of linguistic reference into objects of aesthetic experience; in Dhanika's words, "It is the literary process (*kāvyavyāpāra-*), figures such as hyperbole and metaphor,[34] that actually elevate (*āhitaviśeṣa-*) a thing like the moon into a stimulant factor (*uddīpanavibhāva*), a woman into a foundational factor (*ālambanavibhāva*), despair into a transitory emotion (*vyabhicāribhāva*), and goosebumps, weeping, the play of the eyebrows, and sidelong glances into reactions (*anubhāva*)."[35] With its figures of sense and sound and intentionally patterned sound qualities differentiating it from all other forms of usage, literary language, we might say, defamiliarizes the discourse so as to differentiate it from the everyday world and its real referentiality—the world where, for example, "Sītā" means not "woman as such" but the wife of Rāma.

Another way Bhaṭṭa Nāyaka expresses the radical difference of literary language is by highlighting not its prominence over against everyday usage but its self-subordination to a higher-order process than signification as such. Drawing for the first time a distinction about "primacy" in different forms of discourse that was to be repeated down the centuries (and that no doubt originally linked up with his celebrated analogy of master, friend, and beloved), Bhaṭṭa Nāyaka puts it like this:

> Scripture is distinguished by its dependence on the primacy of the wording [that is, the Veda is more important for *how* it says than *what* it says, and it can therefore never be rephrased]. Historical narrative, for its part, is a matter of factual meaning [that is, *what* it says is more important than *how* it says it, and can be rephrased multiply]. When both these, wording and meaning, are subordinate,[36] and the aesthetic process itself has primacy, we call it literature.[37]

The aesthetic "process" (*vyāpāra*) of *bhāvanā* comprises two remaining components. One of these Bhaṭṭa Nāyaka calls *bhāvakatva*, which as noted earlier must be distinguished from (though it is sometimes confused with) *bhāvanā* as such, the comprehensive term for the literary phenomenon.[38] *Bhāvakatva* is *anyā bhāvanā*, "another order of *bhāvanā*", and perhaps at the same time a "unique" type, different from any other sort of productive capacity associated with language. We saw earlier some of the problems Bhaṭṭa Nāyaka perceived in the old ontology and epistemology of rasa. *Bhāvakatva* is his solution. Although he does not gloss the term himself (appendix #7 is almost certainly inauthentic), *bhāvakatva* is consistently defined as the literary process whereby the emotional states represented in the literary work are made into something in which the reader or spectator can fully participate: *sādhāraṇīkaraṇa*, or "commonalization", a synonym for *bhāvakatva* and apparently another of Bhaṭṭa Nāyaka's coinages,[39] is a conception that obviously depends entirely on the relocation of the substratum of rasa from the character to the reader. The most important exposition of this idea is again offered by Dhanika:

> What then functions as the foundational factor (*ālambanavibhāva*) for rasa when it resides in the audience? Take the case of Sītā, who is a royal (or divine) being: how can there not be something fundamentally contradictory in her acting as such a factor for the spectator? ... Unlike a spiritual adept, a poet does not behold things with the "eye of insight" and present a character like Rāma in a state of sheer individuality (*prātisvikī*), as is the case with historical discourse. Rather, he creates a typological state (*avasthā*)—"the noble" protagonist, say, in the case of Rāma—which is given presence through the poet's imagination (*utprekṣā*) by means of the process of "commonality" that each viewer undergoes (*sarvalokasādhāraṇya*);[40] the state itself simply providing a substratum for a given rasa. Consider here a word like "Sītā": emptied of all its particularities, such as being the daughter of King Janaka, it signifies nothing more than "woman"—and how could anything untoward[41] come of that?[42]

In the real world we have no natural commonality with a figure like Sītā: as a queen (or goddess) and another's wife she cannot rightly be an object of our sexual desire. In literary hermeneutics *bhāvakatva* is therefore not a productive but a "*re*productive" capacity, something that allows us to relive the emotions appropriately in ourselves. Aided by the alchemical powers of literary language,[43] *bhāvakatva* abstracts Sītā from her particularity—this is what Bhaṭṭa Nāyaka calls "the capacity to overcome the resistances of one's deep inner perplexity"[44]—and renders her a foundational factor for the stimulation of the spectator's own stable feeling. One of the best short descriptions of Bhaṭṭa Nāyaka's idea is offered by Siṃhabhūpāla (*c.* 1380):

> Whereas with reference to the historical hero (Rāma, for example) the underlying factor (Sītā) was once completely particularized, the process that in a poem or a play is called "reproduction" consists of "commonalizing" the foundational factor by means of the process of expression (*abhidhā*), and thereby enables it to be imagined by the spectator as connected with himself. It thereby comes to transform itself in the mind of the spectator doing the imagining or "reproducing," without there being any contradiction with its persistence as a foundational factor (for Rāma). Thereby, the stable emotion that Rāma feels can be experienced by the spectator, and without the least disruption through impropriety, in an experience whose nature is a pure blissful absorption.[45]

Bhaṭṭa Nāyaka's third and last component of the literary-aesthetic process is experience (*bhoga*), or—in yet another neologism—"experientialization" (*bhogīkṛttva* or *[tad]bhogīkṛttva* or *-kṛti*, where the *tad-* refers to the now "commonalized" emotional complex). The phenomenon of literary experientialization is far more than "enjoyment", as the usual translation has it. *Bhoga* signifies a complex kind of living-through, of disengaged engagement with, the various emotions. It is characterized as consisting of one of four different reactions depending on the rasa, each of which corresponds to one of the four "mental planes" that constitute our consciousness. Dhanika offers the crucial exposition:

> When there is a "fusion" (*saṃbheda*) between the "elements of the literary work" (*kāvyārtha-*) (that is, the stable emotion "construed with" the factors and the rest) and the mind of the reader—that is, a mutual interpenetration, one in which the self-other differentiation [i.e., between the reader/viewer and the character] has vanished—we have the genesis of the most powerful form of bliss that is the self, namely, savoring (*carvaṇā*). Although in its general form rasa is single, it can occupy one of four

> different mental planes[46] according to the type of fusion produced by the causes—the factors and the rest—that are invariably associated with a particular rasa. These are: expansion (*vikāsa*) in the case of the erotic rasa, enlargement (*vistara*) in the case of the heroic, turbulence (*kṣobha*) in the case of the repugnant, and agitation (*vikṣepa*) in the case of the violent. The remaining four rasas—the comic, the amazing, the horrific, and the tragic—once they have achieved a high degree of enhancement by means of their appropriate complement of aesthetic elements, have each the same four varieties respectively.[47]

We have in fact two traditions of interpretation regarding Bhaṭṭa Nāyaka's aesthetic psychology. Dhanika knew the *HD* intimately, as his exegesis everywhere demonstrates. His account of four mental states is eminently coherent, explaining the psychological response to Bharata's four primary rasas (of which the secondary four, the comic and so on, are thought of as derivates). His version, however, is contradicted by that of Abhinavagupta (and all his followers), which identifies three sorts of *bhoga*: *druti*, *vistāra* (*sic*), and *vikāsa* ("melting, expansion, and radiance," according to his most recent translators)[48] Abhinava does not explain these states, though later interpreters such as Māṇikyacandra attempt to correlate them with different configurations of the three *guṇa*s in the psychological make-up of the reader, though this seems to me a sheer guess extrapolated from Abhinava's vague summation and based on a misleading parallel to the yoga usage.[49] (Mammaṭa eliminated from his account the whole reference—perhaps as being unintelligible as it stands.) But all interpreters agree that for Bhaṭṭa Nāyaka, "experiencing" the emotions that have been made "common" by the power of literary "expression" and thus rendered accessible to the reader—horror without the danger of real horror, or desire without the impropriety of real desire—leads to a kind of absorption in or even cathexis on the literary event.

The term used for this state by Bhaṭṭa Nāyaka, apparently for the first time at least in the literary-critical context, is *viśrānti* (which will becomes so important for Abhinavagupta). This absorptive experience is an event unique to the aesthetic and completely different from normal experience (*anubhava*) and memory. It is, as Mammaṭa restated it, "a full repose in the true nature of one's own consciousness", rendered so completely joyful and luminous that it is akin to the ecstasy of religious self-transcendence given that "the self-other differentiation has vanished", as Dhanika says.[50] We should remember, however, what Bhaṭṭa Nāyaka himself tells us in one of the few preserved fragments, that this religious experience is in fact inferior: "Nothing can compare with [aesthetic rasa], not even the rasa spiritual adepts bring forth" (appendix #3).

In terms of the three-part Mīmāṃsā paradigm, these components represent the means (*abhidhā*), the method (*bhāvakatva*), and the what (*bhogīkṛttva*) of literary "reproduction", and we may synthesize as follows: Aesthetic experience (this is the *kim* or *sādhya*) arises thanks to a conceptual transformation of the literary elements (the foundational factor and so on) via "commonalization" (this is the *kena*, or *sādhana* or *karaṇa*), which for its part is made possible by the unique powers of literary language (this is the *katham* or *itikartavyatā*).[51] The term of art by which the whole process is itself designated, *bhāvanā* or (re)production, is meant to suggest a grand analogy: that the same mechanism enabling us to understand and to become the subject or "agent" of a commandment of scripture enables us to understand and become the subject or agent of a literary text. It is this process itself, as Bhaṭṭa Nāyaka himself says, that constitutes the essential or most distinctive trait of literariness: *vyāpārapradhānye kāvyagīr bhavet*, "when the aesthetic process itself has primacy we call it 'literature'".[52]

Now, in one sense Bhaṭṭa Nāyaka's "hermeneutic" turn would seem to be largely formal: conceiving of the literary text, or rather aesthetic event, as a kind of discourse (*vākya*) enabled him to apply to it the threefold process of "production" that Mīmāṃsā developed for scripture, recoding the components to fit with the new type of "sentence meaning" of an aesthetic phenomenon. But to end with this analytical formalism would be a mistake, for it is only the surface manifestation of far deeper conceptual affiliations with Mīmāṃsā. Until we understand these, key questions of Bhaṭṭa Nāyaka's systems will remain unanswered. What, for example, is the exact relationship between the "reproductive capacity" (*bhāvakatva*) and the overall process, *bhāvanā*? How precisely does "commonalization" (*sādhāraṇīkaraṇa*) enable the reproductive capacity to arise in the experience of a literary text? And why should the entire literary process be designated as "reproduction"?

The answers to these questions, and thereby the true hermeneutical force of Bhaṭṭa Nāyaka's insights, are contained in none of the surviving fragments of his work. But I believe we can see them emerging from the restatement of his views by his most ardent if most reluctant if not ungrateful disciple, Abhinavagupta.

4.

As is well known, Abhinava begins his discourse on rasa in chapter 6 of the *Nāṭyaśāstra* with a celebrated critique of earlier views, including Bhaṭṭa Nāyaka's, to which we owe much of what we know about earlier aesthetic theory. What has been insufficiently registered, however, let alone explained in intellectual-historical terms is why Abhinava should chose to begin his reconstruction (or "purification of principles" *pariśuddhatattvam*) in the way he does.[53] Here is the completely unexpected argument with which it opens:

> yathā hi rātrim āsata tām agnau prādād ity ādāv arthitādilakṣitasyādhikāriṇaḥ pratipattimātrād itivṛttaprarocitāt prathamapravṛttād anantaram adhikaivopāttakālatiraskāreṇaivāse[54] saṃpradadānītyādirūpā saṃkramaṇādisvabhāvā[55] yathādarśanaṃ pratibhā bhāvanāvidhyudyogādibhāṣābhir vyavahṛtā pratipattis, tathaiva kāvyātmakād api śabdād adhikāriṇo 'dhikāsti pratipattiḥ.[56]
>
> [On hearing a sentence of scripture such as "They held a sacrificial session through the night," or "He offered up [the oblation] into the fire," a qualified individual—that is, someone who has the necessary wealth and meets the other prerequisites—has at first a bare comprehension, if one that carries the persuasive power of historical eventfulness. But thereupon a certain surplus comprehension arises, of the nature of a set of grammatical transformations whereby the original tense is suppressed and he thinks, "Let *me hold* a session," or "Let *me offer* up". This sort of comprehension is identified by various terms of art depending on the philosophical school, such as "intellection", "production", "commandment", "injunction", and the like. In precisely the same way, from literary language there arises for the qualified individual a surplus comprehension.]

It is impossible to understand why Abhinava's reconstruction of aesthetics should begin by adducing passages from scripture that contain what is known as an *arthavāda*, a "description of the purpose" of a rite, without some background information from Mīmāṃsā. Such descriptions are held to be supplementary to the actual commandments that make up the core of the Veda and whose capacity to compel us to act is embedded in the deontic language they employ ("One who desires heaven *must sacrifice*"), and toward which much of the discussion of *bhāvanā* is directed. In the case of the *arthavādas*, however, it is far less evident how they are related to the action the Veda enjoins upon us—

as they must be if they are to be considered part of the Veda[57]—for on first glance their purpose is simply narrative. Mīmāṃsā argues that, by providing an incitement (*prarocaka* is a common term) for obeying the commandments and performing a rite, often by making commendatory reference (*stuti*) to a particular quasi-historical event (such as an earlier performance of the sacrifice and the success that the sacrificer thereby achieved), the *arthavāda* persuades the subject to act in the same way.[58] By the use of the *śābdī bhāvanā* analytic, the narrative passage is shown to "form a single sentence with an injunction and have the purpose of commending it".[59] Indeed, from a more abstract perspective, whereas the *what* of *śābdī bhāvanā* as such is some human activity, and the *whereby* is awareness of the syntactical connections of the sentence, the *how* is the incitement stimulated by those descriptive passages of the Veda, the *arthavādas*, that metaphorically or indirectly commend acts that should be done (or condemn those that should not), given that man's natural indolence causes him to turn away from action.[60] Indeed, "modal production" necessarily requires the "method" (*itikartavyatā*) supplied by a descriptive passage.[61]

Abhinava goes on to explain how this process works. When a duly qualified person, one who meets the requirements for participation in a Vedic rite hears a descriptive passage such as "They once attended the all-night rite," or "He once offered the [oblation] in the fire,"[62] he has at first a straightforward understanding of the discourse, one that incites him to act by reason of its historical eventfulness (*itivṛttaprarocita*). Directly afterward, however, he develops a "surplus comprehension" (*adhikā pratipatti*) of the discourse, which has the nature of a set of grammatical transformations[63] leading him to suppress the temporality and agent of the original discourse (the historical past tense, the third person plural/singular), so that he comes to personalize the discourse: "I myself should attend," or "Let me myself offer."[64] Different philosophical schools may have different terms for this process—above all, *bhāvanā*[65]—but they all agree that the discursive function enables a particularized statement such as "they once attended" to be dissociated from its particularity, and thereby to become available for active *recreation* on the part of the sacrificial agent.

It is obvious why Abhinava chose his scriptural examples from the genre of *arthavāda*. There is nothing really mysterious about how the force of the express commandments and prohibitions of the Veda is communicated, since they directly address the reader.[66] But the *arthavāda* is not a commandment, and yet it must speak to us and prompt us to act if it is to be considered part of the Veda. As we have just seen, Mīmāṃsā typically explains this capacity through the discourse analysis of *śābdī bhāvanā*—

indeed, that analytic has special propriety in the case of the *arthavāda*[67]—by showing how such descriptions complement the express commandments with which they form a single *vākya*, by indicating some praise or blame that would enable man to proceed toward or turn away from some action. Embedded in Abhinava's cognitive sequence is, explicitly, an extended sense of *bhāvanā*—perhaps even a new view of *ārthī bhāvanā* (which is strictly speaking *puruṣaniṣṭhā*, located in the agent, rather than *śabdaniṣṭhā*, located in language). Here *bhāvanā* is not primarily a tool of discourse analysis required for a correct interpretation of sentences. It is instead a "surplus comprehension" leading to an incitement to reproduce an act; in other words, a *hermeneutical* force in a scriptural text that, even in the absence of an explicit commandment (one recovered only afterward, through *śābdī bhāvanā*), can impel the reader toward that act. "The very presence of a narrative produces two things," says the Mīmāṃsā exegete Śabara, "both a knowledge of what occurred and an incitement toward or repulsion from some action."[68]

In the same way, the literary work produces in a qualified reader a surplus, departicularized meaning that opens up the discourse to a kind of active engagement. When hearing the first verse of Kālidāsa's play *Śākuntala*, which describes the fear gripping a hunted dear, the spectator after first grasping the actual meaning of the sentence has a kind of apprehension (*pratīti*) that leads him to discard all the specifications in the sentences, whether of time or space or individuality. The deer is stripped of its particularity, and the source of its fear (the hunter, King Duḥṣyanta) of his absolute reality. We are left with the stable emotion of fear, untouched by any time-space particularities; completely different from the sort associated with such everyday notions as "I am afraid; he is afraid; he is enemy, friend, or neutral." Abhinava continues:

> The fear thus grasped unimpeded, transforming itself before one's eyes and entering almost visibly into one's heart, is the *rasa* of horror. In the case of this sort of fear, one's own self is neither completely obscured nor specifically referenced—and the same is true for everyone else. The "commonalization" is therefore not exclusive [to oneself], but rather comprehensive: it is like grasping the invariable concomitance of smoke and fire, or fear and trembling ... All the spectators have the same completely undifferentiated awareness, [a realization] that serves to enhance the *rasa* even more.

"In short," he concludes, "*rasa* is just this stable emotion grasped in an apprehension (*pratīti*) that consists of physical tasting."[69]

5.

The extract from the start of *Abhinavabhāratī*'s reconstruction of aesthetics shows how profoundly it breathes the spirit of Bhaṭṭa Nāyaka, from the idea of "commonalization" to (very possibly) the specific wording of the details of the process.[70] This general influence has been widely recognized, but less so the precise nature and extent of Abhinava's hermeneutical turn, and what these may allow us to infer about Bhaṭṭa Nāyaka's aesthetic system. Aside from its formal linkages with Mīmāṃsā as discourse analysis, *bhāvanā*, once reconceptualized as aesthetic process, enabled Bhaṭṭa Nāyaka to think of the force of the literary text in the same way as the hermeneutists thought of the force of the scriptural text. We can imagine him starting with some simple questions that his two disciplines would have forced upon him: how is it that actions that the Veda shows concern other people at other times and places are actions that we here and now are impelled to re-enact?[71] And by the same token, how is it that we here and now are able in some way to experience a literary discourse that always concerns other people at other times and places? Is there a power in the literary text that makes us re-enact the text ourselves in a way analogous to our experience with scripture? And this led him to conceive of the force operating in each as identical. This force renders the meaning of a particular (past, unique) narrative significant for or applicable to us; we reproduce that meaning, in the sense of recreating it as something that relates to us, and we do this by "commonalizing" its content so that "I" can in some way do or feel what "they" once did.

Preparatory to this, the nature of literary language, with formal properties that make it unlike any other use of language, obliterates the narrative's historical referentiality and "commonalizes" its emotions (through *sādharaṇīkaraṇa*) by "reproducing" them (through *bhāvaktva*).[72] This is what enables the reader to experience (through *bhoga/bhogīkṛttva*) the work himself, thereby "producing" (through *bhāvanā*) not action, but aesthetic pleasure.[73] As Bhaṭṭa Nāyaka was at pains to make clear, the output of literary discourse is thus as different from other discursive genres as its input: just as literature's dual treatment of wording and meaning differs from that of both scripture and *itihāsa* (where wording has primacy in the one case, and meaning in the other), so does literature differ in it effects: whereas scripture leads toward moral action and history to knowledge, literature leads to pleasure (appendix #6). How radically this differs from the Mīmāṃsā textual universe from which Bhaṭṭa Nāyaka emerged is an important if more extraneous question.[74]

Bhaṭṭa Nāyaka's *bhāvanā*, his *vyāpāra* or literary process, must accordingly be seen as a specifically hermeneutical form of knowledge, in the use of the term hermeneutics that points not so much to the conditions of interpretation as to the conditions of understanding. The poem may be about the love of Rāma and Sītā, in the same way as the ritual narrative is about Janamejaya, Brahmā, and the anonymous "they" or "he" who in the descriptive passage in the Vedic *brāhmaṇa* texts are said to have performed the rite in question. Yet through the force of *bhāvanā* the discourse of both scripture and literature comes to be directed to oneself. It is precisely this phenomenon that completes the triple movement of hermeneutical understanding, as Hans-Georg Gadamer was the first to argue out in the Western tradition. Not only are understanding and interpretation mutually constitutive—"interpretation is not an occasional, post facto supplement to understanding; rather, understanding is always interpretation, and hence interpretation is the explicit form of understanding"—but understanding itself always comprises application: It "involves something like applying the text to be understood to the interpreter's present situation ... application [is] just as integral a part of the hermeneutical process as are understanding and interpretation".[75]

The revolutionary move made by Bhaṭṭa Nāyaka was to put the subjective experience of the reader front and center in his aesthetic analysis. As a result, all earlier questions about the aesthetic experience—locked as they were into a linguistic analysis of literature, and text-centric—were pushed to the margin. (And perhaps locked into radically different epistemologies: If Śrī Śaṅkuka, for example, was in fact a Buddhist, did Bhaṭṭa Nāyaka's Mīmāṃsā realism also contest and replace a Buddhist idealism and illusionism?)[76] Once you realize that the key thing about rasa is the reader's or spectator's experience, it no longer matters whether rasa is engendered, inferred, or manifested in the character—indeed, talk of engenderment, inference, and manifestation will no longer make much sense. You begin to ask how literary language transforms a discourse about people you do not know (Rāma, Sītā) into something you as reader can somehow enter into and feel is "applicable" (as Gadamer might put it), or pertinent to your own self, and how that enables an altogether unique kind of experience and knowledge. And what aids you in answering this question is the analytic method developed for scripture, which gives commandments to others that are somehow meant for you, which you make your own, and then proceed to act upon. And in the process of this action, scriptural or literary, transform yourself and your world.

What is worth stressing in conclusion, aside from how profound was Bhaṭṭa Nāyaka's transformation of Indian aesthetic theory, is the quality of his thinking measured against that of contemporary scholars who write on emotions and the aesthetic.[77] I cannot go into that literature here beyond registering my conviction that, except for the more recent advances in cognitive theories of emotion, present-day efforts to make sense of aesthetic response would most certainly have gained in sophistication and depth had it been possible to read in full the "Heart's Mirror" of Bhaṭṭa Nāyaka.

Appendix: From the *Hṛdayadarpaṇa* of Bhaṭṭa Nāyaka[78]

Direct (and probable) citations

.... .

(5) Scripture is distinguished by the fact that for it, wording has primacy. Historical narrative, for its part, is a matter of factual meaning. When both wording and meaning are subordinated and the aesthetic process itself has primacy, we call it literature.[79]

.... .

(6) With respect to literature, every reader in the first instance aims to experience rasa, not to gain knowledge or be persuaded of some moral precept.[80]

.... .

(7) We scholars hold that the literary function is three-fold: expression, reproduction, and experientialization. Beyond that, we do not accept anything, certainly not what has been called "implicature". Expression is an established fact in all domains of communication;[81] production refers to the generalization of the aesthetic elements, the factors and the rest; experientialization refers to the unfettered savoring of rasa.[82]

.... .

(8) Rasa must be completely distinguished from all acts of making and knowing. It is a unique function, something we can call "savoring".[83]

.... .

(9) As for the other process called "implicature", which consists of manifestation, even were it proven to be different from the other two,[84] it would only be a component of literature, not its essential form.[85]

.... .

(11) [In literature] the "three components" are literary expression, a special type of reproduction, and experientialization. To the abode of expression belong the figures of sound and sense. Next, reproduction brings into being the group of

rasas, the erotic and the rest. When a reader is pervaded by the experience of these rasas, he finds aesthetic fulfillment. Although it is something entirely phenomenal [this experience] clearly participates in the nature of spiritual release.[86]

....

(12) Just as in the Veda, where syntactic construal and the other linguistic operations constitute sentence meaning—since sentence meaning is a unity and must bear a relation to some outcome of action[87]—so here in literature does the erotic and every other rasa constitute a kind of sentence meaning.[88]

....

Restatements of Bhaṭṭa Nāyaka's doctrine

(1A) From Abhinavagupta's *Abhinavabhāratī* on *Nāṭyaśāstra* (*c.* 1000), supplemented by Hemacandra's *Kāvyānuśāsana*[89] (*c.* 1175)

Bhaṭṭa Nāyaka, however, argues that rasa can neither be the object of a normal perceptual experience, nor is it a thing that actually comes into being or can be "manifested." If rasa were perceptible, it would have to be perceived either as being in oneself or in someone else. If rasa were perceived as internal to oneself (it would have to be thought as arising in oneself, *DhĀL*). The first problem with this is that, in the case of the tragic rasa, one would feel actual pain oneself (and never return to the theater to see sad plays, *DhĀL*). Second, the perception would not even stand to reason, since a character, Sītā for example, cannot be a foundational factor for the spectator such as would enable him to perceive rasa in himself (she is a factor of that sort only for another character, such as her husband, Rāma, M). Third, the spectator cannot be thinking of his own beloved in the midst of a description of Sītā, because she is a divine/royal being for whom it is senseless to say that she has any kind of property in common with his beloved[90] (and there would therefore be nothing to stimulate the spectator's latent disposition of desire, *DhĀL*). Fourth, in the case of a rasa like the heroic, for example where the stimulant factor is something never experienced, as in the case of Rama's building a bridge across the ocean, the possibility of perceiving the rasa in oneself through the functioning of a commonly shared property is ruled out: there is no stable emotion the spectator shares in common with non-worldly beings like Rāma (*DhĀL*). And one cannot have any memory of Rāma's energy (the stable emotion of the heroic rasa), as empowering him to cross the ocean, because one never had the perception of him in the first place that would be required to ground such a memory. Nor can one be said to have "perceived" Rāma by some other means of valid knowledge, say testimony or inference, in order to provide a basis for one's memory. Such a mediated perception would no more provide an experience of rasa than would glimpsing with one's own eyes the love-making of the actual characters, when the spectator would be expected to be absorbed in one or another state of mind—shame, disgust, or yearning.[91]

If, on the other hand, rasa were perceived as external to the perceiving subject (as present in the actor or the characters), then it could not be a "taste" (that is, something experienced), but an object, like a pot (M), toward which one would be emotionally indifferent.

Accordingly, it makes no[92] sense to say that there is a perception—in the form of an empirical experience or memory or whatever—of rasa. The same criticism applies to the view that rasa actually comes into being. And lastly, if rasa were something that existed only in potential form (since rasa cannot be conceived of as already existing, like some material object, M) and that was subsequently "manifested",[93] it would be subject both to the gradations of actualizing the object that are inherent in any idea of "manifestation",[94] and also to the same dilemmas as before, that is, whether it is manifested in oneself, or another, and so on (*DhĀL*).

Therefore, there must be a second component other than expression, the process known as "reproduction", which is something utterly different from other kinds of language by virtue of the three-fold constitution of literary language (*DhĀL*). This is marked in poetry by language that shows an absence of faults and the presence of language qualities and figures of speech, whereas in drama it is embodied in the four different modes of representation (gestural, verbal, and so on).[95] If literary expression were not complemented by "reproduction", literary figures of speech would be no different from those used in everyday life, and particular literary styles and norms would be meaningless (*DhĀL*). "Reproduction" has the capacity to overcome the resistances of one's deep inner perplexity, and consists in essence in the commonalization of the aesthetic elements, the foundational factor and so on. By this process is produced rasa, which comes to be experienced by a form of "experience" utterly different from empirical experience, memory, and so on; one marked instead by a melting, enlargement, and expansion[96] that depend on the relative degree of volatility and impassivity in the spectator, and marked by an absorption of the spectator's consciousness consisting of a predominance of sensitivity, light, and bliss, and which shares something of the character of savoring the supreme being.

.... .

(2a) From Mammaṭa's *Kāvyaprakāśa* (*c.* 1050)[97]

Rasa is not something cognized, whether as existing in someone external and uninvolved with the viewing subject, or as internal to him. Nor is it something that actually comes into being, or something "manifested". On the contrary, in poetry and drama there is a process in addition to expression called "reproduction", which consists in the "commonalization" of the foundational factor and other aesthetic elements. By this process the stable emotion is reproduced and experienced in a third process called experience, which has the nature of[98] an absorption of consciousness consisting of a predominance of sensitivity, light, and bliss.

....

(3a) From Ruyyaka's *Saṅketa* on *Kāvyaprakāśa*[99] (*c.* 1150)

In Bhaṭṭa Nāyaka's system all three positions concerning rasa—that it actually comes into being; that it is the content of a cognitive experience; that it is "manifested"—are critiqued, and his own position, that rasa is "experienced", is established.... Against all three he levels a common criticism: If rasa arose in or were perceived as truly existing in oneself, it would have to be experienced in precisely the same way (e.g. sorrowfully in the case of the tragic rasa); if it arose in or were perceived as existing in someone else, one would be indifferent and hence have no rasa experience at all; if it were latent and only manifested, it would be subject to the gradations of actualizing the object that are inherent in any idea of "manifestation", and so again one would have no rasa experience. He therefore abandons all three positions and argues in favor of "experience". This consists of relishing rasa and amounts to the same thing as pure pleasure. And it is entirely different from the views that rasa comes into being, and so on: given that their operations must proceed under the constraints of time and space,[100] they all are subject to the many aforementioned criticisms. "Experience", however, is entirely different, hence has a non-worldly quality, and thereby escapes those criticisms.

To be precise: There is a three-fold "process" (*tryaṃśo vyāpāraḥ*) of literature; the three components are called expression, reproduction, and experientialization. Among these the first, namely the language process,[101] is itself two-fold by virtue of the distinction between primary and secondary meaning, that is, whether an unmediated or mediated sense is at issue.[102] This two-fold process is common to scripture and historical discourse as well,[103] which may be likened to master and friend respectively insofar as the wording itself has primacy in the former, and the meaning in the latter. But the other two components are unique to poetry and drama; whereas, at the same time, literature is differentiated in its language-process from scripture and history by being likened to a wife, insofar as both wording and meaning have primacy. With respect to those components, we will first discuss reproduction. Although it is impossible for Sītā, for example, to ever be a foundational factor,[104] reproduction comes into being[105] in order to bring about a state of commonality. This is made possible in poetry by the presence of language qualities and figures of speech[106] and by the absence of faults, and in drama by the use of the four kinds of representation. For the brilliance of the wording and meaning of the literary text is derived from the brilliance of the full complement of aesthetic elements, just as the moonstone is caused to melt by the proximity of moonbeams. In the same way, from the exceptional nature (*vaiśiṣṭya*) of the full complement of aesthetic elements in poetry and drama there comes about this process of reproduction, which may be defined as "commonalization". Once the foundational factor and the rest are "commonalized", commonalization renders the stable emotion an experiential object (*viṣayīkṛta*) on the part of the sensitive reader. The concluding process, "experientialization", can be defined as making this emotion an object for his relishing. It is precisely because literature has the capacity to delight such a reader that is likened to a wife. This experience is in essence a savoring of the highest bliss, and is closely approximated to savoring the supreme being on the part of spiritual masters.

.... .

(4a) From the *Alaṅkārasarvasva* of Ruyyaka (R) (1150), with the commentaries of Jayaratha (J) (fl. 1300) and Samudrabandha (S) (fl. 1300)[107]

(R) When Bhaṭṭa Nāyaka says that the process of manifestation is a component of literature he is admitting it only for the sake of argument and dismissively.[108] He awards primacy to the aesthetic process as such, with the actual forms of wording and meaning subordinated to this. More specifically, over and above[109] the first two literary processes, expression and "reproduction", there is a third one. This is in essence the relishing of rasa, a synonym for which is "enjoyment", and he accepts this as the dominant literary element, insofar it constitutes the place of "absorption" (*viśrānti*).

(J KM 8-9) Some scholars have argued that manifestation is beyond the domain of speech and therefore indefinable.[110] To this view Ruyyaka now turns. "Dismissively", and not by providing a definition. That is why the assertion is dismissive: he accepts something only for the sake of argument, which cannot (he says) be defined. "A component of literature," i.e. not its essence, as (Bhaṭṭa Nāyaka) says, "As for the other process called 'implicature', ..."[111] What Bhaṭṭa Nāyaka means by "process" is poetic creation itself.[112] Otherwise [that is, if literature were not something entirely different, a "process"], it would be impossible to differentiate literature either from the Vedas, where wording itself has primacy, or from historical discourse, where meaning has primacy. As (Bhaṭṭa Nāyaka) has said, "Scripture, in its dependence on the primacy of the word ...". He has declared that literature consists of three components: "Expression, production, and aesthetic experience... ." He sets forth the sphere of the first two components in the verse "To the abode of expression ..." and the third component in the verse "When a reader is pervaded... ." This last component consists of a relishing of the other two that is experienced by lovers of literature. And when he states that "Although it is something phenomenal ..." he accepts this experience as the "abode of absorption", being something similar to relishing the supreme being.

(Samudrabandha TSS 9-10) "Expression", which here includes primary and secondary meaning, is common to literary and nonliterary language. (Bhaṭṭa Nāyaka's) two other processes are specific to literature. The one, "reproduction", is the generalization of the factors and the other components of rasa; the other, "enjoyment", is a literary process that exists over and above/transcends (abl.?) these two, and is described as in essence the relishing of rasa. While both the author of the *Vakroktijīvita* and Bhaṭṭa Nāyaka equally hold linguistic process to have primacy, the former awards this primacy to expression when artistically qualified, whereas the latter awards it to manifestation as related to rasa, for which a synonym is "enjoyment".

(5a) From Mallinātha's Commentary on *Ekāvalī*[113] (fl. 1400)

Bhaṭṭa Nāyaka's doctrine of aesthetic experience is as follows: The "linguistic process", which pertains to literature and plays, assists the "reproduction process", whereby the aesthetic elements, the foundational factor and so on, are "commonalized".[114] Here the stable emotion is brought to consciousness as something common to the reader, since anything that pertains specifically to the actor and so on[115] is eliminated. And it is thereby experienced by the "reproduction" process, also known as aesthetic experience, which consists of an awareness that is pure sensitivity, light, and bliss.

....

Resonances of Bhaṭṭa Nāyaka's doctrine

(1b) From *Rasārṇavasudhākara* of Siṃhabhūpāla (*c.* 1380)[116]

A foundational factor (such as Sītā) attains real existence through linguistic communication, its actual external reality being irrelevant.[117] Furthermore, whereas with reference to the historical hero (Rāma, for example) such a factor was once completely particularized (Sītā being a specific individual for Rāma), the process that in a poem or a play is called "reproduction" consists of generalizing the foundational factor by means of the process of expression,[118] and thereby enables it to be imagined (*vibhāvita*) by the spectator as connected with himself. It thereby comes to visibly manifest itself in the mind of the spectator doing the imagining/reproducing (*bhāvaka*) without there being any contradiction with its persistence as a foundational factor (i.e. for Rāma). Thereby, the stable emotion that Rāma feels can be experienced by the spectator, and without the least disruption through impropriety, in an experience whose nature is a pure blissful absorption (*nirbharānandaviśrānti*).

Notes

Robert Goldman has stressed throughout his career how crucial traditional interpretation is to the modern interpretation of Sanskrit literature. And this of course is the point of studying *alaṅkāraśāstra*. I offer the present essay as a token of long friendship and even longer admiration. I am grateful to Radhavallabh Tripathi and Lawrence McCrea for their criticisms of an earlier draft of this essay.

1. Kane 1971: 196-97. The variant reading is also found in *ABh* mss.

2. *adṛṣṭadarpaṇā mama dhīḥ* (*Vyaktiviveka* v. 4) No commentator on the famous précis in *Kāvyaprakāśa* 4 after Māṇikyacandra and Ruyyaka (both mid-twelfth century) gives any evidence of knowing the original (if even those two did). I include below a citation from Uttuṅgodaya's *Kaumudī*, a thirteenth- or fourteenth-century commentary on the *DhĀL* (Appendix #7) and a summary from Siṃhabhūpāla's *Rasārṇavasudhārakara* (*c.* 1385; Appendix #1b), though without any confidence that these are grounded in the actual text.

3. Their relationship with the earlier writer is seriously understudied. Only vague references are to be found in the standard literature; T. Venkatacharya, the most recent editor of *DR*, is completely silent on the matter.

4. *dvijas tayor nāyakākhyo gaurīśasurasadmanoḥ | cāturvidyaḥ kṛtas tena vāgdevīkulamandiram ||* (*Rājataraṅgiṇī* 5.159; Stein, - *kulamandira*, "familiar dwelling place"; but see such later locutions as *Sārasvateya* and *kavikula*).

5. For the wider intellectual-historical development, see McCrea 2009.

6. Pollock 1998.

7. I say "core" because the text shows evidence of interpolation and manipulation of a very deep and wide sort.

8. Kuntaka accepts the position *sthāyy eva tu raso bhaved*, *Vakroktijīvita* 3.7 ff. (see also Nanavati 1998: 39-40), and views rasa only as a textual phenomenon.

9. Śrī Śaṅkuka's views have been poorly transmitted. All we can safely accept is what is said in the ABh: Rasa is to be defined as the stable emotion, in the form of an imitation of the stable emotion in the main character, being apprehended by inference from the presence of the aesthetic elements (*anukartari rasān āsvādayato 'nukārye bhāvapratītiḥ*, p. 266). The focus remains on the textual/dramatic process, even if the cognitive aspect may have a new prominence. Later elaborations of Abhinava's précis on the part of Mammaṭa, say, or Hemacandra have no automatic claim to authenticity since there is no reason to believe they had access to Śrī Śaṅkuka's work.

10. *DR* and *DRA* 4.38-39. When Viśvanātha in the fourteenth century uses the language of *vyañjanā*, he concedes the point that there is a serious conceptual problem (and seems to be the first one to do so): since rasa is only a process of tasting on the part of the spectator and not some object, it is in fact incoherent to speak of its "manifestation." (*Sāhityadarpaṇa*, pp. 79-81). What complicates this is that eventually the *sthāyibhāva*, the stable emotion, itself comes to be located in the spectator, and rasa will indeed therefore just be the "manifestation" of something that is already there (reference to the *sthāyibhāva* of the *spectator* is found first in *DR* 4.40-41ab; the fuller implications are brought out in *Kāvyadarpaṇa*, p. 150). I leave for another occasion a discussion of the acrobatics required by Abhinava to retrofit *vyañjanā* epistemology for an ontology for which it was never intended.

11. If I understand him correctly, K. Krishnamoorthy seems to have been the first scholar to recognize this (1979: 215).

12. The depth of the confusion about Bhaṭṭa Nāyaka in traditional India may be gauged from the footnotes to the selections (see especially appendix #4a). I forgo here a catalogue of the nebulous formulations typical of modern scholarship.

13. Ingalls et al. 1990: 36. *Bhogakṛttva* is by my lights a persistent misspelling for *bhogīkṛttva*.

14. My translations of Bhaṭṭa Nāyaka's new technical terminology will be clarified below.

15. *paṅgau pūrvavyāpāramahimani* (*Kāvyamālā* ed., p. 29.9); *matasyaitasya pūrvasmān* [sc., *abhinavaguptasya*] *matād bhāvakatvavyāpārāntarasvikāra eva viśeṣaḥ. bhogas tu vyaktiḥ. bhogakṛttvaṃ tu vyañjanād aviśiṣṭam* (*Kāvyamālā* ed., p. 30.2). Madhusudhan Shastri ad loc. interprets *pūrvavyāpāra-* as *bhāvakatva*, but that makes no sense to me.

16. See also appendix #7: "Beyond [expression, reproduction, and experientialization] we do not accept anything, certainly not what has been called 'implicature.'" Bhaṭṭa Nāyaka is cited frequently in the *DhĀL* as providing interpretations (of illustrative verses) that do away with the hypothesis of *dhvani* (cf. e.g., pp. 68, 72). Ruyyaka describes the *HD* as *dhvanidhvaṃsagranthaḥ* in his comment on *Vyaktiviveka*, v. 4. See also his restatement of Bhaṭṭa Nāyaka's views in his commentary on the *Kāvyaprakāśa* (appendix #3a) and most compellingly, Dhanika's elaboration in his commentary on *DR* 4.37.

17. Like Abhinava, Ruyyaka usefully notes that Bhaṭṭa Nāyaka's critique actually pertains to *all* earlier positions (*utpatti*, *jñapti* [= *anumiti*], and *abhivyakti*), see Appendix 3a.

18. *DR* 4.38-39.

19. Cited first by Chintamani 1926: 269 (= Gaekwad Oriental Series ed. 3.309); Kane 1971: 224.

20. *DRA* 4.37.

21. This seems more or less to accord with what Searle meant in saying, "One only *refers* as part of the performance of an illocutionary act" (Searle 1969: 25 [italics added]).

22. As serious a student of Indian philosophy as Daya Krishna had to send out a call for someone to explain the precise difference between the two types of *bhāvanā* (Daya Krishna 2000).

23. I take this account not from Mīmāṃsā but from Nyāya, Dinakara's commentary on the *Kārikāvalī* (vv. 149-52, pp. 817 ff.) I now find that the term "modal" (for *śābdī*) has been used in Balasubrahmanya 1995: 59 (a learned discussion that does not, however, seem to truly grasp the logic of Bhaṭṭa Nāyaka's hermeneutical turn).

24. See *Ślokavārttika*, *Vākyārthadhikaraṇa* v. 275: *anuṣṭheye hi viṣaye vidhiḥ puṃsāṃ pravartakaḥ / aṃśatrayeṇa cāpūrṇāṃ nānutiṣṭhati bhāvanām.*

25. *yāvad veda eva puruṣārthatayā sakalam ātmānaṃ na pratipādayati tāvad apramāṇam ... evaṃ sarvavidhīnāṃ prāk puruṣārthalābhād aparyavasānam* (*Tantravārttika*, pp. 11.6-7, 14-15).

26. *Tantravārttika*, p. 11.14-15; *Śṛṅgāraprakāśa*, p. 320.

27. See further McCrea 2000: 433-37.

28. Appendix #11; so Ruyyaka, *tryaṃśo vyāpāraḥ*, appendix #3a.

29. Thus Mallinātha, appendix #5a. The use of *bhāvanā* at the beginning of Bhoja's *ŚP*, beyond which rasa is said to exist (v.10), raises difficulties of its own that I cannot address here. I now see that I have been anticipated in my use of the phrase "aesthetic process" by Nanavati 1998: 47-51, but he has something else in mind, the notion that *abhidhā* for Bhaṭṭa Nāyaka is supposed to have included all three *vṛttis*, or linguistic functions. The historical record, however, does not support this.

30. *DRA* 4.37 ("aesthetic elements": *vibhāvādi-*).

31. The full analogy seems to be available first only in *DhĀL* p. 40 (at Vāmana's *Kāvyālaṅkāra* 1. 1, the *topos* appears neither in the *sūtra* nor in the *vṛtti* but only in the fifteenth-century *Kāmadhenu* commentary).

32. *DRA* 4.37; see also on 4.46: "By virtue of their treatment in literature 'word meanings' in the form of something like the moon, despair, and goosebumps come to be known as factors, transitory emotions, and reactions, respectively. These enable the stable emotion to be 'reproduced' and hence savored, and that is known as rasa."

33. *abhidhā vilakṣaṇā eva* (*DhĀL* p. 183). *Abhidhā* has been misinterpreted both in both modern and traditional exegeses. "Literal meaning" (Ingalls et al. 1990: 221) and "denotation" (Gnoli 1968: 45) are incorrect (likewise Chintamani's critique of S.K. De, 1926: 271 n. 1). That Uttuṅgodaya interprets Bhaṭṭa Nāyaka's *abhidhā* as "an established fact in all domains of communication" (*siddhādyā* [sc., *abhidhā*] *vyavahārabhūmiṣu*, appendix #7) suggests to me the inauthenticity of the verse; see also Samudrabandha's misreading, appendix #4a.

34. Read *atiśayoktirūpakādikāvyavyāpāra-* (for Adyar's *atiśayoktirūpakāvyavyāpāra-*), see *DRA* 4.2.

35. *DRA* 4.46.

36. This would seem to explain Abhinava's argument that *abhidhā* becomes something completely different from everyday discourse only through its interaction with *bhāvakatva* (*DhĀL*, p. 182).

37. Appendix #5. A somewhat confused gloss is given by Ruyyaka (appendix #3a), where wording and meaning are said to be equally *dominant* (contrast his remarks in appendix #4a), for which compare *Vyaktiviveka*, p. 483.

38. Mallinātha shows a clear grasp of this distinction (appendix #5a).

39. The word is not found in the extant fragments but associated with Bhaṭṭa Nāyaka in all summaries of his position (note that it is unknown to

Ānandavardhana). I believe that Kangle (1973: 380) is correct to deny any such meaning to the idea of *sāmānyaguṇa* at *NŚ* 7.6+ (of which Bharata makes no further use, with the modest exception of 24.184). Dhanika's citation on DR 4.2 is therefore an anachronism, committed in order to provide a more ancient pedigree to Bhaṭṭa Nāyaka's thought (so too Abhinava, *ABh* vol. 1, p. 275, line 6).

40. With this Dhanika is making the point that each viewer thinks the character is similar to himself, not that "commonalization" is available to all people (though Dhanika may well have thought so; contrast n. 69 below).

41. The spectator would be feeling desire toward "woman" as such, not toward the divine mother, Sītā.

42. *DRA* 4.40-41ab.

43. As Bahurūpa Miśra puts it, "[The aesthetic elements like the *ālambanavibhāva*] have their existence as such heightened by virtue of being used in literature through the refinements of language qualities (phonic texture and the like) and figures of sense and sound. These elements, each associated with their specific rasa, enable the stable emotion to be 'reproduced'" (on *DR* 4.46-47ab). See also Mallinātha, appendix #5a. Ruyyaka's understanding (appendix 3a, the aesthetic elements lend *abhidhā* "brilliance," the way moonbeams transform the moonstone) seems inexplicably to reverse the process.

44. *nibiḍanijamohasaṃkaṭatānivāraṇakāriṇā* (*ABh*, vol. 1, p. 271, line 2, very possibly a direct quote). I take this to refer to the initial unconscious perplexity of the viewer reacting to an actor playing a character who should not be a foundational factor for the spectator. No metaphysical concerns need be assumed.

45. See appendix #1b and notes.

46. The term *cittabhūmi* is found first in Buddhist thought (*Abhidharmakośa*) and then in yoga, where the mind is also said to have five *bhūmis* (see n. 49 below). The notion of *cittabhūmis* is found nowhere else in aesthetic discourse.

47. *DRA* 4.43-45ab.

48. Ingalls et al. 1990: 36. See n. 96.

49. For example, Bhoja's understanding of the five mental states, *kṣiptaṃ, mūḍaṃ, vikṣiptam, ekāgraṃ, niruddham iti cittabhūmayaḥ* (*Yogasūtrabhāṣya* 1.1.3), especially his correlation of *vikṣiptam* with *sattva* and the gods, shows that there is no connection with Bhaṭṭa Nāyaka's violence-related *vikṣepa* (see Bhoja's commentary ad loc.)

50. *KP*, p. 560; *DRA*, 4.43.

51. Abhinava tries, quite shamelessly, to reappropriate this triad for his own view (*DhĀL*, p. 189; Ingalls et al., p. 225).

52. Note *vyāpāraprādhānya* in Ruyyaka, appendix #2a; *abhidhādivilakṣaṇavyāpāramātra-* in *Sāhityadarpaṇa*, p. 74. Prabhākara Bhaṭṭa in Mithila in 1583 gracefully summarizes Bhaṭṭa Nāyaka's system (*kāvyārthaparyantābhidhā ratyādiviṣaya bhāvanā sahṛdayaviṣyaś ca bhoga iti* (*Rasapradīpa*, p. 26: "'Expression,' which encompasses literary meaning; 'reproduction,' which pertains to the stable emotions; 'experience,' which pertains to the sensitive reader or viewer"), though it is certain he had no direct access to the *HD*).

53. The one scholar I have found who appreciates the importance of this passage is P.-S. Filliozat (in his edition of *Pratāparudrayaśobhūṣana*, 1963: xi-xii), but his assessment of its meaning is very different from mine. It is vaguely true, I suppose, to say that for Bhaṭṭa Nāyaka "le rasa est autre chose que le sense poétique et la jouissance [bhoga] du rasa autre chose que l'appréhension de ce sens," but that is an odd way of describing Bhaṭṭa Nāyaka's hermeneutical turn. And while Filliozat rightly (and for the first time that I am aware of) flags the importance Abhinavagupta's *śruti* example, instead of describing his goal of appropriation to be "pour la [sc. *bhāvanā*] modeler à nouveau et l'inscrire dans le cadre de sa pensée," it would be more accurate to say that Abhinava brings out the true hermeneutical significance of Bhaṭṭa Nāyaka's thought (unless he is actually still borrowing from him). And what he misses most of all is the core linking concept of *sādharaṇīkaraṇa.*

54. Read *āse*, or possibly *āsāi* or *āsīy* (for *āste*).

55. Read *-svabhāvā* (for *-svābhāvā*) and delete *daṇḍa.*

56. *ABh*, vol. 1, p. 272, lines 21-25.

57. *āmnāyasya kriyārthatvāt* (scriptural tradition is for the purpose of sacrificial action), *Pūrvamīmāṃsāsūtra* 1.2.1.

58. As Kumārila puts it, *buddhipūrvakāriṇo hi puruṣā yāvat praśasto 'yam iti nāvabudhyante tāvan na pravartante. vidhiśaktir* [v. l.l] *avasīdati; tāṃ prāśastyajñānam uttabhnāti* (People who act with any deliberation do not engage in an act until they know it is commendable. The power of the deontic verb itself can falter; when it does it is reinforced by an awareness of some commendation of the act), *Tantravārttika* pp. 12-13.

59. *Pūrvamīmāṃsāsūtra* 1.2.7. Such injunctions must be found or presumed to be present, for otherwise the descriptive passage becomes meaningless (*akal-*

pite vidhāv [arthavādasya] anarthakyaṃ syāt, Tantravārttika p. 19).

60. *ālasyena nivartamānaṃ puruṣaṃ*, Dinakara (p. 820), who goes on to cite the anonymous verse: *liṅa 'bhidhā saiva ca śabdabhāvanā bhāvyā ca tasyāḥ puruṣapravṛttiḥ / saṃbandhabodhaḥ karaṇaṃ tadīyaṃ prarocanā cāṅgatayopayujyate* // (Expression by a modal verb is called "modal production", and what it produces is human action. The instrument of modal production is understanding of the syntax, and incitement [through the *arthavāda*] is used as a subsidiary cause [i.e. as the "method"]). This all builds on *Tantravārttika*, pp. 12-13.

61. *Tantravārttika*, p. 12 (*arthavādāḥ .... śabdātmikayā tu grahiṣyanti*, the descriptive portions are necessarily comprised within modal production).

62. These are typical formulae; I do not believe actual texts are being cited.

63. "Grammatical transformation," *saṃkramaṇa*, but the word seems unattested in precisely this sense. The *-ādi* presumably refers to the interpretative techniques *adhyāhāra*, *vipariṇāma*, and so on (see e.g. Śabara on *Pūrvamīmāṃsāsūtra* 2.1).

64. The Jain Hemacandra replaces the reference to Vedic sacrifice with an account of Śāmba's hymn to the sun, whereby this son of Krishna cured a serious illness: A person hearing that story, according to the verses cited by Hemacandra, comes to think that he too will sing such a hymn to attain healthfulness. This alternate version raises a range of complicated questions, not least whether it was original to Bhaṭṭa Nāyaka, as Gnoli believes (1968: 53), but on what evidence I cannot tell.

65. For Bhoja in *ŚP* 6, these are all really aspects of the same phenomenon, sentence meaning: When sentence meaning has the form of some human activity, it is called *bhāvanā*; when it has the form of a verbal activity it is called a command (or prohibition); when it has the form of intellection, it is called *pratibhā* (p. 322).

66. Mīmāṃsā never seems to put the matter this way, however. The only question Kumārila raises is how an authorless text's commandments work: the deontic verb itself is insentient and cannot actually compel anything, but since the human agent cannot logically compel himself, the deontic verb fulfills that function mediated by the consciousness of the agent (*Tantravārttika*, p. 12.21-22).

67. *Tantravārttika*, p. 12.17: *arthabhāvanā* is not required for *arthavāda* passages; they are however taken up in (required by?) *śabdabhāvanā* (*iha hi liṅādiyukteṣu vākyeṣu dve bhāvane gamyete, śabdātmikā cārthātmikā ca. tatrārthātmikayārthavādā nāpekṣyante, śabdātmikayā tu grahiṣyante*).

68. *anvākhyāne vartamāne dvayaṃ niṣpadyate yac ca vṛttāntajñānaṃ yac ca kasminścit prarocanā dveṣo vā* (*Mīmāṃsādarśana*, p. 33); see also p. 31: *stutiśabdā stuvantaḥ kriyāṃ prarocayamānā anuṣṭhātṝn upakariṣyanti kriyāyāḥ. evam imāni sarvāṇy eva padāni kañcid arthaṃ stuvanti vidadhati.*

69. *ABh*, vol. 1, p. 273, lines 1-14; p. 274, line 6. At the end of this extract Abhinava is presenting a notion of *sādharaṇīkaraṇa*, as a process "made common" among the viewers that I do not believe was maintained by Bhaṭṭa Nāyaka or his followers (compare n. 40 above).

70. "Transforming itself before one's eyes," *cakṣuṣor iva viparivartamānam* (*bhāvam*) is almost certainly Bhaṭṭa Nāyaka's language, see *DRA* 4.1 and 27 (*śrotṛprekṣakāṇām antar* [*bhāvakacetasi*, 37] *viparivartamāno ratyādidir ... sthāyī*); *Rasārṇavasudhākara*, appendix #1b (*vibhāvādibhāvānām ... sākṣād ... viparivartamānānām*). Curiously, Abhinava seems not even to think of some of these ideas as Bhaṭṭa Nāyaka's; in *ABh*, vol. 1, p. 275, line 6, for example, he attributes the idea of *sādharaṇīkaraṇa* to Bharata.

71. Mīmāṃsā itself nowhere, so far as I can see, offers an explicit discussion of the textual psychology described by Abhinava, by which the *lakṣaṇā* or indirection of the *arthavāda* leads the reader to transform an ancient meritorious act into a present possibility.

72. As Ruyyaka says, it is thanks to "the exceptional nature (*vaiśiṣṭya*) of the full complement of aesthetic elements in poetry and drama ([*vibhāvādi-*] *sāmāgrī-*)" that "there comes about this process of reproduction" (Appendix 3a).

73. Here the analogy becomes slightly asymmetrical: the sacrificer *produces exactly* what the primordial "they/he" once did, and receives the same reward. Literary production is *re*production of the emotional state, and of a very different sort from the original, especially in terms of *phala*.

74. For Kumārila, a text like the *Mahābhārata* or the *Rāmāyaṇa* can only be either descriptive (which is useless) or didactic (which is not); if this didactic element is not explicit it has to be taken to be present by implication (*sarvopākhyāneṣu ... kathaṃcid gamyamānastutinindāparigrahaḥ*). The knowledge that these texts provide has nothing to do with their truth (*tattva*) but only with their moral value (*sarve ca stutyarthena pramāṇam*) (*Tantravārttika*, pp. 14-15; he does, however, allow that there are some passages that are utterly irreducible to any moral content and that simply give "pleasure").

75. Gadamer 1996: 307-30

76. Gupta 1963 (I thank Somdev Vasudeva for this reference).

77. For example, Hjort and Laver 1997; Neill 2003; Robinson 2004.

78. Passages not relevant to the argument here have been omitted. The full record is available in Pollock, forthcoming, whose numbering has been preserved here.

79. *śabdaprādhānyam āśritya tatra śāstraṃ pṛthag viduḥ / arthatattvena yuktaṃ tu vadanty ākhyānam etayoḥ / dvayor guṇatve vyāpāraprādhānye kāvyagīr bhavet //* (cited *ABh*, vol. 2, p. 298 [*arthe tattvena yukte tu*], *DhĀL*, p. 87, *Kāvyānuśāna*, p. 5; Jayaratha on *Alaṅkārasarvasva*, p. 9, who reads *-dhīr* for *-gīr*, "we have what we think of as literature"). Abhinava's criticism here turns on the meaning of "process": If the term refers to the relishing of rasa based on implicature then Bhaṭṭa Nāyaka is saying nothing new; and if it refers to signification or expression as such (*abhidhaiva)* then this has already been shown not to have primacy (*DhĀL*, p. 87). Both objections are odd: Bhaṭṭa Nāyaka rejected implicature, as Abhinava well knew, and he also defined "process" far more broadly than mere expression (though Abhinava repeats the narrow interpretation in *ABh*, vol. 2, p. 298, line 9: *bhaṭṭanāyakenāpi kuśa laśikṣitābhidhāvyāpārapradhānaṃ kāvyam.*

80. *kāvye rasayitā sarvo na boddhā na niyogabhāk* (cited *DhĀL*, p. 39). My translation is supported by *DR* 1.6, which echoes this v. Uttuṅgodaya (and independently Rāmaṣāraka) understands that the capacity to experience rasa constitutes the qualification for literature: every person who experiences rasa is qualified for literature, every person who seeks knowledge ... is not (p. 78). But there is no reason to believe, *pace* Ingalls et al. 1990: 73, that Uttuṅgodaya knew the *HD* at first hand (it is hard to believe his text was available in south India in the fourteenth century, and solely to Uttuṅgodaya), and must therefore be regarded as an unimpeachable interpreter; the only independent "citation" of Bhaṭṭa Nāyaka in *Kaumudī* is #7 below, but those are unlikely to be the words of Bhaṭṭa Nāyaka. Another interpretation: every process in literature offers rasa (like a beloved); it does not offer knowledge (like a friend) or give commandments (like a master). Abhinava cites the verse to show that Bhaṭṭa Nāyaka agrees that *rasacarvaṇā* is the principal matter in literary experience. But of course the point of contention between Ānandavardhana and Bhaṭṭa Nāyaka is not whether rasa is the telos of literature, but how rasa works.

81. Given the discussion of *abhidhā* in appendix #11, this definition is erroneous, which casts down on the authenticity of the verse.

82. *vyāpāras trividho budhair abhimataḥ kāvye 'bhidhābhāvanābhogotpādakatātmanā tadadhiko nāsti dhvanir nāma naḥ / siddhādyā vyavahārabhūmiṣu vibhāvādyarthasādharaṇīkārātmā tv aparā nirargalarasāsvādātmikevāntimā //* (cited *Kaumudī* on *DhĀL*, p. 79; cf. Krishnamoorthy 1979: 221). Given the art meter

used here (along with the inadequate grasp of *abhidhā* just noted), it is unlikely that the verse is original to Bhaṭṭa Nāyaka.

83. *vilakṣaṇa evāyaṃ kṛtijñaptibhedebhyaḥ svādanākhyaḥ kaścid vyāpāraḥ* (cited *Sāhityadarpaṇa* p. 74 and not attributed to Bhaṭṭa Nāyaka but bearing all the hallmarks of his idiom; it is not in verse but the *HD* is likely to have been mixed verse and prose; Viśvanātha's use of *vistāra* [*sic*] (p. 71) certainly and *vyāpāramātra* (p. 74) possibly also hearken back to him). "Making" refers to Lollaṭa's *utpatti*- or *poṣaka-pakṣa*, "knowing" to Śaṅkuka's *anumitipakṣa*.

84. That is, primary and secondary meaning. (Rāmaṣāraka erroneously understands as expression and reproduction, but implicature is not of the same order as reproduction and so not to be distinguished from it.)

85. *dhvanir nāmāparo yo 'sau vyāpāro vyañjanātmakaḥ / tasya siddhe 'pi bhede syāt kāvyāṃśatvaṃ na rūpatā //* (*DhĀL*, p. 39; Jayaratha on *Alaṅkārasarvasva*, p. 9). Abhinava cites the verse to indicate that Bhaṭṭa Nāyaka's position has been rejected by the *DhĀ*.

86. *abhidhā bhāvanā cānyā tadbhogīkṛtir eva ca / abhidhādhāmatāṃ yāte śabdārthālaṅkṛtī tataḥ //* (1) *bhāvanābhāvya eṣo 'pi śṛṅgārādigaṇo mataḥ / tadbhogīkṛtirūpeṇa vyāpyate siddhimān naraḥ //* (2) *dṛśyamānāthavā* [corrupt?] *mokṣe yāty aṅgatvam iyaṃ sphutam //* (3) (cited *ABh*, vol. 1, p. 271, line 6; *Kāvyānuśāna*, pp. 90-91 (vv. 1-2); Jayaratha on *Alaṅkārasarvasva*, p. 9; in v. 1, I read -*kṛtir* with Jayaratha instead of H's –*kṛtam*; in v. 2, I read *mataḥ* with Jayaratha instead of *hi yat* with Abhinavagupta and Hemacandra, which seems to misinterpret *tad*- in c as correlative, when it is in fact part of the compound that is a technical term, as v. 1 indicates; and again with Jayaratha –*kṛti*- for --*kṛta*-). "Participates in," literally, "becomes a limb of." In the original text the verses may not have been consecutive.

87. This is standard Mīmāṃsā theory: for the first, *arthaikatvād ekaṃ vākyam* (*Pūrvamīmāṃsāsūtra* 2.1.46); for the second, *bhāvanaiva hi vākyārthaḥ* (*Ślokavārttika Tadbhūtādhikaraṇa* v. 330), and *bhāvanā* by definition is bringing forth a result.

88. *saṃsargādir yathā śāstra ekatvāt phalayogataḥ / vākyārthas, tadvad evātra śṛṅgārādī raso mataḥ //* (cited *ABh*, vol. 1, p. 271; *Kāvyānuśāna*, p. 97). Hemacandra adds (the *ABh* passage is I believe corrupt) the qualification that, unlike Bhaṭṭa Nāyaka's doctrine of *bhāvana* [*sic*], this view has Abhinava's full endorsement. But in *DR*, the idea of rasa as *vākya* is clearly part and parcel of Bhaṭṭa Nāyaka's argument against *vyañjanā* and in favor of the *tātparya* position (Dhanika on *DR* 4.37), a linkage that will be thoroughly misunderstood later in the tradition (see Kumārasvamin on *Pratāparudrayaśobhūṣaṇa* 4.137, and Jagannātha Paṇḍitarāja, *Rasagaṅgādhara* [*Kāvyamālā* ed.], p. 30.2). Normally *saṃsarga* is an idea associated with Nyāya, but the term is used loosely here; less likely the

"intimate association" of two words or things, and the rest of the semantic factors, see *Vākyapadīya* 2.315 ff.; *Kāvyānuśāna* 1.23 ff.

89. Pp. 270-71 and pp. 96-7 respectively, supplemented by the version in *DhĀL*, pp. 180-81 and Māṇikyacandra's précis (Mysore ed., vol. 1, pp. 216-21). The account is so condensed as to be unintelligible without embedding in the translation an exegesis based on these supplements, which I have done.

90. Both texts read *sādhāraṇīkaraṇāyogyatvāt*, but taking it in Bhaṭṭa Nāyaka's technical sense makes for nonsense here: It is precisely in such circumstances that "commonalization" is supposed to work, as Dhanika clearly shows (on 4.40-41ab). Moreover, this is Bhaṭṭa Nāyaka's *siddhānta*—that commonality with such beings is not natural, it is produced by literature—and it would be a petitio principii to adduce it here as an argument against the *pratītivāda*. *DhĀL*'s *pūrvapakṣin* gives the right sense: *kāntātvaṃ sādhāraṇam*; and Māṇikyacandra's text strongly suggests something like *sādhāraṇyāyogyatvāt*, which is what I adopt in the translation. This would also construe well with *asādhāraṇyāt* in the next line. It may simply be that the term is not to be taken in its technical sense (note that later *sādhāraṇya* itself will become a technical term identical to *sādhāraṇīkaraṇa*, *-kṛti*, *Sāhityadarpaṇa* 3.9-11).

91. Although the final clause is found in this position in all four sources, the argument more properly belongs at the end of the following paragraph, describing a problem with perceiving rasa externally. This is how *DR* presents it (4.38-39). I cannot explain its current—to me clearly erroneous—position (and things are not helped by reading, as does Gnoli, *pratyakṣād iva. nāyaka-*).

92. I read *tan na* for *tatra* in both texts (see also Kangle 1973: 147).

93. Ingalls et al. 1990: 227 note that "manifestation" here is used in a more general, non-linguistic sense, of bringing to light a rasa supposed to preexist in latent form in the spectator's psyche, but it is not clear to me that the general and the specific senses were ever clearly distinguished in this discourse.

94. So that one would never be said to have a full rasa experience, see Ruyyaka below (and contrast Ingalls et al. 1990: 221).

95. These are strictly the features of the expression process, but are assimilated to production as contributory elements. See also Ruyyaka appendix #3a.

96. *druti, vistāra, vikāsa* (H reads *vistara*, which is authenticated by *DR* 4.43; Mallinātha on *Ekāvalī* p. 96 notes that the form *vistāra* is a dubious usage in this context; Ingalls et al. 1990: 36 may have misread as *vikāśa* and hence translated as "radiance").

97. *Kāvyaprakāśa*, vol. 2, p. 560.

98. I read *-satattvena* (for *-sattvena*) with Śrīdhara.

99. *Kāvyaprakāśa*, vol. 2, pp. 563.7 ff.

100. I read *-nikarānatikrāntatvāt* (for *-ākarakrāntatvāt*; see Śrīdhara *Kāvyaprakāśa*, vol. 2, p. 565. But what does he mean by this, that the *utpatti* of rasa in Rāma is a historically specific thing to which we here and now have no access?

101. *śabdavyāpāra*. Note that Ruyyaka is clearly using this as a synonym of *abhidhā*.

102. Since for Bhaṭṭa Nāyaka, it is the figures of sound and sense that are involved rather than direct and indirect meaning, we must assume that "indirect meaning" (*sāntarārtha*) is another way of characterizing figures of speech (recall that for thinkers from Daṇḍin to Bhoja, *vakrokti* was a synonym of *alaṅkāra* as such).

103. Ruyyaka's formulation here and in what follows awkward. As extract appendix #5 clearly shows, and as Ruyyaka asserts at the end of the next sentence here, the literary language process, where both wording and meaning have primacy, cannot be "common" to scripture and historical discourse. It is only the use of troped and untroped language that is common, and it is no doubt to the latter that he refers here.

104. That is, for anyone other than her husband Rāma, such as the spectator.

105. *bhavad bhāvanam* strikes me as dubious, though it is given in both editions, and in Śrīdhara's *Kāvyaprakāśa* commentary, which essentially reproduces Ruyyaka.

106. For *guṇālaṅkāratvāt* read *guṇālaṅkārayogāt*, see Śrīdhara, *Kāvyaprakāśa*, vol. 2, p. 565 (also *guṇālaṅkāramayatva* in *ABh*, vol. 1, p. 271, line 1 and *Kāvyānuśāna*, p. 96.19 cited above).

107. I omit the commentator Vidyācakravartin, who has a false reading in the first sentence (*kāvyātmatva*, for *kāvyāṃśatva*) that causes him to completely misunderstand Ruyyaka's argument, and who has nothing of importance to add to our understanding. Clearly by his date (early fourteenth century) direct access to Bhaṭṭa Nāyaka's text was no longer possible.

108. The text has been imperfectly transmitted, with Jayaratha alone preserving the truth: *kāvyāṃśatvaṃ bruvatā* J (translated in text). Completely adrift are Samudrabandha, *kāvye sattvaṃ bruvatā* ("while admitting the existence in literature of the particular linguistic function known as implica-

ture, which he designates as 'fanciful utterance'"), and Vidyācakravartin, *kāvyātmatvaṃ kathayatā* ("while claiming that implicature is the essence of literature").

109. *-uttīrṇa*, borrowed from *DhĀL*, p. 52. *Bhoga* is the result of *bhāvakatva*, and so cannot be "far beyond" it (Ingalls et al. 1990: 81).

110. The reference is to *DhĀ* 1.1c.

111. I read *rupatā* (*rūpitā*).

112. *kavikarmaṇaḥ*. I find this strange, since *vyāpāra* is not itself the literary work (the normal meaning of the term *kavikarma*) but the capacities of the literary work to produce an experience of it.

113. Page 85.

114. I read *sādhāraṇīkṛta-* (for *sādhāraṇīkṛtena*).

115. That is, most importantly, the character.

116. *Rasārṇavasudhākara*, p. 251.

117. See *DRA* 4.2, p. 168.

118. Read *abhidhāvyāpāreṇa* (for the disputed reading *abhidhāparyāyeṇa*, which is impossible).

Abbreviations

ABh = *Abhinavabhāratī*
DR = *Daśarūpaka*
DRA = *Daśarūpakāvaloka*
DhĀ = *Dhvanyāloka*
DhĀL = *Dhvanyālokalocana*
HD = *Hṛdayadarpaṇa*
KP = *Kāvyaprakāśa*
NŚ = *Nāṭyaśāstra*
ŚP = *Śṛṅgāraprakāśa*

Bibliography

Primary Sources

Alaṅkārasarvasva of Rājānaka Ruyyaka, with the commentary of Jayaratha. Edited by Durgaprasad and Kashinath Pandurang Parab. Bombay: Nirnaya Sagar Press, 1893; with the commentary of Samudrabandha, ed. T. Ganapati Sastri. Trivandrum: Travancore Government Press, 1915; with the commentary of Vidyācakravartin, ed. S.S. Janaki. Delhi: Meharchand Lachhmandas, 1965.

Daśarūpaka of Dhanaṃjaya, with the *Avaloka* of Dhanika, and the subcommentary of Bhaṭṭa Nṛsiṃha. Ed. T. Venkatacharya. Madras: Adyar Library and Research Centre, 1969; with the commentary of Bahurūpa Miśra, ed. A.N. Pandey. Varanasi/Delhi: Bharatiya Vidya Prakashan, 1979; with commentary, ed. Sudarsanacarya Panchanadiya. Bombay: Gujarati Printing Press, 1927.

Dhvanyāloka of Ānandavardhana with the *Locana* of Abhinavagupta and the subcommentary of Rāmaṣāraka. Edited by Pattabhirama Sastry. Varanasi: Chowkhamba Sanskrit Series Office, 1940; with the *Kaumudī* of Uttuṅgodaya, ed. Kuppuswami Shastri et al. Madras: Kuppuswami Sastri Research Institute, 1944.

Ekāvalī of Vidyādhara, with commentary of Mallinātha. Edited by Kamalasankara Pranasankara Trivedi. Bombay: Government Central Book Depot, 1903.

Karikāvalī of Viśvanātha Tarkapañcānana, with the commentaries of Dinakara et al. Edited by C. Sankara Rama Sastry. Madras: Balamanorama Press, 1923.

Kāvalaṅkārasūtra and *vṛtti* of Vāmana, with the *Kāmadhenu* commentary of Gopendra Tippa Bhupala. Edited by S.K.S. Vatsyacakaravarti. Srirangam: Sri Vani Vilas Press, 1909.

Kāvyadarpaṇa of Rājacūdāmaṇi Dīkṣita. Edited by S. Subrahmanya Sastri. Srirangam: Vani Vilas Press, 1910.

Kāvyānuśāsana of Hemacandra, 2nd ed. Edited by Rasiklal Chhotalal Parikh and Vinayak Martand Kulkarni. Bombay: Sri Mahavira Jaina Vidyalaya, 1964.

Kāvyaprakāśa [of Mammaṭa], solah ṭīkāoṃ sahit, 6 vols. Edited by Jotsna Mohan. Delhi: Nag Prakashan, 1995-.

Kāvyaprakāśa with the *Saṅketa* commentary of Māṇikyacandra and the *Madhumati* commentary of Ravi Bhattacharya. Edited by N.S. Venktanathachrya. 2 vols. Mysore: Oriental Research Institute, 1974.

Mīmāṃsādarśana with the commentary of Śabara Svāmin. Edited by Ratnagopala Bhatta. Benares: Vidya Vilasa Press, 1910.

Nāṭyaśāstra of Bharata, with the *Abhinavabhāratī* of Abhinavagupta, vol. 1, 4th ed. Edited by K. Krishnamoorthy. Baroda: Oriental Institute, 1992; vol. 2, 2nd edn. Edited by V.M. Kulkarni and Tapasvi Nandi. Baroda: Oriental Institute, 2001. (cited by volume, page, line)

Pratāparudrayaśobhūṣana of Vidyānātha, with the Commentary *Ratnāpaṇa* of Kumārasvāmin. Edited by V. Raghavan. Madras: Samskritvidyasamiti, 1987.

Rasapradīpa of Prabhākara Bhaṭṭa. Edited by Narayana Sastri Khiste. Varanasi: Tara Printing Works, 1925.

Rasagaṅgādhara of Jagannātha Paṇḍitarāja. Edited by Mathuranath Sastri: Bombay: Nirnaya Sagar Press, 1947; edited by Kedarnath Ojha. Varanasi: Sampurnananda Sanskrit University, 1981; edited by Madhusudan Shastri: Varanasi: Banaras Hindu University, v.s. 2020.

Rasārṇavasudhākara of Siṃhabhūpāla. Edited by T. Venkatacharya. Madras: Adyar Library and Research Centre, 1979.

Sāhityadarpaṇa with the commentaries of Anantadāsa and Maheśvara Tarkālaṅkāra Bhaṭṭācārya. [No ed.] Lahore: Motilal Banarsidass, 1938.

Ślokavārttika of Kumārila Bhaṭṭa, with the commentary of Pārthasārathi Miśra. Edited by Swami Dwarikadas Sastri. Varanasi: Tara Publications, 1978.

Śṛṅgāraprakāśa of Bhoja, vol. 1. Edited by Rewaprasad Dwivedi. Delhi: Indira Gandhi National Centre for the Arts, 2007.

Tantravārttika in *Mīmāṃsādarśanam*, vol. 2. Edited by Vasudev Abhyankar. Pune: Anandashrama Press, 1970.

Vakroktijīvita of Kuntaka. Edited by K. Krishnamoorthy. Dharwar: Karanataka University Press, 1977.

Vyaktiviveka of Mahimabhaṭṭa. Edited by Rewaprasad Dwivedi. Varanasi: Chowkhambha Sanskrit Series Office, 1964.

Yogasūtra with the commentaries of Vyāsa and Bhoja. Pune: Anandashrama Press, 1904.

Secondary Sources

Balasubrahmanya, N. 1995. "The Bhavanavada of Bhatta Nayaka." In B. Channakeshava and H.V. Nagaraja Rao, eds. *Ānanda Bhāratī: Dr. K. Krishnamoorthy Felicitation Volume*. Mysore: D.V.K. Murthy.

Bhattacharya, Sivaprasad. 1981. "Three lost Masterpieces of the Alaṁkāraśāstra." In *Studies in Indian Poetics*. Calcutta: Firma KLM, 1964.

Chintamani, T.R. 1926. "Fragments of Bhaṭṭanāyaka." *Journal of Oriental Research, Madras* 1: 267-76.

Daya Krishna. 2000. "Query." *Journal of Indian Council of Philosophical Research* 17 (3): 188.

Filliozat, Pierre-Sylvain, tr. 1963. *Le Pratāparudrīya de Vidyānātha*. Pondicherry: Institut français d'Indologie.

Gadamer, Hans-Georg. 1996. *Truth and Method*, 2nd revised ed. New York: Continuum.

Gnoli, Raniero. 1968. *The Aesthetic Experience According to Abhinavagupta*, 2nd ed. Varanasi: Chowkhamba Sanskrit Series Office.

Gupta, P.S. 1963. "Śaṅkuka, a Buddhist Logician." *Vishveshvaranand Indological Journal* 1 (2): 315-19.

Hjort, Mette, and Sue Laver, eds. 1997. *Emotion and the Arts*. New York: Oxford University Press.

Ingalls, Daniel H.H., J.M. Masson and M.V. Patwardhan, tr. 1990. *The Dhvanyāloka of Ānandavardhana*. Cambridge: Harvard University Press.

Kane, P.V. 1971. *History of Sanskrit Poetics*. Delhi: Motilal Banarsidass.

Kangle, R.P., ed. and tr. 1973. *Rasabhāvavicāra*. Bombay: Maharashtra Rajya Sahitya-Samskrti Mandal. (in Marathi)

Krishnamoorthy, K. 1979. *Studies in Indian Aesthetics and Criticism*. Mysore: D.V.K. Murthy.

McCrea, Lawrence. 2000. "The Hierarchical Organization of Language in Mīmāṃsā Interpretive Theory." *Journal of Indian Philosophy* 28: 429–59.

____. 2009. *The Teleology of Poetics in Medieval Kashmir*. Cambridge: Harvard University Press.

Nanavati, Rajendra I. 1998. *Essays on Sanskrit Poetics*. Vadodara: Oriental Institute.

Neill, Alex. 2003. "Art and Emotions." In Jerrold Levinson, ed. *The Oxford Handbook of Aesthetics*. New York: Oxford University Press.

Pollock, Sheldon. 1998. "Bhoja's *Śṛṅgāraprakāśa* and the Problem of *Rasa*: A Historical Introduction and Translation." *Asiatische Studien/Études asiatiques* 70 (1): 117-92.

____. Forthcoming. *Reader on Rasa: A Historical Sourcebook in Indian Aesthetic Theory*. New York: Columbia University Press.

Robinson, Jenefer. 2004. "The Emotions in Art." In Peter Kivy, ed. *The Blackwell Guide to Aesthetics*. Oxford: Blackwell.

Searle, John. 1969. *Speech Acts: An Essay in the Philosophy of Language*. Cambridge: Cambridge University Press.

The Other Kind of Brahman: Rāma Jāmadagnya and the Psychosocial Construction of Brahman Power in the *Mahābhārata*

ADHEESH SATHAYE

Among the most innovative of Professor Goldman's contributions to our understanding of the Sanskrit epics are his studies of Rāma Jāmadagnya, the *kṣattravṛttir brāhmaṇaḥ* whose infamous genocidal rampage against the Kṣatriyas has left the fringes of the *Mahābhārata* indelibly stained in blood. Working with V.S. Sukthankar's 'Bhṛguization' theory of the epic's textual development, Goldman has provided extensive evidence for a psychological basis for the appearance of the Bhārgava Rāma and his relatives within the epic. Despite a revival of Indological interest in both the textuality of the *Mahābhārata* and its place in early Indian history, and despite a number of recent studies directly "reconsidering" the narratives of Rāma Jāmadagnya, we are only beginning to grasp how the presence of such deeply moving characters at the *Mahābhārata*'s margins granted the epic a unique cultural power in a changing social and political world.

With an interest in this very question, and in appreciation of a scholar and teacher whose work has always been marked by theoretical innovation and a command of the epic text, this essay attempts to bring Professor Goldman's psychoanalytic essays to bear upon current discussions of Rāma Jāmadagnya, Bhṛguization, and the textual production of the Sanskrit *Mahābhārata*. Whereas Goldman has recovered Freudian oedipal themes amidst the Brahman-Kṣatriya conflict at the heart of this sage's life-story, I will re-project these basic fears of familial aggression and desire back into a sociopolitical context in order to arrive at a more nuanced understanding of how Rāma Jāmadagnya, along with his great-uncle Viśvāmitra, represented 'psychosocial' anxieties of Brahman power in early India.

More specifically, I will examine one particular Bhārgava legend, told four times in the *Mahābhārata*, that genealogically links Rāma Jāmadagnya to the equally volatile Viśvāmitra, the king who became a Brahman sage. As it turns out, these sages are blood relatives, and their mixed-up behavior is explained to be entirely a result of a prenatal mistake committed by Viśvāmitra's sister, Satyavatī, when she switched a *caru* (a fertility concoction) that her Bhārgava husband Ṛcīka had prepared for her with one meant especially for her mother, the queen of Kānyakubja.[1] Few Indologists have related the Satyavatī legend to the Bhrguization theory in any significant detail, and even for Goldman, it serves primarily as an example of "metamyth", through which the "Bhārgava mythmakers and epic redactors were able to elaborate the Bhṛguid myths and integrate them, for their own ends, into the pseudohistorical framework of the *Mahābhārata*".[2] A close reading of this story will demonstrate how this metamyth reconciles the Kṣatriya-like behavior of both Rāma Jāmadagnya and Viśvāmitra as a kind of physiological birth defect, in an effort to alleviate Brahman anxieties emerging from the careers of these two notorious sages.

In doing so, this essay seeks to extend an argument I have made elsewhere that the epic and purāṇic legends of Viśvāmitra served to naturalize *varṇa* as a social practice in early India.[3] Viśvāmitra successfully transforms himself into a Brahman, seemingly in contradiction to the fundamental laws of *varṇa*, but as the Satyavatī legend informs us, it happened only because his body was already Brahmanic by birth, not due to any willful breaking of the rules. Rāma Jāmadagnya is similarly shown to be the flip side of the same exotic coin—a Brahman who behaves like a Kṣatriya, but only because he was already born with these tendencies. As the objects of the epic gaze, Viśvāmitra and Rāma Jāmadagnya thus come to represent the 'Other' kind of Brahman, who, much like the 'Oriental' of modern colonial discourse, is both exoticized and subordinated to the Brahman Self through the production of knowledge—that is, through the authoritative telling of stories about them in the *Mahābhārata*. At the same time, since these sages are still treated as Brahmans, they are not wholly 'Othered', and remain paradoxical representatives of the same Brahman Self. It is this ambivalence between identification and antagonism—precisely the inner conflict of the oedipal triangle—that grants a cultural 'force' to the Brahmanic discourse of power in early India. In other words, these stories about Brahmans who behaved like Kṣatriyas allowed real-life Brahmans to speak of themselves as the social elite, while simultaneously distancing 'normal' Brahmanhood from their un-Brahman-like behavior. To arrive at these conclusions, I begin with an examination of Sukthankar's text-historical theory of Bhṛguization and its more recent critics who prefer to see the Bhārgava legends as a 'thread' rather than a 'layer' within the epic. To understand the reasons for why the epic's composers might have picked up this thread, I turn to Goldman's psychoanalytic recovery of oedipal themes within the closely-related careers of Rāma Jāmadagnya and Viśvāmitra. Finally, in what can only be a preliminary effort to explain why the *Mahābhārata* was woven together with such strange narrative threads in the historical context of early India, I will situate Goldman's findings within a discursive analysis of the Satyavatī legend. I hope to show how this genealogy of Brahmans who did not quite fit the mold participated in the regulation of how one could speak of Brahman power within the turbulent sociopolitical sphere of northern India roughly after the fall of the Mauryan empire.

Bhṛguization and Epic Textual History

In one sense, a connection between Brahman power and the Bhārgava legends in the *Mahābhārata* is precisely what lies at the heart of V.S. Sukthankar's Bhṛguization hypothesis. Indologists before Sukthankar had already noticed an overabundance of stories about these sages in the epic text, but this observation was part of a general assessment of the *Mahābhārata* as a heterogenous and disorganized text—in Oldenberg's words, a "monstrous chaos [*ungeheuerliches Chaos*]".[4] Sukthankar was one of the first to demonstrate an inherent logic—and in fact a social-political history—behind this interpolation. Instead of a haphazard, cancerous growth upon the epic body, Sukthankar argued that the legends of Rāma Jāmadagnya and other members of his family were strategically inserted, at a certain time in early Indian history, into the primary Kaurava-Pāṇḍava narrative. Moreover, this Brahmanic editorial project was conducted by a set of redactors belonging to this very Bhārgava clan. The Bhṛguization of the *Mahābhārata*, in other words, was a Bhārgava corporate takeover of Vyāsa's original bardic text—an act of sociopolitical power on the part of a specific set of Brahman writers in the post-Vedic age. Sukthankar was the first scholar to highlight the role of the Bhārgava narratives within a broader process of 'brahmanization'—a model of textual expansion that remains a compelling explanation for the *Mahābhārata's* heterogeneity.

Sukthankar's 1936 essay in the *Annals of the Bhandarkar Oriental Institute* begins with a rather modest ambition, "to collect and collate the Bhārgava references in the *Mahābhārata*".[5] Though he claims to be uninterested in an interpretive agenda, his lengthy investigation offers dramatic and far-reaching implications on how we are to understand the significance of this complex and unwieldy Sanskrit epic. It is worthwhile to highlight three fundamental points within his 'Bhṛguization' hypothesis. First, Sukthankar asserts that stories about the Bhārgava sages are textual interpolations within the Sanskrit epic. As he puts it, "in our version of the *Mahābhārata* there is a conscious—nay deliberate—weaving together or rather stitching together of the Bhārata legends with the Bhārgava stories".[6] The legends themselves are "entirely foreign to the plan of the original saga" and form a cohesive and meaningful cycle of their own. The content of this story cycle leads Sukthankar to a second observation: he notices that these Brahmans often establish matrimonial ties to Kṣatriyas, while a number of Bhārgavas—particularly Rāma Jāmadagnya and his branch of the family—engage in violent conflicts with Kṣatriyas.[7] This ambivalent relationship with the Kṣatriya *varṇa*—one of desire mixed with aggression—is of central importance in the positioning of the Bhārgavas at the margins of Brahmanhood: more so than most sages, they are shown to act in ways that 'good' Brahmans should not. Third, because "the Bhārgava heroes occupy a surprisingly large portion of the canvas," Sukthankar is convinced that the actual redactors of the *Mahābhārata* must have themselves been Brahmans of the Bhārgava clan, and furthermore that this supplementative project had an "ulterior motive".[8] At the heart of the *Mahābhārata's* heterogeneity, suggests Sukthankar, there lay "the colossal idea of converting the popular Epic of the Bhāratas into the *Encyclopedia Brahmanica*".[9] This Brahmanical seizure of intellectual power explains not only the inclusion of Bhārgava material in the epic, but also the copious amounts of didactic material in the *Śānti* and *Anuśāsana Parvans*, for as Sukthankar points out, *dharma* and *nīti* ('moral law' and 'ethics') "are just the two topics in which the Bhrgus had *specialized* and with which their names are prominently associated".[10] By proposing this correlation between the literary text and early Indian cultural history, Sukthankar argued for a coherent logic and real-world motivation behind the growth and development of the epic text.

Indologists have been quick to embrace the Bhṛguization model, though not without modification and more recently, 'reconsideration'. A.P. Karmarkar and Hermann Weller, for example, applied his model towards anthropological questions of Indo-Aryan prehistory.[11] N.J. Shende, noting that the *Mahābhārata* mentions Āṅgirasa Brahmans more frequently than Bhārgavas, proposed a kind of 'Bhṛgvaṅgirasization' theory by suggesting that both families were jointly involved in the final redaction of the epic.[12] More recently, John Brockington's five-stage developmental model of the Sanskrit epics has relied on Sukthankar's thesis both to explain a shift from orality to writtenness (as related to a "shift in transmission from bard to brāhman"), as well as the encyclopedic expansion of the core epic narrative by myths, legends, and didactic material.[13] Sukthankar's theory, as Goldman points out, has been "basic to all subsequent study of the *Mahābhārata*".[14]

No scholar has worked as closely with Sukthankar's idea of Bhṛguization as Goldman, whose doctoral thesis and subsequent monograph explored the thematic unity of the legends which Sukthankar had first identified as a coherent Bhārgava cycle.[15] Noting the Bhārgavas' predilection for marital relations as well as outright hostilities with Kṣatriyas—alongside a host of other un-Brahmanical characteristics—Goldman observes "a pattern of behavior that is aberrant with respect to the norms of brahmanical activities set forth in the dharma literature, including the *Mahābhārata* itself".[16] Goldman suggests that the Bhārgava Brahmans deployed these stories—and particularly Rāma Jāmadagnya's extermination of the Kṣatriyas—as "a sort of trademark, stamped across the face of the vast epic to mark it as the product and possession of the Bhṛgus".[17] These legends, in other words, represent a literary act of Brahman power over what had previously been Kṣatriya-centered bardic tradition.

As Alf Hiltebeitel has also noted, we are here confronted with an important question regarding Bhṛguization, present even in Sukthankar's initial observations.[18] If Bhārgava Brahmans had actively inserted stories about their own ancestors into the *Mahābhārata*, why did they portray themselves so negatively (or at least ambivalently) throughout the epic? If, in other words, these subnarratives do represent an actual Brahman cultural takeover in early India, why would they do so by choosing quintessential examples of how Brahmans ought *not* to behave?

These and other discomforts with Sukthankar's hypotheses have led some to reexamine the Bhṛguization hypothesis. Seeing no historical evidence of a 'Bhārgava movement' in early India, Christopher Minkowski questions Sukthankar's Bhārgava conspiracy theory—"Why," he asks, "should we assume that in India a distinct group could take hostage the product of an entire culture, an epic, moreover, that itself suggests a history of conforming to the interests of its listeners?"[19] Though Minkowski continues to regard the Bhārgava cycle as a distinct set of traditional narratives, he suggests that due to the strong parallels between the Bhārgavas' genocidal annihilation of the Kṣatriyas and the events of the Bhārata war, this cycle was pulled into the primary *Mahābhārata* story through a "thematic attraction".[20] Hiltebeitel's position is more extreme, hypothesizing that the Bhārgavas simply represent Brahmans in general, rather than a specific historical group. Building upon Madeleine Biardeau's suggestion that the *Mahābhārata* was primarily speaking to the *svadharma* of Kṣatriyas,[21] Hiltebeitel argues that the Bhārgava legends serve as testimonia against uncontrolled, vengeful violence. As he explains, "one of the chief objects of the *Mahābhārata* is thus to instruct kings and other Ksatriyas in how to curb endless cycles of violence, particularly as such cycles affect and implicate Brahmans: both Bhārgava Brahmans and non-Bhārgava Brahmans".[22] But where Hiltebeitel most vehemently disagrees with Sukthankar is in the assumption that these legends are later interpolations, arguing instead that the epic ought to be read as a single, unitary work of literature, composed by a committee of intellectuals within one or two generations.[23] Hiltebeitel suggests that the Bhārgava cycle is "inseparable from the 'work' (literary, ritual, and genealogically paternal) of the non-Bhārgava 'author' Vyāsa. ... It can hardly be kept apart as a separable strand of authorship or a layer of textual history."[24] These compelling challenges to Sukthankar's Bhṛguization hypothesis caution against a literary archaeology of textual 'strata' within the *Mahābhārata*, in favor of a historical approach to the formation of the epic as a whole.

On the other hand, whether they have been drawn into the text by 'thematic attraction' or originally belong to Vyāsa's work itself, it is beyond dispute that the Bhārgava legends form a coherent narrative cycle supplemental to the primary *Mahābhārata* narrative; our task therefore becomes to historicize this coherence and supplementarity. Abandoning the concept of textual strata in favor of textual 'threads', James Fitzgerald offers a thought-provoking solution in his 2002 exposition of the 'Rāma Jāmadagnya thread' in the Sanskrit *Mahābhārata*. Declaring, "It is time to go back to the text without Sukthankar's Bhārgava hypothesis in mind," Fitzgerald provides a survey of nearly 130 references to Rāma Jāmadagnya in the epic in order to explore how this particular narrative thread is woven into the fabric of the *Mahābhārata*.[25] Within these sources, he isolates eight themes that connect Rāma Jāmadagnya to primary epic characters (Karṇa, Droṇa, and Bhīṣma), to its major plot events, and to its physical geography, along with three distinct narrative voices through which Rāma Jāmadagnya is presented. In liberating us from the text-historical approach, while nevertheless maintaining a diachronic understanding of the historical context of its textual production, Fitzgerald's analogy of a 'thread' within the epic weave deftly allows us to study two important aspects of the legends of Rāma Jāmadagnya (along with the other Bhārgavas) in isolation: both the 'texture' of this narrative thread as well as 'style' of the epic cloth into which it has been woven. In other words, we may bracket aside the problem of textual development and focus instead on the meaning of these legends and the discourse through which they are told in the *Mahābhārata*.

Rāma Jāmadagnya and the "Indian Oedipus"

No Bhārgava is as important to the *Mahābhārata* as Rāma Jāmadagnya, the "colossus" whose shadow "overspreads the entire epic", who is famous "as an awesomely ferocious brahmin warrior," and who "is the darling of the epic poets, who never tire of repeating his exploits".[26] At the same time, he is a deeply ambivalent character—there is a veneration of his ascetic power and martial knowledge, mixed together with an undeniable anxiety over his terrifying and violent nature. Nowhere does this blend of shock and awe become more apparent than within two particular episodes of Rāma's life: the genocide of the Kṣatriyas and the murder of his own mother Reṇukā.

Both events are recounted at length within a subnarrative appearing in the *Āraṇyaka Parvan* (3.115-17).[27] Naturally endowed with Kṣatriya qualities, Rāma is the youngest of four sons of the Brahman sage Jamadagni, who teaches him the entire *dhanurveda*, "the science of arms". Once, while bathing in the river, Rāma's mother Reṇukā happens to see a king and lusts after him. Jamadagni is able to recognize her infidelitous desire, and orders his sons to kill their mother. The three elder sons refuse and are cursed to lose their sanity; Rāma, however, straight away decapitates his mother with an axe. Jamadagni is pleased with this act of filial obedience and offers Rāma as many boons as he should desire; he chooses that his mother be brought back to life—and that she should forget the whole incident—along with the absolution of his crime and the restoration of his elder brothers. Later, while Jamadagni is alone in the hermitage, the Haihaya king Arjuna Kārtavīrya arrives at the hermitage and steals the calf of the sage's cow. Rāma, learning of the attack on his father's hermitage, flies into vengeful rage and destroys Arjuna, cutting off his thousand arms. In retaliation, the king's sons come and kill the defenseless Jamadagni. At the death of his father, Rāma Jāmadagnya now vows to eliminate the entire Kṣatriya *varṇa*. He clears the earth of all Kṣatriyas twenty-one times over and deposits their corpses in five lakes of blood in the region known as "Samanta-pañcaka", which is to be the future site of the Bhārata war. Eventually ceasing his killings, he offers the earth to the sage Kaśyapa and retires to a celibate life of austerities in the mountains.

As they are for us today, these stories must certainly have been provocative to early Indian audiences; the story of his matricide is most likely what grants him the popular name 'Paraśurāma' in later purāṇic texts, while memories of his vengeful genocide loom large throughout the *Mahābhārata* narrative.[28] But without the ability to interview actual informants from the ancient past, and given the general paucity of historical evidence in which to situate our literary material, how are we to gain a better understanding of why audiences might have found them to be compelling or moving? The contextualist approach to this dilemma, especially popular upon the completion of the critical edition of the *Mahābhārata* in 1970s, is to situate the Sanskrit epics within a broadly synchronic understanding of a 'classical Hindu' or 'Brahmanical' tradition to which the epic belongs.[29] It is with this hermeneutic that Goldman offered a psychological study of Rāma Jāmadagnya within two landmark studies of the oedipal theme in Sanskrit literature. Though they are often overlooked by Indologists, these essays have had a lasting impact upon psychological and anthropological debates regarding the nature of the "Indian Oedipus".[30]

Responding to A.K. Ramanujan's and Philip Spratt's original hypothesis of an absence of the traditional Freudian Oedipus complex within the traditional Indian psyche in favor of a distinctively "Indian Oedipus", Goldman provides an exhaustive survey of three kinds of oedipal themes within Sanskrit epic and purāṇic literature.[31] First, through a careful reading of the epics, Goldman succeeds in locating the 'positive' oedipal theme within a diverse number of epic narratives, in which "a son, almost always a surrogate son, successfully attacks a father figure and through this attack achieves maturity and temporal power".[32] As an example, he highlights a recursion of the positive oedipal theme throughout the *Mahābhārata*: first as a conflict between Bhīṣma and his *guru* Rāma Jāmadagnya, then between Bhīṣma and Arjuna, and finally between Arjuna and his son Babruvāhana. In each case, the 'son' is able to defeat the father-figure, and the dispute is mediated by a mother-figure. Goldman then provides extensive evidence of a second, failed oedipal theme in which the son displays aggression towards the father-figure, but is punished with castration.[33] The third, 'negative' type involves a son who "anticipates and avoids overt oedipal conflict and paternal aggression by freely submitting to the father's will and in effect castrating himself".[34] Goldman finds these kinds of passive sons—who correspond to Ramanujan's understanding of the Indian Oedipus—to be the most widely dispersed, and "without doubt representative of an oedipal type that the culture strongly favors".[35] The impact of Goldman's work was such that Ramanujan explicitly incorporated his findings into a revision of his "Indian Oedipus" essay in 1983, acknowledging in a comparison of Greek and Indian Oedipal patterns that "*both patterns exist in both cultures*, but different cultures emphasise different patterns through their *favourite* tales and psychologies".[36]

The Bhārgava Rāma is the centerpiece of Goldman's analysis. It is not difficult to see how Rāma Jāmadagnya's matricide expresses an oedipal theme—since he obediently beheads his mother at the behest of his father and subsequently lives a celibate life. Rāma Jāmadagnya here represents the classic 'passive' or 'negative' oedipal son, who castrates himself in complete subordination to the desires of the dominant father. But what might inspire such a reading of his Kṣatriya genocide, in which Rāma's aggression is clearly directed outside of his family? Goldman argues that within the Sanskrit epics, there is a regular pattern of symbolic substitution within the Oedipal triangle. As he explains, there is a "very marked tendency in some types of Oedipal story toward the substitution of various male figures, notably the guru or aged brahman sage, and to a much lesser extent the elder brother, for the father and female figures such as the guru's wife, the sister-in-law, and often a cow, for the mother".[37] Most important is an across-the-board homology between the social relations of Brahmans and Kṣatriyas and those of the oedipal father and the son. Thus, if Brahmans function as fathers, and Kṣatriyas function as sons, then Brahman-Kṣatriya conflicts in the Sanskrit epics are symbolic displacements of the three oedipal themes. This theoretical move opens up a world of familial aggression and desire. In the case of Rāma Jāmadagnya's genocide, Goldman argues that Arjuna Kārtavīrya and his sons represent the castrated son within the second oedipal type—after all, Arjuna's thousand arms are severed in a vain attempt to steal Jamadagni's cow (a stand-in for the oedipal mother). Although his sons do succeed in killing the father-figure of Jamadagni, it ultimately spells their own demise at the hands of Rāma Jāmadagnya, the "castrative avenger-father *par excellence*".[38] This observation leads Goldman to suggest that Rāma Jāmadagnya "appears to symbolize, as does the closely related figure of Viśvāmitra, the juxtaposition of the roles of the father (brahman) and son (warrior) in a single individual at the same time".[39]

Goldman explains Viśvāmitra's ambivalence most clearly in his 1982 follow-up study of the oedipal theme in Vālmīki's *Rāmāyaṇa*. Here, he finds that the Brahman Viśvāmitra serves as the aggressive father-figure towards Rāma Dāśarathi (ordering him to slay the mother-surrogate Tāṭakā), within a scene that is a clear parallel to Rāma Jāmadagnya's matricide. However, the opening book of the *Rāmāyaṇa* also includes a "central and elaborate mini-epic of negative oedipal identification", in which Viśvāmitra, as a Kṣatriya, attempts to steal the *kāmadhenu* from the hermitage of the Brahman Vasiṣṭha—only to be defeated resolutely in violent combat with the sage.[40] In this manner, both Rāma Jāmadagnya and Viśvāmitra come to represent two sides of the same problematic coin—powerful and fiery figures who simultaneously represent the subordinate Kṣatriya/son and the dominant Brahman/father.

Freudian methods almost always arouse controversy, and their conclusions are sometimes more obfuscating than revealing; it is not my intention here to delve any further into what these traditional narratives might reveal about the inner workings of the generalized 'Indian mind'—never mind whether the *Mahābhārata* lends itself to such investigations at all. The historical interests of this essay differ in this sense from Goldman's contextualist attempts to understand the "psychological dynamics of Hindu family and social life", and more broadly to explain the "extraordinary hold that the myths and heroes of the Indian epics have exerted on the people of India for at least the last three thousand years".[41] Instead, I would like to relate these oedipal themes to what I am calling 'psychosocial' anxieties.[42] Building on the work of Freud and Lacan, literary theorists have read the oedipal theme of aggression between a father and son as a cultural expression of anxieties surrounding a masculine subject's socialization within structures of dominance and subordination.[43] That is to say, stories about sons wishing to supplant their fathers and fathers wishing to keep their sons in place speak to basic male fears about maturation into the institutions of social hierarchy. Taken in this light, Goldman's psychoanalytic studies make it clear that the literary 'force' driving the epic stories of Rāma

Jāmadagnya and Viśvāmitra is a psychosocial one. But does this bring us any closer to historicizing the value of this force within the textual production of the *Mahābhārata* in early India?

Though the question of when—and where, and by whom—the *Mahābhārata* was composed will always be a matter of intense controversy, Fitzgerald's work is again particularly helpful in situating the epic in a historical context. Treating the composition of the epic as the product of a series of Brahman intellectuals living in northern India roughly during and after the rise and fall of the Mauryan empire, Fitzgerald proposes that the *Mahābhārata* represents "a Brāhmaṇ-inspired response to the tremendous damage (as seen from the point of view of some Brāhmaṇs between approximately 300 and 100 BCE) wrought by the rise of empires at Pāṭalīputra and the 'heathen' (*nāstika*, Jainism and Buddhism, particularly) religions these empires promoted."[44] These external challenges to older Vedic authority, coupled with new modes of religious life within post-Vedic Hinduism (e.g. renunciation, *bhakti*, and *yoga*), led to a crisis of Brahman social identity and power, to which the *Mahābhārata* appears to have been one cultural response.[45]

At a time when the concept of *dharma* was not only appropriated by Buddhist thinkers and politicized by Aśoka's imperial edicts, but was also reinterpreted within Brahmanic thought, the *Mahābhārata* sought to naturalize the śāstraic discourse of *varṇāśramadharma*—a vision of social and cultural life that privileged Brahmans as the purveyors of dharmic (and not just Vedic) knowledge.[46] At a fundamental level, this required a political negotiation with Kṣatriya rulers, and Fitzgerald's explanation of how the *Mahābhārata* played a part in this negotiation is worth quoting in full:

> One of the fundamental messages of the *Mahābhārata* seems to have been that legitimate 'kṣatriyas' should employ the violence they exercise for the protection of brahmins as a distinct elite and thus guarantee the existence of the hierarchical *varṇa* society. Of course the essence of the *varṇa* hierarchy—as distinct from social classes based simply upon power and wealth—is the existence of the brahmin elite, whose entire social capital consists of its monopoly on specifying *dharma*; a monopoly that had been challenged by the Mauryan emperor Aśoka.[47]

The *Mahābhārata* thus enabled Brahman intellectuals to speak of themselves as a social elite possessing a knowledge-based (and not economic or military) capital, and therefore requiring the protection and patronage of Kṣatriyas. Furthermore, this nexus of knowledge/power, to borrow a Foucauldian phrase, did not simply consist of Vedic learning, but now also entailed dharmic and especially narratological expertise. This new self-understanding of Brahmanhood involved two basic features which, I suggest, stir up precisely the social anxieties that motivate the Rāma Jāmadagnya legend: the strict self-regulation of desire (*kāma*) along with a distancing from physical violence (*ahiṃsā*); as Fitzgerald succinctly puts it, "in this bargain, the brahmins gave up all claims to violence on their own behalf".[48]

The stories of Rāma Jāmadagnya and Viśvāmitra juxtapose these Brahman concerns over social identity and violence with more universal anxieties about rivalries between fathers and sons—i.e. the oedipal theme. At the same time, the *Mahābhārata* never presents these stories in a 'raw' form, but instead consistently attempts to alleviate these psychosocial anxieties through 'textual performance'—that is, by regulating how one may authentically tell the stories of Rāma Jāmadagnya and Viśvāmitra.[49] To recover the strategies involved in this textual performance, and how it allows the *Mahābhārata* to speak to the social realities of its time, we must move from an analysis of meaning to an analysis of discourse.

The Genealogy of Rāma Jāmadagnya and Viśvāmitra

In speaking of discourse, that is to say, the attitudes, concerns, and strategies with which the *Mahābhārata* presents Rāma Jāmadagnya (and Viśvāmitra), we enter a speculative field beyond the safe confines of the epic text. But given the limited means for investigating the epic's real-world context, it is a necessary journey if we wish to historicize the production of this literary work. Assuming, as most epic scholars do, that the composers of the Sanskrit *Mahābhārata* were themselves Brahmans, I would like to argue that the supplementation of the legends of Rāma Jāmadagnya and Viśvāmitra—regardless of whether it happened during the epic's initial composition or at a later 'stage' of its development—involved a discourse of Brahman power that regarded *varṇa* hierarchy as a 'natural' property of the social world. Within the pages of the epic, there is an almost obsessive need to classify Rāma Jāmadagnya and Viśvāmitra as Brahmans, even though their aggressive and violent behavior makes them antithetical to the self-controlled Brahman identity being established in north India during the epic's composition. Hiltebeitel is therefore right in asking why Bhārgava redactors would care to portray themselves in such a negative light, and I believe he is also right in declaring that "Bhārgavas represent other Brahmans"—though it might be more accurate to say that they represent the 'Other' Brahman, the exoticized cultural opposite of the Brahman 'Self'.[50]

Unlike the Othering involved in modern Orientalist discourse, the wedge between 'Us' and 'Them' is not driven in completely; the Other kind of Brahman is, after all, still a Brahman.[51] Even though Rāma Jāmadagnya and Viśvāmitra behave like Kṣatriyas—a true Other for the Brahman Self—the *Mahābhārata's* composers appear to have taken special care to incorporate both figures into the Brahmanic fold, and thereby to alleviate the psychosocial anxieties expressed by their ambivalent behavior. The inclusion of Rāma Jāmadagnya (and Viśvāmitra)—that is to say, "Bhṛguization" itself—might be considered a form of narrative therapy, a way for Brahmans to 'talk through' their fears about maintaining elite status within early Indian society. We may observe this in the repeated assertions of Rāma and Viśvāmitra's Brahman status, their inclusion in Brahman lists and lineages, and even when they appear as token Brahmans in the epic background. It is through discourse, I suggest, that the epic tries to normalize these counter-normative Brahmans. Nowhere is this process of normalization more noticeable than in the story of how this *varṇasaṃkara* actually came about—the account of the sages' birth.

The Satyavatī legend appears three times in detail within the *Mahābhārata* (and once more in summary form), and although there is little variation between them, differences in detail nevertheless allow us to identify key points of debate within the story. First and foremost is the narrative frame, where the social anxieties surrounding these two sages are expressed through dialogues between teller and audience. All the versions are told in fact to the same listener, the apparently forgetful Yudhiṣṭhira. First to tell him the story is the Brahman Akṛtavraṇa in the *Āraṇyaka Parvan* (*MBh* 3.115), and next in the *Śānti Parvan* it is Kṛṣṇa himself (*MBh* 12.49). Both are told in order to explain "how Rāma defeated all the Kṣatriyas in battle, and for what purpose".[52] Shortly thereafter, in the *Anuśāsana Parvan*, a dying Bhīṣma tells Yudhiṣṭhira the same story in order to explain how "the mighty Kṣatriya Viśvāmitra was able to attain Brahmanhood, if it is to impossible to attain by men of the three other *varṇas*".[53] The puzzle in all three versions is one of *dharma*—how did these two sages manage to behave in ways that most Brahmans should not? The *Mahābhārata's* solution is to argue for the physicality of *varṇa*: Rāma acted as he did because of the Kṣatriya nature infused in his body, while Viśvāmitra didn't really 'become' a Brahman, his body was already born that way.

As dharmic problems often do, this all began with desire. Once, the Bhārgava sage Ṛcīka came to Gādhi, the King of Kānyakubja who had retired into the forest, to ask for the hand of his beautiful daughter Satyavatī.[54] Gādhi, perhaps unnerved at the thought of a decrepit Brahman ascetic marrying his daughter,[55] insisted upon a bride-price, telling him: "There is a certain custom in our family that has been established by our forebears."[56] The task set before Ṛcīka was practically impossible: to procure one thousand *śyāmakarṇa* horses—white horses each having one black ear. But Bhārgava sage, through the divine intervention of Varuṇa, immediately acquired the bride-price and succeeded in marrying the beautiful princess.

After some time, in order to ensure the fertility of his wife as well as his mother-in-law, Ṛcīka informed Satyavatī that she should first embrace a ficus tree (*udumbara*) and her mother a fig tree (*aśvattha*), before consuming a special *caru* (a *mantra*-infused porridge) that he had prepared for each of them.[57] But for some reason, her mother urged her to switch the *carus* and the trees.[58] As it turned out, each *caru* had respectively contained the 'essence' of Brahmanhood (*brahman*) and of Kṣatriya valor (*kṣattra-vīrya*), and because of the switch, Satyavatī became pregnant with a son endowed with Kṣatriya qualities, while her Kṣatriya mother was fated to have a son who would behave like a Brahman. Satyavatī was horrified, and begged her husband that this fate be made to skip a generation; and so it was their grandson, Rāma, who became the terrifying slayer of Kṣatriyas, while Satyavatī's brother, Viśvāmitra, grew up to become a Brahman sage.[59]

This metamyth about *varṇa* intermixture is motivated by a desire to reconcile the life-stories of Rāma Jāmadagnya and Viśvāmitra, or as Goldman explains, a "desire to trace to a single cause the two most important examples of social aberrance in the traditional literature".[60] Because the essence of *varṇa* has been substantialized in the form of the *carus*, this aberrant behavior can no longer be attributed to the willful desires of either character—instead, it is clearly a consequence of the physical intermixture that happened at conception. The *caru*-switch motif supports an argument that *varṇa* is a physical and inalienable property of the body by asserting that these sages' behavior is a teleological result of the substances infused within their bodies. Further alleviating Brahman anxieties, there is no longer any trace of the violent Brahman-Kṣatriya conflicts that mar the other legends of Rāma Jāmadagnya and Viśvāmitra; it is instead replaced by a tale of Kṣatriya subterfuge and mistrust. The plot twists around Gādhi's asking a bride-price and the divisive behavior of Satyavatī's mother; the fact that these are precisely the locations where we find the most variation among the different tellings of the story indicates the continuing concern with establishing 'natural' social differences between Brahmans and Kṣatriyas as well as the hierarchical relationship between them. But in all the versions, the threat of the violently coercive Kṣatriya is quite absent.

The *Mahābhārata* thus uses this genealogical narrative to normalize Rāma Jāmadagnya and Viśvāmitra. The Satyavatī legend leads to what one might call a 'Selfing' of the Other kind of Brahman through the production of authoritative genealogical knowledge. For once we know the physical makeup of the bodies of Rāma Jāmadagnya and Viśvāmitra, it is impossible to deny that they are, in fact, Brahmans. In the context of post-Mauryan India, in the midst of a cultural struggle for elite status, it is not difficult to see how these stories of counter-normative Brahmans participated in the formation of a Brahmanic social discourse—both as cautionary examples of the perils of *varṇa* intermixture as well as fantastic representations of the hidden potential for aggressive and retributive violence of a social class that was otherwise giving up "all claims to violence on their own behalf".

This discursive examination of the *Mahābhārata's* Satyavatī 'meta-myth' allows us to address the question of the epic's cultural impact in early Indian history without being constrained by the lack of external material and documentary evidence necessary for making historical assessments. With the idea that the supplementary Bhārgava legends constitute a narrative 'thread' rather than a text-historical layer, then it becomes clear that the epic composers used genealogical 'capstone' narratives such as the Satyavatī legend to weave together preexisting narrative traditions. Instead of penciling off distinct archaeological strata within the Pune Critical Edition as reflecting different periods of early Indian history, we may thus begin to speak more effectively about how its composers impacted the socio-political and religious world around them. In particular, Goldman's identification of oedipal themes in the Rāma Jāmadagnya and Viśvāmitra legends yields a glimpse of the fears and anxieties of composers who were quite skilled at masking these insecurities within a resolutely normative epic. Once we re-project the universal anxieties of interfamilial aggression and desire back into the socio-political context of early India, it seems evident that these legends speak most directly to the Brahman fears of maintaining their place as the dominant father-figures in *varṇa*-based society. By representing the violent potential of Brahman power in a world in which *ahiṃsā* had been established as a 'new' dharmic norm, the *Mahābhārata* worked discursively to alleviate these psychosocial anxieties while reinforcing the elite status of Brahmans that was increasingly under threat.[61]

Though there is still much to be understood about the precise nature of Brahman power during and after the fall of the Mauryan empire, it is clear that this hegemony was secured through the control of various forms of knowledge—dharmic, śāstraic, vedic. And particularly in a climate in which other religious and socio-political groups were challenging these Brahman intellectual monopolies, the consolidation of knowledge and power (following Foucault) required the establishment of a normative discourse.[62] As this study of the legends of Rāma Jāmadagnya and Viśvāmitra has tried to show, one way this appears to have happened was through the control of historical knowledge—of *itihāsa*. By regulating the narratives through which one could authoritatively speak about the significant past, the *Mahābhārata* participated in the formation of the discourse of *varṇa* that was in its very essence hierarchical, in which an individual's public life was invariably determined by his or her birth, and in which one could not imagine Brahmans—no matter how passive they may have appeared in real life—as anything but father-figures.

Notes

1. As the sage Cyavana prophecies to Satyavatī's grandfather Kuśika, "two women will become the cause for this inversion [*striyau tu kāraṇaṃ tatra parivarte bhaviṣyataḥ* /]" (*MBh* 13.56.13ab).
2. Goldman 1977: 104.
3. Sathaye 2007.
4. Oldenberg 1922: 1 (cited in Hiltebeitel 2001: 1).
5. Sukthankar 1936: 3.
6. Sukthankar 1936: 70.
7. Sukthankar 1936: 16, 63.
8. Sukthankar 1936: 67.
9. Sukthankar 1966: 68.
10. Sukthankar 1936: 73, emphasis in original.
11. Weller 1937; Karmarkar 1938.

12. Shende 1943 (cited in Brockington 1998: 156). Norvin Hein also raises the possibility of other Brahman editorial groups collaborating with the Bhārgava redactors (Hein 1986; cited in Brockington 1998: 157), while Goldman's comparative analysis of two versions of the Rāma Jāmadagnya genocide narrative raises the possibility that "other interests than the Bhārgavas" may have been involved in their interpolation (Goldman 1970: 173).

13. Brockington 1998: 395, 484.

14. Goldman 1977: 2.

15. Also of note here is Goldman's application of the Bhṛguization theory to Vālmīki's *Rāmāyaṇa* (Goldman 1976).

16. Goldman 1977: 5.

17. Goldman 1977: 140.

18. Hiltebeitel 1999: 162.

19. Minkowski 1991: 400.

20. Minkowski 1991: 398.

21. Biardeau 1981: 76.

22. Hiltebeitel 1999: 166.

23. Hiltebeitel 2001: 20.

24. Hiltebeitel 1999: 166.

25. Fitzgerald 2002: 89.

26. Sukthankar 1936: 18; Fitzgerald 2002: 95; Goldman 1977: 85.

27. This is the only telling of the matricide narrative; the genocide story, on the other hand, is found throughout the epic; for a comprehensive discussion of these passages, see Fitzgerald 2002.

28. On the origins of the name 'Paraśurāma,' see Goldman 1972a; for the thematic presence of Rāma throughout the *Mahābhārata*, see Fitzgerald 2002: 115-16.

29. Ronald Inden has offered an important critique of the contextualist approach, calling instead for a 'dialogical' approach towards the cultural

production of a text as "an intervention on the part of an agent in the world" (Inden, Walters, and Ali 2000: 13).

30. For a recent study challenging some of Goldman's findings, see Adarkar 2008: 133-37.

31. Ramanujan 1972; Spratt 1966.

32. Goldman 1978: 362.

33. Goldman 1978: 363.

34. Goldman 1978: 363.

35. Goldman 1978: 364.

36. Ramanujan 1999: 394, emphasis in original. Within the lively debate on the universality of the Oedipal complex among comparative Freudians and anthropologists (e.g. Spiro 1982; Kurtz 1992; Ingham 1996; Johnson and Price-Williams 1996; Bhugra and Bhui 2002), Goldman's findings have served to discredit purely relativistic models that would exempt Indian children "from what is a universal element of the human psyche" (Goldman 1978: 325), and informs Gananath Obeyesekere's useful theorization of Wittgensteinian 'family resemblances' of Oedipal myths across cultures (Obeyesekere 1990: 105-106).

37. Goldman 1978: 327.

38. Goldman 1978: 391.

39. Goldman 1978: 391.

40. Goldman 1982: 128. Viśvāmitra's subsequent self-transformation from Kṣatriya to Brahman thus becomes thematically parallel to Rāma Dāśarathi's development into manhood, though as Goldman points out, Rāma does not simply stop at the level of the "classic Indian self-castrative hero", (as does Viśvāmitra), but is able to "to throw off the oppressive yoke of paternal dominance and participate in a mature and fulfilling love relationship with his wife" (Goldman 1982: 131).

41. Goldman 1978: 365; Goldman 1982: 131.

42. Through the use of the term 'psychosocial', my approach is indebted to—but not, strictly speaking, a direct application of—Erik Erikson's understanding of psychosocial development in the formation of ego identity (see Erikson 1980: 108-75).

43. See for example Jameson 1977; Astle 1979; Felman 1983; Borch-Jacobsen 1994.

44. Fitzgerald 2004a: 54.

45. See Fitzgerald 2004b: 100.

46. See Fitzgerald 2004b: 103-04.

47. Fitzgerald 2002: 118.

48. Fitzgerald 2002: 118.

49. For a illustration of what I mean by "textual performance" in the Viśvāmitra legends in the Sanskrit epics, see Sathaye—In Press.

50. Hiltebeitel 1999: 162.

51. Said 1979: 39-44.

52. "*yathā rāmeṇa nirjitāḥ / āhave kṣatriyāḥ sarve katham kena ca hetunā //*" *MBh* 3.115.8bcd; see also *MBh* 12.49.1-2. In analyzing the differences between these two Rāma Jāmadagnya-centered versions, Goldman has noted the possible presence of both Brahman and Kṣatriya voices in the epic (Goldman 1973). He suggests that Kṛṣṇa's disparaging portrayal of Rāma Jāmadagnya in the *Śānti Parvan* may represent a Kṣatriya defense of Arjuna Kārtavīrya. It is hard, however, to imagine that there was a kind of literary tug-of-war taking place within the pages of the *Mahābhārata* between Brahman and Kṣatriya authors, and instead I find it more likely this version told by Kṛṣṇa was composed by Brahmans but directed towards an explicitly Kṣatriya set of issues, given that it is told at a point in the *Śānti Parvan* where Kṛṣṇa urges Yudhiṣṭhira to seek Bhīṣma's counsel in reconciling kingly rule with *dharma* in the Kali Age (Fitzgerald 2004b: 94).

53. "*brāhmaṇyaṃ yadi duṣprāpaṃ tribhir varṇair narādhipa / kathaṃ prāptaṃ mahārāja kṣatriyeṇa mahātmanā //*" *MBh* 13.3.1. The story is later mentioned again by Bhīṣma in the *Anuśāsana Parvan* as a prophecy during his narration of the Cyavana-Kuśika dialogue (*MBh* 13.56.32-36; see Goldman 1977: 71).

54. Gādhi is known as Gāthin in Vedic literature. In a number of epic and purāṇic versions of the story, including the *Śānti Parvan* (*MBh* 12.49.3-6), he is said to be an incarnation of Indra.

55. This sentiment is brought out in a later version found in the *Nāgara Khaṇḍa* of the *Skanda Purāṇa*: "Hearing this, the exalted King Gādhi became agitated by fear. Though he considered him to be of unequal *varṇa*, and poor and old,

he nonetheless feared a curse if he did not give her to him, and so he uttered this pretext [*tacchrutvā bhayasaṃtrasto gādhiḥ pārthivasattamaḥ || asavarṇaṃ ca taṃ matvā daridraṃ vṛddham eva ca || adāne śāpabhītas tu tato vyājam uvāca saḥ || *]" (*SkandaP* 6.165.28).

56. "*ucitaṃ naḥ kule kiṃ cit pūrvair yat saṃpravartitam* ||" *MBh* 3.115.11cd. The bride-price is not found in the *Śānti Parvan* version, and in the *Āraṇyaka Parvan's* version, it is left as optional—Gādhi explains that it is his family's custom, but that he could not ask someone like Ṛcīka (i.e. a Brahman) to give him anything (*MBh* 3.115.13).

57. The three versions of this legend each represent this scene slightly differently. What I have described takes place in the *Anuśāsana Parvan* version (*MBh* 13.4.27-28); in the *Śānti Parvan* version, Ṛcīka only gives them the two *carus*, while in the *Āraṇyaka Parvan*, where they are told only to embrace the two trees, it is Ṛcīka's great grandfather Bhṛgu who instructs them to do so.

58. It is here where we find the greatest point of debate between the three versions of the legend. In both the *Śānti* and *Āraṇyaka Parvan* versions, we do not gain any insight into why her mother pulled the switch—only that Satyavatī was "tricked [*vyaṃsitā*]" (*MBh* 12.49.18). In the *Anuśāsana Parvan*, on the other hand—and in all later purāṇic versions that are focalized on the birth of Viśvāmitra—Satyavatī's mother explains her reasoning in more detail: Feeling that Ṛcīka would naturally have *caru* meant for his son more special, she urges her daughter to make the switch, "so that her brother might become distinguished [*viśiṣṭa*]" (*MBh* 13.4.33).

59. In the *Āraṇyaka Parvan*, it is again Bhṛgu who notices the switching of the trees, who rebukes Satyavatī, and who delays the results for one generation.

60. Goldman 1977: 20, n. 3.

61. See Fitzgerald 2004b: x.

62. See in particular Foucault's "Truth and Power" (Foucault 1980: 109-33) on the discursive formation of the nexus of knowledge and power.

Bibliography

Primary Sources

Māhābhārata of Vyāsa. Critically edited by V.S. Sukthankar et al. Pune: Bhandarkar Oriental Research Institute, 1927-66.

Skanda Purāṇa. Delhi: Nag Publishers, 1986-89. (Original edition, Bombay: Sri Venkateshvara Steam Press, 1908-10).

Secondary Sources

Adarkar, Aditya. 2008. "Psychological Growth and Heroic Steadfastness in the *Mahābhārata*," in Rita D. Sherma and Arvind Sharma, eds. *Hermeneutics and Hindu Thought: Toward a Fusion of Horizons*. Dordrecht and London: Springer.

Astle, Richard. 1979. "Dracula as Totemic Monster: Lacan, Freud, Oedipus and History." *SubStance* 8: 98-105.

Bhugra, Dinesh and Kamaldeep Bhui. 2002. "Is the Oedipal Complex Universal? Problems for Sexual and Relationship Psychotherapy across Cultures," *Sexual and Relationship Therapy* 17: 69-86.

Biardeau, Madeleine. 1981. "The Salvation of the King in the *Mahābhārata*." *Contributions to Indian Sociology* (n.s.) 15: 75-97.

Borch-Jacobsen, Mikkel. 1994. "The Oedipus Problem in Freud and Lacan." *Critical Inquiry* 20: 267-82. Translated by Douglas Brick.

Brockington, John. 1998. *The Sanskrit Epics*. Leiden: Brill.

Erikson, Erik H. 1980. *Identity and the Life Cycle*. New York and London: Norton. (Original edition, New York: International Universities Press, 1959).

Felman, Shoshana. 1983. "Beyond Oedipus: The Specimen Story of Psychoanalysis." *MLN* 98: 1021-53.

Fitzgerald, James. 2002. "The Rāma Jāmadagnya Thread of the Mahābhārata: A New Survey of Rama Jāmadagnya in the Pune Text." In Mary Brockington, ed. *Stages and Transitions: Temporal and Historical Frameworks in Epic and Purāṇic Literature, Proceedings of the Second Dubrovnik International Conference on the Sanskrit Epics and Puranas, August 1999*. Zagreb: Croatian Academy of Sciences and Arts.

———. 2004a. "Mahābhārata." In Sushil Mittal and Gene Thursby, eds. *The Hindu World*. New York: Routledge.

———, tr. 2004b. *The Mahābhārata. Book 11: The Book of the Women. Book 12: The Book of Peace, Part One*. Chicago: University of Chicago Press.

Foucault, Michel. 1980. *Power/Knowledge: Selected Interviews and Other Writings, 1972-1977*. New York: Pantheon Books.

Goldman, Robert P. 1972. "Some Observations on the *paraśu* of 'Paraśurāma.'" *Journal of the Oriental Institute of Baroda* 21: 153-65.

____. 1973. "Akṛtavraṇa vs. Śrīkṛṣṇa as Narrators of the Legend of the Bhārgava Rāma: *A propos* Some Observations of Dr. V.S. Sukthankar." *Annals of the Bhandarkar Oriental Research Institute* 53: 161-73.

____. 1976. "Vālmīki and the Bhṛgu Connection." *Journal of the American Oriental Society* 96: 97–101.

____. 1977. *Gods, Priests, and Warriors: The Bhṛgus of the Mahābhārata.* Studies in Oriental Culture 12. New York: Columbia University Press.

____. 1978. "Fathers, Sons, and Gurus: Oedipal Conflict in the Sanskrit Epics." *Journal of Indian Philosophy* 6: 325–92.

____. 1982. "Matricide, Renunciation, and Compensation in the Legends of Two Warrior Heroes of the Sanskrit Epics." *Indologica Taurinensia* 10: 117–31.

Hein, Norvin. 1986. "Epic sarvabhūtahite rataḥ: A Byword of Non-Bhārgava Editors." *Annals of the Bhandarkar Oriental Research Institute* 67: 17-34.

Hiltebeitel, Alf. 1999. "Reconsidering Bhṛguization." In Mary Brockington and Peter Schreiner, eds. *Composing a Tradition: Concepts, Techniques, and Relationships: Proceedings of the First Dubrovnik International Conference on the Sanskrit Epics and Purāṇas*. Zagreb: Croatian Academy of Sciences and Arts.

____. 2001. *Rethinking the Mahābhārata: A Reader's Guide to the Education of the Dharma King*. Chicago: University of Chicago Press.

Inden, Ronald, Jonathan Walters, and Daud Ali. 2000. *Querying the Medieval: Texts and the History of Practices in South Asia.* New York: Oxford University Press.

Ingham, John. 1996. "Oedipality in Pragmatic Discourse: The Trobriands and Hindu India." *Ethos* 24: 559-87.

Jameson, Frederic. 1977. "Imaginary and Symbolic in Lacan: Marxism, Psychoanalytic Criticism, and the Problem of the Subject." *Yale French Studies* 55-56: 338-95.

Johnson, Allen and Douglass Richard Price-Williams 1996. *Oedipus Ubiquitous: The Family Complex in World Folk Literature.* Stanford: Stanford University Press.

Karmarkar, A.P. 1938. "Dr. V.S. Sukthankar's Theory of the Bhṛguization of the Original Bhārata and the Light It Throws on the Dravidian Problem." *Annals of the Bhandarkar Oriental Research Institute* 20 (3): 19-26.

Kurtz, Stanley. 1992. *All the Mothers Are One: Hindu India and the Cultural Reshaping of Psychoanalysis.* New York: Columbia University Press.

Minkowski, Christopher. 1991. "Snakes, *Sattras* and the *Mahābhārata*." In Arvind Sharma, ed. *Essays on the Mahābhārata*. Leiden: E.J. Brill.

Obeyesekere, Gananath. 1990. *The Work of Culture: Symbolic Transformation in Psychoanalysis and Anthropology*. Chicago: University of Chicago Press.

Oldenberg, Hermann. 1922. *Das Mahābhārata: Seine Entstehung, sein Inhalt, seine Form*. Göttingen: Vandenhoek and Ruprecht.

Ramanujan, A.K. 1972. "The Indian 'Oedipus.'" *Transactions of the Indian Institute of Advanced Studies* 16: 127-37.

____. 1999. "The Indian 'Oedipus.'" In V. Dharwadker, ed. *The Collected Essays of A.K. Ramanujan*. Delhi: Oxford University Press. Originally published in *Oedipus: A Folklore Casebook*, edited by Lowell Edmunds and Alan Dundes. New York: Garland, 1983, pp. 234-49.

Said, Edward. 1979. *Orientalism*. New York: Vintage Books.

Sathaye, Adheesh. 2007. "How to Become a Brahman: The Construction of *Varṇa* as Social Place in the *Mahābhārata's* Legends of Viśvāmitra." *Acta Orientalia Vilnensia* 8: 41-67.

____. In Press. "Magic Cows and Cannibal Kings: The Textual Performance of the Viśvāmitra Legends in the Mahābhārata." In John Brockington, ed. *Battles, Bards, and Brahmans: Papers from the Epics Section of the 13th World Sanskrit Conference*. Delhi: Motilal Banarsidass.

Shende, N. J. 1943. "The Authorship of the *Mahābhārata*." *Annals of the Bhandarkar Oriental Research Institute* 24: 67-82.

Spiro, M.E. 1982. *Oedipus in the Trobriands*. Chicago: University of Chicago Press.

Spratt, Philip. 1966. *Hindu Culture and Personality: A Psycho-Analytic Study*. Bombay: Manaktala.

Sukthankar, V.S. 1936. "Epic Studies 6: The Bhṛgus and the Bhārata: A Text-Historical Study." *Annals of the Bhandarkar Oriental Research Institute* 18: 1-76.

Weller, Hermann. 1937. "Who were the Bhriguids?" *Annals of the Bhandarkar Oriental Research Institute* 18: 296-302.

Illusory Evidence:
The Construction of *Māyā* in Vālmīki's *Rāmāyaṇa*[1]

SALLY J. SUTHERLAND GOLDMAN

The word *māyā* typically conjures up, as it were, the vedāntic connotation of the term in its sense of, "unreality *or* the notion by which one considers the unreal universe as really existent and as distinct from the Supreme spirit".[2] This use has, perhaps, one of its earliest articulations in the Upaniṣadic utterance,

> *māyāṃ tu prakṛtiṃ vidyān māyinaṃ tu maheśvaram /*
> *tasyāvayavabhūtais tu vyāptaṃ sarvam idaṃ jagat //*[3]

and finds its most influential development in the works of the eighth-century philosopher and founder of the *advaita* school of vedāntic philosophy, Śaṅkarācārya. A brief survey of literature that concerns itself with the word *māyā* reveals that studies are largely concerned with and limited to its use in this context or to the historical process through which the term has come to be used by the *advaitins* or contested by the school's detractors.[4]

The term *māyā*, like the vast majority of Sanskrit words, is polysemic and has a range of meanings that include, but are not limited to, "fraud, deceit, trick", "witchcraft, an illusion of magic", "phantom, unreal apparition", "pseudo-", "pity", and "extraordinary power, wisdom".[5] The word is known from the period of the vedic literature, and in this context has been the initial point of discussion for a number of scholars.[6] Studies by Gonda, Goudriaan, and Shastri have demonstrated that for the *Ṛgveda*, at least, the term *māyā* has strong magical connotations, and this magical association is also present in later vedic texts, in particular the *Atharvaveda.*[7] Shastri, for example, has held that in the Ṛgvedic context *māyā* refers to, "a wonderful, supernatural power, an extraordinary skill" or "a supernatural power",[8] while Gonda has defined it for this period as, "incomprehensible wisdom and power enabling its possessor, or being able itself, to create, devise, contrive, effect, or do something".[9] These magical associations become even stronger in the *Atharvaveda,*[10] where the term is used in the sense of "tricking one's enemies" and is strongly associated with the asuric world (*AV* 8.10.22), although Gonda has cautioned against considering this link to impart a primarily negative connotation with the word *māyā.*[11]

It is not my purpose in the context of this paper to discuss the history of the term *māyā* in the *vedic* literature since this has been addressed by earlier scholars, particularly Gonda and Goudriaan. Of note, for my concerns are, however, two important semantic constructions of the term *māyā* that emanate from the vedic literataure (1) *māyā*'s early and fundamental association with magic and transformative powers; and (2) that while *māyā* can be understood as neutral—that is to say that *māyā* is neither divine nor earthly, neither positive nor negative—it is clearly, although not exclusively, associated with and employed by not just the demonic world in general but the *rākṣasa* race in particular.

Despite Gonda's quite appropriate cautionary note, from the time of the *Ṛgveda*, the term *māyā* is linked with "magic" as a negative construction and is understood as a power associated with groups that stand in opposition to the gods. At *ṚV* 7.104, for example, Indra and Soma are exhorted to slay the demons [*rākṣasas/yātudhānas*], who are said to employ *māyā*: [verse 24]

> *índra jahí púmāṃsaṃ yātudhā́nam utá stríyaṃ māyáyā śā́śadānām /*
> *vígrīvāso mū́radevā ṛdantu mā́ té dṛśán sū́ryam uccárantam //*[12]

> O Indra, kill that male *yātudhāna* and the female, who annihilates by means of [her] *māyā*; Let [these] foolish divinities,[13] with crooked necks, fall and not see the rising sun.

In fact, in this hymn we learn that the demons in question are not the *asuras*, the more familiar anti-*deva* race commonly associated with the vedic world and the power of *māyā* in the *veda*, but rather belong to the race known as the *rākṣasas* (7.104.1, 4, 7, 17, 18, 19, 23, 25). The hymn employs other terms, such as *yātudhāna* and *kimīdins*, seemingly as synonyms for these demonic creatures.[14] Of note here, too, is the association of the term *māyā* with a female figure (*stríyaṃ māyáyā śā́śadānām*), an association to which we will return shortly.

Both the *Māhābhārata* and the *Rāmāyaṇa* employ the term *māyā*. The use of the term in the epics is said to be multivalent, but scholarly references to and discussions of the *māyā* of the epics are largely restricted to the *Mahābhārata* while references to the word in the *Rāmāyaṇa* are almost an afterthought. Thus Hopkins, Gonda, and others focus their attention on the *Mahābhārata*, giving the use of the word in the *Rāmāyaṇa* only the slightest nod,[15] while Goudriaan mentions the "lesser" epic in passing. Their focus on the longer epic is not unreasonable, since these scholars are mostly concerned with the philosophical constructions of *māyā* and its use in Vaiṣṇava theology. Nevertheless, in the larger epic, the term is truly multivalent and multi-referential. Thus gods, demons, semi-divine figures, and humans and even perhaps animals—if one counts Takṣaka and his son—all are said to possess *māyā*. But it is to the *māyā* of the *Gītā* that scholars have primarily turned.[16]

Perhaps most telling of the lack of interest in the *Rāmāyaṇa*'s use of this term is, in fact, the example that both Hopkins and Gonda choose to cite as of particular interest to their projects. Hopkins, arguing that for many of the *Gītā* passages, it is not the *māyā* of Śaṅkara that is referred to but rather that "the simpler meaning suffices of either trick or delusion (false understanding) applied to the relation of the individual soul and God, and this is probably the meaning".[17]

Hopkins then continues in this line, noting that in the *Gītā*, when Kṛṣṇa states, " 'that he is born by *ātmamāyā*', it must be remembered that in describing the parallel situation in the *Rāmāyaṇa*, where Vishnu is born as Rāma, the word *chadman*, disguise, cover, is used as the equivalent of *māyā*."[18] Hopkins's reference is taken from Gorresio's edition of the *Vālmīki Rāmāyaṇa* 6.11.32, which reads,

> *viṣṇuṃ rāmam ahaṃ manye mānuṣaṃ chadmarūpiṇam* /
>
> I think that Rāma is Viṣṇu, a man in a deceptive form.

However, the phrase *chadmarūpiṇam*, "having a deceptive form," is known only to a few northern manuscripts (Ñ2,B2,3,D3), while the critical reading (6.26.31) and the one best supported by the manuscript evidence that was collated for the critical edition reads,

> *viṣṇuṃ manyāmahe rāmaṃ mānuṣaṃ deham āsthitam /*
>
> We truly believe that Rāma is none other than Viṣṇu who has taken on the body of a man.

The verse, while it has important implications for our understanding of the epic's self-awareness of the divinity of Rāma, undermines Hopkins's argument that the *māyā* in the *Rāmāyaṇa* is a relational one between god and the individual and is parallel to the use of that term in the *Mahābhārata*. It is his only example of the term in the *Rāmāyaṇa*.

Gonda, referring to Hopkins's remark, argues similarly, that, "Here [in the Gītā], *māyā* obviously assumes the character of a veil which hides the real and eternal from men's sight and understanding; God, veiled by his *yogamāyā*-, is not revealed at all (7.25)."[19] Gonda then cites Hopkins noting,

> Hopkins ... rightly drew attention to the parallel situation in the Rāmāyaṇa, where in the description of Viṣṇu being born as Rāma the term chadman—"cover, disguise" is used as the equivalent of māyā (Gorr 6, 11, 32).[20]

Like Hopkins's, Gonda's comments become moot in the context of the textual evidence. Both use the *Rāmāyaṇa* to support their understanding of *māyā* in the "greater epic", and have only the most tangential interest in the *Rāmāyaṇa*'s construction of the term, which, given their respective projects, may be justified. For the *Rāmāyaṇa*, I would argue, while it may well assume such a relationship between god and individual, has little interest in making such a relationship explicit and even less for terming it god's *māyā*. The term *yogamāyā* is only used once, to the best of my knowledge, in the *Rāmāyaṇa*, and there it seems to indicate, as it does in the passages noted by Gonda and Hopkins, such a relationship. This reference occurs in the *Bālakāṇḍa*, at 1.28.7, in the context of one of the so-called purāṇic stories. The narrative is of the *Vāmanāvatara* of Viṣṇu, where Viṣṇu is asked to use his, "*māyāyoga*", to incarnate as a dwarf.

The *Bālakaṇḍa* connects Viṣṇu with *māyā* elsewhere, although not explicitly, and arguably, the term may encompass different semantic ranges. At 1.15.13, for example, the *pāyasa*, or "porridge" that contains the essence of Viṣṇu is as if, "*māyāmayīm* (made of *māyā*)". Again, at 1.16, Brahmā tells the gods to "create powerful allies able to take on any form at will to aid the hero Viṣṇu. Let them be heroes with magic powers, whose swiftness shall rival that of the wind. They must be ... equal in valor to Viṣṇu himself."[21] The term for "magic powers" used here is *māyāvid*. This is the only passage in the epic where the monkeys possess or are explicitly connected with *māyā*,[22] although in one instance one of their members is accused of possessing it.[23]

Otherwise, even in the final *sargas* of the final *kāṇḍa* of the epic, where Rāma is identified with Viṣṇu, the association of Viṣṇu and *māyā* is very limited, occurring, it appears, in only two places in the critical text. The first makes an explicit connection between god and *māyā*, while the second is explicit as well but a bit more puzzling. The first reference occurs at 7.94.4-5, where Kāla has come to Rāma and, recognizing him as Viṣṇu, relates to him verbatim Brahmā's message:

saṃkṣipya ca purā lokān māyayā svayam eva hi /
mahārṇave śayāno 'psu māṃ tvaṃ pūrvam ajījanaḥ //

bhogavantaṃ tato nāgam anantam udake śayam /
māyayā janayitvā tvaṃ dvau ca sattvau mahābalau //[24]

Formerly having destroyed the worlds through your own *māyā*, you, sleeping on the great ocean, caused me to take birth.

Through your *māyā*, you having caused Ananta, that great serpent, with his coils, sleeping on the waters, to take birth, as well as two powerful creatures [Madhu and Kaiṭabha] ...

The final reference to *māyā* in the epic occurs in its last *sarga*, where Rāma ascends to heaven. The passage provides an explicit identification between Rāma Rāghava and Viṣṇu. Both names are in the *saṃbodhanam* and stand in apposition. God must resume his natural, divine form and return to his divine abode. Additionally the verses contain an explicit reference to *māyā*, but here, *māyā* is personified as god's consort (*parigrahā*):

āgaccha viṣṇo bhadraṃ te diṣṭyā prāpto 'si rāghava //

bhrātṛbhiḥ saha devābhaiḥ praviśasva svakāṃ tanum /
vaiṣṇavīṃ tāṃ mahātejas tad ākāśaṃ sanātanam //

tvaṃ hi lokagatir deva na tvāṃ kecit prajānate /
ṛte māyāṃ viśālākṣa tava pūrvaparigrahām //[25]

> Viṣṇu! Rāghava! Come! Bless you, thank heavens you have arrived.
>
> Along with your brothers, in their divine manifestations, inhabit your own body, that of Viṣṇu, [and] that eternal, glorious space.
>
> You, long-eyed lord, are the goal of world. Except for Māyā, your consort of old, no one recognizes you.[26]

The lines appear to be intentionally enigmatic, but again the connection between Viṣṇu and *māyā* is explicit and reinforces Gonda's interpretation of *māyā* in the *Gītā* as "a veil which hides the real and eternal from men's sight". But this last association of *māyā* as the consort of Viṣṇu in the closing lines of the epic is somewhat puzzling and an issue to which I will return shortly.

In the *Bālakāṇḍa*, the term *māyā* is used number of times in contexts that present it as a more "neutral" or non-aligned concept. We find the word used twice in its sense of "extraordinary power", or in a context where "creative energy" is foregrounded. For example, at 1.15.13, as noted above, the *pāyasa*, or "porridge" that contains the essence of Viṣṇu, is as if "*māyāmayīm* (made of *māyā*)" and at 1.48.14, Ahalyā is said to be as if "created through the creative energy of Brahmā (*prayatnān nirmitā dhātrā divyāṃ māyāmayīm iva*)". In a different context, and one found only in this instance, the term appears as part of the proper name of a weapon, Māyādhara, "bearer of illusion", given to Rāma by Viśvāmitra, but never deployed in the epic (1.28.7).[27]

Elsewhere in the poem, there is little doubt that *māyā* lies exclusively within the domain of the evil. Outside of the *rākṣasa* world, the remaining occurrences of the term *māyā* in Vālmīki's text are limited to the following:

(1) It refers to the name of an *asura*, Māyāvin, the firstborn son of the *asura* Dundubhi (4.9.4; 4.10.9)].

(2) It is considered a possession of the *asura* Maya. It is this demon who, through his *māyā*, creates the cave in which Aṅgada's search party wanders during their search for Sītā (4.50.10; 4.52.15,32; 4.56.17). It is from Maya that Rāvaṇa is said to have obtained his *māyā* (6.22.6-8). It is Maya who is said to have employed it to build the city of Hemapura, the "Golden City" (7.12.6-8). And it is Maya who is said to have forged an infallible javelin with it (6.88.30-31).

(3) In one case, is used of a human—Mantharā, in whose hump are stored her magical powers (2.9.34).

(4) In one instance, Rāvaṇa, in addressing the monkey Nīla, accuses him of being swift because of *māyā* (6.47.82).

Outside of these references and those discussed in the opening *kāṇḍa* and at the very end of the last *kāṇḍa*, *Vālmīki's Rāmāyaṇa* limits the usage of the term *māyā* to fairly restricted environments. The possessors of *māyā* are virtually all demonic figures[28] or those associated with evil or demonic concerns, while the objects of their *māyā* are normally human or animal (albeit, divinities in these forms). The meaning of the term in these environments is restricted more or less to the notion of "magical illusion". This stands in contrast to the *Mahābhārata*, where, although the vast majority of those who possess the power are divine or semi-divine, both the subjects and objects of *māyā* may be from any of numerous worlds or realms and where the multivalence of the term permeates all levels of the text. This in itself, I would argue, is significant, as it marks a difference in both what was felt as an appropriate construction of and reaction to the term by both the composer and audience of the *Rāmāyaṇa*, who can be said to understand *māyā* as a power strongly associated with the darker forces.

Even within the *rākṣasa* world, the use of the term *māyā* is used fairly restrictively. Only a few of these demonic creatures are actually identified as possessing or using *māyā* and even fewer as actually employing it.

The family of Tāṭakā seems particularly infused with the power of *māyā*. At *Bālakāṇḍa* 1.25.11 Tāṭakā is called *māyābalā*, "having strength through her *māyā*", (armed as she is with magic powers), while both of her sons, Subāhu and Mārīca, are early on identified as employing *māyā*.

> *āvārya gaganaṃ megho yathā prāvṛṣi nirgataḥ /*
> *tathā māyāṃ vikurvāṇau rākṣasāv abhyadhāvatām //*[29]
>
> Like a storm cloud comes forth in the rainy season covering the sky, those two *rākṣasas*, displaying their magical illusion, raced forth.

Mārīca, of course, is the most famous among this *rākṣasa* clan, for it is no other than he who assumes the form of the magical or illusory deer that is used to infatuate Sītā. The term employed when Mārīca assumes the form of the golden deer or when this form is alluded to is consistently *māyā* (1.1.42; 3.41.6, 7, 36; 3.43.14; 3.44.36; cf. 3.64.9), and the deer itself is referred to as *māyāmayaḥ* (3.40.31). The text is silent as to how or when he comes into the possession of *māyā*.

Rāvaṇa's family is similarly marked by possession of *māyā*. At 6.57.11 we are told that all the sons of Rāvaṇa are skilled in *māyā* (*sarve sarve māyāviśāradāḥ*). More specifically, Indrajit, the powerful son of Rāvaṇa, and Vibhīṣaṇa, the demon king's brother, also are said to possess and use *māyā* (6.11.19; 6.36.8, 9, passim).

Rāvaṇa, the most prominent of the *rākṣasas*, while certainly associated with *māyā*, is only infrequently explicitly said to possess or be a master of it, and is even more rarely said to actually employ it. In the *Araṇyakāṇḍa*, Rāvaṇa, although associated with the term *māyā* (3.47.18—his chariot is fashioned of *māyā*; 3.52.13—he is compared to the demon Maya who possesses *māyā*), is not said specifically to employ *māyā* when he assumes the form of a mendicant (see, for example, 3.44.2,8; 3.45.1; 3.47.1,6). However, Rāvaṇa is described as an actual practitioner of *māyā* at the end of the *kāṇḍa*, where, Jaṭāyus with his dying breaths tells Rāma,

> *sā hṛtā rākṣasendreṇa rāvaṇena vihāyasā /*
> *māyām āsthāya vipulāṃ vātadurdinasaṃkulām //*[30]
>
> She was carried off through the sky by Rāvaṇa, the king of the *rākṣasas*, who took on a prodigious illusion, replete with gales and storms.[31]

In the *Yuddhakāṇḍa*, Rāvaṇa is reminded that he has received his magical powers from Maya, his father-in-law (6.7.7,10), whereas in the *Uttarakāṇḍa* we are told that Rāvaṇa learned ninety-nine illusory tricks (*māyānāṃ śatam ekonam*) from the Nivātakavacas while he was living in their city for a year (7.23.12-14). He is described as *māyāvid* twice (6.22.6; 6.24.12) and *māyābalaḥ* once (6.25.8). He once questions his charioteer, asking if he considers him to lack such powers (6.93.3). He is accused of employing his illusory magic at 3.51.5, where Sītā thinks that he has employed *māyā* to assume the form of the *māyāmṛga*, and at 6.31.55, where Rāma accuses Rāvaṇa of using it when he abducted Sītā.

Rāvaṇa, in fact, only actually employs *māyā* on a limited number of occasions. During the culminating battle of the epic, in which the demon king fights Rāma, he is said to infuse *māyā* into his weapons, which then assume various animal shapes:

> *śarān kharamukhāṃś cānyān varāhamukhasaṃsthitān /*
> *śvānakukkuṭavaktrāṃś makarāśīviṣānanān //*
>
> *etāṃś cānyāṃś ca māyābhiḥ sasarja niśitāñ śarān /*
> *rāmaṃ prati mahātejāḥ kruddhaḥ sarpa iva śvasan //* [32]
>
> Hissing like an angry serpent, the immensely powerful *rākṣasa*, employing his powers of illusion, then loosed still more sharp arrows at Rāma. Some of these arrows had the heads of donkeys, while others were shaped like the heads of boars. Some had the heads of dogs and cocks, while others had the heads of sea monsters and venomous serpents.

On the other hand, at 6.95.18, Rāvaṇa's weapons are said to be invested with *māyā*, but no agent is noted and, at 6.88.30-35, he is said to strike down Lakṣmaṇa with an infallible javelin that Maya forged and infused with *māyā*. Outside of these contexts, it is only in the *Uttarakāṇḍa* (7.15.26), where Rāvaṇa is explicitly said to use his powers of magical illusion, literally to "enter *māyā*", to defeat the Yakṣas (*tato māyāṃ praviṣṭo 'sau rākṣasīṃ rākṣaseśvaraḥ*).

In one of the most famous scenes of the *Yuddhakāṇḍa*, where the illusory head and sword of Rāma are created and displayed before Sītā, it is not Rāvaṇa who creates the magic but his foremost sorcerer, Vidyujjihva (6.22.6-8).

For the *Rāmāyaṇa*, the true master of and most powerful controller of *māyā* is not Rāvaṇa but his eldest son, Indrajit Rāvaṇi. It is to this figure that the largest number of references and actual uses of *māyā* are attributed. And it is from Indrajit's possession of and empolyment of *māyā* that we can understand most clearly the *Rāmāyaṇa*'s construction of the term. We are only first made aware of Indrajit's powers of *māyā* in the *Yuddhakāṇḍa*, for although he fights Hanumān in *sarga* 46 of the *Sundarakāṇḍa*, no mention is made there of his possession of or employment of any powers of illusion. Indrajit, in fact, realizing that he would not be able to kill the monkey, employs the *brahmāstra* to capture him. It is only later that this *astra* and the boon that allowed it to be acquired is connected with Indrajit's *māyā*. Hanumān is explicitly said to have permitted himself to be captured since Brahmā had shown him such kindness and since, in any case, he would be able to free himself momentarily (5.46.40).

At 6.27.18, Indrajit, one of the warriors that Rāvaṇa assigns to guard the gates of Laṅkā, is called, "*māhāmāyam*", but it is not until the battle has started that Indrajit's mastery over *māyā* is made manifest. At *sarga* 34, as the night battle rages on, Aṅgada attacks the horses and charioteer of Indrajit, and

indrajit tu rathaṃ tyaktvā hatāśvo hatasārathiḥ /
aṅgadena mahāmāyas tatraivāntaradhīyata //

so 'ntardhānagataḥ pāpo rāvaṇī raṇakarkaśaḥ /
brahmadattavaro vīro rāvaṇiḥ krodhamūrchitaḥ /
adṛśyo niśitān bāṇān mumocāśanivarcasaḥ //

sa rāmaṃ lakṣmaṇaṃ caiva ghorair nāgamayaiḥ śaraiḥ /
bibheda samare kruddhaḥ sarvagātreṣu rākṣasaḥ // [33]

> His horses and charioteer slain by Aṅgada, Indrajit, who possessed great powers of illusion, vanished on the spot.
>
> The evil Indrajit Rāvaṇi, a hero ruthless in battle, possessed a boon from Brahmā. Seething with rage, he concealed himself; and, unseen, he loosed sharp arrows, blazing like lightning bolts.
>
> In a rage, the *rākṣasa* pierced Rāma and Lakṣmaṇa in every part of their bodies with dreadful arrows in the form of great serpents.

As the battle continues we are told that the invisible Indrajit completely overwhelms Rāma and Lakṣmaṇa (6.35.7) until "their bodies were thus thickly covered with arrows that had not a hair's breadth between them" (8). Indrajit continues his attack until both heroes, riddled with arrows, lie as if dead on the battlefield (26). In the following *sarga*, the monkeys, as would be expected, are deluded by Indrajit's illusory magic, but Vibhīṣaṇa is not:

> *antarikṣaṃ nirīkṣanto diśaḥ sarvāś ca vānarāḥ /*
> *na cainaṃ māyayā channaṃ dadṛsū rāvaṇiṃ raṇe //*
>
> *taṃ tu māyāpraticchannaṃ māyayaiva vibhīṣaṇaḥ /*
> *vīkṣamāṇo dadarśātha bhrātuḥ putram avasthitam //*[34]
>
> Although the monkeys scanned the sky and all directions, they could not see Indrajit Rāvaṇi, who had concealed himself in the battle with his powers of illusion.
>
> But Vibhīṣaṇa, in looking about, was able, through his own magical powers, to discern his brother's son, who stood there, concealed by his powers of illusion.

The passage marks, but not for the first time (6.11.19), the possession of *māyā* not only by Indrajit but by his uncle Vibhīṣaṇa, who has defected to Rāma's camp. It is clear that only one who possesses such a power can see through it. And as we are to discover, so long as Indrajit is in possession of and is able to employ his *māyā*, he cannot be defeated.

Indrajit's powers are so great that even Rāma and Lakṣmaṇa are unable to counter them. Indrajit once again resorts to the power of his *māyā*, generally manifested as the power to become invisible, to baffle and defeat Rāma and his forces in battle two more times in the *kāṇḍa*, once explicitly and once implicitly. At *sarga* 60, Indrajit, resorting to his magical power of invisibility, strikes down the entire monkey army—with the exception of Hanumān and Vibhīṣaṇa—as well as Rāma and Lakṣmaṇa. It is following this scene, that Hanumān brings the *oṣadhaparvata* and revives the monkey forces. Here the monkeys are said to be *māyāhatāḥ*, "slain by *māyā*", and *māyānigūḍhāḥ*, "baffled by *māyā*". At *sarga* 67, Indrajit, although not explicitly said to employ his *māyā*, is said to be able to render himself and/or his horses and chariots invisible and does so (4, 15, 17), once again riddling Rāma and Lakṣmaṇa with arrows (21).

It is in *sargas* 60 and 67, moreover, that we are introduced to the mechanism through which Indrajit is said to acquire his powers of invisibility. It is a sacrifice. Both *sargas* have parallel, sometimes verbatim, descriptions of Indrajit's sacrifice. The first is the more elaborate and the more specific. These sacrifices are said to take place in the Nikumbhilā grove (6.60.18), a grove dedicated to a goddess of the same name. The word is first introduced in the *Sundarakāṇḍa* as either the name of a deity that the *rākṣasīs* worship or the name of the grove where they worship (5.22.41). There the commentators identify the goddess as Bhadrakālī, whose shrine is said to be located in western Laṅkā. In *sarga* 60 we are told that Indrajit proceeds to the shrine of Nikumbhilā, where he performs a sacrifice. This sacrifice, like the ones that follow, is vedic in nature, in that it is offered to Agni (6.60.20, 21, 25; 6.67.9), but it is also infused with elements of black magic (6.60.22, 23; 6.67.5, 6, 7). We are told at 6.67.15 that the oblations are accompanied by *rākṣasair mantraiḥ*, "*rākṣasa mantras*". In both passages the text makes it clear that the warrior gains "invisibility" through his efforts (6.60.28, 29; 6.67.10,15). Moreover, at 6.60.30,31 we are given to understand that this invisibility is directly linked to Indrajit's *māyā*.[35]

> *te kevalaṃ saṃdadṛśuḥ śitāgrān bāṇān raṇe vānaravāhinīṣu /*
> *māyānigūḍhaṃ ca surendraśatruṃ na cātra taṃ rākṣasam abhyapaśyan //*[36]

> All they could see in the battle were the sharp-tipped arrows raining on the monkey troops. For they could not see the *rākṣasa*, the foe of the lord of the gods, concealed as he was by magical illusion.

The sacrifice, moreover, appears to allow Indrajit to invoke and infuse his weapons with sacred *mantras* thus empowering the *brahmāstra* (6.60.26; 6.67.14). Once again, at *sarga* 69 (6.69.23) Indrajit undertakes a sacrifice[37] to renew his powers. At *sarga* 71, as Indrajit is commencing yet another of his sacrifices, Vibhīṣaṇa, the only member of Rāma's forces who can see through Indrajit's (and other's) *māyā*, realizes his nephew's intentions and makes clear to his companions that this powerful son of

Rāvaṇa cannot be defeated if his sacrifice is completed (6.71.15, 18, 22).

The history of Indrajit's sacrifice and austerities is given in the *Uttarakāṇḍa* (25.2-13). Rāvaṇa sends his sister Śūrpaṇakhā, whom he had recently widowed, with Khara to the Daṇḍaka forest. He himself goes to the Nikumbhilā grove. There he sees his son Indrajit, who is called Meghanāda, wearing the clothes of an ascetic (7.25.4). Rāvaṇa addresses him, but Indrajit Rāvaṇi, who has taken a vow of silence, remains silent. Uśanas Kāvya, the *purohita* of the *asuras*, responds instead. He informs Rāvaṇa that Indrajit has performed seven vedic sacrifices and as a result has received boons from Śiva, among which is the *tāmasī māyā* (10-11). However, it is clear from the context of the *Yuddhakāṇḍa* that Indrajit's *māyā* must, as it were, be recharged periodically. The acquisition of *māyā* is linked to sacrfice and asceticism, but its creation and deployment in the *rākṣasa* world is limited and tied to the temporal.

Thus, for the vast majority of cases in Vālmīki's text, and in particular in the *Yuddhakāṇḍa*, the semantic range of *māyā* must be limited to a type of black magic or power of illusion. This is the case in the two remaining incidents in which *rākṣasas* employ *māyā*. The first, mentioned above, occurs early in the *kāṇḍa* at *sarga* 22. Rāvaṇa, having just been given a detail account of the gathered monkey forces, becomes "somewhat agitated" (6.22.2) and takes counsel with one of his ministers, a *rākṣasa* named Vidyujjihva.[38]

> *vidyujjihvaṃ ca māyājñam abravīd rākṣasādhipaḥ /*
> *mohayiṣyāmahe sītāṃ māyayā janakātmajām //*
>
> *śiro māyāmayaṃ gṛhya rāghavasya niśācaraḥ /*
> *māṃ tvaṃ samupatiṣṭhasya mahac ca saśaraṃ dhanuḥ //*
>
> *evam uktas tathety āha vidyujjihvo niśācara /*
> *tasya tuṣṭo 'bhavad rājā pradadau ca vibhūṣaṇam //* [39]
>
> The lord of the *rākṣasas* addressed Vidyujjihva, master of illusion, saying, "Let us delude Sītā, Janaka's daughter, with an illusion.
>
> "Night-roaming *rākṣasa*, you must come to me bearing Rāghava's head along with his great bow and arrows—all fashioned through the power of illusion."
>
> When he had been addressed in this fashion, the night-roaming *rākṣasa* Vidyujjihva responded, "So be it". The king was pleased with him and presented him with a piece of jewelry.

Rāvaṇa then approaches Sītā and, in graphic detail, tells her of the battle in which he has slain Rāma. Rāvaṇa then orders:

> *rākṣasaṃ krūrakarmāṇaṃ vidyujjihvaṃ tvam ānaya /*
> *yena tad rāghavaśiraḥ saṃgrāmāt svayam āhṛtam //*
>
> *vidyujjihvas tato gṛhya śiras tat saśarāsanam /*
> *praṇāmaṃ śirasā kṛtvā rāvaṇasyāgrataḥ sthitaḥ //*
>
> *tam abravīt tato rājā rāvaṇo rākṣasaṃ sthitam /*
> *vidyujjihvaṃ mahājihvaṃ samīpaparivartinam //*
>
> *agrataḥ kuru sītāyāḥ śighraṃ dāśaratheḥ śiraḥ /*
> *avasthāṃ paścimāṃ bhartuḥ kṛpaṇā sādhu paśyatu //*
>
> *evam uktaṃ tu tad rakṣaḥ śiras tatpriyadarśanam /*
> *upanikṣipya sītāyāḥ kṣipram antaradhīyata //* [40]
>
> "Go and fetch Vidyujjihva, that *rākṣasa* of cruel deeds, the very one who has brought the head of Rāghava from the battlefield."
>
> Then Vidyujjihva, grasping that head along with that bow, presented himself before Rāvaṇa, bowing his head in reverence.
>
> Then King Rāvaṇa addressed the long-tongued *rākṣasa*, Vidyujjihva, who stood close beside him.
>
> "Place the head of Dāśarathi before Sītā at once. Let the wretched woman clearly see her husband's final state."
>
> Addressed in this fashion, the *rākṣasa* placed that beautiful head before Sītā and swiftly withdrew.

The text makes it clear that Vidyujjihva is still present (6.22.43). Sītā, distraught, begins to lament her fate as she gazes upon her husband's head. But in the midst of her lamentation, Prahasta, a minister of Rāvaṇa, seeks an audience and, with a matter of some urgency (6.23.34-35), Rāvaṇa departs:

> *antardhānaṃ tu tac chīrṣaṃ tac ca kārmukam uttamam /*
> *jagāma rāvaṇasyaiva niryāṇasamanantaram //* [41]
>
> But no sooner had Rāvaṇa departed than that head and splendid bow vanished.

While nothing more is said of the movements of Vidyujjihva, there is a clear connection between the physical presence of Rāvaṇa and, presumably, Vidyujjihva and the power of the *māyā* to create an illusory head and bow. As in the case of Indrajit's invisibility, the *māyā* creates an illusion, but that illusion is tied to a character and its employment is bound by temporality.

Māyā is employed one more time in the *Yuddhakāṇḍa* to create an illusory figure. This time the creator of the illusion is Indrajit and, in order to demoralize the opposing forces, he creates a simulacrum of Sītā. At *sarga* 68, threatened by the tenacity of Rāma and Lakṣmaṇa, Indrajit resorts to trickery. Here we are given a graphic description of both of the illusory Sītā and her/ its apparent slaying, as well as Hanumān's and the monkeys' reaction to it. However, we are given little in the way of information of the mechanism for the illusion's creation. The monkey army, it is clear, is deluded by Indrajit's *māyā*. And its leader, Hanumān, is likewise completely baffled by Indrajit's *māyā* and believes Sītā to have been murdered. Hanumān and his army first devastate the enemy troops, after which he orders a withdrawal from the battlefield and returns to Rāma:

> *samare yudhyamānām asmākaṃ prekṣatāṃ ca saḥ /*
> *jaghāna rudatīṃ sītām indrajid rāvaṇātmajaḥ //*
>
> *udbhrāntacittas tāṃ dṛṣṭvā viṣaṇṇo 'ham arindama /*
> *tad ahaṃ bhavato vṛttaṃ vijñāpayitum āgataḥ //*[42]
>
> While we were engaged in battle, Indrajit, son of Rāvaṇa, slew the wailing Sītā right before our eyes.
>
> When I saw her like that, I was devastated and despondent, tamer of your foes. Then I came straightaway to report this news to you, sir.

Rāma, believing what Hanumān said to be true, immediately sinks into a profound swoon (6.70.10). Lakṣmaṇa, deeply grieved, then launches into one of the epic's many comments on the nature of *dharma* and questions its very existence, since it is impossible to "perceive":

> *bhūtānāṃ sthāvarāṇāṃ ca jaṅgamānāṃ ca darśanam /*
> *yathāsti na tathā dharmas tena nāstīti me matiḥ //*
>
> *yathaiva sthāvaraṃ vyaktaṃ jaṅgamaṃ ca tathāvidham /*
> *nāyam arthas tathā yuktas tvadvidho na vipadyate //*[43]

For, since we cannot directly perceive the force of righteousness in the same way that we perceive moving and fixed objects, it is my opinion that it does not exist.

This thing called "righteousness" is not demonstrable in the same way that moving and fixed objects are. Otherwise, a person like you would not experience such suffering.[44]

Vālmīki is concerned with and understands that there are forces in this world that are not visible and/or directly perceptible. Moreover, Lakṣmaṇa's speech here is one of the numerous and noteworthy instances in the epic where Vālmīki pauses to challenge the hegemonic brāhmaṇic discourse.[45] Here Lakṣmaṇa's agnostic views are dispelled by Vibhīṣaṇa not Rāma. These views are expressed in a context that is textually closely linked with the employment of the *rākṣasas' māyā*, and parallels can easily be inferred. Lakṣmaṇa's heretical ideas are wrong and threatening to brāhmaṇic world, much as is the *māyā* of the *rākṣasas*. It is not until Vibhīṣaṇa speaks that Rāma, Lakṣmaṇa, and the monkeys are made aware of the illusion perpetuated by Indrajit:

abhiprāyaṃ tu jānāmi rāvaṇasya durātmanaḥ /
sītāṃ prati mahābāho na ca ghātaṃ kariṣyati //

naiva sāmnā na bhedena na dānena kuto yudhā /
sā draṣṭum api śakyeta naiva cānyena kenacit //

vānarān mohayitvā tu pratiyātaḥ sa rākṣasaḥ /
caityaṃ nikumbhilāṃ nāma yatra homaṃ kariṣyati // [46]

For I know full well the plans that the evil-minded Rāvaṇa has for Sītā, great-armed warrior. He would never countenance her killing.

But no one can so much as get a glimpse of her, whether through conciliation, sowing dissension, bribery, or any other means much less through violence.

After deluding the monkeys, the *rākṣasa* Indrajit has returned to the shrine known as Nikumbhilā, where he will perform a sacrifice.

Again, only a *rākṣasa* is able see through another *rākṣasa*'s *māyā* and provide an appropriate antidote, as it were. Symbolic though the passage may seem, the *māyā* employed by Indrajit is no more than a trick, black magic, created though the power derived from his sacrifice at the Nikumbhilā grove.

For the *Vālmīki Rāmāyaṇa* then, while *māyā* does not necessarily exclusively belong to the demonic realm, it can be understood to be principally aligned with the forces of evil, and most specifically with the *rākṣasas*, that is to say that it is in the possession of and chiefly employed by the force that the text has constructed to represent *adharma*, unrighteousness, and evil. For Vālmīki, the term rarely can be understood to have a semantic range outside its most basic meaning of "trick *or* magic". The real force of the term is more adequately rendered as "black magic *or* illusory magic". This restrictive use of *māyā*, although it has vedic antecedents, is notable. For unlike the vedic tradition and its sister epic, Vālmīki's *Rāmāyaṇa* distances itself from associating the word *māyā* with anything positive. This association and the limited semantic realm of the term as used by Vālmīki suggests that at least this poet and his audiences were most comfortable when the word *māyā* is aligned with the powers of darkness.

The term *māyā* thus comes to haunt certain very important junctures in the epic text and becomes associated with certain figures. Throughout the text the vast majority of figures who possess and practice *māyā* are male—Maya, Mārīca, Rāvaṇa, Indrajit, Vidyujjihva, etc., and only rarely, in fact only twice, are women so described. Once, of course, is in reference to Tāṭakā, the monstrous and gargantuan *rākṣasī*, and mother of Mārīca, who, as noted above, is called *māyābalā*, "who has the power of *māyā*" (1.25.11). Perhaps more worthy of note is the only other mention of a woman as possessing *māyā*. In the *Ayodhyākāṇḍa*, Kaikeyī, pleased with Mantharā's plan, describes the hunchback's hump:

> *tavedaṃ sthagu yad dīrghaṃ rathaghoṇam ivāyatam /*
> *matayaḥ kṣatravidyāś ca māyāś cātra vasanti te //*[47]
>
> This hump of yours, long and wide like a chariot's hub, this is where your clever ideas, your knowledge of political strategy, and your *māyā*, "magic powers", must reside.

That Mantharā's hump marks her as deformed, and therefore evil, has been discussed elsewhere and need not be elaborated upon here.[48] That the hump, marked as the locus of Mantharā's evil, is also the locus of her *māyā*, only further strengthens the bond in Vālmīki's epic between *māyā* and evil. Furthermore, Mantharā is the only "human", although still marked as "other", to be considered truly evil (Kaikeyī, merely being a temporary puppet under her influence), and it comes as no surprise that she is also said to possess *māyā*.[49]

Although many of the epic's characters are subject to the power of *māyā*, Vālmīki's text makes its female characters particularly so. Kaikeyī, for example, can be understood to have fallen under Mantharā's sway (*kubjāvākyavaśaṃ gatā* 2.9.44), but is finally rehabilitated by the epic, and, once the intrigue in Ayodhyā is resolved, is reabsorbed as a more or less unmarked character of the epic.[50] It is, however, Sītā who is most susceptible to the power of *māyā* as well as other similar types of changes of form. This is not to argue that male characters are not subject to its power. They are, and, in particular, Rāma, Lakṣmaṇa, and Hanumān all fall at least temporarily under the sway of the *rākṣasas' māyā* at one point or another in the epic. But it is principally and consistently Sītā who is subjected to and deluded by the *rākṣasas' māyā*. And it is she who is deluded by the *māyā* of Mārīca both in the form of the golden deer (3.40.32; 3.41.9-21) and by the imitation of Rāma's voice (6.4.31-33), while Lakṣmaṇa and Rāma are fully aware of the possibility that the deer and the voice are illusions (6.41.4-7, 36-46ab; 6.42.20; 6.43.15). It is she who cannot see through Rāvaṇa's disguise (3.44.31-35). And, it is, after all, Sītā's inability to accept and/or acknowledge the illusory and magical powers of the *rākṣasa* world that gives rise to her abduction. Sītā mistakes Rāvaṇa's powers—she thinks that it is he who has created the *māyāmṛga* (3.51.4) and she thinks that Hanumān is really Rāvaṇa who has changed his form through his *māyā* (5.32.14).

Finally, it is Sītā who, upon seeing Rāma's head and bow, gives up hope, lamenting her loss as if she were a widow. There the poet describes her as *mohitām*, "deluded, confused", and *naṣṭacetanām*, "with her wits destroyed" (6.24.1, 3). And, there, it is Saramā who convinces her that Rāma is not dead and that she has been a victim of magical illusion:

> *ayuktabuddhikṛtyena sarvabhūtavirodhinā /*
> *iyaṃ prayuktā raudreṇa māyā māyāvidā tvayi //*[51]

> This was just an illusion perpetrated upon you by that savage master of illusion, whose every thought and deed is reprehensible and who is inimical to all creatures.

Note again, that it is a member of the *rākṣasa* race who identifies and dispels the *māyā*. That the heroine of the epic is particularly marked by this flaw, I would argue, is intentional on the part of the poet.

Moreover, this strong link between Sītā and *māyā* extends beyond her being the one who falls victim to *māyā*. Finally, in the last moments of her captivity, Sītā becomes the actual object of the illusion; it is, after all, a simulacrum of her that Indrajit manifests and appears to kill. This mapping of *māyā* onto Sītā is seen elsewhere in the text. At 3.52.13 there is what might appear to be a rather strange verse. Rāvaṇa has brought Sītā back to Laṅkā:

> *tatra tām asitāpāṅgīṃ śokamohaparāyaṇām /*
> *nidadhe rāvaṇaḥ sītāṃ mayo māyām ivāsurīm //*
>
> There Rāvaṇa placed Sītā, that black-eyed woman, lost in grief and utter confusion, just as the *asura* Maya did Māyā.

Pollock, in his note to the passage,[52] rationalizes, "the simile itself is odd in sense, but the alliterative wordplay and the apposite genders of the words (*maya-* being masculine; *māyā*, feminine) mitigate this to some degree" and notes that the commentators, too, seem uncomfortable with figure. While the reference of the simile is still obscure, in light of the above discussion on *māyā*, the choice of Maya and *māyā* is perhaps not as odd as Pollock suggests. For, as we have seen, the epic has consistently closely linked Sītā with *māyā*. Through his use of such a simile, the poet has drawn upon a theme and concern that he wishes to further exploit.

This very close association between Sītā and *māyā* has one more manifestation. In the final *sarga* of the epic, one discussed above, Rāma, who is now directly identified with Viṣṇu, is said not to be recognized by anyone, except for "*māyām ... pūrvaparigrahām* (Māyā, his consort of old)". In this context, where Viṣṇu is so closely tied to his Rāmāvatāra, the earthly referent for *māyā* can refer to none other than Sītā.[53]

For Vālmīki, *māyā* is largely possessed and employed by *rākṣasa* males (and by Mantharā, the phallicised feminine other) to delude and gain power over one's enemy. *Māyā*, therefore, resides in and is confined largely to the domain of the demonic. That it is closely tied to and overlaps with the heroine of the epic is, I would argue, intentional and systematic on the part of the poet. Sītā, constructed in part to be the perfectly devoted wife, is, nevertheless, because of her feminine nature still depicted by the text as easily deluded, fickle, and threatening, while *māyā* is unknowable/delusional, negative, and threatening. Both are in the possession of the *rākṣasas*. Such an association of *māyā* with Sītā reinforces for the epic audience the dangers and evil inherent in women, even the most perfect of them, and how easily one might be deluded and led astray. Rāma, of course, will defeat the *rākṣasas*, whose *māyā* haunts the text. Once they are defeated, *māyā* would seem no longer to pose a threat. But so long as that threat is present in the form of Sītā, Rāma is still subject to danger. That Rāma will reject and eventually banish Sītā becomes a necessary resolution of the epic story, but that she reappears at the very concluding moments identified as Māyā becomes logical and integral to the narrative's construction of evil, the uncanny, the other, and the feminine.

Notes

1. This paper was originally presented at the annual meeting of the American Oriental Society, March 2006, in Seattle, Washington.

2. See Apte, s.v.

3. "One should know that *prakṛti*, 'nature', is *māyā*, 'illusion', and the Great Lord is *māyin*, 'possessed of *māyā*'. This entire world is pervaded by beings [made up of] his parts." *Śvetāśvatara Upaniṣad* 4.10. See Gonda 1965: 170–71.

4. See, for example, Reyna 1962 and Shastri 1911. Note, too, Bergaigne 1883: 80 and Regnaud 1885: 237.

5. For an expanded list, see Apte, s.v., Monier-Williams, s.v., and Böhtlingk and Roth, s.v.

6. Reyna 1962: ibid. See, too, Gonda 1952: 3–62; Goudriaan 1978; Shastri 1911; Oldenberg 1919: 129; and Zimmer 1936.

7. Goudriaan 1978: 1.

8. Shastri 1911: 14, 30ff.

9. Gonda 1965: 166.

10. Goudriaan 1978: 1.

11. Gonda 1965: 168–69.

12. *ṚV* 7.104.24.

13. *māradevāḥ*: The compound is glossed by Sāyaṇa as *mārakrīḍā rākṣasāḥ*, "*rākṣasas* who play with death".

14. The use of the word *yātudhāna* to refer to a *rākṣasa* is not uncommon in Vālmīki. See, for example, *Rām* 5.23.26; 6.3.27; 6.31.74; 6.47.39; 6.48.28;

6.55.49.

15. Hopkins 1920: 139; Gonda 1965: 173.

16. See, for example, *BhG* 7.14-25, where *māyā* is said to be *daivī*, "divine", and caused by the *guṇas* (*guṇamayī*), "characterizing people, wicked and foolish". Hopkins 1902: 138. See, too. *BhG* 4.6, 7.14-15, 25 and 18.61. See Gonda 1965: 172-74.

17. Hopkins 1920: 138-39.

18. Hopkins 1920: 139.

19. Gonda 1965: 173. Here the reference is to *BhG* 7.25, and it is at the end of this passage where he references Hopkins in a footnote.

20. Gonda 1965: 173.

21. *Rām* 1.16.2ab–3.
viṣṇoḥ sahāyān balinaḥ sṛjadhvaṃ kāmarūpiṇaḥ//
māyāvidaś ca śrāṃś ca vāyuvegasamāñjave/
nayajñān buddhisampannān viṣṇutulyaparākramān//

22. The monkeys, however, are said throughout the epic to be *kāmarūpins*, i.e. able to take on any form at will, and they do take on human forms at the end of the *Yuddhakāṇḍa* (6.115.35; cf. 6.113.18). The notion of *māyā* as a creative energy is found elsewhere in the *Rāmāyaṇa*. For example, at 1.48.14, where Ahalyā is described, we are told "it seemed as if the creator himself had wrought her ... out of pure creative energy (*māyayā*)". Here the reference is to Brahmā.

23. See n. 28 below.

24. 7.94.4-5.

25. 7.100.6cd-8.

26. Nagojibhaṭṭa understands *māyā* here to refer to *jñānaśaktirūpām*, "having the form of the power of knowledge", while Govindarāja identifies *māyā* as Lakṣmī. Śivasahāya glosses *māyā* as *kṛpāmayī*, "consisting of compassion", and *pūrvaparigrhām*, "consort of old", as *nityastriyaṃ sitām* [*sic*], "the eternal woman, Sītā".

27. A number of the weapons given to Rāma here are used later in the epic, while a number are never again mentioned.

28. There is one questionable exception. At 6.47.82, the monkey Nīla so im-

presses Rāvaṇa with his quickness that the *rākṣasa* overlord says to him, "Your swiftness derives from this extraordinary trickery of yours, monkey (*kape lāghavayukto 'si māyayā parayānayā*)." Nevertheless, Nīla is no match for Rāvaṇa's own magic in battle, and is defeated by the *rākṣasa* overlord. One might note the use of the term at 6.99.10 where Mandodarī, lamenting Rāvaṇa's death, wonders if this were not all accomplished by Vāsava's *māyā*.

29. *Rām* 1.29.10.

30. *Rām* 3.64.9.

31. On the other hand, Hanumān, who frequently changes his size (Goldman and Goldman 1996: 44-47)—a talent also attributed to *rākṣasas* (e.g. Kumbhakarṇa 6.49.4)—is said to actually change forms only twice, once in the *Kiṣkindhākāṇḍa* and once in the *Yuddhakāṇḍa*. Each time he assumes the form of a man. At his initial meeting with Rāma and Lakṣmaṇa, he assumes the form of a mendicant (4.3.3). In the *Yuddhakāṇḍa* he is said to appear as a human (6.113.18). The term *māyā* is never explicitly used in association with Hanumān.

32. *Rām* 6.87.41-42.

33. *Rām* 6.34.28-30.

34. *Rām* 6.36.8-9.

35. See Goldman in press.

36. *Rām* 6.60.31.

37. The monkeys have retreated. Having witnessed Indrajit's apparent slaying of her, they think that Sītā has been slain. See below.

38. This is also the name of the husband of Śūrpaṇakhā (7.12.2), but this counselor of Rāvaṇa is likely a different figure than Śūrpaṇakhā's husband. This is supported by a passage in the *Uttarakāṇḍa*, where Rāvaṇa is said to have slain Śūrpaṇakhā's husband and then sent his sister with Khara to the Daṇḍaka forest (7.24.12-35). These events are intended to provide a rationale for the *rākṣasī*'s appearance in the forest without a husband. Her widowhood serves to further intensify her development as an oversexed, evil, and inauspicious figure.

39. *Rām* 6.22.7-9.

40. *Rām* 6.22.36-40.

41. *Rām* 6.23.38.

42. *Rām* 6.70.8-9.

43. *Rām* 6.70.15-16.

44. "the force of righteousness ... it does not exist" *dharmaḥ ... nāsti*: Literally, "*dharma* does not exist".
"This thing called 'righteousness'" *ayam arthaḥ*: Literally, "this matter". "is not demonstrable in the same way that moving and fixed objects are" *yathaiva sthāvaraṃ vyaktaṃ jaṅgamaṃ ca tathāvidham / na ... tathā yuktaḥ*: Literally, "is not proven in the way that a fixed object is manifest and a moving one of the same sort." "Otherwise, a person like you would not experience such suffering" *tvadvidho na vipadyate*: Literally, "one such as you does not experience misfortune." For a discussion of our translation and interpretation of this passage, see Goldman et al. 2009: 1170-71.

45. See Goldman et al. 2009: 55-56, 357-61, 1168-80.

46. *Rām* 6.71.10,12-13.

47. *Rām* 2.9.34.

48. See Sutherland 1992: 243-51.

49. Two other female figures are closely associated with *māyā* in Vālmīki's epic. The first is the ascetic woman Svayaṃprabhā, and the second is the *apsaras* Hemā. Both are known from the same episode, although neither is said explicitly to possess or use *māyā*. Searching for Sītā, Hanumān and his search party, tired and exhausted, come across a cave, from which water flows. They enter the cave and wander about until, at last, they spy an old ascetic woman. Hanumān asks her who she is, and where they are. She tells the monkeys that she watches over "this wonderful forest, this golden mansion", which belongs to the *apsaras* Hemā and was a gift from Brahmā. Further questioned by Hanumān, Svayaṃprabhā tells her own history as well as the history of this magical place. It was fashioned by the *dānava* Maya, who possessed magical powers [*māyā*]. He performed austerities for thousands of years and gained the wealth of Uśanas from Brahmā. He created the entire forest and lived there happily for a long time. He was in love with the *apsaras* Hemā, but Indra killed him. Then Brahmā gave this place to Hemā. The ascetic woman identifies herself as Svayaṃprabhā, the daughter of Merusāvarṇi.
Specific to this discussion is Svayaṃprabhā's relationship with Hemā and the cave. According to Lefeber (1994: 324), for the *Kiṣkindhākāṇḍa* at least, the term used for cavern here, *bila*, literally, "cave, hole, *or* a burrow [of an animal]", is used exclusively to mark the dwellings of the demons

Maya and Māyāvin. It is clear that the cave along with its elaborate interiors, palaces, gardens, etc., has demonic associations, as it was originally fashioned by the *dānava* Maya through *māyā*. That *māyā* is used for this purpose further ties it with the demonic world. While Maya's relationship with Hemā is given little attention, we are told only that "*tam apsarasi hemāyāṃ saktam*, (him, who was attached to the *apsaras* Hemā)" (4.50.14), it marks the *apsaras* as aligned with the demonic as well. The nature or duration of this relationship is, however, left to the audience's imagination. It is clear though that her relationship is strong enough that Brahmā feels it appropriate to give her the magical residence upon her paramour's death, along with the forest, and everlasting enjoyment of the objects of her desire (4.50.15—*idaṃ ca brahmaṇā dattaṃ hemāyai vanam uttamam / śāśvataḥ kāmabhogaś ca gṛhaṃ cedaṃ hiraṇyam/* cf., Lefeber's translation). It is with Hemā that Svayaṃprabhā is associated. Svayaṃprabhā is her dear friend (*priyasakhī hemā*), and Svayaṃprabhā was given a boon by Hemā to guard this excellent residence (4.50.17).

50. Once her son refuses to accede to her plans, Kaikeyī is more or less rehabilitated by Vālmīki. See Sutherland 1992.

51. *Rām* 6.24.12.

52. Pollock 1991: 328.

53. See n. 26 above, where Śivasahāya clearly understands the referent to be Sītā.

Bibliography

Primary Sources

The Bhagavad-Gita. With eleven commentaries. Edited by Shastri Gajanana Shambhu Sadhale. Bombay: Gujarati Printing Press, 1935.

Mahābhārata. 6 vols. With the commentary of Nīlakaṇṭha. Poona: Chitrashala Press, 1929.

Mahābhārata: Critical Edition. With *Harivaṃśa* (1969-71). Critically edited by V.S. Sukthankar et al. 24 vols. Poona: Bhandarkar Oriental Research Institute, 1933-70.

Ramayana, poema indiano di Valmici. Edited by Gaspare Gorresio. Paris: Stamperia Reale, 1843-67.

Rāmāyan of Vālmīki. With three commentaries called *Tilaka*, *Shiromani*, and *Bhooshana*. Edited by Shastri Shrinivas Katti Mudholkar. 7 vols. Bombay: Gujarati Printing Press, 1914-20.

The Rāmāyaṇa of Vālmīki. With the commentary (*Tilaka*) of Rāma. Edited by

Wāsudeva Laxmaṇ Śāstrī Paṇaśīkar. 4th rev. ed. Bombay: Nirṇayasāgar Press, 1930.

Ṛgveda-Samhitā. With the commentary of Sāyaṇāchārya. 5 vols. Poona: Vaidic Samshodhan Mandal, 1933.

Śrīmad Vālmīki-Rāmāyaṇa. 3 vols. Gorakhpur: Gita Press, 1969.

Śrimadvālmīkirāmāyaṇam. Edited by T.R. Krishnacharya and T.R. Vyasacharya. 7 vols. Also called the Kumbakonam Edition. Bombay: Nirṇayasāgar Press, 1911-13. Reprint 1930.

Śrīmadvālmīkirāmāyaṇam. Edited by Gaṅgāviṣṇu Śrīkṛṣṇadāsa. With the commentaries of Govindarāja, Rāmānuja, and Maheśvaratīrtha and the commentary known as *Taniślokī*. 3 vols. Bombay: Lakṣmīveṅkaṭeśvara Mudraṇālaya, 1935.

Śvetāśvatara Upaniṣad. Edited by V.P. Limaye and R.D. Vāḍekar *Eighteen Prinicipal Upaniṣads*, vol. 1, Puṇyapattanam: Vaidikasaṃśodhanamaṇḍalam, 1958.

The Vālmīki Rāmāyaṇa: Critical Edition. General editors G.H. Bhatt and U.P. Shah. 7 vols. Baroda: Oriental Institute, 1960-75.

Secondary Sources

Apte, V.S. 1957-59. *The Practical Sanskrit-English Dictionary*. 3 vols. Poona: Prasad Prakashan.

Bergaigne, A. 1883. *La religion védique*, II. Paris: F. Vieweg.

Böhtlingk, Otto, and Rudolph Roth. 1855-75. *Sanskrit-Wörterbuch*. 7 vols. St. Petersburg: Kaiserlichen Akademie der Wissenschaften. Reprint in 7 vols., Osnabrück/Wiesbaden, 1966.

Goldman, Robert P., Sally J. Sutherland Goldman, and Barend van Nooten. 2009. The *Rāmāyaṇa of Vālmīki: An Epic of Ancient India. Volume VI: Yuddhakāṇḍa*. Translation and Annotation by Robert P. Goldman, Sally J. Sutherland Goldman, and Barend van Nooten. Introduction by Sally J. Sutherland Goldman and Robert P. Goldman. Princeton: Princeton University Press.

Goldman, Robert P., and Sally J. Sutherland Goldman. 1996. *The Rāmāyaṇa of Vālmīki: An Epic of Ancient India. Volume V: Sundarakāṇḍa:* Introduction, Translation, and Annotation by Sally J. Sutherland Goldman and R.P. Goldman. Princeton: Princeton University Press.

Goldman, Sally J. Sutherland. In Press. "Nikumbhilā's Grove: *Rākṣasa* Rites in Vālmīki's *Rāmāyaṇa*." In J. Brockington, ed. *Proceedings of the XIIIth World Sanskrit Conference*, Edinburgh: Epic Studies. Delhi: Motilal Banarsidass, 255-75.

Gonda, J. 1952. "Māyā." *Tijdscrift voor filosofie* 14: 3-62. Lueven.

____. 1965. "The concept of Maya: An Essay in Historical Survey of the Hindu Theory of Maya." In *Change and Continuity in Indian Religion*. The Hague: Mouton.

Goudriaan, T. 1978. *Māyā: Divine and Human*. Delhi: Motilal Banarsidass, 1978.

Hopkins, E.W. 1920. *The Great Epic of India*. New Haven: Yale University Press.

Lefeber, Rosalind. 1994. *The Rāmāyaṇa of Vālmīki: An Epic of Ancient India. Volume IV: Kiṣkindhākāṇḍa*. Edited by Robert P. Goldman. Princeton: Princeton University Press.

Monier-Williams, Monier. 1899. *A Sanskrit-English Dictionary*. Oxford: Oxford University Press. Reprint 1964.

Oldenberg, H. 1919. *Vorwissenschaftliche Wissenschaft. Die Weltanschauung der Brāhmaṇa-Texte*. Göttingen: Vandenhoeck & Ruprecht.

Pollock, Sheldon I. 1991. *The Rāmāyaṇa of Vālmīki: An Epic of Ancient India. Volume III: Araṇyakāṇḍa*. Edited by Robert P. Goldman. Introduction and annotation by Sheldon Pollock. Princeton: Princeton University Press.

Regnaud, Paul. 1885. "La *maya*." In *Revue de l'histoire des religions* 12, Paris.

Reyna, Ruth. 1962. *The Concept of Māyā: From the Vedas to the 20th Century*. Bombay: Asia Publishing House.

Shastri, Prabhu Dutt. 1911. *The Doctine of Māyā in the Philosophy of the Vedānta*. London: Luzac and Co.

Sutherland, S.J. (Goldman). 1992. "Seduction and Counter-Seduction: Bedroom Politics in the Ancient Epics." *Journal of Indian Philosophy* 20: 243-51.

Zimmer, H. 1936. *Maya: Der Indische Mythos*. Stuttgart: Deutsche Verlags-Anstalt.

The *Dāna-stuti* Hymns of the *Ṛgveda*

ROMILA THAPAR

My attempt in this short essay is to examine the *dāna-stuti* hymns of the *Ṛgveda* to ascertain whether they can provide clues to the historical context of Ṛgvedic society. Being essentially a collection of ritual hymns it is to ritual that attention has been drawn in studies of the *Ṛgveda*. That they also reflect a society different from what preceded it and what came after has received less attention. Whether Ṛgvedic society carried some elements that had prevailed previously or the extent to which subsequent compositions reflect a degree of continuity requires more investigation than can be covered here. But some pointers towards this may be possible. The argument is not that these were historically attested societies but that in recording them or looking back at them from later in time, there was some presence of at least a modicum of historical consciousness.

Prior to the *Ṛgveda* was the urban culture of the north-west and subsequent to it that of the Ganges plain. Ṛgvedic society presents a contrast. This in part determines the gist of my argument that perceptions of the past and how these are recorded are related to the form of the society recording them. The *dāna-stuti* hymns, although few in number, had their own importance and because of this were preserved by being embedded as it were in a compilation of essentially ritual hymns. Their importance lay in the implicit claim that they were indirectly recording *itihāsa* (literally, 'thus indeed it was') in listing *rājās* and their gifts.

Fragmentary forms of narratives occur in various sections of the Vedic corpus. The *dāna-stutis*, literally in praise of gift-giving, are eulogies to the generosity of earlier or current patrons and were the prototype of what later became praise poems and stories involving heroes, actual or fictive, in the later corpus. They are included in the *Ṛgveda* but mention is also made of them as a specific category in subsequent texts that comment on some of the narratives of the *Ṛgveda* such as the *Bṛhad-devatā*, *Nirukta* and *Anukramaṇī*. Mention is also made of *gāthās*, *nārāśaṃsīs* and *raibhīs* of the same genre as the *dāna-stutis* but found more frequently in the later Vedic corpus. It is interesting that despite being recognised as a distinctive category they were not collated into one *maṇḍala* as were the Soma hymns. The *dāna-stuti* hymns, like all sources of patronage, come to be treated almost as property and claimed by particular families, the assumption being that even the recitation of ancestral generosity could bring a gift—at least a milch cow.[1]

The Society of the *Ṛgveda*

The *Ṛgveda* assumes a clan-based society that is therefore different from the urban cultures that came before and after. The unit of society was the *viś*, the clan, located in small localised settlements. A group of these formed the *jana*, sometimes translated as 'tribe' although there is a growing preference now for rendering it as 'a segmentary society'.[2] Recruitment to the clan was by birth, which provided the individual with an identity. Being largely agro-pastoralists the mainstay of the Ṛgvedic clan wealth was cattle supplemented by sheep and goat herding with additional resources from horse live-stock. (Horses of quality, however, have never been successfully bred in India and have generally been imported from Central Asia or later from Arabia.) The horse as a commodity was essential to herding and raiding and to relatively fast transportation which made it more valuable than the other animals. Increase in wealth required a proficiency in herding involving proximity to pasture lands and water resources. Controlling access to these led to constant competition. Where these were not easy to come by, cattle-raiding became the simpler way out and is frequently mentioned. The person who protected the resources or led the raid was crucial to the clan and this was in most cases the role of the chief, the *rājā/rājan*.

A more peaceful arrangement for access to resources is the symbiotic relationship between pastoralists and cultivators. In this the pastoralists follow a defined circuit which coincides with their moving their herds to recently harvested fields. The animals feed on the stubble and their droppings manure the fields. This is not a relationship that is described in the hymns but may well have been practised. If the cultivators spoke a language different from that of the pastoralists then some degree of bilingualism may have emerged and this may have been one factor accounting for non-Indo-Aryan elements in the language of the hymns. A number of non-Indo-Aryan words are linked to agricultural processes.[3]

For clan societies kinship connections were primary. The recording of generations changed from just mentioning individuals as fathers or sons to listing an ancestor or two and a couple of descendents. Generations therefore become time-markers. Depending on the context such references can be helpful in suggesting earlier or later dates for hymns.

Clan societies generally record the activities of the families of chiefs.[4] In this case it would be the activities of the *rājās / rājans*. They had status which came initially from birth into a clan of some standing. This was enhanced through a heroic act beyond the ordinary which led to the hero being eulogised and if the heroic act was successful the hero brought in additional wealth. Gradually and in addition the performance of *yajñas* which became more complex. Extending over longer periods and promising increasing powers, they also became a reason for praise. A bond was established between the chief and the ritual specialist, the fulcrum of which was the act of giving by both to each other. The gifts so exchanged were not identical. The poet composed verses in praise of the *rājā* and received a reward in the form of a gift from the *rājā*. In the case of the *yajña* the priest bestowed an intangible but recognisable status on the *rājā* through rituals, some of which claimed divine sanction, and the *rājā* in turn provided the priest with tangible wealth in the form of a gift or *dāna*. When the performance of *yajñas* became essential to status, there was a *dakṣinā* or fee.

The *rājā / rājan* was the head of the clan and this was generally the title of a single person, although clans with multiple *rājās* are mentioned in later sources that refer to them more as governing families.[5] The term is generally translated as 'king' but in the context of the *Ṛgveda* 'chief' seems more appropriate. Chiefships could last for a considerable time before mutating into kingships or else fading out. The *gaṇa-saṅghas* and the *gaṇa-rājyas* are mentioned in texts and inscriptions until at least the mid-first millennium CE and their subjugation by kings is regarded as a major political achievement. Sacrificial ceremonies such as the *abhiṣeka*, *rājasūya*, *aśvamedha* could as well be the initiation and articulation of chiefly power and need not be seen as exclusively indicative of kingdoms. The constituents of the state mentioned in texts when states and kingdoms had come to be established are not evident in these earlier compositions.[6] Elements of impending kingship probably date to a period closer to the mid-first millennium BCE.

From having once been close to the *viś* the *rājā* was gradually distanced from it by his special status. This was doubtless enhanced by his acquisition of greater wealth after a successful raid since it was from his share of the division of spoils that he made gifts to those who pleased him. The prestige of the chief drew from his success in these raids and this was encapsulated as it were in poems of praise composed by the priests and the panegyrists, as well as by the poets, the *kavi*, *rebha* and *kāru*.[7] If the poem and the eulogy pleased the chief the poet was rewarded, thus creating a nexus between the two, a nexus that became central to what have been called the *dāna-stuti* hymns.

These hymns either in their entirety or in specific verses celebrate a heroic act and record the gift of wealth. Implicit in some is the invisible presence of a deity whose sanction ensured victory in the heroic act. The poet claimed that the deity had come at his urging. The event recorded and the purpose of these compositions—the successful raid and the successful acquisition of wealth subsequently—was rather mundane and hardly occasions inclusion in a compilation of ritual hymns. However, there is an association with deity, which may in some instances be the justification. It has been suggested that they may have been added later.[8] However, the sentiments they evoke are intrinsic to clan societies and appropriate to many of their concerns. Equally, if not more significantly, is their role as records of what was assumed to have happened—what is said to be *itihāsa*. Since the record was to be preserved, it was likely to be better preserved if embedded in a ritual text.

The significance of the past in clan societies would be recognisable, but the ordering of the past as history was not a requirement. Nevertheless elements of what eventually went into the making of a historical tradition were woven into what was projected as the past in the sources of these early societies. In post Ṛgvedic compositions references to the *itihāsa-purāṇa* described it as the fifth *Veda*, a category which included esoteric knowledge such as that on *sarpavidyā* and *asuravidyā*, and at another level the *Mahābhārata* and the *Nāṭyaśāstra*. The notion of the fifth *Veda* would suggest a possible association with divine sanction but more than that the requirement that it be carefully maintained. Another text speaks of the *itihāsa-veda* and the *purāṇa-veda*.[9] The *Nirukta* of Yāska explains the term *aitihāsika* as one who uses *itihāsa* to explain the *mantras* through narratives from the past such as that of Devāpi and Śantanu. [10]

The *dāna-stutis* can be verses which form a part of a hymn in which a *rājā* is praised for his munificence in bestowing gifts on the composer who had praised the action of a *rājā*.[11] They can also be complete hymns with the intention being the same, although these are fewer in number. Specific verses tend to come at the end of the hymn[12] but their intention is knit into the purpose of the hymns as they are likely to have been close in time to the subject, particularly where the subject is a living *rājā*.[13] If the patron was alive as many were, then the *dāna-stuti* was not likely to have been a later addition. Many are placed in the late *maṇḍalas*, the First and the Tenth, although the concentration is in the Eighth Book of the Kaṇvas. Some of those in the late *maṇḍalas* refer to patrons of earlier times.

The idea could have originated in the praise of a deity, generally Indra or Agni, for an assumed heroic exploit. *Dāna-stutis* in the form of verses at the end of a hymn are probably earlier than those hymns that are specifically *dāna-stutis*. The extensive praise of deities bestowing wealth may also have preceded the eulogies of *rājās*. Hero lauds are referred to as *stuti*, *stoma* or *stotra*.[14]

The composer of the *dāna-stuti*, a *kavi* or a *rebha*, a poet-bard or part priest attached to the clan of the *rājan*, claimed that *rājans* so praised are immortal (*śrotā rājano amṛtasya*).[15] If immortality is understood as undying fame, then this is a valid claim since we today know of these *rājās* largely through this category of hymns. Praising the donor and listing the gifts received by the composer was said to ensure the glory of the *rājā* even in heaven.[16] Some continue to be quoted in later times as eulogistic comments on contemporary *rājās*. In a late hymn a bard states that he was the eulogist to Mitrātithi the grandfather of the current *rājā* Upamaśravas.[17] This suggests that some bards were attached to the family or the clan of the *rājā*, a tradition that has a long continuity up to the recent present. Authorship could be that of a single poet or a group of poets.[18]

It would be worth looking more closely at who the authors of these fragments were. Some came from established *brāhmaṇa* families. Others were associated with groups originally regarded as alien if not marginal. These were introduced into the texts as an extraneous but significant element. Poets were regarded as more than just professionals singing the praises of the *rājā*. They are respected *kārus* and *kavis*.[19] *Stutis* can be fantasy but the reference to person and event is less open to doubt.

In the format of the *dāna-stutis* there could be an invocation of the deity with an appeal that the composer should rapidly acquire a generous patron. Of the deities invoked, the two most popular were Indra and Agni, although the Maruts, Vāyu, Uṣas, the Aśvins and Mitra-Varuṇa were also described as assisting the donor to victory, or as witnessing the gift given, or even as exemplars in gift-giving.[20] The association with deities led to the claim that the human hero was successful in his enterprise because of the interlocution of the composer with the gods. The argument becomes somewhat circular. The poet invokes Indra and offers him oblations of *soma* among other things. Indra aids the *rājā* and ensures his victory over his foes. This brings a generous gift from the *rājā* to the poet, both for invoking Indra and as a reward for eulogising the *rājā*. Embedding it in a ritual text assumed that it would be repeated as long as the ritual was performed or the hymns recited.

The more generous of the *rājās* were projected almost as gods in their generosity. Deities can be unimaginably generous judging by what they are supposed to have given in the hymns, and this was meant to encourage extravagance among the *rājās*. There is an eliding from praise of the deity to praise of the donor. The status of the donor had to be high, even if he was a *dāsa*, and his name had to be mentioned. This gives the narrative a hint of authenticity. The notion of the bard as the moral conscience of the hero was as yet absent.

The Patrons

A recitation of the exploits, past or current, of the human hero follows together with a listing of the gifts which the composer had received. The hero's success was necessary in an inter-clan conflict or a cattle-raid and his victory was celebrated by the distribution of the booty which included gifts for those who immortalised the hero. Divodāsa gives the poet the booty taken from Śambara, elsewhere described as a *dāsa*.[21] On another occasion the *dāsas* Balbuth and Tarukṣa are mentioned as givers of wealth.[22] A particularly generous patron Kuruśravana is gratefully remembered by the bard after his death and the patron's son and grandson are reminded of his generosity.[23] The Bharadvāja priests were said to have been handsomely rewarded.[24]

The past is recalled in the exploits of patrons of earlier times and their propensity for making gifts is exaggerated in an attempt to nudge, as it were, the contemporary patron into spectacular generosity. Evidently the element of competition was not lacking and the assumption was that if the gifts from past occasions were magnified those from the present would be larger. A later text commenting on poems of a similar kind, the *nārāśaṃsī* and *gāthās*, asserts that the statements they make are untrue.[25] Presumably the reference is to the exaggeration of the wealth received from the composer. In describing the munificence of the patron, the poet was indirectly underlining his own contribution to the patron's enterprise through the efficacy of his verses.

Of the many patrons some are singled out for special mention. Abhyāvartin Cāyamāna attacked the Vṛśivants at Hariyūpīyā.[26] Successive generations of a family—Sṛñjaya, Sahadeva and Somaka—are referred to.[27] Sudās, the son of Pijavana,[28] was of the Bharata clan. Sudās defeated the *rājās* Varcin and Śambara. The Sṛñjayas were his allies and helped in his overcoming the alliance of ten *rājās*, *dāśarājña*, which is repeatedly alluded to.[29] The ten clans opposing Sudās are described as those who do not perform *yajñas*, which gives them an ambiguous cultural identity. The ten consist of those mentioned often, the Yadu, Turvaśa, Anu, Druhyu and Pūru as well as those mentioned infrequently, the Pakthas, Bhalānas, Alinas, Śivas and Viṣāṇins. Of the first five, the Anu and the Druhyu seem less important. The Bhṛgus are the priests of the Druhyu but are linked also to the *yatis* whom Indra tried to feed to jackals.[30] The Yadu and the Turvaśa are often coupled, especially when being rescued from a flood by Indra.[31] The Yadu were generous patrons and fought against both Sudās and Śambara. Of the Pūrus, Trasadasyu, whose father was Purukutsa and son was Kuruśravana, were settled in the Suvastu region of the north-west. The poet looks back and reminds the present chief of the generosity of his father and grandfather.[32] Another *rājā*, Bhāvya, dwelt on the banks of the Sindhu.[33] Pṛthuśravas the son of Kanīta gave handsomely.[34] Kaśu the son of the Cedi *rājā* is said to be particularly generous.[35]

The *dāsas* Balbutha and Tarukṣa are also noted donors.[36] Among the *dāsa* chiefs Śambara was feared, since he was targeted among those attacked with the aid of Indra. He controlled a large number of *pur*, enclosed settlements.[37] His main foe was Divodāsa Atithigva. Śambara referred to himself as *devaka*, a more honourable title than is given to most and he is remembered for his immense treasures.[38] The battle lines were not drawn on the basis of ethnic identities, if these existed, and the panegyrists were happy to receive gifts from whomever was willing to make them.

Repeating the same names associated with particular events may have been meant to suggest historicity. What adds to this is that where the patrons are niggardly they are described in a satirical manner, such as Śara Śauradevya, who gave only one calf to three poets.[39] Possibly such a gift was the more realistic order of wealth that came the way of the poets once the extravagant descriptions are pared away.

In the information provided on the *rājās*, genealogical depth is shallow and rarely exceeds four or five generations and these are not listed as a succession. Descent is usually not given in one hymn but has to be collated from scattered references. Repeated references to the same fathers and sons but in different contexts as in the case of Sṛñjaya or Sudās, could suggest that some of these at least may have been known persons and not mythical figures. A trace of authenticity could come from some aspects of genealogical links. In an earlier hymn Trasadasyu is described as the son of Purukutsa and in a later hymn mention is made of Upamaśravas as a descendent.

The Bharatas and the Pūrus seem to span at least five generations and this has some significance for references to *rājās* in later texts such as the *Brāhmaṇas* and the *Mahābhārata*, and for the confederacy that was to gain prominence, that of the Kuru-Pañcāla.

A genealogical reconstruction associated with the Bharatas, from the Ṛgvedic hymns could be as follows:

Devavant
Vadhryaśva
Divodāsa
Pijavana
Sudās

The Bharatas are important in the *Ṛgveda* as also in later texts.
Divodāsa is mentioned a few times but the more authoritative *rājā* was Sudās.[40]

The Pūru descent referred to in the *Ṛgveda* could be:[41]

Purukutsa
Trasadasyu
Mitrātithi
Kuruśravana
Upamaśravas

There is a suggested identity between the Pūrus and Purukutsa.[42] The latter is a contemporary of Sudās but the Pūrus were part of the alliance against him. The epithet *mṛdhravāc* is used for Pūru, whose ancestor is said to be an *asura rākṣasa*.[43] The clans who allied against Sudās are described as *ayajyavaḥ*, those that do not perform the sacrificial rites.[44] Elsewhere it is the *dāsas* that are described as "... *amanturanyavrato amānuṣaḥ* ...".[45] The description therefore of people not performing rites would most likely refer to *dāsas*. But these clans were not called *dāsas*, although their identity is ambiguous. The composer of the later hymn is said to be Kavaṣa and possibly this was the Kavaṣa Ailūṣa mentioned in the *Aitareya Brāhmaṇa* as the son of a *dāsi*. Was the Purukutsa lineage connected with the *dāsas*?

The *Ṛgveda* tends to speak of single clans which are at times in conflict with or in alliance with others. The need for self-protection and for exploiting resources is likely to have encouraged the idea of confederation among clans. The alliance of the ten clans would have been one of these. Such confederations are mentioned in the later corpus, the pre-eminent among them being that of the Kuru-Pañcālas. Confederations were not permanent and alliances changed, in part because the enemy was not constant and in part because migrations were essential to the search for pastures and water.

The *rājās* referred to were contemporary or removed by a couple of generations. The exploits therefore, were of present times except where they were deliberately fanciful. Some names such as Pūru, Yadu and Cedi occur in later texts as ancestors of lineages but these do not necessarily tally with the statements in the *Ṛgveda*. The Cedis marked out for special praise are said to have included a hundred buffaloes as their gift,[46] an animal not mentioned often although known to the north-west. The exploits of Indra—the attacker of *purs*, the winner of cattle and the lord of wealth—are imitated by the *rājās*.[47]

Of the conflicts two in particular stand out. One is the much discussed *dāśarājña* when Sudās leading the Bharatas and Tṛtsus defeated a confederacy of ten clans.[48] Although it is translated as a 'battle' it was hardly a formal battle and was more a defence of the water sources on the Paruṣṇī River with a skirmish on its banks. The description of this event comes from hymns in the Seventh *maṇḍala* attributed to the Vasiṣṭhas. The latter were closely associated with the Tṛtsus and this may have contributed to the narration of the rout of the enemies. Another conflict involved Abhayāvartin Cāyamāna defeating the Vṛśivant led by their *rājā* Varśikha who was an ally of Sṛñjaya, at Hariyūpīyā.[49] These were victories over other clans and chiefs who were not invariably fantasised into demons, even though the conflict was sometimes between those described as *āryas* and at other times between *āryas* and *dāsas*. Major conflicts are often located on rivers and understandably so given the need to control water sources. In some cases it is possible to trace the migration of clans.[50]

The Authors

Some distinction in authorship is likely between poets and ritual specialists, although there is often an overlap. Kakṣivant is described as both a presser of *soma* and a eulogist.[51] In one hymn there is a personification of *raibhī, nārāśaṃsī* and *gāthā*.[52] Also associated with these were the *chandas*, songs of praise recited by *kavis*.[53] Some eulogies were incorporated into ritual occasions, more commonly so in the later corpus. Where the *gotra* of the composer is mentioned there is no ambiguity about his status. Whereas in the *Ṛgveda* there is some overlap between the functions of the priest and the poet, this was gradually bifurcated and the *brāhmaṇa* was distinct from the *sūta*.

Many poets are named but some are more respected than others. Babhru received gifts from Ṛṇaṃcaya.[54] The patron of Śyāvāśva was Purumīlha, who is associated with the story that he himself wished for gifts but was debarred since he was neither a priest nor a poet, and therefore took the gifts rather than received them.[55] Nābhānediṣṭha[56] is referred to as the son of Manu. Kakṣivant, in some accounts the son of Dīrghatamas, whose story is narrated in the *Bṛhad-devatā*,[57] is also described as a *vipra, kavi* and *stotṛ*, and who claims Nāhuṣa and the Sindhu *rājā* Svanaya Bhāvya among his patrons.[58] Kakṣivant is referred to more often in a late section of the *Ṛgveda* and with reverence.[59] One hymn narrates the restoration of his youth—a common enough legend in many early literatures.[60] Kakṣivant is referred to as Kakṣivant Auśija, a descendent of Uśij, a *dāsi* who is said to have been sent to Dīrghatamas and the child Kakṣivant was born.[61] This would make him yet another *brāhmaṇa* born of a *dāsi*.

The largest number of *dāna-stutis* is in the Eighth *maṇḍala* associated with the Kaṇvas. The Kaṇvas in turn were linked to the Aṅgiras who together with the Bhṛgus are regarded as keepers of the narratives relating to past events. The late *maṇḍalas* of the *Ṛgveda*—the First and Tenth—also have *dāna-stutis*, suggesting in some cases a looking back to the past. Such a looking back is more evident in the later corpus where *rājās* are mentioned as having performed sacrificial rituals in earlier times and are held up as exemplars. Among the names a few are common to the *Ṛgveda* as, for instance, Sudās Paijavana.[62]

The Gift

The heroic exploit that compelled the composition of a eulogy is described in glowing terms. This is followed by an enumeration of the objects of wealth bestowed by the *rājā* on the poet as reward for the eulogy. Wealth is listed as cattle, horses, camels, chariots, wagons, garments, treasure chests, pieces of gold and jars with gold, and *dāsis*; with dogs, sheep, calves, colts and asses carrying less value. Mention is also made of copper utensils, bamboo objects and the skin from the *soma* pressing.[63] By far the most valuable of these were horses and cattle, sometimes listed in clearly exaggerated figures. Horses range from a single steed to many thousands. Some poets claim to have received a thousand cows and others sixty-thousand head of cattle.[64] Such figures are formulaic, as are 100, 1000, 10,000, since the same figure is at times repeated for an entire list, as with Divodāsa's raid on the *dāsa* Śambara's treasure which he then bestowed on the bard.[65] This included ten horses, ten treasure chests, ten garments, ten lumps of gold and ten chariots.

The reference to *vadhu,* fifty in number, among the gifts of Kuruśravana,[66] was read as 'women' by Sāyaṇa but others have read it as the female of any species. *Dāsas* are rarely listed as wealth in these hymns but *dāsis* are. Did the *dāsi* at this point refer to a captured woman from the *dāsa* community, as seems likely in this context, or was the term already being used for a woman slave? Since many *dāsas* were rich and feared as was Śambara, it is perhaps more appropriate to render its meaning as 'the Other'. Servitude was probably that of household work.

The wealth as listed was largely associated with pastoralism and with chiefdoms. It consisted of animals acquired through breeding or raiding, chariots that were made locally, garments and gold objects that did not require elaborate craftsmanship and *dāsis*. These items would be directly put to use. None of the archaeological sites of northern India excavated so far ranging over the period from 1700 to 600 BC have revealed any great treasures. Burials from this period are, unfortunately for historians, largely absent, but would not in all likelihood have led to dramatic discoveries of wealth. Objects produced for trade and exchange are seldom part of local wealth and such objects are not mentioned in other contexts in the hymns. The wealth gifted is utility wealth. A comparison can be made with the wealth staked by Yudhiṣṭhira at the game of dice in the *Mahābhārata* where the parallels are striking.[67]

Among the characteristics of the notion of an exchange of wealth was the idea of reciprocity. Exchange creates a bond between donor and recipient and this in turn creates a variety of greater or lesser obligations.

The reciprocal gifts can be of equal value or, as in this case, of unequal material value but of equal significance, although different in form and kind. There is however, a nucleus of the concept of redistribution in the processing of this wealth. The booty collected from skirmishes and raids seems to have been taken to a central place, possibly the assembly of the *vidatha* where it is distributed. Hymns addressed to Bhāga, the personification of sharing, clarify that a gift is also part of the process of distribution and the personified Bhāga is the distributor.[68] The poet, however, was given his gift directly by the *rājā*. The figures mentioned by the poets are extremely doubtful in many instances. It would have been unlikely for an agro-pastoral community to produce such wealth even if only animal wealth. Later too when the performance of a *yajña* demanded the expending of wealth the actual wealth used would have been less than what is described. The elaborate forms of *yajñas* as described in the later corpus call for presentations and offerings—the *bali*, *bhāga* and *śulka*—and these come from the *viś* and are directed to the *yajamāna*. The *rājā's* control over the *viś* had increased by this time, facilitating the extraction of wealth.[69] Nevertheless the *yajña* could curb the acquisition of wealth by a *rājā*, thereby enabling a balance between the authority of the *rājā* and the *brāhmaṇa*.

The *dāna-stutis* reflect the wishful thinking of a society eager for wealth. The exaggeration was doubtless part of the formula for ensuring that some wealth was likely and an element of sympathetic magic might encourage more. The frequency of cattle wealth depended on the success of cattle raids rather than just herding and became a way of augmenting wealth. The wish for more and more cows is the dream of cattle-herders. The niggardly deserve contempt. The gifting of land which was to be introduced a few centuries later is conspicuously absent, as it also is in the listing of wealth in the *Mahābhārata*.[70] The clan had the right to use the land it claimed to control but none had the right of individual ownership. Even in the later corpus where mention is made indirectly to land being given by the patron to the ritual specialist to establish a settlement, it is not an outright gift, and furthermore requires the approval of the *viś*.[71] Grant of land even as *dakṣiṇā* is debated and at one point strongly contested.[72] Generally the best in *dāna* and *dakṣiṇā* consisted of gold, cattle, garments and horses which are of course in conformity with the activities of a productive nature in this society.[73]

Wealth actually or even supposedly given on such occasions becomes a form of social gradation as well as a part of the gift exchange implicit in the relationship between patron and poet.[74] There is an awareness of those with wealth and the rest of the clan. The patrons are generally the *rājās* and rarely others. The access to wealth and its acquisition was an evident concern. It has been argued that the word *arya* refers to one who is wealthy.[75] This is also suggested in Pāṇini who glosses *arya* as *aryaḥ svāmivaiśyayoḥ*.[76] Can the argument be taken further that the association with a magnanimous gift, even if fictive, could be used as a way of raising the status of those whose origins were obscure and were being inducted into the society of the *āryas*?

These hymns are said to have a different linguistic style characterized by ellipses and by an ironical tone.[77] Since their concerns were more down-to-earth, they were different from the ritual hymns. The link here is between the panegyric, the person to be exalted and the quantity of the gift. It is the same *rājās* who are also the patrons of the sacrificial ritual although at this earlier stage the performance of ritual is less central than the heroic act. This of course changed over time.

The context of gift-giving gradually came to include more than the heroic act. From being a gift given largely for composing a eulogy on a heroic act and the ensuing generosity of a *rājā*, it incorporated the *dakṣiṇā*, a fee, for performing a ritual of legitimation for the *rājā* by a ritual specialist. The gift was a fee for the priest interceding with the deity on behalf of the *rājā*. A hymn addressed to *Dakṣiṇā*, the fee personified, from a late *maṇḍala*, indicates this change.[78] To drive home the point it is said that *dakṣiṇā* does not come from misers, it comes from those who wish to avoid the dishonour of being called so.[79] It becomes a matter of prestige and deliberate exchange.

Nevertheless, gift-giving was to remain a nexus between political authority and priestly function and if anything was intensified when the *yajña* became the pivot in this relationship. The potential competition in claiming authority between the priest and the chief was controlled through various ways and this was one mechanism. In a vertical division of society into lineages and an absence of central authority, gift obligations keep a check on those desirous of acquiring the maximum resources. Since gift-giving symbolises mutual dependence and reciprocal relations, the gift can up to a point take on the dimensions of a ritual item and its quantity need not be taken literally.[80] What is important, however, are the social and economic consequences of the act.

It is axiomatic that the wealthy one must give of his generosity when requested: *dado maghāni maghavaniyānaḥ*.[81] Essential to the notion of gift-exchange is that those with wealth have to give away some of it. If the figures given by the poets were in any way accurate then they too in turn would be required to gift wealth to others, but we hear none of this which indicates that the actual wealth so gifted was probably a small amount. The nuances change somewhat when the gift-giving is linked to the *yajña*. The axis of the sacrificial act could be the gift.[82] This is summarised in the statement: *dehi me dadāmi te ni me dehi ni te dadhe.*[83]

The dual relationship of the poet and the patron common to most clan-based societies is here mutated somewhat to include the invisible presence of the deity. It tends to become a triangular relationship even if the deity gradually recedes from the forefront. A *rājā* required a poet to immortalise him and the poet in turn required wealth. This would be enhanced if the poet could claim that his invoking of the deity ensured the patron's victory. Even if on occasion a deity is claimed as the patron, the itemising of wealth parallels the patronage of the *rājā*. The immortality that came to the hero via the hymn would have provided an additional incentive to the hero to fight. It also established the legitimacy of the *rājā* to the office of chief.

The Continuity

The *dāna-stuti* hymns together with other fragmentary material are a preface to more complex epic forms. Some of the clans reappear as ancestral to the later heroes of the *Mahābhārata* even if the chronology is confused. The Yadus, Druhyus, Turvaśas, Anus and Pūrus are now kin-related, which they were not in the *Ṛgveda*. Kinship would seem to have been a later assumption based perhaps on the closeness of the five as part of the alliance of ten clans against the Bharatas. The Yadus and the Pūrus were to become the dominant clans. Many others, such as Ikṣvāku, Yayāti the son of Nāhuṣa and the descendents of Divodāsa are woven into the descent groups as structured in the *Mahābhārata* and the *Vaṃśānucarita* section of the *Purāṇas*.

Some clans seem to have migrated and the locations are often given with reference to rivers. The Pūrus, originally located in the Suvastu/Swat valley in the north-west became part of the large Kuru tribe linked to the Pañcāla in the western Ganges plain and Haryana. The Bharatas on the Paruṣṇī River move to the Vipāś and Śutudrī and finally to the western Ganges plain again as part of the Kuru tribe. In the *Mahābhārata,* Dhṛtrāṣtra is occasionally given the epithet of Bharata. Some clans opposed to each other in the *dāśarājña* were unified a few centuries later. Despite Pūru's *mṛdhravāc*, the language of the Kuru-Pañcāla is now said to be excellent and they observe the required Vedic rituals although earlier they were said to be *ayajyavaḥ*.[84] Had the language and rituals changed to accommodate the non-purists? The Kurus are often mentioned as the most eminent among the clans, the pace-setters of the culture that was now emerging.

A comparison of gift-giving in the *Ṛgveda* and in the *Brāhmaṇas* suggests that although the cultural emphases of language and rituals had undergone change, nevertheless the *rājās* of earlier times were evoked. The preservation of separate identities among clans from past times gave way to a considerable mingling of peoples in the creation of new identities. The trend was towards confederation involving larger territorial units. Cattle raids continued but were not so central and gift-giving focused on the *yajña*. This was one among other factors that encouraged the creation of kings and kingdoms by the mid-first millennium BCE. The emerging culture was an amalgam of *ārya* and *dāsa* and their diverse languages and ritual practices.

A continuation of the idea of the *dāna-stuti* and perhaps recognition of the usefulness of the form in creating a perspective on the past is referred to in the *Śatapatha Brāhamaṇa*.[85] The reference is to the two *vīnāgāthins*, a *rājanya* and a *brāhmaṇa*, who sing the praises of the patron, the sacrifices he offered, his victories and the gifts he distributed. The bifurcation of the task of eulogising the patron gave a new dimension to the relationship and in some ways made it more important with both a *brāhmaṇa* and a *rājanya* now reciting the *rājā's stuti*.

The Genre

The genre as such was continued in the composition of the *nārāśaṃsīs* and the *gāthās* which became more frequent in the later corpus as also did the *ākhyana* narratives of the *yajñas* involving the authority of the *rājan*. The performance of the rituals associated with political and charismatic power continued for more than a millennium.

The epics and more so the *Mahābhārata* incorporated some of what might be called bardic fragments from the Vedic corpus and associated texts and wove them into narratives constituting epic events and personalities. Genealogies were given some semblance of form even if it meant changing relationships. This material available in the Ādiparvan of the *Mahābhārata* and the Bālakāṇḍa of the *Rāmāyaṇa*, was then reworked into a more systematic version of the past in the *Vaṃśānucarita* section of the *Viṣṇu Purāṇa*, and some other *Purāṇas*, compiling the lineages and setting them out in two broad categories of the Sūryavaṃśa and the Candravaṃśa. This made the supposed network of lineages and clans available to those who wished to establish genealogical links with ancient heroes.

From the Gupta period onwards, royal families claimed connections with the descent groups of the early period—the *kṣatriya vaṃśa* as it is sometimes called. This was most easily done by latching onto some point in the genealogies of the early clans. Many inscriptions of this time, and more so those recording grants, carried a *praśasti* section in which such claims were sought to be established and statements made about the dynasty and its achievements. The patron who made the grant was praised, the grant/gift was described, and the scribe gave his credentials, often an officer of the administration or a poet at the court. The *dāna-stuti* hymns were in many ways seminal to the *praśasti.* The degree to which there was continuity in its essential form there was recognition of historical consciousness.

Notes

1. *Ṛgveda* 2.2.9; 10.64.12. F. Max Müller (ed.), *Rig-Veda-Samhita*, London, 1890 (Reprint Varanasi); K.F. Geldner, *Der Rig-Veda*, Cambridge (MA), 1951, HOS XXXIII; R.T.H. Griffith, *The Hymns of the Ṛgveda*, Varanasi, 1963 (4th ed).

2. This is in part because the term 'tribe' has now come to include so many types of societies as to be almost impossible to define.

3. T. Burrow, *The Sanskrit Language*, London 1965, 373 ff; F.B.J. Kuiper, *Aryans in the Ṛgveda*, Amsterdam, 1991.

4. T. Earle (ed.), *Chiefdoms: Power, Economy and Ideology*, Cambridge, 1991.

5. As for example, the many Cedi *rājās* mentioned in the *Cetiya Jātaka*, no. 422.

6. *Arthaśāstra*, 6.1.1 ff.

7. *Ṛgveda* 8.8.11; 8.31.1; p. 76; 1.127.10, 8.97.11; 1.148.2, 5.33.7.

8. H. Grassman, *Worterbuch zum Rigveda*, II, Wiesbaden, 1976 (reprint); A.B. Keith, *History of Sanskrit Literature*, Oxford, 1928, 49 ff.

9. *Gopatha Brāhmaṇa*, 1.10.

10. L. Renou, *Etudes Vediques et Paninéennes*, Paris, 1960, Tome VI, 62 ff.

11. Manilal Patel, *The Dānastutis of the Rgveda*, Bombay, 1961 (reprint); translation of M. Patel's thesis entitled, *Die Danastutis des Rigveda*, Marburg, 1929;

P.V. Kane, *History of Dharmaśāstra*, II, 2, Poona, 1974, 2nd ed., 837 ff.

12. *Ṛgveda* 8.1.31-33; 2.41-42.

13. *Bṛhad-devatā*, 3.142 ff ; 5.62 ff.

14. *Ṛgveda* 7.32.18-19; 5.18.5.

15. *Ṛgveda* 1.122.7-15.

16. *Ṛgveda* 1.126.2.

17. *Ṛgveda* 10.33.6-7.

18. *Ṛgveda* 8.1.16; 1.126.4; 7.18.

19. *Ṛgveda* 1.177.5; 178.3; 3.33.8 ; 5.33.7.

20. *Ṛgveda* 6.47.22; 6.27.8; 6.37.4; 5.52.17; 1.122.14; 8.24.28-30; 6.63.9-10; 8.5.37; 5.18.3; 5.27.1; 5.34.9; 1.122.7-9.

21. *Ṛgveda* 6.47.22. *Vedic Index*, II, 355.

22. *Ṛgveda* 8.46.32.

23. *Ṛgveda* 10.33.4. cf. 10.32.9.

24. *Ṛgveda* 6.47.22-25; 8.46.21-23; 10.33.4-5.

25. *Kāṭhaka Samhitā*, 14.5.

26. *Ṛgveda* 6.27.4-8; 4.15.4-10.

27. *Ṛgveda* 6.47; 4.15.4-10.

28. *Nirukta* 2.24.

29. *Ṛgveda* 7.18; 7.33; 7.83.

30. *Ṛgveda* 8.3.9; 6.18; *Aitareya Brāhmaṇa* 7.28.1.

31. *Ṛgveda* 1.174.9; 4.30.17; 5.31.8.

32. *Ṛgveda* 10.33.4.

33. *Ṛgveda* 1.126.1.

34. *Ṛgveda* 1.116. 21; 8.46.21.

35. *Ṛgveda* 8.5.37.

36. *Ṛgveda* 8.46.32.

37. W. Rau, "The meaning of *pur* in Vedic Literature," *AMGG*, 1983, 1.

38. *Ṛgveda* 1.51.6.

39. *Ṛgveda* 8.59.15.

40. *Ṛgveda* 3.53.9; 33.11-12; 7.18; 7.20; 7.33.

41. *Ṛgveda* 8.19; 10.33.6-7; *Bṛhad-devatā* 7.35-36.

42. *Ṛgveda* 6.20.10 and 1.63.7.

43. *Ṛgveda* 7.18. 13. Even if he was speaking Prākrit, as has been suggested, it was different from Vedic Sanskrit. *Śatapatha Brāhmaṇa* 6.8.1.14.

44. *Ṛgveda* 7.83.7.

45. *Ṛgveda* 10.22.8.

46. *Ṛgveda* 8.5.37-39.

47. *Ṛgveda* 8.5.10 ff.

48. *Ṛgveda* 7. 18.

49. *Ṛgveda* 6.27.4-8.

50. *Ṛgveda* 3.23.42.33; *Śatapatha Brāhmaṇa* 13. 5. 4.11 ff.

51. *Ṛgveda* 1.18.1; 1.112.11.

52. *Ṛgveda* 10.85.6; *Atharvaveda* 14.1.7.

53. *Ṛgveda* 10.114.5.

54. *Ṛgveda* 5.30.12; 8.22.10; *Atharvaveda* 4.29.21.

55. *Ṛgveda* 5.52-61; 8.35.19ff; 9.32; 8.2.40; *Pañcaviṃśa Brāhmaṇa* 13.7.12.

56. *Ṛgveda* 10. 62.

57. 4.11 ff

58. *Ṛgveda* 4.26.1; 10.143.1; 1.116.10; 117.13; 118.6; 112.11; 1.126.

59. *Ṛgveda* 1.116.7; 117.6; 119.9; 120.3;122.4; 126.

60. *Ṛgveda* 10.143.1.

61. *Ṛgveda* 1.18.1 ; *Pañcaviṃśa Brāhmaṇa* 14.11.16; *Bṛhad-devatā* 4.21 ff.

62. *Aitareya Brāhmaṇa* 8.21.

63. M. Patel, op. cit., pp. 64 ff.

64. *Ṛgveda* 8.4.19-20; 6.63.10.

65. *Ṛgveda* 6.47.22-25.

66. *Ṛgveda* 8.19.36.

67. R. Thapar, "Some Aspects of the Economic Data in the *Mahābhārata*," *Cultural Pasts*, Delhi, 2003, 630-46.

68. *Ṛgveda* 7.41.2; 9.97.55.

69. *Śatapatha Brāhamaṇa* 8.7.2.3; 5.1.3.3 ; 13.2.2.15.

70. *Mahābhārata*, Sabhāparvan 47-48.

71. *Śatapatha Brāhmaṇa* 7.1.1.4.

72. *Śatapatha Brāhmaṇa* 13.7.1.13-15.

73. *Śatapatha Brāhamaṇa* 4.3.4.7.

74. R. Thapar, "*Dāna* and *Dakṣinā* as Forms of Exchange," *Cultural Pasts*, Delhi, 2000, 521-35.

75. H. W. Bailey, "Iranian *Arya* and *Daha*," in *Transactions of the Philological Society*, 1959, 71ff.

76. Pāṇini 3.1.103.

77. Patel, op. cit., p. 73.

78. *Ṛgveda* 10. 107.

79. *Ṛgveda* 10.107.3.

80. M. Mauss, *The Gift*, (trans.) London, 1954; C.A. Gregory, *Gifts and Commodities*, London, 1982; Thapar, "*Dāna* and *Dakṣinā* as Forms of Exchange," op. cit., 521-35.

81. *Ṛgveda* 7.29.1.

82. J. Gonda, "Gifts and Giving in the Rigveda," *Selected Studies*, IV, Leiden, 1975.

83. *Taittiriya Samhitā* 1.8.4.1; cf. *Śatapatha Brāhmaṇa* 2.5.3.19.

84. *Śatapatha Brāhmaṇa* 3.2.3.15; i.7.2.8; 5.2.3.5.

85. *Śatapatha Brāhamaṇa* 13.1.5.1-6.

Memories of Bob

Bob is my oldest friend. We met when we were both graduate students: he at Columbia; I at Harvard. We met in Poona, as it was then called (now it is Pune), in 1968. We were studying for a Ph.D. in Sanskrit: he was writing about the epic and I about poetics. He and his first wife had rented a house near the river. I was on the other side of the river, in Koregaon Park (a few years later, in 1974, it was to achieve dubious fame as the seat of the ashram of Osho, or Rajneesh, as he was first known). It was friendship at first sight. Like high school students, we immediately became each other's best friend and have remained such for the last forty years. Why not? We were both Jewish, vegetarians, and Sanskritists. How many such could there be in the world? An even deeper bonding glue was discovered immediately: we both had reservations about any kind of spirituality. This made us very different from most of the people who studied Sanskrit.

Also, as I quickly discovered, Bob has a wicked wit. Anyone reading this already knows this fact, and I am sure each of you has a story attesting to it. I was witness to it on a daily basis, and it has made me question the origin of humor. Where does it come from? Why are some people so gifted and others deficient? Sometimes his wit was benign, but I have a theory that true wit is rarely kind. When an esteemed colleague, no longer with us, was learning Sanskrit at Berkeley when Bob was chairman, he stopped both of us in the hall (I was a visiting professor at the time): "Bob and Jeff, you won't believe the nightmare I had last night! I dreamt that I had to give a lecture, in Sanskrit, and you were both in the audience." Bob: "Funny, I had the same nightmare." Studying Sanskrit with Bob around suddenly became more fun.

There was another similarity, one you don't hear much about these days: we both developed an interest in spoken Sanskrit. It sounds obvious. We were in the very center of Sanskrit learning in India, surrounded by old Pandits who spoke only two languages: their own (often a South Indian Dravidian language) and Sanskrit. Why attempt to speak with our teachers in broken Hindi (actually Bob's Hindi was miraculously good. I say it was a wonder because, as far as I know, he never studied it; just picked it up by osmosis, I guess, from people around him), or in English, which they rarely knew beyond a few words? Surely it made sense to learn Sanskrit.

Bob and I quickly discovered that Sanskrit was far from a dead language. It was very much alive, at least in the minds and mouths of these elderly Pandits. One in particular struck Bob and me as not only immensely learned but also a man with a great heart. His name was Pandit T. Shrinivas Shastri. He must have been about fifty at the time, celibate, of course, and completely devoted to Sanskrit learning. He was the senior Pandit at the Deccan College. He knew a vast number of texts by heart, but he could also think analytically about them. He had an amazing command of spoken Sanskrit. I don't think I ever met anyone who spoke it so fluently, with such ease, and so mellifluously. He liked teaching Bob and me because he could be playful with us, something he could not do with his more conservative colleagues or students. He once confessed to us the great secret of his early life: he was the mouthpiece of the young Shankaracharya in Sringeri, in Karnataka, on the banks of the river Tunga. Whenever the young guru was asked a question he could not answer, he was taught to respond with the lovely Sanskrit phrase: *vicārya, vacmi*, "after thinking it over, I will answer". He then would disappear behind a curtain where he would find our teacher, who would tell him the answer. When we pointed out that this made the young Shankara less than infallible, Guruji merely smiled. He had an infinite curiosity. As a single man, I was dating young, visiting American students at the time. After each date, when I would see him, he would say in Sanskrit: *viśeṣataḥ vaktavyam*, basically, "give me all the details". He never pretended to know all the answers, and whenever Bob and I would ask him a difficult question about a puzzling passage in a Sanskrit text, he would answer, like his holy pupil, that he would need to think it over.

Bob and I loved studying with Shrinivas. He would chant the *Rāmāyaṇa* to us in such a beautiful manner—am I wrong in thinking this is how Bob first became interested in translating the Vālmīki *Rāmāyaṇa* (in my opinion, the single most significant translation of a major Sanskrit text into English of our time)? It was only from him that we both began to see the beauty of an ancient tradition that has been flawlessly preserved. (Bob and Sally were later to dedicate their translation of the *Sundarakāṇḍa* to Shrinivas Shastri.) While we could not entirely adopt the philosophy, we took great delight in the language and the aesthetics of the culture that lay behind it. We attended Sanskrit plays together and practiced our newly won skills in spoken Sanskrit with each other on the bus to the college. You cannot imagine the excitement this engendered in our fellow passengers when they realized we were speaking their ancient sacred language. Bob took great pleasure in reciting *ślokas* from the *Rāmāyaṇa* or more complicated meters from Kālidāsa and watching the faces of his audience. They would, invariably, ask him if we were Kashmiri Brahmins and Bob took perverse delight in nodding his head back and forth to indicate, "indeed, we are".

One story about Shrinivas Shastri that I cannot refrain from telling (to everyone, over and over) is about my dog Puppy. I will make it as brief as possible. I saw an accident on the road in front of my house in Pune: a dog was hit by a car and lay dying. Next to her was a small puppy. I took her in. She had terrible habits, worse even than Marley, but was entirely loveable. As the time came for me to leave, I decided it best to give her away a few months early to somebody who lived far away, miles past the Deccan College where I would go to study with Bob and Shrinivas. She never came with me because dogs were considered unclean, especially to orthodox Pandits, and besides, as everyone knew, this dog *was* unclean (never mind—suffice it to say her eating habits endeared her to no one). A few days after she left, I was sitting with Bob and Shrinivas very early in the morning, about 6 a.m., studying Sanskrit, when there was an unexpected knock on the door. I opened it, and who should come in, but Puppy! Shrinivas leapt up onto his chair to avoid contamination with this polluting creature. Bob and I were perplexed how she could possibly have found us. She was miles away and had never been either to the university or to Shrinivas's room. Yet find me she did. When I told this to Shrinivas, he had tears in his eyes, and he invented a beautiful *śloka* in Sanskrit on the spot, the gist of which was that our karmas were intertwined, and I was never to abandon Puppy again! Alas, a few weeks after I took her back home, she was on my lap, looking up at me, and gave a deep sigh and died. I never understood why.

I became romantically involved with one of Bob's and his wife's best friends from Columbia and paid for her ticket to visit Pune. The four of us then rented a beautiful villa in the hill station of Mahabaleshwar. The greatest pleasure was to sit in the large garden and watch the silver Hanuman langurs leap from tree to tree. Bob insisted I read *Lord of the Rings*, and to my surprise I became completely absorbed in this slightly fascistic tale. Bob would read over my shoulder, savoring the parts he remembered best, and commenting with great wit about each and every character. Gifted with a fantastic memory, Bob could not only recite hundreds of Sanskrit verses by heart but he also knew literally thousands of songs and numerous poems and prose passages from the oddest assortment of texts. So as I read Tolkien, he would glance at the page, walk off, and recite the rest of it by heart. Plots of movies, plots of novels, and poems, and old Irish folk songs—all of these things came easily to Bob. His wife, too, seemed to know an endless number of beautiful songs. The two of them would sing them together, and I would curse my lack of talent but took delight in theirs.

The nights were long in Mahabaleshwar, and I remember Bob talking to me at length about animals, both those we saw there, such as the Hanuman langurs, and other animals of India, especially elephants. Bob seemed to know everything about all animals. How he knew so much I never discovered, but he was a walking encyclopedia and I never tired of asking him questions. Whales? Sure: did I have ten minutes for a quick rundown of the facts? Could this be the first inkling of my later book *When Elephants Weep,* about the emotional lives of animals? I think so.

As I discovered, Bob also has endless curiosity about the life around him. Once, while we were walking in the small town, we noticed a man dressed as a tiger walk into a shop and walk out again, carrying a considerable sum of money. He walked into another shop and the same thing happened. Bob couldn't stand it any longer. He walked into the shop and asked who the man was. "That," said the shopkeeper, "was a man dressed as a tiger." "I know that," said Bob, "but why did you give him money?" "Because he was dressed as a tiger and asked for money, so I gave it to him." Bob and I puzzled over this but were not satisfied with the shopkeeper's answer. Bob entered the next store, and this time he asked in Marathi (as I explained, Bob just absorbed languages without trying, and he speaks Hindi, Gujarati, and Marathi, as well as being fluent in Sanskrit). Different language, same answer. We gave up, or at least I did. But I'll wager that somewhere in the thousands of notes to Bob's and Sally's translation of the *Ramayana* some learned reference will be found to men dressing as tigers. Animal behavior is often referred to in their notes, something one rarely finds in a scholarly apparatus. Moreover, when you read these notes, it is like getting an education in an entire culture. Not only are they fun to read, they are well written too. Of how many scholarly texts can one say that in any language? (The great Paul Demieville comes to mind for his magnificent *Le Concile de Lhasa.*)

Strangely enough, it was also during this time in the foothills that Bob introduced me to what was to become a leading passion of mine and an entirely new career: psychoanalysis. Bob brought with him to Mahabaleshwar the three volumes by Ernest Jones of *The Life and Work of Sigmund Freud*. We read them together, partly for their own sake, but partly also for what they might reveal about Indian literature. Was it possible to understand some of the bizarre aspects of the epics, for example, by using Freudian paradigms? Both Bob and I thought so (neither of us are quite so sure forty years later), and in many publications we attempted to apply psychological theories to Indian texts, not always successfully or to everyone's delight. Bob wrote an often-cited paper, "Fathers, Sons, and Gurus: Oedipal Conflict in the Sanskrit Epics" (*Journal of Indian Philosophy*, vol. 6, 1978, pp. 325-92) and other articles, such as "Karma, Guilt, and Buried Memories: Public Fantasy and Private Reality in Traditional India" (*Journal of the American Oriental Society*, vol. 105, no. 3, 1985, pp. 413-25), and I wrote the much-disliked *The Oceanic Feeling*. Nonetheless, I have noted over the years that whatever Bob writes is invariably of interest to people beyond the narrow confines of Sanskrit literature. He makes a point of bringing out the universal themes in any text he writes about, often with remarkable perspicacity.

It would be difficult for me to catalogue all the ways in which Bob has influenced my life and my studies. Nobody I know ranges so widely in his interests. He would always tell me: let us find what is of universal interest in anything we decide to study. He has a hatred of parochialism, as do I, and we agreed that if we could not interest a general audience in what we were studying, then we were doing something wrong. This is not to say that Bob does not have a remarkable grasp of the details of any text, especially texts that are difficult to understand, but he does not relish difficulty for its own sake. He always wanted to discover the universal significance of what we were reading. Thus, although he was interested in the critical reading of a text, like so many of our teachers

(Ingalls, Renou, Lamotte), he always wanted to go beyond that. Reading a text "against the grain", as he called it, meant that we could read a commentary on the Upaniṣads by Śaṅkara and see things in it that would cast light on matters far beyond the immediate concerns of Śaṅkara.

By the way, Bob was one of the first scholars to recognize the great value of later commentaries. Whereas many Western scholars tended to dismiss them (often without bothering to read them), Bob pored over them for the many interesting items they contained that could be found nowhere else. Not only did these commentators often understand the original text far better than we could, they also had original comments that were of value in and of themselves. (For a particularly neat explanation of the value of these commentaries by Bob, see his fascinating article "How Fast Do Monkeys Fly? How Long Do Demons Sleep?" *Rivista di Studi Sudasiatici*, Rome, no. 1, 2006, pp. 185-207.) Nobody else I had studied with realized this. Bob opened this world of commentaries to me when we were graduate students, and this is why I eventually decided to translate the great *Locana* by Abhinavagupta on the *Dhvanyāloka* of Ānandavardhana. Granted, this was more than an ordinary commentary; still, without Bob's interest, enthusiasm, and direction, I doubt I would have even thought about working with such a difficult text. Even traditional Pandits found it hard to understand, but I was immensely lucky in being able to work with one of the finest Sanskrit scholars of India, the late M.V. Patwardhan (who had the same gift as Shrinivas—he never claimed to understand something he did not). The book was eventually to appear in the Harvard Oriental Series, with a translation by M.V. Patwardhan, Daniel H.H. Ingalls, and me. The inspiration for this work came from Bob.

There are so few scholars with this broad range of interests. One whom Bob and I much admired was Richard Robinson, who was Professor of Buddhism at the University of Wisconsin at Madison. I remember how he would insist that if I truly wanted to understand Buddhism, it was not enough to know Pali and Sanskrit and Tibetan, I must read good American novels about baseball as well, and he recommended that I read the 1952 novel, *The Natural*, by Bernard Malamud. I did, and loved it, but I never did understand the connection to Buddhism. I was hoping to study with Dick, but alas, he died in a tragic gas explosion in his house in 1970 while Bob and I were in Pune.

We spent two years together in India. That time formed the basis of our subsequent friendship. Although I drifted away from Sanskrit studies, Bob and I have remained close. We still have an interest in progressive politics in common, whether practiced in government or in the university, and have found we have very similar views of people, policies, and places. If he were Obama today, I would be his Secretary of State! In a way, Bob is the Obama of Sanskrit studies: measured, rational, calm, humorous, and insightful. Bob has never written anything that is dull. I have often urged him to write a novel, and as he finishes up nearly four decades of dedication to the field, I have some hopes that in looking back at the time he has spent in India, he just might do that. I know where it will take place. And I know many of the themes that will inform it. And I know the spirit in which it will be written. It will be coruscating with wit, candor, and depth. How much longer must we wait?

Auckland, New Zealand JEFFREY MOUSSAIEFF MASSON

Contributors

Greg Bailey is associate professor of Asian Studies at La Trobe University.

John Brockington is professor of Sanskrit emeritus at the University of Edinburgh.

James L. Fitzgerald is St. Purandara Das Distinguished Professor of Classics at Brown University.

Luis González-Reimann is lecturer in South and Southeast Asian Studies at the University of California at Berkeley.

Phyllis Granoff is professor of Religious Studies at Yale University.

Alf Hiltebeitel is professor of Religion at the George Washington University.

Jeffrey Moussaieff Masson is an Auckland, New Zealand-based author.

CHRISTOPHER MINKOWSKI is Boden Professor of Sanskrit at the University of Oxford.

DEVEN M. PATEL is assistant professor of South Asia Studies at the University of Pennsylvania.

SHELDON POLLOCK is William B. Ransford Professor of Sanskrit and Indian Studies at Columbia University.

ADHEESH SATHAYE is assistant professor of Asian Studies at the University of British Columbia.

SALLY J. SUTHERLAND GOLDMAN is lecturer in Sanskrit at the University of California at Berkeley.

ROMILA THAPAR is professor of History emerita at Jawaharlal Nehru University.